Kaplan Publi[illegible]ntly finding new ways to mak[illegible]our studies and our exciting onli[illegible]y do offer something different to students looking for exam success.



**This book comes with free EN-gage online resources so that you can study anytime, anywhere.**

Having purchased this book, you have access to the following online study materials:



| CONTENT | ACCA [illegible] | | AAT [illegible] | | FIA (excluding FFA,FAB,FMA) | |
|---|---|---|---|---|---|---|
| [illegible] | [illegible] | [illegible] | [illegible] | [illegible] | Text | Kit |
| iPaper version of the book | [illegible] | [illegible] | [illegible] | [illegible] | ✓ | ✓ |
| Interactive electronic versio[illegible] | [illegible] | [illegible] | [illegible] | [illegible] | | |
| Fixed tests / progress tests [illegible] | [illegible] | [illegible] | [illegible] | [illegible] | | |
| Mock assessments online [illegible] | [illegible] | [illegible] | [illegible] | [illegible] | | |
| Material updates | [illegible] | ✓ | ✓ | [illegible] | ✓ | ✓ |
| Latest official ACCA exam questions | | ✓ | | | | |
| Extra question assistance using the signpost icon* | | ✓ | | | | |
| Timed questions with an online tutor debrief using the clock icon* | | ✓ | | | | |
| Interim assessment including questions and answers | | ✓ | | | ✓ | |
| Technical articles | ✓ | ✓ | | | ✓ | ✓ |

* Excludes F1, F2, F3, FFA, FAB, FMA

## How to access your online resources

Kaplan Financial students will already have a Kaplan EN-gage account and these extra resources will be available to you online. You do not need to register again, as this process was completed when you enrolled. If you are having problems accessing online materials, please ask your course administrator.

If you are already a registered Kaplan EN-gage user go to www.EN-gage.co.uk and log in. Select the 'add a book' feature and enter the ISBN number of this book and the unique pass key at the bottom of this card. Then click 'finished' or 'add another book'. You may add as many books as you have purchased from this screen.

If you purchased through Kaplan Flexible Learning or via the Kaplan Publishing website you will automatically receive an e-mail invitation to Kaplan EN·gage online. Please register your details using this email to gain access to your content. If you do not receive the e-mail or book content, please contact Kaplan Flexible Learning.

If you are a new Kaplan EN-gage user register at www.EN-gage.co.uk and click on the link contained in the email we sent you to activate your account. Then select the 'add a book' feature, enter the ISBN number of this book and the unique pass key at the bottom of this card. Then click 'finished' or 'add another book'.

### Your Code and Information

This code can only be used once for the registration of one book online. This registration and your online content will expire when the final sittings for the examinations covered by this book have taken place. Please allow one hour from the time you submit your book details for us to process your request.

Please scratch the film to access your EN-gage code.

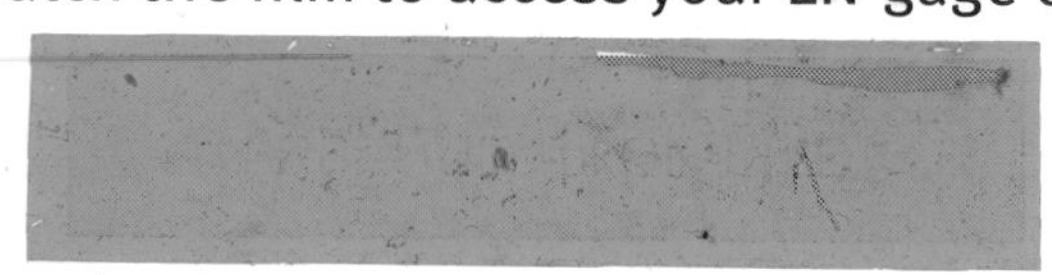

Please be aware that this code is case-sensitive and you will need to include the dashes within the passcode, but not when entering the ISBN. For further technical support, please visit www.EN-gage.co.uk

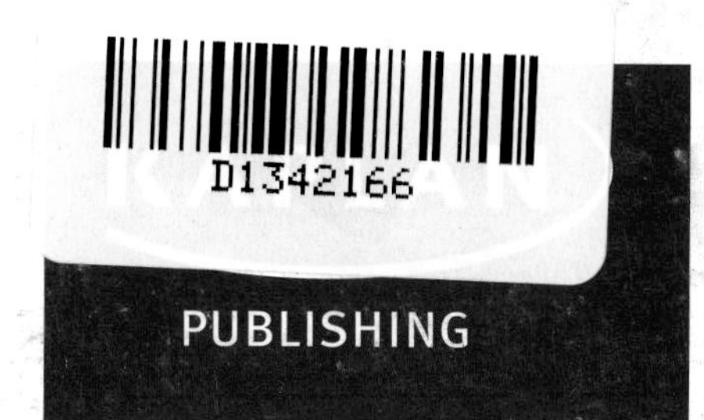

# ACCA

# Paper F8 (INT/UK)

# Audit and Assurance

# Complete Text

## British library cataloguing-in-publication data

A catalogue record for this book is available from the British Library.

Published by:
Kaplan Publishing UK
Unit 2 The Business Centre
Molly Millars Lane
Wokingham
Berkshire
RG41 2QZ

ISBN 978-0-85732-663-8



The text in this material and any others made available by any Kaplan Group company does not amount to advice on a particular matter and should not be taken as such. No reliance should be placed on the content as the basis for any investment or other decision or in connection with any advice given to third parties. Please consult your appropriate professional adviser as necessary. Kaplan Publishing Limited and all other Kaplan group companies expressly disclaim all liability to any person in respect of any losses or other claims, whether direct, indirect, incidental, consequential or otherwise arising in relation to the use of such materials.

Printed and bound in Great Britain.

**Acknowledgements**

We are grateful to the Association of Chartered Certified Accountants and the Chartered Institute of Management Accountants for permisssion to reproduce past examination questions. The answers have been prepared by Kaplan Publishing.

## Contents

# Paper Introduction

# How to Use the Materials

These Kaplan Publishing learning materials have been carefully designed to make your learning experience as easy as possible and to give you the best chances of success in your examinations.

The product range contains a number of features to help you in the study process. They include:

(1) Detailed study guide and syllabus objectives

(2) Description of the examination

(3) Study skills and revision guidance

(4) Complete text or essential text

(5) Question practice

The sections on the study guide, the syllabus objectives, the examination and study skills should all be read before you commence your studies. They are designed to familiarise you with the nature and content of the examination and give you tips on how to best to approach your learning.

The **complete text or essential text** comprises the main learning materials and gives guidance as to the importance of topics and where other related resources can be found. Each chapter includes:

- The **learning objectives** contained in each chapter, which have been carefully mapped to the examining body's own syllabus learning objectives or outcomes. You should use these to check you have a clear understanding of all the topics on which you might be assessed in the examination.
- The **chapter diagram** provides a visual reference for the content in the chapter, giving an overview of the topics and how they link together.
- The **content** for each topic area commences with a brief explanation or definition to put the topic into context before covering the topic in detail. You should follow your studying of the content with a review of the illustration/s. These are worked examples which will help you to understand better how to apply the content for the topic.
- **Test your understanding** sections provide an opportunity to assess your understanding of the key topics by applying what you have learned to short questions. Answers can be found at the back of each chapter.

- **Summary diagrams** complete each chapter to show the important links between topics and the overall content of the paper. These diagrams should be used to check that you have covered and understood the core topics before moving on.
- **Question practice** is provided at the back of each text.

**Icon Explanations**

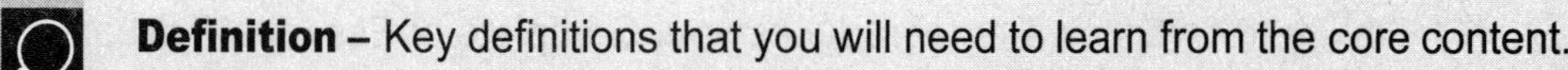

**Definition** – Key definitions that you will need to learn from the core content.

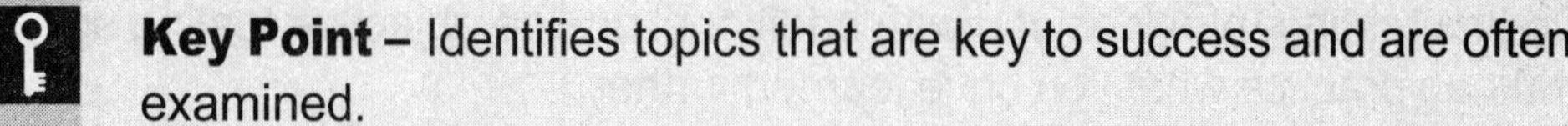

**Key Point** – Identifies topics that are key to success and are often examined.

**New** – Identifies topics that are brand new in papers that build on, and therefore also contain, learning covered in earlier papers.

**Expandable Text** – Expandable text provides you with additional information about a topic area and may help you gain a better understanding of the core content. Essential text users can access this additional content on-line (read it where you need further guidance or skip over when you are happy with the topic)

**Test Your Understanding** – Exercises for you to complete to ensure that you have understood the topics just learned.

**Illustration** – Worked examples help you understand the core content better.

**Tricky topic** – When reviewing these areas care should be taken and all illustrations and test your understanding exercises should be completed to ensure that the topic is understood.

**Tutorial note** – Included to explain some of the technical points in more detail.

**Footsteps** – Helpful tutor tips.

## On-line subscribers

Our on-line resources are designed to increase the flexibility of your learning materials and provide you with immediate feedback on how your studies are progressing.

If you are subscribed to our on-line resources you will find:

(1) On-line referenceware: reproduces your Complete or Essential Text on-line, giving you anytime, anywhere access.

(2) On-line testing: provides you with additional on-line objective testing so you can practice what you have learned further.

(3) On-line performance management: immediate access to your on-line testing results. Review your performance by key topics and chart your achievement through the course relative to your peer group.

Ask your local customer services staff if you are not already a subscriber and wish to join.

# Syllabus

## Paper background

The aim of ACCA Paper F8 (INT & UK), Audit and Assurance, is to develop knowledge and understanding of the process of carrying out the assurance engagement and its application in the context of the professional regulatory framework.

## Objectives of the syllabus

- Explain the nature, purpose and scope of assurance engagements including the role of the external audit and its regulatory and ethical framework.
- Explain the nature of internal audit and describe its role as part of overall performance management and its relationship with the external audit.
- Demonstrate how the auditor obtains an understanding of the entity and its environment, assesses the risk of material misstatement, whether arising from fraud or other irregularities, and plans an audit of financial statements.
- Describe and evaluate information systems and internal controls to identify and communicate control risks and their potential consequences, making appropriate recommendations.
- Identify and describe the work and evidence required to meet the objectives of audit engagements and the application of the International Standards on Auditing.

- Evaluate findings and modify the audit plan as necessary.
- Explain how the conclusions from audit work are reflected in different types of audit report, explain the elements of each type of report.

**Core areas of the syllabus**

- Audit framework and regulation.
- Internal audit.
- Planning and risk assessment.
- Internal control.
- Audit evidence.
- Review.
- Reporting.

**Approach to INT and UK syllabus elements**

Due to the alignment of the INT and UK syllabus elements one text has been produced to address both variants. Both streams apply the principles of International Standards on Auditing (ISA's) and International Financial Reporting Standards (IFRS).

The International variant has been used as the basis of the text. Any variances relevant only to the UK syllabus (such as compliance with the Companies Act 2006) have been included at the end of each chapter in expandable text boxes headed "UK Syllabus Focus." All test your understandings have also been appended to reflect any UK specific variations.

## Syllabus objectives and chapter references

We have reproduced the ACCA's syllabus below, showing where the objectives are explored within this book. Within the chapters, we have broken down the extensive information found in the syllabus into easily digestible and relevant sections, called Content Objectives. These correspond to the objectives at the beginning of each chapter.

### Syllabus learning objective

### A AUDIT FRAMEWORK AND REGULATION

#### 1 The concept of audit and other assurance engagements

(a) Identify and describe the objective and general principles of external audit engagements.[2] **Ch. 1**

(b) Explain the nature and development of audit and other assurance engagements.[1] **Ch. 1**

(c) Discuss the concepts of accountability, stewardship and agency.[2] **Ch. 1**

(d) Discuss the concepts of true and fair presentation and reasonable assurance.[2] **Ch. 1**

(e) Explain reporting as a means of communication to different stakeholders.[1] **Ch. 1**

(f) Define and provide the objectives of an assurance engagement.[1] **Ch. 1**

(g) Explain the five elements of an assurance engagement.[2] **Ch. 1**

(h) Explain the level of assurance provided by audit and other review assignments.[1] **Ch. 1**

#### 2 Statutory audits

(a) Describe the regulatory environment within which statutory audits take place.[1] **Ch. 2**

(b) Discuss the reasons and mechanisms for the regulation of auditors. [2] **Ch. 2**

(c) Explain the statutory regulations governing the appointment, rights, removal and resignation of auditors.[1] **Ch. 2**

(d) State the objectives and principal activities of statutory audit and assess its value (e.g. in assisting management to reduce risk and improve performance).[1] **Ch. 1**

(e) Describe the limitations of statutory audits.[1] **Ch. 1**

**3 The regulatory environment and corporate governance**

(a) Explain the development and status of International Standards on Auditing.[1] **Ch. 2**

(b) Explain the relationship between International Standards on Auditing and national standards *(UK syllabus: between ISA's and the Financial Reporting Council)*.[1] **Ch. 2**

(c) Discuss the objective, relevance and importance of corporate governance.[2] **Ch. 11**

(d) Discuss the need for auditors to communicate with those charged with governance.[2] **Ch. 10**

(e) Discuss the provisions of international codes of corporate governance (such as OECD) *(UK syllabus: such as the UK Corporate Governance Code)* that are most relevant to auditors.[2] **Ch. 11**

(f) Describe good corporate governance requirements relating to directors' responsibilities (e.g. for risk management and internal control) and the reporting responsibilities of auditors.[1] **Ch. 11**

(g) Analyse the structure and roles of audit committees and discuss their benefits and limitations.[2] **Ch. 11**

(h) Explain the importance of internal control and risk management.[1] **Ch. 11**

(i) Compare the responsibilities of management and auditors for the design and operation of systems and controls.[2] **Ch.11**

**4 Professional ethics and ACCA's Code of Ethics and Conduct *(UK syllabus: including the APB ethical standards)***

(a) Define and apply the fundamental principles of professional ethics of integrity, objectivity, professional competence and due care, confidentiality and professional behaviour.[2] **Ch. 3**

(b) Define and apply the conceptual framework including the threats to the fundamental principles of self-interest, self-review, advocacy, familiarity, and intimidation.[2] **Ch. 3**

(c) Discuss the safeguards to offset the threats to the fundamental principles.[2] **Ch. 3**

(d) Describe the auditor's responsibility with regard to auditor independence, conflicts of interest and confidentiality.[1] **Ch. 3**

(e) Discuss the preconditions, requirements of professional ethics, and other requirements in relation to the acceptance of new audit engagements.[2] **Ch. 3**

(f) Discuss the process by which an auditor obtains an audit engagement.[2] **Ch. 3**

(g) Explain the importance of engagement letters and state their contents. [1] **Ch. 3**

**B INTERNAL AUDIT**

**1 Internal audit and corporate governance**

(a) Discuss the factors to be taken into account when assessing the need for internal audit.[2] **Ch. 12**

(b) Discuss the elements of best practice in the structure and operations of internal audit with reference to appropriate international codes of corporate governance.[2] **Ch. 12**

**2 Differences between the external auditor and the internal audit function**

(a) Compare and contrast the role of external and internal audit.[2] **Ch. 12**

**3 The scope of the internal audit function**

(a) Discuss the scope of internal audit and the limitations of the internal audit function.[2] **Ch. 12**

**4 Outsourcing the internal audit department**

(a) Explain the advantages and disadvantages of outsourcing internal audit.[1] **Ch. 12**

**5 Internal audit assignments**

(a) Discuss the nature and purpose of internal audit assignments including value for money, IT, best value and financial.[2] **Ch. 12**

(b) Discuss the nature and purpose of operational internal audit assignments including procurement.[2] **Ch. 12**

**C PLANNING AND RISK ASSESSMENT**

**1 Objective and general principles**

(a) Identify the overall objectives of the auditor.[2] **Ch. 4**

(b) Identify and describe the need to plan and perform audits with an attitude of professional scepticism, and to exercise professional judgement.[2] **Ch. 4**

(c) Explain the need to conduct audits in accordance with ISAs.[1] **Ch. 2**

### 2 Assessing the risks of material misstatement

(a) Explain the components of audit risk.[1] **Ch. 4**

(b) Explain the audit risks in the financial statements and explain the auditor's response to each risk. [2] **Ch. 4**

### 3 Understanding the entity and its environment

(a) Explain how auditors obtain an initial understanding of the entity and knowledge of its environment.[2] **Ch. 4**

(b) Describe risk assessment procedures for the identification and assessment of the risks of material misstatement.[2] **Ch. 4**

### 4 Materiality, fraud, laws and regulations

(a) Define and explain the concepts of materiality and performance materiality.[2] **Ch. 4**

(b) Explain and calculate materiality levels from financial information.[2] **Ch. 4**

(c) Discuss the effect of fraud and misstatements on the audit strategy and extent of audit work.[2] **Ch. 5**

(d) Discuss the responsibilities of internal and external auditors for the prevention and detection of fraud and error. [2] **Ch. 5**

(e) Explain the auditor's responsibility to consider laws and regulations. [2] **Ch. 5**

### 5 Analytical procedures

(a) Describe and explain the nature and purpose of analytical procedures in planning.[2] **Ch. 4**

(b) Compute and interpret key ratios used in analytical procedures.[2] **Ch. 4**

### 6 Planning an audit

(a) Identify and explain the need for planning an audit.[2] **Ch. 5**

(b) Identify and describe the contents of the overall audit strategy and audit plan.[2] **Ch. 5**

(c) Explain and describe the relationship between the overall audit strategy and the audit plan.[2] **Ch. 5**

(d) Explain the difference between interim and final audit.[1] **Ch. 5**

(e) Describe the purpose of an interim audit and the procedures likely to be adopted at this stage in the audit.[2] **Ch. 5**

(f) Describe the impact of the work performed during the interim audit on the final audit.[2] **Ch. 5**

### 7 Audit documentation

(a) Explain the need for and the importance of audit documentation.[1] **Ch. 5**

(b) Describe the contents of working papers and supporting documentation.[2] **Ch. 5**

(c) Explain the procedures to ensure safe custody and retention of working papers.[1] **Ch. 5**

## D INTERNAL CONTROL

The following transaction cycles and account balances are relevant to this capability:

- revenue
- purchases
- inventory
- revenue and capital expenditure
- payroll
- bank and cash.

### 1 Internal control systems

(a) Explain why an auditor needs to obtain an understanding of internal control activities relevant to the audit.[1] **Ch. 6**

(b) Describe and explain the five key components of an internal control system of the control environment, the entity's risk assessment process, the information system, including related business processes relevant to financial reporting, and communication, control activities relevant to the audit, and monitoring of controls.[1] **Ch. 7**

(c) Discuss the difference between tests of control and substantive procedures.[2] **Ch. 6**

### 2 The use of internal control systems by auditors

(a) Explain how auditors record internal control systems including the use of internal control questionnaires and internal control evaluation questionnaires.[1] **Ch. 7**

(b) Explain how auditors identify deficiencies and significant deficiencies in internal control systems and how those deficiencies limit the extent of auditors' reliance on those systems.[2] **Ch. 7**

### 3 Transaction cycles

(a) Explain, analyse and provide examples of internal control procedures and control activities.[2] **Ch. 7**

(b) Provide examples of computer system controls.[2] **Ch. 7**

### 4 Tests of control

(a) Explain and tabulate tests of control suitable for inclusion in audit working papers.[2] **Ch. 7**

(b) List examples of application controls and general IT controls.[2] **Ch. 7**

### 5 The evaluation of internal control components

(a) Analyse the limitations of internal control components in the context of fraud and error.[2] **Ch. 7**

(b) Explain the need to modify the audit strategy and audit plan following the results of tests of control.[1] **Ch. 6**

(c) Identify and explain management's risk assessment process with reference to internal control components.[1] **Ch. 6**

### 6 Communication on internal control

(a) Discuss and provide examples of how the reporting of internal control significant deficiencies are provided to management.[2] **Ch. 7**

## E AUDIT EVIDENCE

### 1 The use of assertions by auditors

(a) Explain the assertions contained in the financial statements.[2] **Ch. 6**

(b) Explain the assertions in relation to classes of transactions, account balances, and presentation and disclosure.[1] **Ch. 6**

(c) Explain the use of assertions in obtaining audit evidence.[2] **Ch. 6**

### 2 Audit procedures

(a) Discuss the quality and quantity of audit evidence.[2] **Ch. 6**

(b) Discuss the relevance and reliability of audit evidence. [2] **Ch. 6**

(c) Discuss the procedures for obtaining audit evidence. [2] **Ch. 6**

(d) Discuss and provide examples of how analytical procedures are used as substantive procedures.[2] **Ch. 6**

(e) Discuss the problems associated with the audit and review of accounting estimates.[2] **Ch. 8**

(f) Describe why smaller entities may have different control environments and describe the types of evidence likely to be available in smaller entities.[1] **Ch. 8**

(g) Explain the auditor's responsibilities and describe procedures to be applied in relation to opening balances and comparative information. [2] **Ch. 9**

**3 The audit of specific items**

For each of the account balances stated in this sub-capability:

- explain the purpose of substantive procedures in relation to financial statement assertions
- explain the substantive procedures used in auditing each balance.

(a) Receivables:[2] **Ch. 8**
   (i) direct confirmation of accounts receivable
   (ii) other evidence in relation to receivables, and
   (iii) the related profit or loss section entries.

(b) Inventory:[2] **Ch. 8**
   (i) inventory counting procedures in relation to year-end and continuous inventory systems
   (ii) cut-off
   (iii) auditor's attendance at inventory counting
   (iv) direct confirmation of inventory held by third parties,
   (v) other evidence in relation to inventory.

(c) Payables, accruals, provisions and contingencies:[2] **Ch. 8**
   (i) supplier statement reconciliations and direct confirmation of accounts payable
   (ii) obtain evidence in relation to payables and accruals, and
   (iii) the related profit or loss section entries.

(d) Bank and cash:[2] **Ch. 8**
   (i) bank confirmation reports used in obtaining evidence in relation to bank and cash
   (ii) other evidence in relation to bank and cash, and
   (iii) the related profit or loss section entries.

(e) Tangible and intangible non-current assets and non-current liabilities: [2] **Ch. 8**

   (i) evidence in relation to non-current assets,

   (ii) non-current liabilities,

   (iii) provisions, and

   (iv) the related profit or loss section entries.

(f) Share capital, reserves and directors' emoluments:[2] **Ch. 8**

   (i) evidence in relation to share capital, reserves and directors' emoluments, and

   (ii) the related profit or loss section entries.

### 4 Audit sampling and other means of testing

(a) Define audit sampling and explain the need for sampling.[1] **Ch. 6**

(b) Identify and discuss the differences between statistical and non-statistical sampling.[2] **Ch. 6**

(c) Discuss and provide relevant examples of, the application of the basic principles of statistical sampling and other selective testing procedures. [2] **Ch. 6**

(d) Discuss the results of statistical sampling, including consideration of whether additional testing is required.[2] **Ch. 6**

### 5 Computer-assisted audit techniques

(a) Explain the use of computer-assisted audit techniques in the context of an audit.[1] **Ch. 6**

(b) Discuss and provide relevant examples of the use of test data and audit software for the transaction cycles and balances mentioned in sub-capability 3.[2] **Ch. 6**

### 6 The work of others

(a) Discuss the extent to which auditors are able to rely on the work of experts.[2] **Ch. 6**

(b) Discuss the extent to which external auditors are able to rely on the work of internal audit.[2] **Ch. 6**

(c) Discuss the audit considerations relating to entities using service organisations.[2] **Ch. 6**

(d) Discuss why auditors rely on the work of others.[2] **Ch. 6**

(e) Explain the extent to which reference to the work of others can be made in audit reports.[1] **Ch. 6**

### 7 Not-for-profit organisations

(a) Apply audit techniques to small not-for-profit organisations.[2] **Ch. 8**

(b) Explain how the audit of small not-for-profit organisations differs from the audit of for-profit organisations.[1] **Ch. 8**

## F REVIEW

### 1 Subsequent events

(a) Explain the purpose of a subsequent events review.[1] **Ch. 9**

(b) Explain the responsibilities of auditors regarding subsequent events.[1] **Ch. 9**

(c) Discuss the procedures to be undertaken in performing a subsequent events review.[2] **Ch. 9**

### 2 Going concern

(a) Define and discuss the significance of the going concern concept. [2] **Ch. 9**

(b) Explain the importance of and the need for going concern reviews. [2] **Ch. 9**

(c) Identify and explain potential indicators that an entity is not a going concern.[2] **Ch. 9**

(d) Explain the respective responsibilities of auditors and management regarding going concern.[1] **Ch. 9**

(e) Discuss the procedures to be applied in performing going concern reviews.[2] **Ch. 9**

(f) Discuss the disclosure requirements in relation to going concern issues.[2] **Ch. 9**

(g) Discuss the reporting implications of the findings of going concern reviews.[2] **Ch. 9**

### 3 Written representations

(a) Explain the purpose of and procedure for obtaining written representations.[2] **Ch. 9**

(b) Discuss the quality and reliability of written representations as audit evidence.[2] **Ch. 9**

(c) Discuss the circumstances where written representations are necessary and the matters on which representations are commonly obtained.[2] **Ch. 9**

**4 Audit finalisation and the final review**

(a) Discuss the importance of the overall review of evidence obtained. [2] **Ch. 9**

(b) Describe procedures an auditor should perform in conducting their overall review of financial statements.[2].**Ch. 9**

(c) Explain the significance of uncorrected misstatements.[1] **Ch. 9**

(d) Evaluate the effect of dealing with uncorrected misstatements. [2] **Ch. 9**

**G REPORTING**

**1 Audit reports**

(a) Describe and analyse the format and content of unmodified audit reports.[2] **Ch. 10**

(b) Describe and analyse the format and content of modified audit reports. [2] **Ch. 10**

(c) Describe the format and content of and emphasis of matter and other matter paragraphs.[2] **Ch. 10**

**2 Reports to management**

(a) Identify and analyse internal control and system deficiencies and significant deficiencies and their potential effects and make appropriate recommendations to management.[2] **Ch. 7**

**3 Internal audit reports**

(a) Describe and explain the format and content of internal audit review reports and other reports dealing with the enhancement of performance. [1] **Ch. 12**

The superscript numbers in square brackets indicate the intellectual depth at which the subject area could be assessed within the examination. Level 1 (knowledge and comprehension) broadly equates with the Knowledge module, Level 2 (application and analysis) with the Skills module and Level 3 (synthesis and evaluation) to the Professional level. However, lower level skills can continue to be assessed as you progress through each module and level.

For a list of examinable documents, see the ACCA web site: (www.accaglobal.com/en/student).

## The Examination

### Examination format

The examination is a three-hour paper covering five compulsory questions. The bulk of the questions will be discursive but some questions involving computational elements will be set from time to time.

The questions will cover all areas of the syllabus:

| | **Number of marks** |
|---|---|
| Question 1 (scenario based) | 30 |
| Question 2 (knowledge based) | 10 |
| Questions 3-5 (each question will be worth 20 marks each) | 60 |
| | **100** |

Total time allowed: reading and planning 15 minutes; writing 3 hours.

### Paper-based examination tips

Spend the first few minutes of the examination reading the paper.

**Divide the time** you spend on questions in proportion to the marks on offer. One suggestion **for this examination** is to allocate 1.8 minutes to each mark available, so a 10-mark question should be completed in approximately 18 minutes.

Unless you know exactly how to answer the question, spend some time planning your answer. Stick to the question and tailor your answer to what you are asked. Pay particular attention to the verbs in the question.

Spend the last five minutes reading through your answers and making any additions or corrections.

If you **get completely stuck** with a question, leave space in your answer book and return to it later.

If you do not understand what a question is asking, state your assumptions. Even if you do not answer in precisely the way the examiner hoped, you should be given some credit, if your assumptions are reasonable.

You should do everything you can to make things easy for the marker. The marker will find it easier to identify the points you have made if your answers are legible.

**Written questions:** Your essay should have a clear structure. It should contain a brief introduction, a main section and a conclusion. Be concise. It is better to write a little about a lot of different points than a great deal about one or two points.

**Reports, memos and other documents:** some questions ask you to present your answer in the form of a report or a memo or other document. So use the correct format - there are easy marks to gain here.

## Study skills and revision guidance

This section aims to give guidance on how to study for your ACCA exams and to give ideas on how to improve your existing study techniques.

### Preparing to study

### Set your objectives

Before starting to study decide what you want to achieve - the type of pass you wish to obtain. This will decide the level of commitment and time you need to dedicate to your studies.

### Devise a study plan

Determine which times of the week you will study.

Split these times into sessions of at least one hour for study of new material. Any shorter periods could be used for revision or practice.

Put the times you plan to study onto a study plan for the weeks from now until the exam and set yourself targets for each period of study – in your sessions make sure you cover the course, course assignments and revision.

If you are studying for more than one paper at a time, try to vary your subjects as this can help you to keep interested and see subjects as part of wider knowledge.

When working through your course, compare your progress with your plan and, if necessary, re-plan your work (perhaps including extra sessions) or, if you are ahead, do some extra revision/practice questions.

## Effective studying

### Active reading

You are not expected to learn the text by rote, rather, you must understand what you are reading and be able to use it to pass the exam and develop good practice. A good technique to use is SQ3Rs – Survey, Question, Read, Recall, Review:

(1) **Survey the chapter** – look at the headings and read the introduction, summary and objectives, so as to get an overview of what the chapter deals with.

(2) **Question** – whilst undertaking the survey, ask yourself the questions that you hope the chapter will answer for you.

(3) **Read** through the chapter thoroughly, answering the questions and making sure you can meet the objectives. Attempt the exercises and activities in the text, and work through all the examples.

(4) **Recall** – at the end of each section and at the end of the chapter, try to recall the main ideas of the section/chapter without referring to the text. This is best done after a short break of a couple of minutes after the reading stage.

(5) **Review** – check that your recall notes are correct.

You may also find it helpful to re-read the chapter to try to see the topic(s) it deals with as a whole.

### Note-taking

Taking notes is a useful way of learning, but do not simply copy out the text. The notes must:

- be in your own words
- be concise
- cover the key points
- be well-organised
- be modified as you study further chapters in this text or in related ones.

Trying to summarise a chapter without referring to the text can be a useful way of determining which areas you know and which you don't.

**Three ways of taking notes:**

**Summarise the key points of a chapter.**

**Make linear notes** – a list of headings, divided up with subheadings listing the key points. If you use linear notes, you can use different colours to highlight key points and keep topic areas together. Use plenty of space to make your notes easy to use.

**Try a diagrammatic form** – the most common of which is a mind-map. To make a mind-map, put the main heading in the centre of the paper and put a circle around it. Then draw short lines radiating from this to the main sub-headings, which again have circles around them. Then continue the process from the sub-headings to sub-sub-headings, advantages, disadvantages, etc.

**Highlighting and underlining**

You may find it useful to underline or highlight key points in your study text – but do be selective. You may also wish to make notes in the margins.

**Revision**

The best approach to revision is to revise the course as you work through it. Also try to leave four to six weeks before the exam for final revision. Make sure you cover the whole syllabus and pay special attention to those areas where your knowledge is weak. Here are some recommendations:

Read through the text and your notes again and condense your notes into key phrases. It may help to put key revision points onto index cards to look at when you have a few minutes to spare.

Review any assignments you have completed and look at where you lost marks – put more work into those areas where you were weak.

Practise exam standard questions under timed conditions. If you are short of time, list the points that you would cover in your answer and then read the model answer, but do try to complete at least a few questions under exam conditions.

Also practise producing answer plans and comparing them to the model answer.

If you are stuck on a topic find somebody (a tutor) to explain it to you.

Read good newspapers and professional journals, especially ACCA's Student Accountant – this can give you an advantage in the exam.

Ensure you know the structure of the exam – how many questions and of what type you will be expected to answer. During your revision attempt all the different styles of questions you may be asked.

**Further reading**

You can find further reading and technical articles under the student section of ACCA's website.

chapter

1

# Introduction to assurance

## Chapter learning objectives

When you have completed this chapter you will be able to:

- Explain the concept of assurance and the five elements of an assurance engagement.
- Explain reporting as a means of communication to different stakeholders.
- Explain the level of assurance provided by an external audit and other review engagements.
- Identify and describe the objective and general principles of external audit engagements.
- Define and provide the objectives of a review engagement.
- Assess the value of external audits and describe the limitations of external audits.

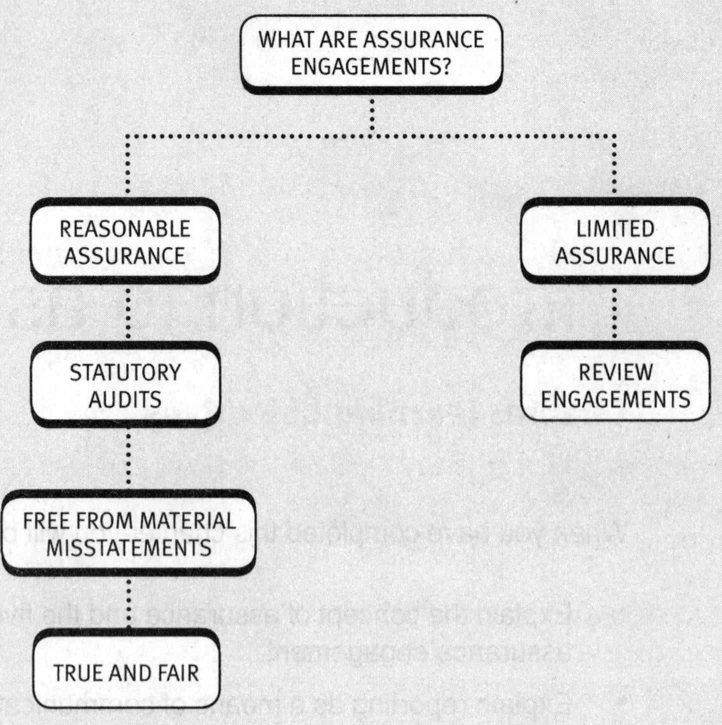


## 1 What is assurance?

An assurance engagement is: 'An engagement in which a practitioner expresses a conclusion designed to enhance the degree of confidence of the intended users other than the responsible party about the outcome of the evaluation or measurement of a subject matter against criteria.' (International Audit and Assurance Standards Board Handbook)

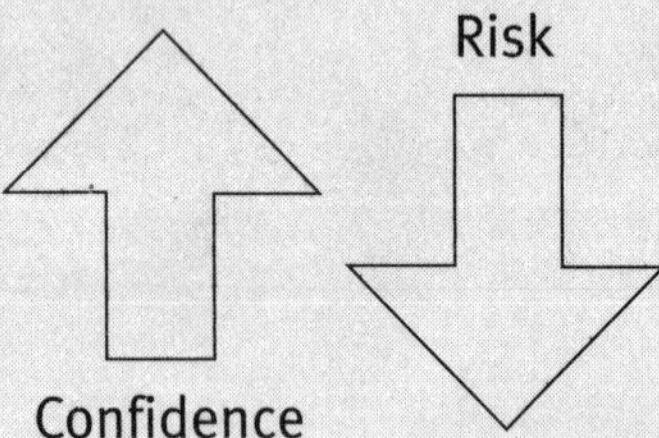


Giving assurance means: offering an opinion about specific information so the users of that information are able to make **confident decisions** knowing that the **risk** of the information being 'incorrect' is **reduced**.

There are five elements of an assurance engagement:

(i) the three parties involved:

- the practitioner (i.e. the reviewer of the subject matter who provides the assurance)
- the intended users (of the information)
- the responsible party (i.e. those responsible for the subject matter)

(ii) an appropriate subject matter

(iii) suitable criteria, against which the subject matter is evaluated/measured

(iv) sufficient appropriate evidence

(v) a written assurance report in an appropriate form.

**Illustration 1: Buying a house**

Consider someone who is buying a house.

Most members of the public lack the technical expertise to assess the structural condition of property. There is therefore a risk that someone pays a large sum of money to purchase a structurally unsafe property which needs further expenditure to make it useable.

To reduce this risk, it is normal for house buyers (the users) to pay a property surveyor (the practitioner) to perform a structural assessment of the house (the subject matter). The surveyor would then report back (written report) to the house buyer identifying any structural deficiencies (measured against building regulations/best practice and other criteria). With this information the potential buyer can then make their decision to buy or not to buy the house with confidence that they know what the structural condition of the house is.

In this example, the responsible party is the current house owner, and the evidence would largely be obtained by visually inspecting the property.

**The elements of an audit engagement**

**The five elements of an external audit engagement**

(i) The three parties involved:
   - the preparers – management/directors;
   - the users – shareholders; and
   - the practitioner – the auditors.

(ii) The subject matter: the financial statements (prepared by management).

(iii) Sufficient appropriate evidence: obtained by performing audit procedures and reviewing the financial statements.

(iv) This includes evaluating whether they are prepared in accordance with a relevant financial reporting framework (i.e. suitable criteria).

(v) The audit report: which is presented to the shareholders. This report summarises the auditor's opinion as to whether the financial statements are "presented fairly" (or "true and fair").

**Assurance services**

- an audit of financial statements
- a review of financial statements
- risk assessment reviews
- systems reliability reports
- verification of social and environmental issues (e.g. to validate an employer's claims about being an equal opportunities employer or a company's claims about sustainable sourcing of materials)
- reviews of internal controls
- value for money audit in public sector organisations.

## 2 Assurance in the context of a company

The users of corporate information are referred to as **stakeholders**. These are people, or groups, who are influenced by, or can influence, the company's decisions and actions.

**Examples of stakeholder groups**

Examples of stakeholder groups are:

- shareholders
- management and those charged with the governance of a business
- other employees
- customers
- suppliers
- government offices
- lenders of funds
- community organisations.

These stakeholders will need information about the company in order to make decisions. Of course, the decisions they make will all be different.

**Illustration 2: Stakeholder decisions**

- Shareholders need to decide whether to alter their shareholdings.
- Employees need to make career decisions.
- Customers need to manage their supply chain.

One of the primary sources of information about a company is the **financial statements**. This contains information that almost all of the stakeholder groups will find useful. In particular, the shareholders (the primary stakeholder group) will need reliable financial statements to appraise the performance of their shareholding.

The directors are responsible for managing the company in order to achieve the objectives of that company (normally the maximisation of shareholder wealth). However, directors often directly benefit from increasing profit; director's remuneration may include bonuses, linked to the level of profits achieved.

The directors are also responsible for preparing the financial statements; this creates a conflict of interest as the directors benefit from reporting higher profits.

There is therefore a need for an independent review of these financial statements, i.e. assurance from an external practitioner to ensure the financial statements give a true and fair view.

**Usefulness of financial statements**

- Employees may be able to judge whether they think their levels of pay are adequate compared to the directors and results of the company.
- Those charged with governance can see whether they think management have struck the right balance between their own need for reward (remuneration, share options, etc) and the needs of other stakeholders.
- Customers, suppliers and lenders can make judgements about whether the company has sufficient financial strength (i.e. liquidity) to justify future trading/financial relationships.
- The government can decide whether the right amounts of tax have been paid, etc.

**The development of assurance engagements**

**Incorporation and the separation of ownership and control**



Businesses can operate through a number of different vehicles. It is common for investors in those businesses to seek the protection of limited company status. This means that whilst they could lose the funds they invest in a business they cannot be held personally responsible for satisfying the remaining corporate debts. The creation of a limited company is referred to as **incorporation**.

Incorporation has the following implications:

- the creation of a legal distinction between the owners of the business and the business itself;
- the opportunity for the owners/investors to detach themselves from the operation of the business; and
- the need for managers to operate the business on a daily basis.

Whilst this has provided financial protection for shareholders it does lead to one significant conflict:

- Shareholders seek to maximise their wealth through the increasing value of their shareholding. This is driven by the profitability (both current and potential) of the company.

- Directors/management seek to maximise their wealth through salary, bonuses and other employment benefits. This reduces company profitability.

This conflict led to the legal requirement for **financial statements** to be produced by directors to account for their **stewardship** of the company. These are sent to shareholders to allow them to assess the performance of management.

**Key definitions:**

**Stewardship** is the responsibility to take good care of resources. A steward is a person entrusted with management of another person's property, for example, when one person is paid to look after another person's house while the owner goes abroad on holiday.

This relationship, where one person has a duty of care towards someone else is known as a '**fiduciary relationship**'.

The steward is **accountable** for the way he carries out his role.

A **fiduciary relationship** is a relationship of 'good faith' such as that between the directors of a company and the shareholders of the company. There is a 'separation of ownership and control' in the sense that the shareholders own the company, while the directors make the decisions. The directors must make their decisions in the interests of the shareholders rather than in their own selfish personal interests.

**Accountability** means that people in positions of power can be held to account for their actions, i.e. they can be compelled to explain their decisions and can be criticised or punished if they have abused their position.

Accountability is central to the concept of good **corporate governance** – the process of ensuring that companies are well run – which we will look at in more detail in a later chapter.

**Agency** occurs when one party, the principal, employs another party, the agent, to perform a task on their behalf.

## 3 Types of assurance engagement

The IAASB International Framework for Assurance Engagements permits two types of assurance engagement:

- reasonable
- limited.

### Reasonable assurance engagements

In a reasonable assurance engagement, the practitioner:

- Gathers **sufficient appropriate evidence** to be able to draw reasonable conclusions.
- Concludes that the subject matter **conforms in all material respects** with identified suitable criteria.
- Gives a **positively** worded assurance opinion.

**Illustration 3: Positively worded assurance opinion**

In our opinion, the financial statements give a true and fair view of (or *present fairly, in all material respects*) the financial position of Murray Company as at December 31 2012, and of its financial performance and its cash flows for the year then ended in accordance with International Financial Reporting Standards.

### Limited assurance engagement

In a limited assurance assignment, the practitioner:

- Gathers **sufficient appropriate evidence** to be able to draw limited conclusions.
- Concludes that the subject matter, with respect to identified suitable criteria, **is plausible in the circumstances**.
- Gives a **negatively** worded assurance opinion.

**Illustration 4: Negatively worded assurance opinion**

Nothing has come to our attention that causes us to believe that the financial statements of Murray Company as of 31 December 2012 are not prepared, in all material respects, in accordance with an applicable financial reporting framework.

**Levels of assurance**

There is no precise definition of what is meant by reasonable or limited assurance. However, it is clear that the confidence inspired by a reasonable assurance report is designed to be greater than that inspired by a limited one.

Therefore:

- there are more regulations/standards governing a reasonable assurance assignment
- the procedures carried out in a reasonable assignment will be more thorough
- the evidence gathered will need to be of a higher quality.

## 4 Audit engagements

In most developed countries, publicly quoted companies and large companies are required by law to produce annual financial statements and have them audited by an external auditor: a **statutory audit**.

Companies that are not required to have a statutory audit may have an **external audit** because the company's shareholders or other influential stakeholders want one and because of the **benefits of an audit**:

- An audit improves the quality and reliability of information, giving investors faith in and improving the reputation of the market.
- Independent scrutiny and verification may be valuable to management.
- An audit may reduce the risk of management bias, fraud and error by acting as a deterrent.
- An audit enhances the credibility of the financial statements, e.g. for tax authorities/lenders.
- Deficiencies in the internal control system may be highlighted by the auditor.

An **external audit** is an example of a **reasonable assurance** engagement.

The purpose of an audit is to enhance the degree of confidence of the intended users in the financial statements.

The objective of an external audit engagement is to enable the auditor to express an opinion on whether the financial statements

- give a true and fair view (or present fairly in all material respects).
- are prepared, in all material respects, in accordance with an applicable financial reporting framework.

The financial reporting framework to be applied will vary from country to country: in F8, it is assumed that International Financial Reporting Standards are the basis of preparing the financial statements.

The financial reporting framework to be applied will vary from country to country: in F8, it is assumed that International Financial Reporting Standards are the basis of preparing the financial statements.

**True and fair**

There is no definition in the International Standards on Auditing of true and fair, but it is generally considered to have the following meaning:

- **True**: factual, conforms with accounting standards and relevant legislation and agrees with underlying records.
- **Fair**: clear, impartial and unbiased and reflects the commercial substance of the transactions of the entity.

## 5 Review engagements

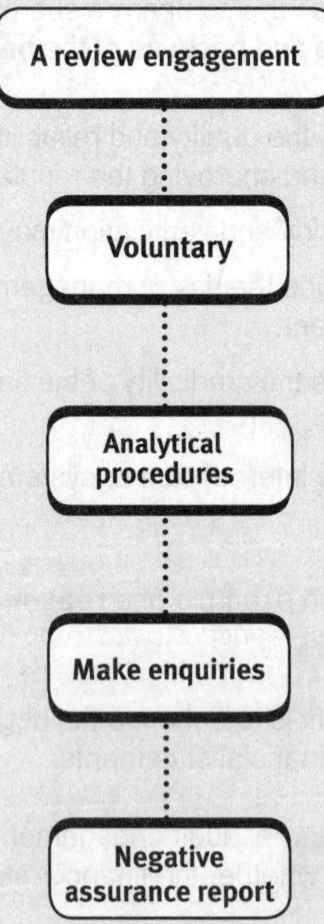


It is possible for small companies, who are not legally required to have a full audit, to have a review of their financial statements to enable them to present their accounts (for example) to potential lenders.

A **review engagement** is an example of a **limited assurance** engagement.

The **objective of a review of financial statements** is to enable an auditor to state whether, on the basis of procedures which do not provide all the evidence required in an audit, anything has come to the auditor's attention that causes the auditor to believe that the financial statements are not prepared in accordance with the applicable financial reporting framework (i.e. negative/limited assurance).

**Review engagements**

Guidance on how to perform this type of assignment is given by the IAASB in International Standard on Review Engagements (ISRE) 2400, Engagements to Review Financial Statements.

**Characteristics of a review engagement**

Typically review engagements will be carried out using much more limited procedures than an audit. Typically the following procedures are used:

- analytical review
- enquiry.

These and other audit procedures will be explained in a later chapter.

## 6 Expectations gap

Some users incorrectly believe that an audit provides absolute assurance; that the audit opinion is a guarantee the financial statements are 'correct'. This and other misconceptions about the role of an auditor are referred to as the '**expectations gap**'.

The greatest level of assurance auditors can provide is reasonable. The **limitations of an audit** mean that it is not possible to provide 'absolute' assurance. These limitations include:

- The financial statements include subjective estimates and other judgemental matters.
- Assurance may be obtained from the operating effectiveness of internal controls, which are inherently limited.
- Representations from management may have to be relied upon as the only source of evidence in some areas.
- Evidence is often persuasive not conclusive.
- Auditors do not test all transactions and balances, they test on a sample basis.

Other examples of the expectations gap include:

- a belief that auditors test all transactions and balances; they test on a sample basis.
- a belief that auditors are required to detect fraud; auditors are required to provide reasonable assurance that the financial statements are free from material misstatement, which may be caused by fraud.
- a belief that auditors are responsible for preparing the financial statements; this is the responsibility of management.

**Test your understanding 1**

Auditors are frequently required to provide assurance for a range of non-audit engagements.

**Required:**

**List and explain the elements of an assurance engagement.**

*Real exam question: June 2010*

**(5 marks)**

**Test your understanding 2**

Explain the term 'limited assurance' in the context of a review of a company's cash flow forecast and explain how this differs from the assurance provided by a statutory audit.

**(5 marks)**

## 7 Chapter summary

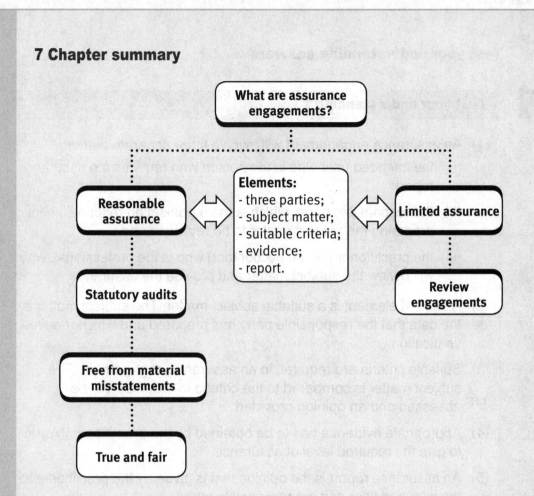

What are assurance engagements?

Reasonable assurance

Elements:
- three parties;
- subject matter;
- suitable criteria;
- evidence;
- report.

Limited assurance

Statutory audits

Review engagements

Free from material misstatements

True and fair

## Test your understanding answers

### Test your understanding 1

(1) An assurance engagement will involve three separate parties:

(i) the intended user who is the person who requires the assurance report

(ii) the responsible party, which is the organisation responsible for preparing the subject matter to be reviewed and

(iii) the practitioner (i.e. an accountant) who is the professional, who will review the subject matter and provide the assurance.

(2) A second element is a suitable subject matter. The subject matter is the data that the responsible party has prepared and which requires verification.

(3) Suitable criteria are required in an assurance engagement. The subject matter is compared to the criteria in order for it to be assessed and an opinion provided.

(4) Appropriate evidence has to be obtained by the practitioner in order to give the required level of assurance.

(5) An assurance report is the opinion that is given by the practitioner to the intended user and the responsible party.

**Test your understanding 2**

| Limited Assurance | Assurance provided by statutory audit |
|---|---|
| Limited assurance is a moderate level of assurance. | A statutory audit provides reasonable assurance, which is a high level. |
| The objective of a limited assurance engagement is to obtain sufficient appropriate evidence that the cash flow forecast is plausible in the circumstances. | The objective of a statutory audit is to obtain sufficient appropriate evidence that the financial statements conform in all material respects with the relevant financial reporting framework. |
| A limited assurance report provides a negative opinion. The practitioner will state that nothing has come to their attention which indicates that the cash flow forecast contains any material errors.<br><br>The assurance is therefore given on the absence of any indication to the contrary. | The statutory audit report provides a positive opinion; that is the financial statements do show a true and fair view. |
| With limited assurance, limited procedures are performed; often only enquiry and analytical procedures. | More evidence will need to be obtained to provide reasonable assurance, and a wider range of procedures performed, including tests of controls. |
| A cash flow relates to the future, which is inherently uncertain, and therefore it would not be possible to obtain assurance that it is free from material misstatement. | Financial statements relate to the past, and so the auditor should be able to obtain sufficient appropriate evidence. |
| Less reliance can therefore be placed on the forecast than the financial statements, where the positive assurance was given. | |

| Limited Assurance | Assurance provided by statutory audit |
|---|---|
| Limited assurance is a moderate level of assurance. | A statutory audit provides reasonable assurance, which is a high level. |
| The objective of a limited assurance engagement is to obtain sufficient appropriate evidence that the cash flow forecast is plausible in the circumstances. | The objective of a statutory audit is to obtain sufficient appropriate evidence that the financial statements conform in all material respects with the relevant financial reporting framework. |
| A limited assurance report provides a negative opinion. The practitioner will state that nothing has come to their attention which indicates that the cash flow forecast contains any material errors. The assurance is therefore given on the absence of any indication to the contrary. | The statutory auditor provides a positive opinion that the financial statements do show a true and fair view. |
| With limited assurance, limited procedures are performed, often only enquiry and analytical procedures. | More evidence will need to be obtained to provide reasonable assurance, and a wider range of procedures performed, including tests of controls. |
| A cash flow relates to the future which is inherently uncertain, and therefore it would not be possible to obtain assurance that it is free from material misstatement. | Financial statements relate to the past, and so the auditor should be able to obtain sufficient appropriate evidence. |
| Less reliance can be placed on the forecast than the historical statements, where the positive assurance was given. | |

chapter

# 2

# Rules and regulation

## Chapter learning objectives

When you have completed this chapter you will be able to:

- Describe the regulatory environment within which external audits take place.
- Discuss the reasons and mechanisms for the regulation of auditors.
- Explain the development and status of International Standards on Auditing.
- Explain the relationship between International Standards on Auditing and national standards *(UK syllabus: between ISAs and the work of the Financial Reporting Council).*
- Explain the statutory regulations governing the appointment, rights, removal and resignation of auditors.

## 1 The need for regulation

The role of the auditor has come under increased scrutiny over the last thirty years due to an increase in high profile, economically damaging fraud cases. The most high profile case, and the catalyst for regulatory change, was the collapse of Enron and its auditor Arthur Andersen.

In order to try and regain trust in the auditing profession national and international standard setters and regulators have tried to introduce three initiatives:

- **Harmonisation** of auditing procedures, so that users of audit services are confident in the nature of audits being conducted around the world.
- Focus **on audit quality**, so that the expectations of users are met.
- Adherence to a strict **ethical code** of conduct, to try and improve the perception of auditors as independent, unbiased service providers.

In order to achieve this practitioners now have to follow two sets of regulatory guidance in addition to **national corporate law**:

- the **Code of Ethics**.
- **Auditing Standards** (the basis of this text is International Standards on Auditing).

**Examples of national laws/guidance**

- The Companies Act 2006 in the UK
- The Sarbanes Oxley Act in the US (enforcing standards of corporate governance)
- The UK Corporate Governance Code (formerly the Combined Code).

## 2 Auditing standards

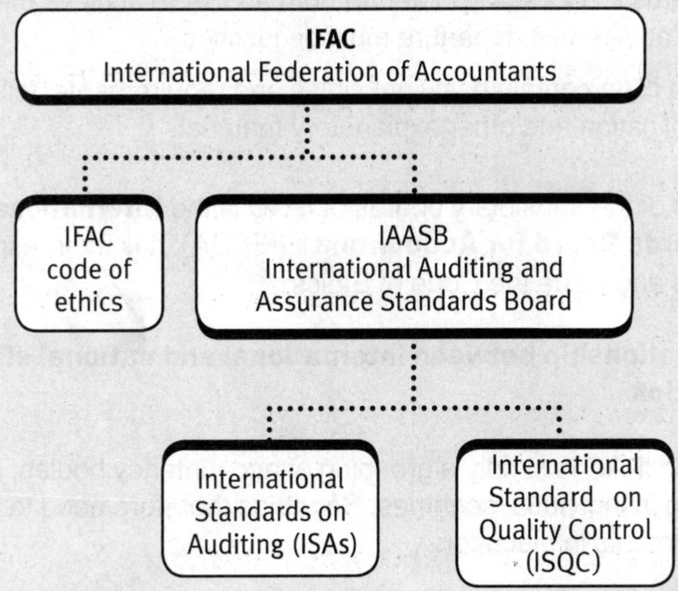


### IFAC

The International Federation of Accountants (IFAC) is the global organisation for the accountancy profession.

**More about IFAC**

IFAC was formed in 1977 and is based in New York. IFAC has more than 160 member bodies of accountants (including the ACCA), representing 2.5 million accountants from over 120 separate countries.

IFAC's overall mission is to serve the public interest, strengthen the worldwide accountancy profession, and contribute to the development of strong international economies by establishing and promoting adherence to high-quality professional standards.

One of the subsidiary boards of IFAC is the **International Audit and Assurance Standards Board** (IAASB). It is their responsibility to develop and promote International Standards on Auditing (ISAs). There are currently 36 ISAs and one International Standard of Quality Control.

You do not need to learn the names or numbers of the auditing standards, but you will need to know and be able to apply the key principles and requirements of the standards.

- ISAs are written in the context of an audit of financial statements but can be applied to the audit of other historical financial information.

- ISAs must be applied in all but exceptional cases, where the auditor deems it necessary to depart from an ISA to achieve the overall aim of the audit – this departure must be justified.
- The ISAs contain basic principles and requirements, followed by application and other explanatory material.

Another of the subsidiary boards of IFAC is the **International Ethics Standards Board for Accountants** (IESBA). It is their responsibility to develop and issue the Code of Ethics.

**The relationship between international and national standards and regulation**

Because IFAC is simply a grouping of accountancy bodies, it has no legal standing in individual countries. Countries therefore need to have arrangements in place for:

- regulating the audit profession and
- implementing auditing standards.

**National regulatory bodies**

National regulatory bodies:

- enforce the implementation of auditing standards
- have disciplinary powers to enforce quality of audit work
- have rights to inspect audit files to monitor audit quality.

There are two possible schemes for regulation at the national level:

- self regulation by the audit/accountancy profession
- regulation by government or by some independent body set up by government for the purpose.

**All audits carried out in EU member states are now carried out in accordance with ISAs.**

Following the decision by the EU to implement ISAs for all accounting periods beginning on or after 1 January 2005, countries with their own standard setting bodies such as the UK had to decide whether to:

- modify their own standards to bring them into line with ISAs
- adopt ISAs and modify them to suit national requirements.

In the UK the national standard setter (the Auditing Practices Board, now the Financial Reporting Council, Codes and Standards division) decided to adopt and modify ISAs.

**National standard setters**

- may set their own auditing standards
- may adopt and implement ISAs, possibly after modifying them to suit national needs.

In accordance with ISA 200 *Overall Objectives of the Independent Auditor and the Conduct of an Audit in Accordance with International Standards on Auditing* the auditor's fundamental objectives are to:

- Obtain reasonable assurance about whether the financial statements as a whole are free from material misstatement, whether due to fraud or error.
- Express an opinion on whether the financial statements are prepared, in all material respects, in accordance with an applicable financial reporting framework.
- Report on the financial statements, and communicate as required by ISAs, in accordance with the auditor's findings.

**Assurance engagements other than audits**

ISAE 3000 *Assurance engagements other than audits or reviews of historical financial information* is the International Standard on Assurance Engagements (ISAE) that 'establishes the basic principles and essential procedures for, and provides guidance to, professional accountants... for the performance of assurance engagements other than audits or reviews of historical financial information.'

## 3 The law

National law includes:

- which companies are required to have an audit
- who can and cannot carry out an audit
- auditor appointment, resignation and removal
- the rights and duties of an auditor.

## Who needs an audit and why?

In most countries companies are required by law to have an audit. However, small or owner-managed companies are often exempt (e.g. in the UK companies with annual turnover < £6.5 million). This is because there is less value in an audit for these companies.

Note that these exemptions often do not apply to companies in certain regulated sectors, e.g. financial services companies.

**Audit exemptions**

The main reasons for exempting small companies are:

- The owners and managers of the company are often the same people.
- The advice and value which accountants can add to a small company is more likely to concern other services, such as accounting and tax.
- The impact of misstatements in the accounts of small companies is unlikely to be material to the wider economy.
- The audit fee and disruption of an audit are seen as too great a cost for any benefits the audit might bring.

## Who may act as auditor?

To be **eligible to act as auditor**, a person must be:

- a member of a Recognised Supervisory Body (RSB), e.g. ACCA, and allowed by the rules of that body to be an auditor **or**
- someone directly authorised by the state.

**Conducting audit work**

Individuals who are authorised to conduct audit work may be:

- sole practitioners
- partners in a partnership
- members of a limited liability partnership
- directors of an audit company.

To be eligible to offer audit services, a firm must be:

- controlled by members of a suitably authorised supervisory body or
- a firm directly authorised by the state.

**Note**: In some countries only individuals can be authorised to act as auditor and need to be directly authorised by the state.

### Who may not act as auditor?

**Excluded by law:** The law in most countries excludes those involved with managing the company and those who have business or personal connections with them from auditing that company.

**Excluded by law: UK example**

For example, in the UK the following are excluded by company law:

- an officer (director or secretary) of the company
- an employee of the company
- a business partner or employee of the above.

**Excluded by the Code of Ethics:** Auditors must also comply with a Code of Ethics. The Code of Ethics requires the auditor to consider any factors that would prevent them acting as auditor, such as independence, competence or issues regarding confidentiality. This is considered in more detail in a later chapter.

## 4 How are auditors appointed and removed?

### Who appoints the auditor?

In most jurisdictions the members (shareholders) of the company appoint the auditor by voting them in at the Annual General Meeting (AGM). Directors can appoint the first auditor to fill a 'casual vacancy' this requires the members' approval at the next AGM, and in some countries the auditors may be appointed by the directors as a matter of course.

Auditors are appointed from one AGM until the end of the next one.

However, private companies can elect to dispense with the requirement for an AGM. In these circumstances the auditor is automatically reappointed unless a shareholder objects.

### Removing the auditor

Arrangements for removing the auditor have to be structured in such a way that:

- the auditor has sufficiently secure tenure of office, to maintain independence of management
- existing auditors can be removed if there are doubts about their continuing abilities to carry out their duties effectively.

To enable this balance to be maintained, the removal of auditors can usually be achieved by a simple majority at a general meeting of the company. There are some safeguards, such as a specified notice period, to prevent the resolution to remove the auditors being 'sprung' on the meeting.

### Resigning as auditor

In practice, if the auditors and management find it difficult to work together, the auditors will usually resign.

To prevent the circumstances of the resignation being hidden from the company's members, the auditors have to submit a statement of the circumstances surrounding their resignation.

### Notifying ACCA

If an auditor resigns or is removed from office before the end of their term of office, they must notify ACCA.

**The auditor's responsibilities on removal/resignation**

The following is taken from UK law, but provides an example of the typical responsibilities of the auditor.

- Deposit at the company's registered office:
  - a statement of the circumstances connected with the removal/resignation or
  - a statement that there are no such circumstances.
- Deal promptly with requests for clearance from new auditors.

## 5 The auditor's rights

**During appointment as auditor**

- Access to the company's books and records at any reasonable time.
- To receive information and explanations necessary for the audit.
- To receive notice of and attend any general meeting of members of the company.
- To be heard at such meetings on matters of concern to the auditor.
- To receive copies of any written resolutions of the company.

**On resignation**

- To request an Extraordinary General Meeting (EGM) of the company to explain the circumstances of the resignation.
- To require the company to circulate the notice of circumstances relating to the resignation.

## 6 The auditor's duties

The auditors primary statutory duty is to audit the financial statements and provide an opinion on whether the financial statements, as presented to the shareholders at the general meeting of the company give a true and fair view (or are fairly presented in all material respects).

They may have additional reporting responsibilities required by local national law, such as confirming that the financial statements are properly prepared in accordance with those laws.

**UK syllabus focus**

**Regulation of Auditing**

Regulation of auditing in the UK changed on 2 July 2012.

Audit and Assurance in the United Kingdom is regulated by the **Financial Reporting Council** (FRC). The FRC has two divisions, one of which is the **Codes and Standards** division. The Codes and Standards division is responsible for maintaining an effective framework of UK codes and standards for Corporate Governance, Stewardship, Accounting, Auditing and Assurance, and Actuary. The codes and standards division has three councils: the Auditing and Assurance Council, the Accounting Council, and the Actuarial Council. The Auditing and Assurance Council considers and advises the FRC Board and the Codes and Standards Committee on audit and assurance matters.

The FRC issues International Standards on Auditing for use within the United Kingdom and Republic of Ireland. The standards are supplemented and revised before issuing them, mainly in order to ensure that they remain compliant with national laws, such as the Companies Act 2006.

In addition the FRC:

- Develop and maintain ethical standards and guidance for auditors' and reporting accountants' integrity, objectivity and independence to facilitate the adoption of the Code of Ethics in the UK (see Ethics and Acceptance chapter for more detail).
- Has statutory responsibility for the oversight and regulations of the accountancy profession and of statutory auditors, which is managed by the Professional Oversight team, part of the Conduct division.
- Monitors the quality of the audits of listed and other major public interest entities; this is the responsibility of the Audit Quality Review team.
- Ensures that appropriate standards are maintained by members and member firms, by operating an independent professional disciplinary scheme for accountants, overseen by the Conduct division.

**Audit Exemption**

In accordance with the Companies Act 2006 those companies falling below the small company threshold are not required, in law, to have an annual audit. Although they may still choose to have one voluntarily.

The main criteria for small company status are:

- Turnover not exceeding £6.5m
- Gross assets not exceeding £3.26m and
- The number of employees must not exceed 50.

In order to qualify the company must meet two out of the three criteria.

**Reporting by exception**

In the UK auditors take on additional reporting responsibilities. The matters are reported on by exception, meaning that the auditor would only make a separate report if the matters have not been concluded satisfactorily. These matters are that:

- adequate accounting records have been kept
- returns adequate for the audit have been received from branches not visited by the auditor

- the accounts agree with accounting records and returns
- director's remuneration has been adequately disclosed as required by law
- all information and explanations required for the audit have been received.

ISA 700 (UK & Ireland) also adds additional reporting responsibilities (by exception) for auditor's of listed companies in the UK, they are:

- A statement given by the directors that they consider the annual report and accounts taken as a whole is fair, balanced and understandable and provides the information necessary for shareholders to assess the entity's performance, business model and strategy, that is inconsistent with the knowledge acquired by the auditor in the course of performing the audit.
- A section describing the work of the audit committee that does not appropriately address matters communicated by the auditor to the audit committee.
- An explanation, as to why the annual report does not include such a statement or section, that is materially inconsistent with the knowledge acquired by the auditor in the course of performing the audit.
- Other information that, in the auditor's judgment, contains a material inconsistency or a material misstatement of fact.

**UK Corporate Governance Code**

The UK Corporate Governance Code states:

- The audit committee should have primary responsibility for making a recommendation on the appointment, reappointment and removal of the external auditors.
- **FTSE 350 companies should put the external audit contract out to tender at least every ten years** (but can retain the current auditor if they provide the best quality and most effective audit).
- If the board does not accept the audit committee's recommendation, it should include in the annual report, and in any papers recommending appointment or re-appointment, a statement from the audit committee explaining the recommendation and should set out reasons why the board has taken a different position.

**Test your understanding 1**

Auditors have various duties to perform in their role as auditors, for example, to assess the truth and fairness of the financial statements.

**Required:**

**Explain THREE rights that enable auditors to carry out their duties.**

*Real exam question: December 2008*

**(3 marks)**

**Test your understanding 2**

The purpose of an external audit and its role are not well understood. You have been asked to write some material for inclusion in your firm's training materials dealing with these issues in the audit of large companies.

**Required:**

**Draft an explanation dealing with the purpose of an external audit and its role in the audit of large companies, for inclusion in your firm's training materials.**

**(10 marks)**

## 7 Chapter summary

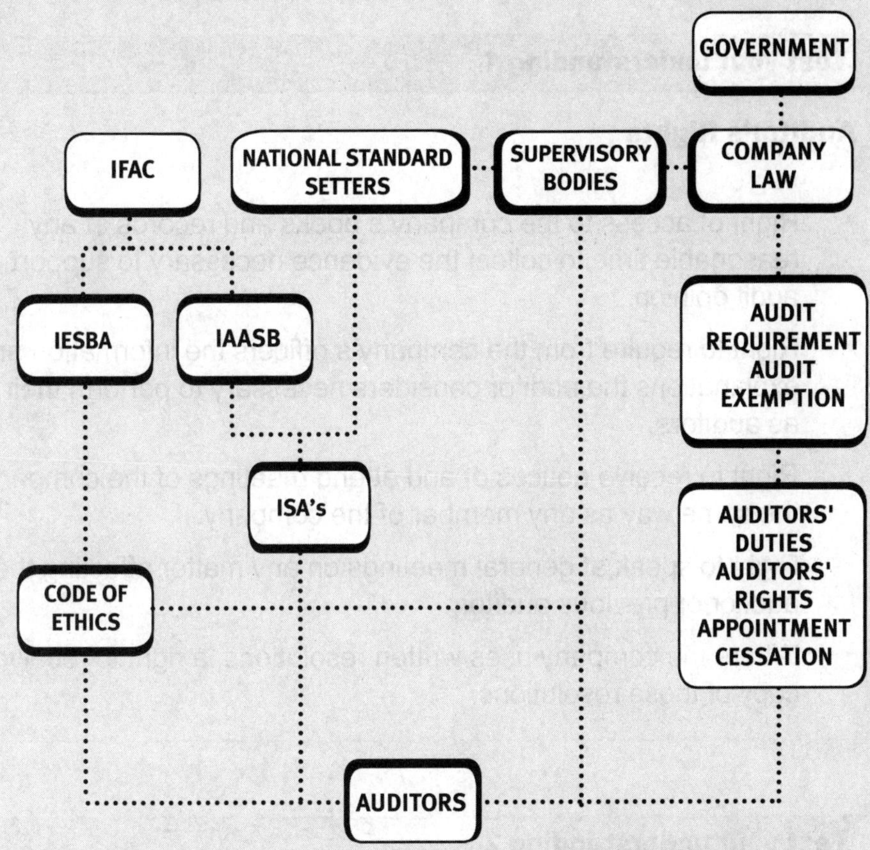

## Test your understanding answers

### Test your understanding 1

**Auditor's Rights**

- Right of access to the company's books and records at any reasonable time to collect the evidence necessary to support the audit opinion.
- Right to require from the company's officers the information and explanations the auditor considers necessary to perform their duties as auditors.
- Right to receive notices of and attend meetings of the company in the same way as any member of the company.
- Right to speak at general meetings on any matter affecting the auditor or previous auditor.
- Where the company uses written resolutions, a right to receive a copy of those resolutions.

### Test your understanding 2

**Training material: purpose of external audit and its role**

(i) The external audit has a long history that derives largely from the separation of the ownership and management of assets. Those who own assets wish to ensure that those to whom they have entrusted control are using those assets wisely. This is known as the 'stewardship' function.

(ii) The requirement for an independent audit helps ensure that financial statements are free of bias and manipulation for the benefit of users of financial information.

(iii) Companies are owned by shareholders but they are managed by directors (in very small companies, owners and managers are the same, but many such companies are not subject to statutory audit requirements).

(iv) The requirement for a statutory audit is a public interest issue: the public is invited to invest in enterprises, it is in the interests of the capital markets (and society as a whole) that those investing do so in the knowledge that they will be provided with 'true and fair' information about the enterprise. This should result in the efficient allocation of capital as investors are able to make rational decisions on the basis of transparent financial information.

(v) The requirement for an audit can help prevent investors from being defrauded, although there is no guarantee of this because the external audit has inherent limitations. Reducing the possibility of false information being provided by managers to owners is achieved by the requirement for external auditors to be independent of the managers upon whose financial statements they are reporting.

(vi) The purpose of the external audit under International Standards on Auditing is for the auditor to obtain sufficient appropriate audit evidence on which to base the audit opinion. This opinion is on whether the financial statements give a 'true and fair view' (or 'present fairly in all material respects') of the position, performance (and cash flows) of the entity. This opinion is prepared for the benefit of shareholders.

chapter

3

# Ethics and acceptance

## Chapter learning objectives

When you have completed this chapter you will be able to:

- Define and apply the fundamental principles of professional ethics.
- Describe the auditor's responsibility with regard to auditor independence, conflicts of interest and confidentiality.
- Identify and explain threats to the fundamental principles and safeguards to manage those threats.
- Discuss the preconditions, requirements of professional ethics and other requirements in relation to the acceptance of new audit engagements.
- Explain the importance of engagement letters and state their contents.

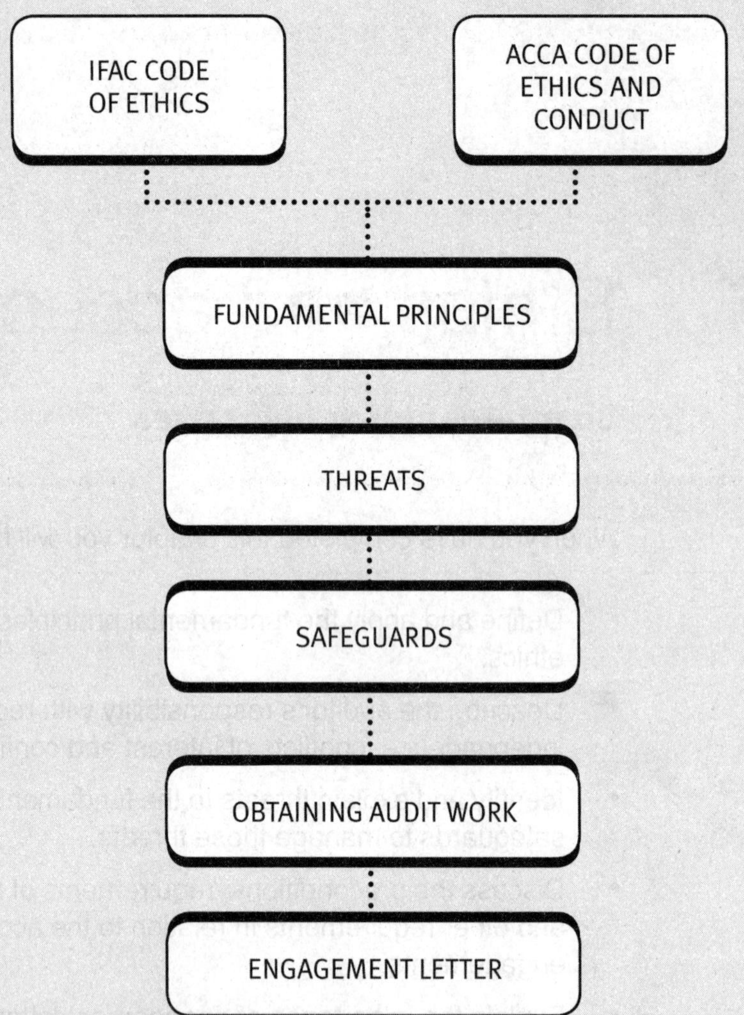


## 1 The need for professional ethics

Professional accountants have a responsibility to act in the public interest. The purpose of assurance engagements is to increase the confidence of the intended users, therefore the users need to trust the professional who is providing the assurance.

In order to be trusted the assurance provider needs to be **independent** of their client. Independence can be defined as having 'freedom from situations and relationships where objectivity would be perceived to be impaired by a reasonable and informed third party.'

Therefore, assurance providers need to and must operate (and be perceived to operate) in accordance with an accepted code of ethics.

## 2 The IFAC and ACCA codes and the conceptual framework

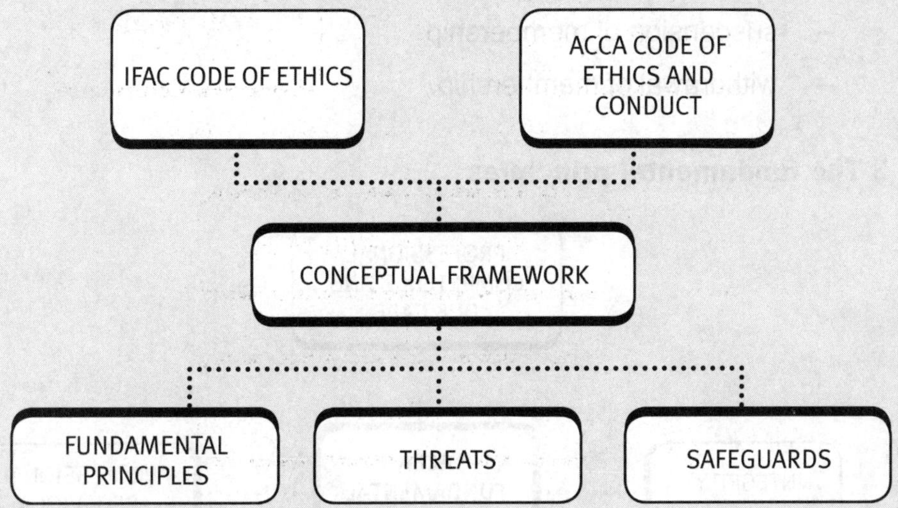


IFAC, through the IESBA, has issued a code of ethics, as has the ACCA. The ACCA Code of Ethics is covered in this chapter. However, both the IESBA and ACCA codes have the same roots and are, to all intents and purposes identical.

Both follow a conceptual framework which identifies:

- fundamental principles of ethical behaviour
- potential threats to compliance with these fundamental principles
- possible safeguards which can be implemented to eliminate the threats identified, or reduce them to an acceptable level.

A conceptual framework relies on a principles rather than a rules based approach. This provides guidance so that the principles may be applied to wide ranging and potentially unique circumstances.

This requires the assurance provider to apply **professional judgement** in applying the code of ethics.

### Consequences

Practitioners should apply the spirit of the code to every day practice. However, the framework and principles would be of little use if they could not be enforced.

Professional bodies like the ACCA therefore reserve the right to discipline members who fail to comply with the code of ethics through a process of:

- Disciplinary hearings which can result in:
  – fines
  – suspension of membership
  – withdrawal of membership.

**3 The fundamental principles**

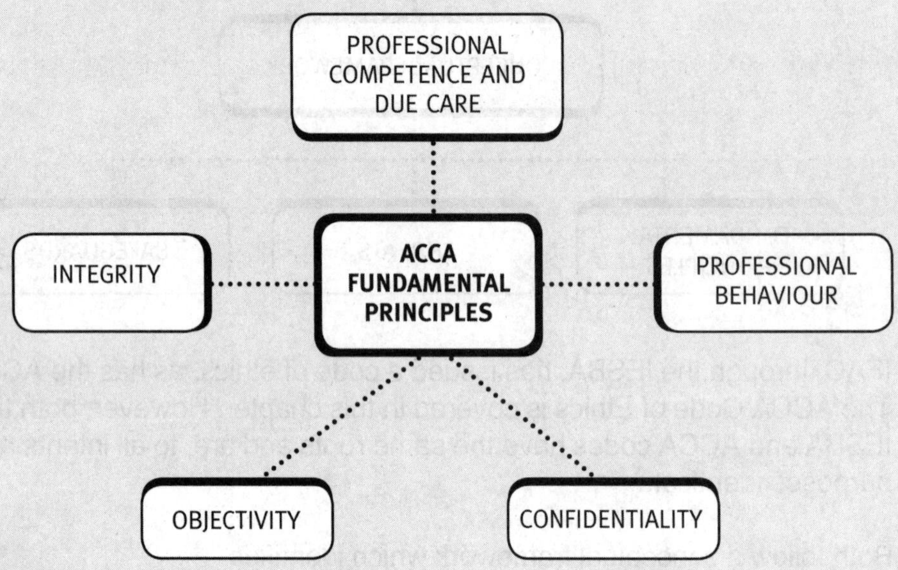


The formal definitions of the fundamental principles are as follows:

- **Objectivity**: Members should not allow bias, conflicts of interest or undue influence of others to override professional or business judgements.
- **Professional behaviour**: Members should comply with relevant laws and regulations and should avoid any action that discredits the profession.
- **Professional competence and due care**: Members should maintain professional knowledge and skill at a level required to ensure that a client or employer receives competent professional services based on current developments in practice, legislation and techniques.

  Members should act diligently and in accordance with applicable technical and professional standards.
- **Integrity**: Members should be straightforward and honest in all professional and business relationships.

- **Confidentiality**: Members should respect the confidentiality of information acquired as a result of professional and business relationships and should not disclose any such information to third parties without proper and specific authority or unless there is a legal or professional right or duty to disclose. Confidential information acquired as a result of professional and business relationships should not be used for the personal advantage of members or third parties.

Practitioners need to **behave and be seen to behave** in an ethical, professional manner. This means taking active steps to comply with the Code of Ethics in every professional situation.

e.g

**Illustration 1: Fundamental principles**

The following are real précis hearings held and decisions made and published by the ACCA Disciplinary Committee:

(1) A member was found guilty of misconduct because they signed the audit report of a company without conducting any audit work, contrary to the fundamental principle of..........................................?

(2) A member was found guilty of misconduct because they failed to advise a client to have an audit when an audit was required by law, contrary to the fundamental principle of..........................................?

(3) A member was found guilty of misconduct because they 'failed to reply to correspondence sent by a third party and ACCA' contrary to the fundamental principle of..........................................?

(4) A member was found guilty of misconduct because they 'lost possession of a client's books and records to a third party' contrary to the fundamental principle of..........................................?

(5) A member was found guilty of misconduct because they 'carried out an audit of a company' in which they owned shares 'without implementing appropriate safeguards' contrary to the fundamental principle of..........................................?

**Exercise:**

**Discuss the scenarios described above and identify which of the fundamental principles has been breached in each circumstance.**

**Case Study Solution: Fundamental principles**

The following are real précis hearings held and decisions made by the ACCA Disciplinary Committee:

(1) A member was found guilty of misconduct because they signed the audit report of a company without conducting any audit work, contrary to the fundamental principle of **integrity**.

(2) A member was found guilty of misconduct because they failed to advise a client to have an audit when an audit was required by law, contrary to the fundamental principle of **professional competence and due care**.

(3) A member was found guilty of misconduct because they 'failed to reply to correspondence sent by a third party and ACCA' contrary to the fundamental principle of **professional behaviour**.

(4) A member was found guilty of misconduct because they 'lost possession of a client's books and records to a third party' contrary to the fundamental principle of **confidentiality**.

(5) A member was found guilty of misconduct because they 'carried out an audit of a company' in which they owned shares 'without implementing appropriate safeguards' contrary to the fundamental principle of **objectivity**.

As a result, a combination of the following sanctions were ordered by ACCA Disciplinary Committee in each case:

- suspension of membership
- exclusion from ACCA
- a fine
- a costs order
- publication of the results of the decision and the member's name on the ACCA website
- publication of the results of the decision and the member's name in the local press.

## 4 Threats and safeguards

**Definitions and examples of threats**

**Self interest threat:** a financial or other interest that will inappropriately influence the judgement or behaviour of the assurance provider, e.g. if a firm were to charge a contingent fee (i.e. a fee calculated based on the result of the work performed) – contingent fees are not permitted for assurance engagements.

**Self-review threat:** not appropriately evaluating the results of work performed by the assurance provider or another individual or team within their firm as part of a separate engagement, e.g. if a firm were to provide valuation services for a client – valuation of matters which are material to the financial statements and involve a significant degree of subjectivity must not be provided for audit clients.

**Advocacy threat:** promoting the position of a client, e.g. if a firm promoted shares in audit client (which they must not).

**Familiarity threat:** being too sympathetic to or too trusting of a client, due to a long or close relationship, e.g. if a member of the audit team joins an audit client (this would also create an intimidation threat).

**Intimidation threat:** actual or perceived pressures from the client, or attempts to exercise undue influence over the assurance provider, e.g. actual or threatened litigation between the auditor and audit client (in which case it may be necessary to resign from the engagement).

**Identifying the threats**

Firms must establish procedures to:

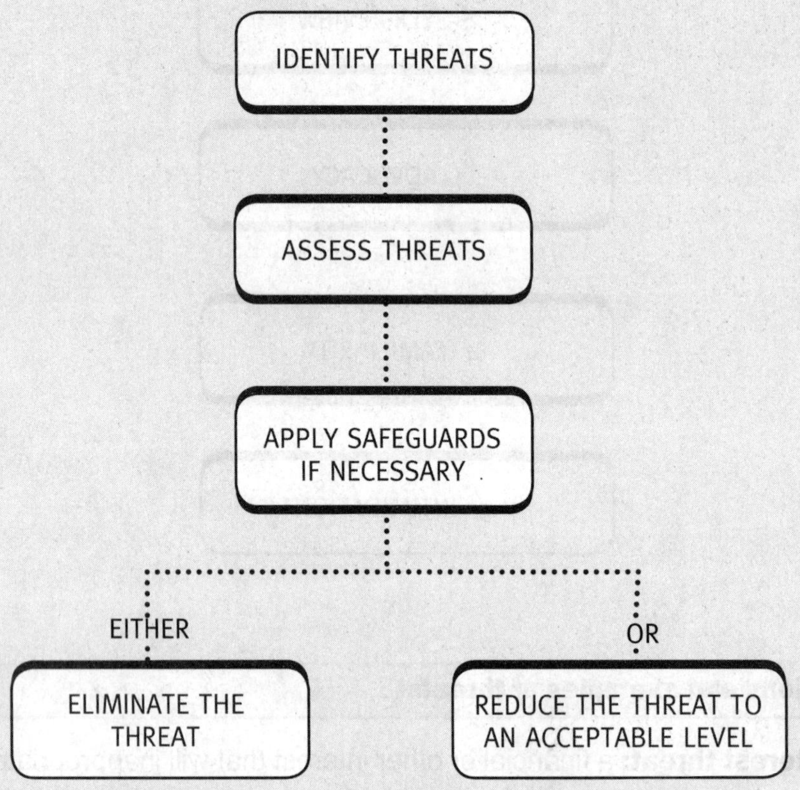

A **safeguard** is an action or measure that eliminates a threat, or reduces it to an acceptable level.

If the threat cannot be eliminated or reduced to an acceptable level, the assurance provider must decline or resign from the engagement.

The ACCA Code of Ethics divides safeguards into two broad categories:

- **Safeguards created by the profession, legislation or regulation**, these include: requirements for entry into the profession, continuing professional development, corporate governance, professional standards, and monitoring and disciplinary procedures, etc.
- **Safeguards created by the work environment**, these include: rotation/removal of relevant staff from the engagement team, independent quality control reviews, using separate teams, etc.

## Illustration 2: Wimble & Co ethics

You are an audit manager in Wimble & Co, a large audit firm which specialises in providing audit and accountancy services to manufacturing companies. Murray Co has asked your firm to accept appointment as external auditor. Murray Co manufactures sports equipment. Your firm also audits Barker Co, another manufacturer of sports equipment, and therefore your firm is confident it has the experience to carry out the audit.

You have been asked to take on the role of audit manager for Murray Co, should your firm accept the engagement. You own a small number of shares in Murray Co, as you used to be an employee of the company. Don Henman, who has been the engagement partner for Barker Co for twelve years, will take the role of engagement partner for Murray Co. The audit senior will be Tim Andrews, as his sister is the Financial Controller at Murray Co and therefore he knows the business well.

Your firm recently purchased some bibs, footballs and other equipment from Murray Co for the firm's annual football tournament. Murray Co has offered to provide this equipment free of charge to the firm if they accept the role as auditor.

Murray Co would also like your firm to provide taxation and accounting services. Specifically, the company would like you to prepare the financial statements and represent the company in a dispute with the taxation authorities.

The fees for last year's audit of Barker Co have not yet been paid, and you have been asked by Don Henman to look into the matter.

**Exercise:**

**Using the information provided, explain the ethical threats which may affect the independence of Wimble & Co in respect of the audit of Murray Co or Barker Co, and for each threat identify ways in which the threat might be reduced.**

## Solution: Wimble & Co ethics

**Conflict of Interest**

**Wimble & Co also audits Barker Co, another manufacturer of sports equipment. The engagement partner for Barker Co will be the engagement partner for Murray Co.**

Acting for directly competing clients is a threat to objectivity (and confidentiality). It is normal for firms to have clients that are in competition with each other; firms need relevant professional experience in the client's industry in order to comply with the fundamental principle of professional competence and accept appointment as auditor.

In order to manage such a conflict of interest, Wimble & Co should ensure that separate teams are used for each engagement – more detail is provided later in this chapter.

**Financial interest**

**The audit manager owns shares in Murray Co.**

The audit firm or a member of the assurance team (or their immediate family) are not allowed to own a direct financial interest in a client.

This creates a **self-interest threat**: the audit manager may be reluctant to identify misstatements or modify the audit opinion for fear of damaging the value of their shareholding.

The audit manager must be required to dispose of the shares, or another audit manager should be appointed to the engagement team instead.

**Business relationship**

**Wimble & Co recently purchased some bibs, footballs and other equipment from Murray Co.**

Purchasing goods and services from an audit client, does not generally create a threat to independence if the transaction is in the normal course of business and at arm's length.

However, a close business relationship between a firm or an audit team member (or their immediate family) and the client, such as a joint venture, creates a **self-interest threat**. Such relationships are not normally acceptable unless clearly insignificant.

**Gifts and hospitality**

**Murray Co has offered free equipment to the auditor.**

Accepting gifts or hospitality from an audit client may create **self-interest** and **familiarity** threats.

The partners of the firm should evaluate the gift offered and unless trivial and inconsequential, the audit team must not accept the equipment.

**Long association**

**The engagement partner for Barker Co has been in place for twelve years.**

**Familiarity** and **self-interest** threats are created by using the same senior personnel on an assurance engagement for a long period of time. Possible safeguards include:

- rotating the senior personnel off the assurance team
- independent review of the senior personnel's work
- independent quality control reviews of the engagement.

If it is a **listed company or another public interest entity**, individuals cannot act as **key audit partners** for more than **seven years** before being rotated off the audit for a minimum of **two years** (in exceptional circumstances in the interest of audit quality, an individual can act as key audit partner for eight years).

**Personal relationship**

**The audit senior's sister is the Financial Controller at Murray Co.**

Family and personal relationships between a member of an assurance team and a director of the client, or an employee of the client in a position to exert significant influence over the subject matter, may create **self-interest**, **familiarity** or **intimidation threats**.

Tim Andrew's sister is the Financial Controller at Murray Co and is therefore in a position to exert significant influence over the financial statements. Tim Andrews should not be on the audit team for Murray Co.

**Provision of other services**

The provision of other services may create threats to objectivity and independence. The threats, and significance of those threats is dependent on the services being provided.

However, there are some threats that may be created regardless of the type of service, such as:

- When the total fees from an audit client represent a large proportion of a firm's total income (or a specific partner or office's income), i.e. **fee dependence**, a **self-interest** or **intimidation** threat to objectivity may be created; the auditor may be reluctant to identify misstatements in the financial statements or to modify the audit opinion, for fear of losing the client. Possible safeguards include:
  - reducing dependence on the client
  - independent quality control reviews of the engagement.
- When the audit client is a **listed client or other public interest entity**, and the total fees represent **more than 15%** of the firm's total income for **two consecutive years**, the firm must:
  - disclose this to those charged with governance
  - arrange for an external quality control review of the engagement (either before or after issuing the audit report).
- Assuming management responsibilities for an assurance client may create threats to independence. The provision of other services may require the assurance firm to assume management responsibilities but an assurance firm **must not assume management responsibilities** as part of an assurance engagement or **for an audit client**.
  - Activities that are routine and administrative, or involve matters that are insignificant, generally are deemed not to be a management responsibility.
  - Providing advice and recommendations to assist management in discharging its responsibilities is not assuming management responsibilities.

In addition:

(1) **Murray Co would like the audit firm to prepare the financial statements.**

Preparing the financial statements and then auditing them creates a significant **self-review** threat to objectivity. However, audit firms may provide such services, as long as the client is not a listed or other public-interest entity, with adequate safeguards in place, including:

- Using staff who are not part of the audit team to prepare the financial statements or
- if performed by a member of the audit team, arranging an independent partner or senior staff member to review the work performed.

If an **audit client** is a **listed or other public-interest entity**, the firm **must not provide any accounting or bookkeeping services**, including payroll services or preparation of the financial statements.

(2) **Murray Co would like the audit firm to and represent the company in a dispute with the taxation authorities.**

This would create **advocacy** and **self-review** threats.

**Firms must not represent audit clients in such disputes.**

**Overdue fees**

**The fee for last year's audit of Barker Co have not yet been paid.**

Overdue fees create a **self-interest threat** where they remain unpaid for some time.

In addition, overdue fees could be perceived to be a loan. **An audit firm must not enter into any loan arrangement with a client.**

A firm should take steps to ensure audit fees are paid before the audit report is issued. If fees remain outstanding for any engagement, possible safeguards include an independent quality control review.

## 5 Confidentiality

External auditors are in a unique position of having a legal right of access to all information about their clients. The client must be able to trust the auditor not to disclose anything about their business to anyone as it could be detrimental to their operations.

Members of an assurance team should not disclose any information to anyone outside of the engagement team, whether or not they work for the same firm.

Information should only be disclosed with proper and specific authority or when there is a legal or professional right or duty to disclose.

**Duty to disclose:**

- Breaches of specific laws to the appropriate public authority, e.g. money laundering, terrorism, treason, or drug trafficking.
- If a court order has been obtained.
- If it is required by ACCA or another professional body.

**Right to disclose:**

- If the client has given their permission.
- To protect a member or firm's interests, e.g. to defend themselves in court or at a disciplinary hearing.
- Where authorised by law.
- Breaches of regulations to a non-governmental regulatory body that has the power to compel disclosure, e.g. financial services authority.
- If it is in the public interest to do so.*

**Public interest**

*There is no definition of 'public interest'. Whether or not it is in the public interest is difficult to prove and the auditor must proceed with caution if thinking of disclosing information for this reason. Such examples could include fraud, environmental pollution, or simply companies acting against the public good.

Legal advice should be sought beforehand to avoid the risk of being sued. Matters should only be reported to an appropriate authority.

Before disclosing information in the public interest, the auditor should consider, for example, whether that matter is likely to be repeated and how serious the effects of the client's actions are.

**Conflicts of interest**

Professional accountants should always act in the best interests of the client. However, where conflicts of interest exist, such as when a firm acts for competing clients (which is common) the firm's work should be arranged to **avoid the interests of one being adversely affected** by those of another and to prevent a breach of **confidentiality**.

In order to ensure this, the firm must notify all affected clients of the conflict and **obtain their consent to act**. The following additional safeguards should be considered:

- advise the clients to seek independent advice
- separate engagement teams (with different engagement partners and team members)
- procedures to prevent access to information, e.g. physical separation of the team members and confidential/secure data filing
- signed confidentiality agreements
- regular review of the application of safeguards by an independent person of appropriate seniority.

If adequate safeguards cannot be implemented, the firm must decline, or resign from one or more conflicting engagements.

## 6 Accepting new audit engagements

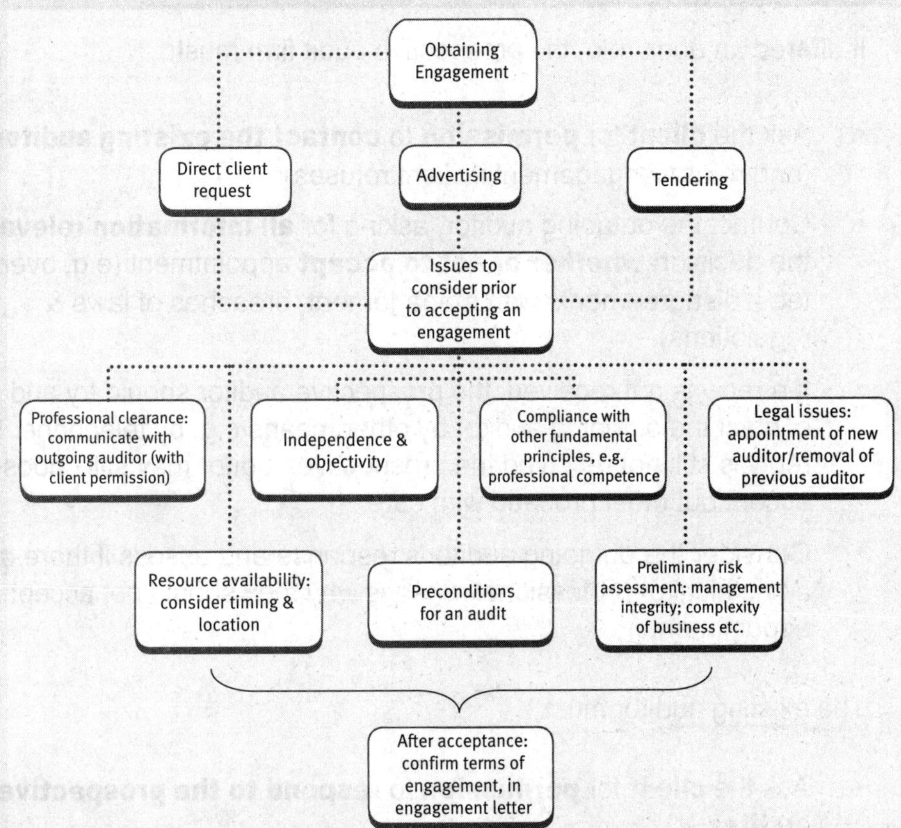

**Preconditions for an audit**

Auditors should only accept a new audit engagement, or continue an existing audit engagement if the 'preconditions for an audit' required by ISA 210 *Agreeing the terms of audit engagements* are present.

ISA 210 requires the auditor to:

- Determine whether the financial reporting framework to be applied in the preparation of the financial statements is appropriate.
- Obtain the agreement of management that it acknowledges and understands its responsibilities.

If the preconditions for an audit are not present, the auditor should discuss the matter with management, and should not accept the engagement unless required to do so by law or regulation.

**Professional clearance**

If offered an audit role, the prospective audit firm must:

- Ask the **client** for **permission** to **contact the existing auditor** (and refuse engagement if client refuses).
- Contact the outgoing auditor, asking for **all information relevant** to the decision **whether or not to accept** appointment (e.g. overdue fees, disagreements with management, breaches of laws & regulations).
- If a reply is not received, the prospective auditor should try and contact the outgoing auditor by other means e.g. by telephone. If a reply is still not received the prospective auditor may still choose to accept but must proceed with care.
- Consider the outgoing auditor's response and assess if there are any ethical or professional reasons why they should not accept appointment.

The existing auditor must:

- Ask the **client** for **permission** to **respond to the prospective auditor**.
- If the client refuses permission, the existing auditor should notify the prospective auditor of this fact.

## 7 Engagement letters

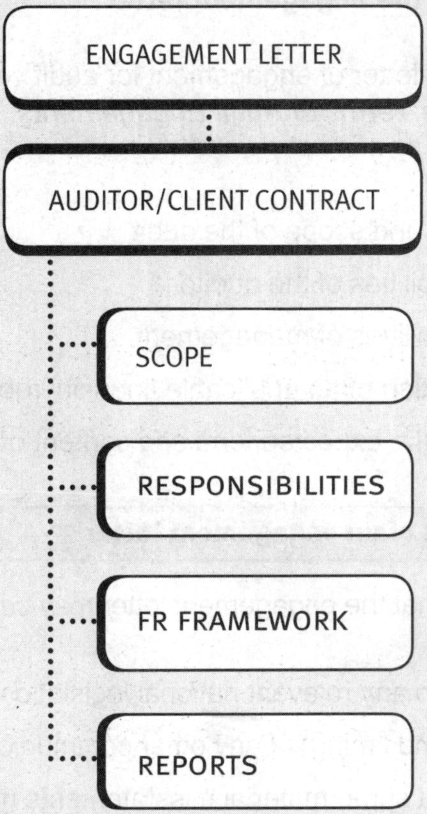


### Engagement letters – main considerations

The engagement letter will be **sent before the audit**. It specifies the nature of the **contract** between the audit firm and the client and minimises the risk of any misunderstanding of the auditor's role.

It should be **reviewed every year** to ensure that it is up to date but does not need to be reissued every year unless there are changes to the terms of the engagement. The auditor must issue a **new engagement letter if the scope or context** of the assignment **changes** after initial appointment.

ISA 210 requires the auditor to consider whether there is a need to remind the entity of the existing terms of the audit engagement for recurring audits and many firms choose to send a new letter every year, to emphasise its importance to clients.

**Reasons for changes**

Reasons for changes include:

- Changes to statutory duties due to new legislation.
- Changes to professional duties, perhaps due to new ISAs.
- Changes to 'other services' as requested by clients.

## The contents of the engagement letter

The contents of a letter of engagement for audit services are listed in ISA 210 *Agreeing the Terms of Audit Engagements*. The contents should include:

- the objective and scope of the audit
- the responsibilities of the auditor
- the responsibilities of management
- the identification of an applicable financial reporting framework
- reference to the expected form and content of any reports to be issued.

**Other contents of an engagement letter**

Other matters that the engagement letter may cover include:

- reference to any relevant national legislation
- the form (and timing) of any other communication during the audit
- the fact that some material misstatements may not be detected
- key members of the audit team
- period of engagement
- the basis on which fees are calculated and any billing arrangements
- arrangements concerning the involvement of internal auditors and other staff of the entity
- limitations to the auditor's liability
- a request for management to acknowledge receipt of the audit engagement letter and to agree to the terms of the engagement.

**Illustration 3: Murray Co engagement letter**

Wimble & Co
14 The Grove
Kingston
KI4 6AP

25 November 2011

To the Board of Directors of Murray Company.

This letter and the attached terms of business dated 25 November 2011 set out the basis on which we are to provide services as auditors and your and our respective responsibilities.

**The objective and scope of the audit:** You have requested that we audit the financial statements of Murray Company, which comprise the statement of financial position as at December 31, and the statement of profit or loss, statement of changes in equity and cash flow statement for the year then ended, and a summary of significant accounting policies and other explanatory information.

We are pleased to confirm our acceptance and our understanding of this audit engagement by means of this letter. Our audit will be conducted with the objective of our expressing an opinion on the financial statements.

**The responsibilities of the auditor:** We will conduct our audit in accordance with International Standards on Auditing (ISAs). Those standards require that we comply with ethical requirements and plan and perform the audit to obtain reasonable assurance about whether the financial statements are free from material misstatement. An audit involves performing procedures to obtain audit evidence about the amounts and disclosures in the financial statements. The procedures selected depend on the auditor's judgment, including the assessment of the risks of material misstatement of the financial statements, whether due to fraud or error. An audit also includes evaluating the appropriateness of accounting policies used and the reasonableness of accounting estimates made by management, as well as evaluating the overall presentation of the financial statements.

Because of the inherent limitations of an audit, together with the inherent limitations of internal control, there is an unavoidable risk that some material misstatements may not be detected, even though the audit is properly planned and performed in accordance with ISAs.

In making our risk assessments, we consider internal control relevant to Murray Company's preparation of the financial statements in order to design audit procedures that are appropriate in the circumstances, but not for the purpose of expressing an opinion on the effectiveness of Murray Company's internal control. However, we will communicate to you in writing concerning any significant deficiencies in internal control relevant to the audit of the financial statements that we have identified during the audit.

**The responsibilities of management:** Our audit will be conducted on the basis that management acknowledge and understand that they have responsibility:

(a) For the preparation and fair presentation of the financial statements in accordance with International Financial Reporting Standards.

(b) For such internal control as management determines is necessary to enable the preparation of financial statements that are free from material misstatement, whether due to fraud or error.

(c) To provide us with:

(i) Access to all information of which management is aware that is relevant to the preparation of the financial statements such as records, documentation and other matters.

(ii) Additional information that we may request from management for the purpose of the audit.

(iii) Unrestricted access to persons within the entity from whom we determine it necessary to obtain audit evidence.

As part of our audit process, we will request from management written confirmation concerning representations made to us in connection with the audit.

We look forward to full cooperation from your staff during our audit.

**Report:** We will report to the members of Murray Company as a body, whether in our opinion the financial statements present fairly in all material respects, the financial position of Murray Company as at December 31, and its financial performance and its cash flows for the year then ended in accordance with International Financial Reporting Standards. The form and content of our report may need to be amended in the light of our audit findings.

**Fees:** Our fees, which will be billed as work progresses, are based on the time required by the individuals assigned to the engagement plus out-of-pocket expenses. Individual hourly rates vary according to the degree of responsibility involved and the experience and skill required.

**Period of engagement:** This engagement will start on 01 January 2012 with the company's accounting period ending on 31 December. We will not be responsible for earlier years. The company's previous advisers, Roland, Garros & Co will deal with outstanding returns, assessments and other matters relating to earlier periods.

This letter supersedes any previous engagement letter for the period covered. Once agreed, this letter will remain effective for future years from the date of signature unless it is terminated, amended or superseded. You or we may agree to vary or terminate our authority to act on your behalf at any time without penalty. Notice of variation or termination must be given in writing.

**Limitation of liability:** To the fullest extent permitted by law, we will not be responsible for any losses, where you or others supply incorrect or incomplete information, or fail to supply any appropriate information or where you fail to act on our advice or respond promptly to communications from us.

Our work is not, unless there is a legal or regulatory requirement, to be made available to third parties without our written permission and we will accept no responsibility to third parties for any aspect of our professional services or work that is made available to them.

**Confirmation of your agreement:** Please sign and return the attached copy of this letter to indicate your acknowledgement of, and agreement with, the arrangements for our audit of the financial statements including our respective responsibilities.

If this letter and the attached terms of business are not in accordance with your understanding of our terms of appointment, please let us know.

*Wimble & Co*

Wimble & Co

Acknowledged and agreed on behalf of Murray Company by (signed)

..........................
Name and Title
Date

**Murray Co engagement letter**

*To the Board of Directors of Murray Company...*

- Although the audit report is issued to the shareholders, the engagement letter is addressed to and signed by the directors of a company.

*The responsibilities of the auditor... The responsibilities of management...*

- It is important to set out the directors and auditors responsibilities for clarity and to reduce any expectation gap.
- The responsibilities of the auditor include the scope of the audit, i.e. the process by which the auditor will form their opinion. The same description of the scope of an audit is included in the audit report.

*We will report to the members of Murray Company as a body...*

- It is important to define who the intended users of the report are, i.e. who can place reliance on it.

*This engagement will start on 01 January 2012 with the company's accounting period ending on 31 December. We will not be responsible for earlier years...*

- The auditor's responsibility starts at the beginning of the period for which they are providing the first audit report.

*Confirmation of your agreement...*

- Both the client and the auditor must sign and retain a copy of the engagement letter for reference and to support the contract agreed.

## UK Syllabus Focus

The Financial Reporting Council has issued a set of ethical standards designed to ensure practitioners comply with the IFAC Code of Ethics in the UK. However, you will be examined on the IFAC Code of Ethics. The FRC ethical standards can be summarised as follows:

**Ethical Standard 1 – integrity, objectivity and independence**

- The audit firm shall establish policies and procedures to ensure that the firm, and all those involved in the audit, act with integrity, objectivity and independence.
- The leadership of the audit firm shall take responsibility for establishing a control environment that places adherence to ethical principles above commercial considerations.
- The audit firm shall designate an ethics partner.
- The audit firm shall establish policies and procedures to prevent employees from taking decisions that are the responsibility of management of the audited entity.
- The audit firm shall establish policies and procedures to assess the significance of threats to the auditor's objectivity:
  - (i) when considering whether to accept or retain an audit or non-audit service
  - (ii) when planning the audit
  - (iii) when forming an opinion on the financial statements
  - (iv) when potential threats are reported.
- The audit engagement partner shall not accept or shall not continue an audit engagement if he or she concludes that any threats to the auditor's objectivity and independence cannot be reduced to an acceptable level.
- In the case of listed companies the engagement quality control reviewer shall:
  - (i) consider the audit firm's compliance with the FRC Ethical Standards and
  - (ii) form an independent opinion as to the appropriateness and adequacy of the safeguards applied.

**Ethical Standard 2 – financial, business, employment and personal relationships**

- The audit firm, or employees, shall not hold any financial interest in an audited entity.
- Audit firms and employees shall not make loans to, or guarantee the borrowings of, an audited entity (and vice versa).
- Audit firms and employees shall not enter into business relationships with an audited entity.
- An audit firm shall not second partners or employees to an audit client unless:
  (i) the agreement is for a short period of time and
  (ii) the audited entity agrees that the individual concerned will not hold a management position.
- Where a partner or employee returns to a firm on completion of a secondment to an audit client, that individual shall not be given any role on the audit involving any function or activity that they performed or supervised during that assignment.
- Where a partner joins an audited entity, the audit firm shall take action to ensure that no connections remain between the firm and the individual.
- Where a partner leaves a firm and is appointed as a director or to a key management position with an audited entity, having acted as audit engagement partner at any time in the two years prior to this appointment, the firm shall resign as auditor.
- A partner, or employee of the audit firm who undertakes audit work, shall not accept appointment:
  (i) to the board of directors of the audited entity or
  (ii) to any subcommittee of that board.

**ES 3 – Long association with the audit engagement**

- The audit firm shall establish policies and procedures to monitor the length of time that senior staff serve as members of the engagement team for each audit.
- Where senior staff have a long association with the audit, the audit firm shall assess the threats to the auditor's objectivity and independence and shall apply safeguards to reduce the threats to an acceptable level. Where appropriate safeguards cannot be applied, the audit firm shall either resign as auditor or not stand for reappointment, as appropriate.

- Once an audit engagement partner has held this role for ten years, careful consideration must be given as to whether their objectivity would be perceived to be impaired.
- In the case of listed companies the audit firm shall establish policies and procedures to ensure that no one shall act as audit engagement partner for more than five years (this can be extended by up to two years with audit commitee approval in order to safeguard audit quality).
- In the case of listed companies, the audit engagement partner shall review the safeguards put in place to address the threats arising where senior staff have been involved in the audit for a period longer than seven years.

**ES 4 – Fees, remuneration and evaluation policies, litigation, gifts and hospitality**

- The audit engagement partner shall ensure that audit fees are not influenced or determined by the provision of non-audit services;
- An audit shall not be undertaken on a contingent fee basis.
- Audit fee for the previous audit and the arrangements for its payment shall be agreed with the audited entity before the audit firm formally accepts appointment as auditor in respect of the following period.
- Where it is expected that the total fees receivable from a listed audited entity will regularly exceed 10% of the annual fee income (15% if non-listed) of the audit firm, the firm shall not act as the auditor of that entity.
- The audit firm shall establish policies and procedures to ensure that the objectives and appraisal of members of the audit team do not include selling non-audit services.
- Where litigation with a client is already in progress, or where it is probable, the audit firm shall either not continue with or not accept the audit engagement.
- The audit firm, including employees, shall not accept gifts from the audited entity, unless the value is clearly insignificant.
- Audit firm employees shall not accept hospitality from the audited entity, unless it is reasonable in terms of its frequency, nature and cost.

**ES 5 – non-audit services provided to audited entities**

- Before the audit firm accepts a proposed engagement to provide non-audit services to an audit client, the audit engagement partner shall:

(i) consider whether a reasonable third party would regard the objectives of the proposed engagement as being inconsistent with the objectives of the audit

(ii) identify and assess any threats to the auditor's objectivity, including any perceived loss of independence

(iii) identify and assess the effectiveness of the available safeguards to eliminate the threats or reduce them to an acceptable level.

- Where the audit partner considers it probable that a reasonable third party would regard the objectives of the proposed non-audit service engagement as being inconsistent with the objectives of the audit, the audit firm shall either:

  (i) not undertake the non-audit service engagement or

  (ii) not accept or withdraw from the audit engagement.

- Specifically, the audit firm shall not undertake an engagement to provide internal audit services to an audited entity where it is reasonably foreseeable that:

  (i) for the purposes of the audit of the financial statements, the auditor would place significant reliance on the internal audit work performed by the audit firm or

  (ii) for the purposes of the internal audit services, the audit firm would undertake part of the role of management.

- The audit firm shall not undertake an engagement to design, provide or implement information technology systems for an audited entity where:

  (i) the systems concerned would be important to any significant part of the accounting system and the auditor would place significant reliance upon them as part of the audit of the financial statements or

  (ii) for the purposes of the information technology services, the audit firm would undertake part of the role of management.

**ES – Provisions Available for Small Entities (PASE)**

When auditing the financial statements of a small entity the audit firm is not required to:

- Comply with the requirement that an external independent quality control review is performed.
- Apply safeguards to address self-review threat provided:

  (i) the audited entity has 'informed management' and

  (ii) the audit firm extends the cyclical inspection of completed engagements that is performed for quality control purposes.

- Adhere to the prohibitions in Ethical Standard 5, relating to providing non-audit services that involve the audit firm undertaking part of the role of management, provided that it discusses objectivity and independence issues related to the provision of non-audit services with those charged with governance, confirming that management accept responsibility for any decisions taken.
- Comply with Ethical Standard 5, paragraph 82 (acting as an advocate by providing tax services to an audit client during an appeal/tribunal).
- Comply with Ethical Standard 2, paragraph 48 (partner leaving firm and being appointed as director of audit client) provided that it takes appropriate steps to determine that there has been no significant threat to the audit team's integrity, objectivity and independence.

**Test your understanding 1**

**Explain each of the FIVE fundamental principles of ACCA's Code of Ethics and Conduct.**

*Real exam question: December 2007*

**(5 marks)**

**Test your understanding 2**

(a) There are legal and professional arrangements for the appointment and removal of auditors.

(i) **State the circumstances in which a person is not eligible to act as an auditor**

**(2 marks)**

(ii) **Describe the steps required to remove an auditor from an engagement.**

**(3 marks)**

You are a manager in the audit department of Whilling and Abel. A potential new client, Truckers Co, a haulage company, has approached your firm to do the statutory audit in addition to some other non-audit services for the financial year ended 30 September 2013. Your audit firm was recommended to Truckers Co by an existing client, O&P, a shipping company who is also a major customer of Truckers Co.

You have been chosen to lead the assignment as you have experience of auditing haulage companies and you also manage the audit of O&P. Whilst arranging the initial meeting with the directors of Truckers Co you discover that you studied accountancy with the finance director at university.

During the meeting, you establish that Truckers Co has not made a profit for the last 2 years. The directors explain that this is largely due to escalating costs in the industry including fuel price rises. They are confident they have now controlled their costs for the current year to 30 September 2012. They have also been approached to tender for a large profitable contract which would improve their financial performance going forward. They would like you to assist them with the preparation of this tender and present with them on the day.

The current year's financial statements and audit are being finalised with another audit firm. The finance director tells you that the current auditors have identified material misstatements but the board of directors are refusing to make these adjustments. If adjusted, it would turn the break even position into a loss. The finance director told you this information informally whilst catching up on old times at the local pub.

The current auditors have replied to your professional clearance letter and have informed you that they are still owed fees relating to the year ended 30 September 2012. This is under dispute with the client.

Once back from the meeting you calculate that the potential fees from Truckers Co would amount to about 14% of your firm's total fee income.

**Required:**

(b) **Identify and explain the threats to independence if Whilling and Abel accept Truckers Co as a new audit client. For each threat, recommend how the threat can be managed.**

**(15 marks)**

**(Total: 20 marks)**

**Test your understanding 3**

You are a manager in the audit firm of JT & Co and this is your first time you have worked on one of the firm's established clients, Pink Co. The main activity of Pink Co is providing investment advice to individuals regarding saving for retirement, purchase of shares and securities and investing in tax efficient savings schemes. Pink Co is a listed company regulated by the relevant financial services authority.

You have been asked to start the audit planning for Pink Co, by Mrs Goodall, a partner in JT & Co. Mrs Goodall has been the engagement partner for Pink Co, for the previous seven years and so has a sound knowledge of the client. Mrs Goodall has informed you that she would like her son Simon to be part of the audit team this year; Simon is currently studying for his first set of fundamentals papers for his ACCA qualification. Mrs Goodall also informs you that Mr Supper, the audit senior, received investment advice from Pink Co during the year and intends to do the same next year.

In an initial meeting with the finance director of Pink Co, you learn that the audit team will not be entertained on Pink Co's yacht this year as this could appear to be an attempt to influence the opinion of the audit. Instead, he has arranged a day at the horse races costing less than two fifth's of the expense of using the yacht and hopes this will be acceptable.

JT & Co have done some consultive work previously and the invoice is still outstanding.

**Required:**

**Identify and explain the threats to independence in relation to the audit of Pink Co by JT & Co. For each threat, recommend how the threat can be managed.**

**(10 marks)**

**Test your understanding 4**

Client confidentiality underpins the relationship between Chartered Certified Accountants in practice and their clients.

It is a core element of ACCA's Rules of Professional Conduct.

**Required:**

(a) **Explain the circumstances in which ACCA's Rules of Professional Conduct permit or require external auditors to disclose information relating to their clients to third parties without the knowledge or consent of the client.**

**(8 marks)**

(b) A waste disposal company has breached tax regulations, environmental regulations and health and safety regulations. The auditor has been approached by the tax authorities, the government body supervising the award of licences to such companies and a trade union representative. All of them have asked the auditor to provide them with information about the company. The auditor has also been approached by the police. They are investigating a suspected fraud perpetrated by the managing director of the company and they wish to ask the auditor certain questions about him.

**Describe how the auditor should respond to these types of request.**

**(12 marks)**

**(Total: 20 marks)**

## 8 Chapter summary

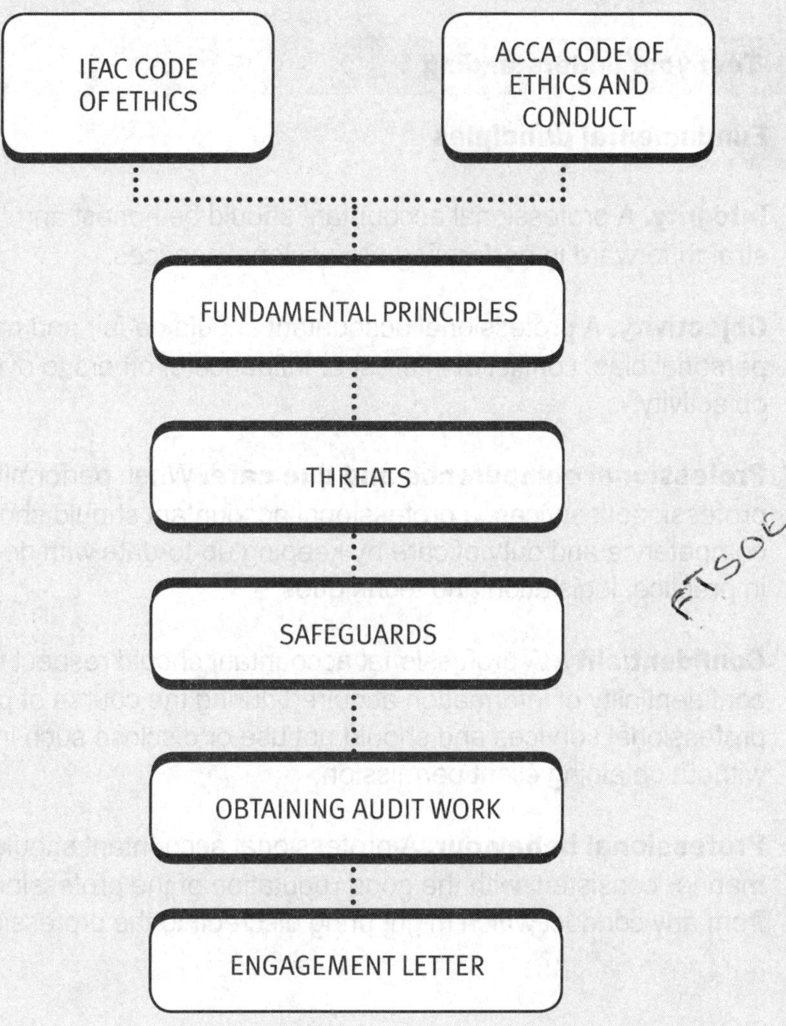

## Test your understanding answers

### Test your understanding 1

**Fundamental principles**

**Integrity.** A professional accountant should be honest and straightforward in performing professional services.

**Objectivity.** A professional accountant should be fair and not allow personal bias, conflict of interest or influence of others to override objectivity.

**Professional competence and due care.** When performing professional services, a professional accountant should show competence and duty of care by keeping up-to-date with developments in practice, legislation and techniques.

**Confidentiality.** A professional accountant should respect the confidentiality of information acquired during the course of providing professional services and should not use or disclose such information without obtaining client permission.

**Professional behaviour.** A professional accountant should act in a manner consistent with the good reputation of the profession and refrain from any conduct which might bring discredit to the profession.

### Test your understanding 2

(a)

(i) A person is not eligible to act as an auditor in the following circumstances:

- They are not a member of an RSB (recognised supervisory body) or not allowed to practice under the rules of an RSB.
- They are an officer or employee of the company.
- They are a business partner or employee of the company.

(ii) Steps required to remove an auditor from an engagement

- A decision must be made by the shareholders at a general meeting usually with a majority vote being required.
- Advance notice must be given to the company and the auditors prior to any general meeting
- Auditors have the right to attend and speak at the general meeting or have representations read out on their behalf.

(b) **Threats to independence**

| **Threat** | **Managing the threat** |
|---|---|
| Audit manager knows one of the directors socially. This creates a familiarity threat; the auditor may be too trusting of the client or too sympathetic to the client's needs. | A different audit manager should be assigned to the audit of Truckers Co. |
| You are the audit manager of one of Trucker Co's major customers. This creates a conflict of interest and a risk that confidential information may be passed between the clients. | A different audit manager should be assigned to the audit of Truckers Co.<br><br>Different teams should be used for the audit of Truckers Co and O&P. |
| The audit manager has been asked to present at the tender for clients contract. This would give rise to an advocacy threat as the audit firm would be promoting the client. | The auditors should politely decline the invitation to present at the tender explaining their reasons. |
| There are outstanding fees still owed to previous auditors for the year ending 30 September 2012. This situation could arise again for the new auditor leading to a self-interest threat where the auditor may not wish to identify misstatements or modify the audit opinion for fear of not receiving outstanding fees. | Discuss reasons for non payment with client and consider whether you should accept the assignment.<br><br>If accepted new work should not be commenced when significant fees remain outstanding. |

| | |
|---|---|
| The audit firm will provide non audit services in addition to the statutory audit. This represents a self-review threat. The audit firm may ignore or overlook their own errors when auditing the financial statements. | The audit firm should ensure separate teams work on each engagement.<br><br>An independent partner review of the files for each engagement should be arranged. |
| Total fees received from Trucker Co will represent 14% of the audit firm's total income. Fee dependence creates a self-interest threat. | Whilling & Abel should consider declining additional non-audit services from Trucker Co to reduce fee dependence.<br><br>An independent partner review of the audit work should be arranged. |

**Test your understanding 3**

| **Threat** | **Managing the threat** |
|---|---|
| Mrs Goodall has been the engagement partner for the last seven years. This creates a familiarity threat. Mrs Goodall may be too trusting of or too close to the client to be able to make objective decisions due to this long association. | Mrs Goodall should be rotated from the engagement team.<br><br>It may be possible to allow Mrs Goodall to continue as engagement partner for one further year in order to safeguard audit quality.<br><br>Audit committee approval must be obtained in order to allow this and an independent partner review of the audit files for Pink Co should be arranged. |
| There is no ethical rule which stops Mrs Goodall recommending Simon for the audit, or letting Simon take part in the audit.<br><br>However, there may be the impression of lack of independence as Simon is related to the engagement partner. Simon could be tempted not to identify errors in case this prejudiced his Mum's relationship with the client. | To demonstrate complete independence, Simon should not be part of any audit or assurance team for which Mrs Goodall is partner. |

| | |
|---|---|
| As long as Mr Supper paid a full fee to Pink Co for the investment advice (i.e. it is on an arm's length basis) there is no ethical threat as investment advice is in the normal course of business for Pink Co.<br><br>However, if Mr Supper were to receive a discount on the services of Pink Co as a benefit of being part of the audit team, this would create a self-interest threat.<br><br>In either case, continued use of client services could be perceived as a lack of independence as Mr Supper could be given the investment advice for a reduced fee (or free) as a benefit of being part of the audit team. | Mr Supper should be asked not to use the services of Pink Co again unless this is first agreed with the engagement partner. |
| The audit team has been offered a day at the horse races at the end of the audit.<br><br>Acceptance of gifts or hospitality from a client creates a self-interest threat, and unless of an insignificant amount, is not allowed. The fact that the horse race day costs less than the yacht expense is irrelevant, independence could still be impaired. | The day out should not be accepted. In addition, the rationale for accepting hospitality in previous years should be investigated. |
| There are outstanding fees. This creates a self-interest threat to objectivity. JT & Co may be reluctant to identify misstatements for fear of not getting paid.<br><br>In addition, outstanding fees may be considered to be a loan. Loans to clients are not permitted. | Payment for work should be arranged before the audit is commenced, or a payment plan agreed. |

**Test your understanding 4**

(a) **Disclosure of information relating to clients to third parties**

(i) Auditors are permitted or required to disclose information about their clients to third parties without their knowledge or consent in very limited circumstances.

(ii) Generally, auditors can be required to, or are permitted to, disclose information to certain regulatory bodies, including certain specialist units within police forces under legislation. Such legislation in many countries includes financial services legislation, legislation concerning banks and insurance companies, legislation concerning money laundering and legislation concerning the investigation of serious fraud or tax evasion.

(iii) Auditors are also permitted or required to disclose information where they are personally involved in litigation, including litigation that involves the recovery of fees from clients, or where they are subject to disciplinary proceedings brought by ACCA or other, similar professional bodies.

(iv) Auditors are also permitted to disclose information where they consider it to be in the 'public interest' or in the interests of national security. Factors to take into account include the seriousness of the matter, the likelihood of repetition and the extent to which the public is involved. This right is rarely used in practice.

(b) **Response to requests**

(i) It is not unusual in practice for various bodies to request information from auditors 'informally' because it relieves them of the obligation to obtain the necessary statutory authorities which may be time consuming or difficult.

(ii) Auditors must not disclose information without the consent of the client or unless the necessary statutory documentation is provided by the person(s) requesting the information.

(iii) Unless the auditor has reason to believe that there is a statutory duty not to inform the client that an approach has been made, the client should first be approached to see if consent can be obtained, and to see if the client is aware of the investigations, as should normally be the case. The auditor should ensure that the client is aware of the fact the voluntary disclosure may work in the client's favour, in the long run, but if the client refuses, the auditor should inform the client if the auditor has a statutory duty of disclosure.

(iv) Auditors should take legal advice in all of the cases described.

(v) Where the auditor is made aware of potential actions against the client that may have an affect on the financial statements, the auditor must consider the affect on the audit report. If the client is aware of the investigation, the auditor will be able to seek audit evidence to support any necessary provisions or disclosures in the financial statements.

(vi) The auditors should consider whether the suspected fraud relating to the managing director relates to the company and affects the financial statements.

(vii) Auditors will be in a very difficult situation if they become aware of an action that may materially affect the financial statements, but where the client is not, and where auditors are under a statutory duty not to inform the client. This situation will not be improved by the resignation of auditors as they may be obliged to make a statement on resignation. This puts auditors in a very difficult position and legal advice is essential in such circumstances.

(viii) Tax authorities normally have powers to ask clients to disclose information voluntarily. Such voluntary disclosure is often looked on favourably by the tax authorities and the courts. Tax authorities normally also have statutory powers to demand information from both clients and auditors. The same is generally true of environmental and health and safety inspectors.

(ix) The power of the police to demand information is sometimes less clear and auditors and clients should take care to ensure that the appropriate authorities are in place. Those sections of the police investigating serious frauds usually have more powers than the general police. It is unlikely that trade union representatives have any statutory powers to demand information.

(vi) Where the auditor is made aware of potential actions against the client that may have an impact on the financial statements the auditor must consider the effect on the audit report. If the auditor is aware of the investigation, the auditor will be able to seek audit evidence to support any necessary provisions or disclosures in the financial statements.

(vii) The auditors should consider whether the suspected fraud [illegible] relates to the company and affects the financial statements.

(viii) Auditors will be in a very difficult situation if they become aware of an action that may materially affect the financial statements but where the auditors [illegible] and where police [illegible] not to inform the client. This situation will not be improved by the resignation of auditors as they may be obliged to issue a statement of circumstances. The [illegible] auditors in a very [illegible] position and legal advice is essential in such circumstances.

(ix) Tax authorities normally have powers to ask clients to disclose information voluntarily, and voluntary disclosure is often favoured by the tax authorities and the courts. Tax authorities typically also have statutory powers to demand information from clients and auditors. The same is generally true of environmental and health and safety regulators.

(x) The power of the police to demand information is sometimes less clear and auditors and clients should therefore ensure that the appropriate authorities are in place. Those sections of the police investigating serious fraud generally have more powers than the general police. It is unlikely that [illegible] have any statutory powers to demand information.

chapter

# 4

# Risk

## Chapter learning objectives

When you have completed this chapter you will be able to:

- Explain the importance of risk assessment and the components of audit risk.
- Explain the concepts of materiality and performance materiality.
- Explain the audit risks in the financial statements and explain the auditor's response to each risk.
- Describe risk assessment procedures for the identification and assessment of audit risks.
- Describe and explain the nature, and purpose of, analytical procedures in planning.
- Compute and interpret key ratios used in analytical procedures.

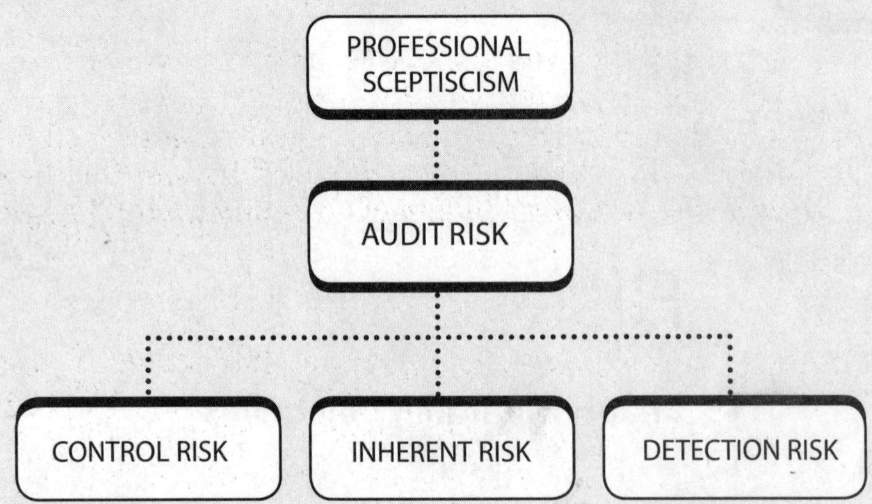


## 1 The importance of risk assessment

The overriding principle of auditing is introduced in ISA 200 *Overall Objectives of the Independent Auditor and the Conduct of an Audit in Accordance with ISA's*:

'To obtain reasonable assurance, **the auditor shall obtain sufficient appropriate evidence to reduce audit risk to an acceptably low level**...'

**Audit risk** is the risk that the auditor expresses an **inappropriate audit opinion**.

This is further developed by ISA 315 (Revised) *Identifying and Assessing the Risks of Material Misstatement Through Understanding the Entity and its Environment* (issued March 2012, effective for audits of financial statements for periods ending on or after December 15, 2013) which states:

'The **objective** of the auditor is **to identify and assess the risk of material misstatement,** whether due to fraud or error, at the financial statement and assertion levels, through understanding the entity and its environment, including the entity's internal control, thereby providing a basis for **designing and implementing responses to the assessed risks of material misstatement.**'

The auditor must identify the risks of material misstatement; and use this to guide the design of their audit procedures.

### What is a misstatement?

'A **difference between** the amount, classification, presentation, or disclosure of a reported **financial statement** item and the amount, classification, presentation, or disclosure that is required for the item to be in accordance with the applicable **financial reporting framework**. Misstatements can arise from error or fraud.' (ISA 450 *Evaluation of Misstatements Identified during the Audit)*

In conducting a thorough assessment of risk, auditors will be able to:

- Identify areas of the financial statements where misstatements are likely to occur early in the audit.
- Plan procedures that address the significant risk areas identified.
- Carry out an efficient, focussed and effective audit.
- Minimise the risk of issuing an inappropriate audit opinion to an acceptable level.
- Reduce the risk of reputational and punitive damage.

**Types of misstatements**

There are three categories of misstatements:

(i) Factual misstatements: a misstatement about which there is no doubt.

(ii) Judgemental misstatements: a difference in an accounting estimates that the auditor considers unreasonable, or the selection or application of accounting policies that the auditor considers inappropriate.

(iii) Projected misstatements: a projected misstatement is the auditor's best estimate of the total misstatement in a population through the projection of misstatements identified in a sample.

## 2 Materiality

### What is materiality?

'Misstatements, including omissions, are considered to be material if they, individually or in the aggregate, could reasonably be expected to influence the economic decisions of users taken on the basis of the financial statements'

(ISA 320 *Materiality in Planning and Performing an Audit*)

## What is the significance of materiality?

The auditor is responsible for providing 'an opinion on whether the financial statements are prepared, in all **material** respects, in accordance with an applicable financial reporting framework.' (ISA 200 *Overall Objectives of the Independent Auditor and the Conduct of an Audit in Accordance with International Standards on Auditing*)

If financial statements contain material misstatement they cannot be deemed to show a true and fair view.

As a result the focus of an audit is identifying the significant risks of material misstatement in the financial statements and then designing procedures aimed at identifying and quantifying material misstatement.

## How is materiality determined?

The guidance in ISA 320 states that the determination of materiality is a **matter of professional judgement** and that the auditor must consider:

- the circumstances surrounding the entity
- both the size and nature of misstatements
- the information needs of the users as a group.

It is a subjective and potentially complex process and it is vital that materiality is considered in light of the client's needs.

However, ISA 320 does recognise the need to establish a financial threshold to guide audit planning and procedures. For this reason it does allow the use of standard benchmarks but only as a starting point. The auditor must consider all of the factors listed above.

**Illustration 1: Traditional benchmarks for materiality**

Traditional benchmarks include:

- ½ – 1% of revenue
- 5% – 10% of profit before tax
- 1 – 2% of gross assets.

Note that these benchmarks do not come from the auditing standards. Materiality is a matter of professional judgement. The above are common benchmarks used, but different audit firms may use different benchmarks or a firm may use different thresholds for each client.

In addition, materiality is not just a purely financial concern. Disclosures in the financial statements relating to possible future legal claims, for example, could influence users' decisions and may be purely narrative. In this case a numerical calculation is not relevant.

**Material by nature or impact**

Examples of items which are material by nature or material by impact include:

- Misstatements that, when adjusted, would turn a reported profit into a loss for the year.
- Misstatements that, when adjusted, would turn a reported net-asset position into a net-liability position (or net-current asset to net-current liability)
- Transactions with directors, e.g. salary and benefits, personal use of assets, etc.
- Related party transactions.

**Illustration 2: Murray Co materiality**

$000

| **Financial Statement Extracts** | 2012 | 2011 |
|---|---|---|
| Revenue | 21,960 | 19,580 |
| Total assets | 9,697 | 7,288 |
| Profit before tax | 1,048 | 248 |

| **Materiality** | | |
|---|---|---|
| **Revenue** | ½% | 1% |
| 2012 | 110 | 220 |
| 2011 | 98 | 196 |
| **Profit before taxation** | 5% | 10% |
| 2012 | 52 | 105 |
| 2011 | 12 | 25 |
| **Total assets** | 1% | 2% |
| 2012 | 97 | 194 |
| 2011 | 73 | 146 |

A suitable range for **preliminary materiality** is **$97,000 - $105,000**.

**Murray Co materiality**

Materiality is not normally based on revenue, except in circumstances when it would not be meaningful to base materiality on profit, e.g. because the entity being audited is a not-for-profit entity or where there is a small profit (or a loss) as this will result in over-auditing of the financial statements (such as was the case for Murray Co in 2011).

More than $105,000 profit is material to the statement of comprehensive income, therefore preliminary materiality is likely to be set so as not to exceed this amount. Less than $52,000 is not material to profit (or to the statement of financial position) so preliminary materiality should not be less than this amount.

A suitable preliminary materiality level is most likely to be one that lies within the overlap of the ranges calculated for profit and total assets. $97,000 (1% of total assets) represents 9% profit. As this is at the lower end of the assets range, this would be a relatively prudent measure of materiality (resulting in a higher level of audit work).

$105,000 (10% of profit) represents 1.1% of total assets. Preliminary materiality might be set at this end of the range had this been a recurring audit. However, as this is a first audit, preliminary materiality is likely to be lower.

The financial statements are draft and therefore greater errors should be expected than if they were actual. Consequently, sample sizes for audit testing should be increased (i.e. preliminary materiality should be set at a relatively lower level).

Preliminary materiality is therefore likely to be set at $97,000.

## The practical application of materiality

It is unlikely, in practice, that auditors will be able to design tests that identify individually material misstatements. It is much more common that misstatements in aggregate (i.e. in combination) are material.

Auditors also only test on a sample basis, so they have to evaluate their findings and determine how likely it is that errors identified in the sample are representative of material errors in the whole population under scrutiny (i.e. projected misstatements).

Materiality, as determined for the financial statements as a whole, may not be the best guide in determining the nature and extent of audit tests. For this reason, ISAs introduce a further concept: **performance materiality**.

**Performance materiality** is defined in ISA 320 as:

'The amount set by the auditor at less than materiality for the financial statements as a whole to reduce to an appropriately low level the probability that the aggregate of uncorrected and undetected misstatements exceeds materiality for the financial statements as a whole.'

- The auditor sets **performance materiality** at a **value lower than overall materiality**, and uses this lower threshold when designing and performing audit procedures.
- In using this lower threshold, the auditor is more likely to identify misstatements.
- This **reduces** the **risk** that the auditor will fail to identify misstatements that are material in combination.

**Murray Co performance materiality**

The audit engagement team has planned the audit of the financial statements for the year ended 31 December 2012. The team has determined a materiality level for the financial statements as a whole, of $97,000. Performance materiality needs to be applied to work-in-progress inventories, as this is an area of audit risk.

Performance materiality could be determined as a percentage of financial statement materiality, say 75%, i.e. a performance materiality of ($97,000x75%) $72,750 (the audit team could use a higher or lower percentage, or use a different calculation, depending on their professional judgement).

The aim of performance materiality is to reduce the risk that the combination of immaterial misstatements exceed materiality for the financial statements as a whole.

For example, if a misstatement was identified of, say $80,000, without performance materiality the auditor would conclude that work-in-progress is not materially misstated. However, the audit may not have detected further misstatements which when added to the $80,000 identified would result in a material misstatement. By using performance materiality, the auditor would conclude that a misstatement of $80,000 is material, and consequently would require the directors to amend the finanancial statements to correct this misstatement, reducing the risk of giving an inappropriate opinion.

## 3 Audit Risk

**Audit risk** is the risk that the auditor expresses an **inappropriate audit opinion**, i.e. that they give an unmodified audit opinion when the financial statements contain a material misstatement.

Audit risk is made up of two components: **risk of material misstatement** and **detection risk**.

**Risk of material misstatement** is the risk that the financial statements are materially misstated prior to audit and consists of two components, **inherent risk** and **control risk**.

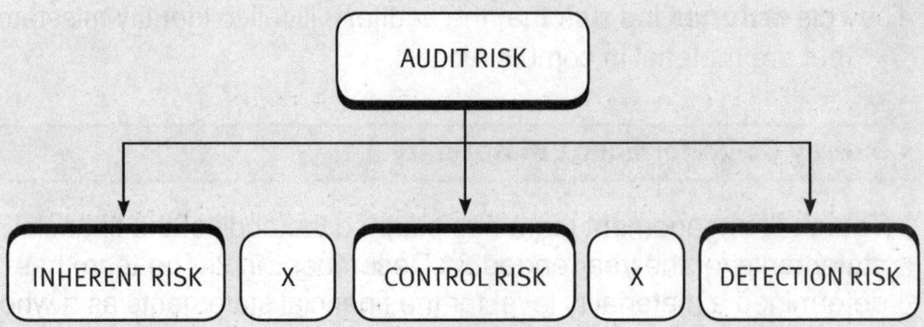

**Inherent risk** is the susceptibility of an assertion about a class of transaction, account balance or disclosure to misstatement that could be material, before consideration of any related controls.

- Inherent risk is the risk of a material misstatement in the financial statements because of the nature of the industry, entity or the nature of the item itself.

**Control risk** is the risk that a misstatement that could occur and that could be material will not be prevented, or detected and corrected on a timely basis by the entity's internal controls.

- Control risk may be high either because the design of the internal control system is insufficient in the circumstances of the business or because the controls have not been applied effectively during the period. This is covered in more detail in a later chapter.

**Detection risk** is the risk that the procedures performed by the auditor to reduce audit risk to an acceptably low level will not detect a misstatement that exists and that could be material.

Detection risk comprises **sampling risk** and **non-sampling risk**:

- **Sampling risk** is the risk that the auditor's conclusion based on a sample is different from the conclusion that would be reached if the whole population were tested.
- **Non-sampling risk** is the risk that the auditor's conclusion is inappropriate for any other reason, e.g. the application of inappropriate procedures or the failure to recognise a misstatement.

## Auditor's response

The auditor must amend the audit approach in response to risk assessment. They can achieve this by:

- assigning more experienced staff to risk areas
- increasing supervision levels
- increasing the element of unpredictability in sample selection
- changing the nature, timing and extent of procedures
- increasing the emphasis on substantive tests of detail
- emphasising the need for **professional scepticism**.

**Professional scepticism** is: 'An attitude that includes a questioning mind, being alert to conditions which may indicate possible misstatement due to fraud or error, and a critical assessment of audit evidence.' (ISA 200 *Overall Objectives of the Independent Auditor and the Conduct of an Audit in Accordance with International Standards on Auditing*).

### Professional scepticism

Professional scepticism requires the auditor to be alert to:

- Audit **evidence that contradicts other** audit **evidence**.
- Information that brings into question **the reliability of documents and responses to enquiries** to be used as audit evidence.
- Conditions that may indiciate **possible fraud**.
- Circumstances that suggest **the need for audit procedures in addition to those required by ISAs**.

Clearly this requires the audit team to have a good knowledge of how the client's activities are likely to affect its financial statements, and the audit team should discuss these matters in a **planning meeting** before deciding on the detailed approach and audit work to be used.

**Illustration 3: Murray Co risk assessment**

Your firm Wimble & Co has recently accepted appointment as auditor of Murray Co (a manufacturer of Sports equipment).

Having sold your shares in Murray Co, you have been assigned as audit manager and you have started planning the audit (although you were an employee of Murray Co, this was many years ago and you did not have any involvement in preparation of the financial statements). You have held a meeting with the client and have ascertained the following:

Murray Co manufactures sports equipment in its UK factory (the currency of the UK is the Pound Sterling). Components are sourced from suppliers in Europe, who invoice Murray Co in the Euro. Most items of equipment, such as tennis rackets, hockey sticks and goals, take less than one day to manufacture. Murray Co's largest revenue generating product, ergometers (rowing machines), takes up to one week to manufacture. Murray Co refurbished the assembly line for the ergometers during the year. Murray Co uses a third party warehouse provider to store the manufactured ergometers and approximately one quarter of the other equipment.

Historically, Murray Co has only sold to retailers. For the first time this year, Murray Co has made sales directly to consumers, via a new website. The website is directly linked to the finance system, recording sales automatically. Website customers pay on ordering. The website development costs have been capitalised. This initiative was implemented to respond to market demands, as retailer sales have fallen dramatically in the last two years. Some of Murray Co's retail customers are struggling to pay their outstanding balances. Several of the sales team were made redundant last month as a result of the falling retailer sales.

Murray Co is planning to list on the stock exchange next year.

**Exercise:**

**Using the information provided, describe SIX audit risks and explain the auditor's response to each risk in planning the audit of Murray Co.**

**Solution: Murray Co risk assessment**

| **Audit Risks** | **Auditor's Response** |
|---|---|
| *This is the first year Wimble & Co have audited Murray Co.*<br><br>There is a lack of cumulative audit knowledge and experience, increasing detection risk. Opening balances may be misstated. | More time and resource will need to be devoted to obtaining an understanding of Murray Co at the start of the audit. More substantive procedures will need to be planned and performed, and larger samples tested in order to lower detection risk. |
| *Components are sourced from suppliers in Europe, who invoice Murray Co in the Euro.*<br><br>There is a risk of arithmetical error or the wrong exchange rate being used when translating foreign currency transactions. Payables, purchases and inventory may be misstated. | Recalculation of a sample of transactions to confirm mathematical accuracy.<br><br>Agreement of the rates used to a reliable external source (e.g. The Financial Times). |
| *Inventory is stored at a third party warehouse.*<br><br>It may be difficult to obtain sufficient appropriate evidence over the quantity and condition of inventory held. There is increased detection risk over completeness, existence and valuation of inventory. | Additional procedures to ensure that inventory quantities and condition have been confirmed for both third party and company owned locations, e.g:<br><br>• Attend the inventory count (if one is to be performed) at the third party warehouses to review the controls in operation<br>• Inspect any reports produced by the auditors of third party warehouses in relation to the adequacy of controls over inventory. |
| *Ergometers take up to one week to manufacture.*<br><br>There is likely to be a material work in progress (WIP) inventory balance at the year end. Determining the value and quantity of WIP is complex. There is a risk of misstatement of WIP inventory. | Consideration should be given as to whether an independent expert is required to value WIP. If so, this will need to be arranged with consent from management and in time for the year-end count. |

| | |
|---|---|
| *Murray Co refurbished the assembly line for the ergometers during the year.*<br><br>There is a risk that the expenditure incurred has been incorrectly treated as capital in nature and included within assets or expensed as repairs. | Review a breakdown of the costs and agree to invoices to assess the nature of the expenditure and if capital agree to inclusion within the asset register, and if repairs agree to expense in the statement of profit or loss. |
| *There is a new website directly linked to the finance system, which records sales automatically.*<br><br>There is increased risk over completeness of income if the system fails to record all sales made on the website; revenue may be understated. | Extended controls testing to be performed over the sales cycle, including the use of test data where possible. Detailed testing to be performed over the completeness of income. |
| *The website development costs have been capitalised.*<br><br>In order to be capitalised, it must meet all of the criteria under IAS 38 *Intangible Assets.* Research costs should be expensed rather than capitalised. There is a risk that intangible assets are overstated. | A breakdown of the development expenditure should be reviewed and tested in detail to ensure that only projects which meet the capitalisation criteria are included as an intangible asset, with the balance being expensed. |
| *Retailer sales have fallen dramatically in the last two years.*<br><br>If retailer sales continue to fall and direct consumer sales do not compensate for the loss of retailer revenue, Murray Co may not be able to continue to operate for the foreseeable future. There is a risk that disclosures of material uncertainties relating to going concern may be inadequate. | Perform a detailed going concern review, including: obtain and review the company's cash flow forecast and evaluate the reasonableness of the assumptions used to understand if management will have sufficient cash.<br><br>Review post year end order books from retailers and post year end direct consumer sales to assess if the revenue figures in the cash flow are reasonable. |
| *Several of the sales team were made redundant last month as a result of the falling retailer sales.*<br><br>Under IAS 37 *Provisions, Contingent Liabilities and Contingent Assets,* a redundancy provision will be required for any staff not yet paid at the year end. There is a risk of understated liabilities. | Discuss with management the progress of the redundancy programme and review and recalculate the redundancy provision. |

| | |
|---|---|
| *Some retail customers are struggling to pay their outstanding balances to Murray Co.*<br><br>There is a risk of overstatement of receivables and understatement of irrecoverable debt allowance. | Extended post-year end cash receipts testing and a review of the aged receivables ledger to be performed to assess valuation<br><br>An allowance for receivables to be discussed with management. |
| *Murray Co is planning to list on the stock exchange next year.*<br><br>There is an increased risk of manipulation of the financial statements. There is a risk of overstatement of assets and profits, and understatement of expenses and liabilities. | Plan and perform procedures to ensure accounting estimates and judgemental areas are reasonable.<br><br>Maintain professional scepticism and be alert to the risks identified in order to achieve a successful listing. |

## 4 Risk assessment procedures

ISA 315 (Revised) requires auditors to perform the following risk assessment procedures:

- **Enquiries** with management, of appropriate individuals within the internal audit function (if there is one), and others (with relevant information) within the client entity (e.g. about external and internal changes the company has experienced)
- **Analytical procedures**
- **Observation** (e.g. of control procedures) and **inspection** (e.g. of key strategic documents and procedural manuals).

### Understanding the entity and its environment

In order to identify the risks of material misstatement in the financial statements the auditor is required to obtain an understanding of: their clients; their clients' environments; and their clients' internal controls. This generally includes:

- relevant industry, regulatory and other external factors (including the financial reporting framework)

- the nature of the entity, including:
  - its operations
  - its ownership and governance structures
  - the types of investment it makes
  - the way it is structured and financed
- the entity's selection and application of accounting policies
- the entity's objectives, strategies and related business risks
- the measurement and review of the entity's financial performance
- the internal controls relevant to the audit.

(ISA 315 (Revised) *Identifying and Assessing the Risks of Material Misstatement through understanding the entity and its environment*)

If the entity has an internal audit function, obtaining an understanding of that function also contributes to the auditor's understanding of the entity and its environment, including internal control, in particular the role that the function plays in the entity's monitoring of internal control over financial reporting. This understanding, together with the information obtained from the auditor's inquiries described above may also provide information that is directly relevant to the auditor's identification and assessment of the risks of material misstatement.

The information used to obtain this understanding can come from a wide range of sources, including:

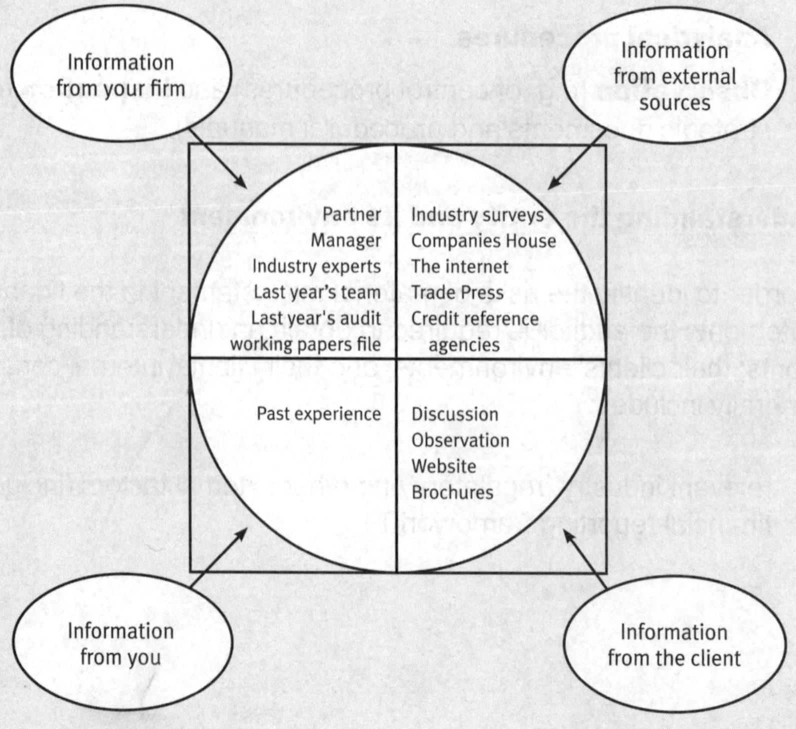

## Analytical procedures

Analytical procedures are defined in ISA 520 *Analytical Procedures* as:

'Evaluations of financial information through **analysis of plausible relationships** among both financial and non-financial data' and investigation of identified fluctuations, inconsistent relationships or amounts that differ from expected values.

Analytical procedures are fundamental to the auditing process.

The auditor is **required to perform analytical procedures as risk assessment procedures** in order to:

- obtain an **understanding of the entity and its environment**
- assist in **assessing the risks of material misstatement** in order to provide a basis for designing and implementing responses to the assessed risks
- help **identify** the existence of **unusual transactions or events, and amounts, ratios, and trends** that might indicate matters that have audit implications
- assist the auditor in identifying risks of material misstatement due to **fraud**.

Analytical procedures include comparisons of the entity's financial information with, for example:

- comparable information for **prior periods**.
- **anticipated results** of the entity, such as budgets or forecasts, or expectations of the auditor, such as an estimation of depreciation
- similar **industry information**, such as a comparison of the entity's ratio of sales to accounts receivable with industry averages or with other entities of comparable size in the same industry.

Analytical procedures also include consideration of **relationships**, for example:

- among elements of financial information that would be expected to conform to a predictable pattern based on the entity's experience, such as gross margin percentages
- between financial information and relevant non-financial information, such as payroll costs to number of employees.

Computer aided auditing techniques are now often used to perform data analysis.

## Analytical procedures

Analytical procedures can be used at all stages of an audit.

However, ISA 315 *Identifying and Assessing the Risks of Material Misstatement through Understanding the Entity and Its Environment* requires the auditor to perform analytical procedures as risk assessment procedures in order to help the auditor to obtain an understanding of the entity and assess the risk of material misstatement.

The auditor can choose to use analytical procedures as substantive procedures during the final audit to obtain relevant and reliable audit evidence.

The auditor must also use analytical procedures at the final review stage, near the end of the audit, when forming an overall conclusion as to whether the financial statements are consistent with the auditor's understanding of the entity.

## Ratios

**Key ratios**

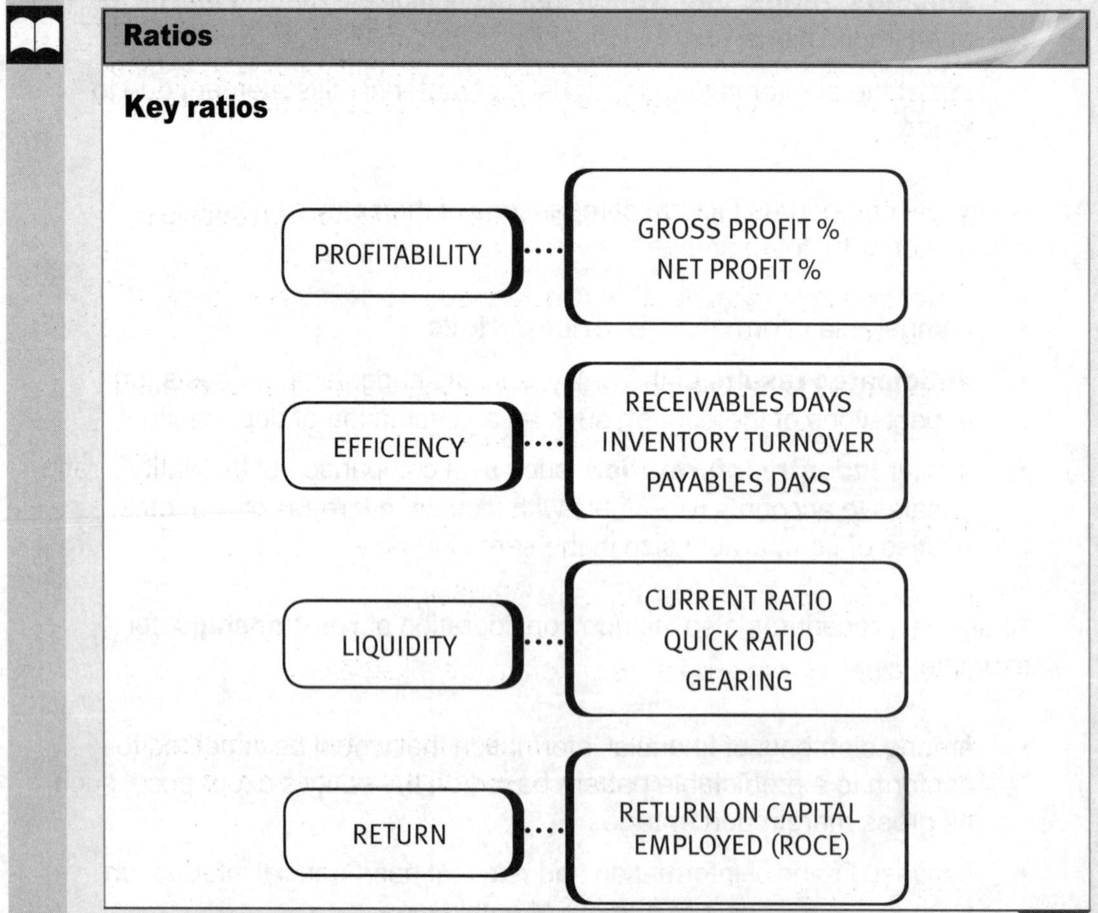

**Profitability ratios**

Gross margin: gross profit/sales revenue×100%

Net margin: profit before tax/sales revenue×100%

Auditors would expect the relationships between costs and revenues to stay relatively stable. Things that can affect these ratios include: changes in sales prices, bulk purchase discounts, economies of scale, new marketing initiatives, changing energy costs, wage inflation.

**Efficiency Ratios**

Receivables days: receivables/sales revenue×365

Payables days: payables/purchases×365

Inventory days: inventory/cost of sales×365

These ratios show how long, on average, companies take to collect cash from customers and pay suppliers and how long they hold inventory for. Companies should strive to reduce receivables and inventory days to an acceptable level and increase payables days because this strategy maximises cash flow.

Any changes can indicate significant issues to the auditor, such as:

- worsening credit control and increased need for receivables allowance
- ageing and possible obsolete inventory that could be overvalued
- poor cash flow leading to going concern problems.

**Liquidity Ratios**

Current ratio: current assets/current liabilities

Quick ratio: (current assets-inventory)/current liabilities

These ratios indicate how able a company is to meet its short term debts. As a result these are key indicators when assessing going concern.

**Investor Ratios**

Gearing: borrowings/share capital+reserves

Return on capital employed (ROCE): profit before interest and tax/(share capital+reserves+borrowings)

Gearing is a measure of external debt finance to internal equity finance. ROCE indicates the returns those investments generate.

Any change in gearing or ROCE could indicate a change in the financing structure of the business or it could indicate changes in overall performance of the business. These ratios are important for identifying potentially material changes to the statement of financial position (new/repaid loans or share issues) and for obtaining an overall picture of the annual performance of the business.

**Illustration 4: Murray Co Analytical Procedures**

**Murray Co Draft Financial Statements for the year ended 31 December 2012**

**Draft Statement of Financial Position as at 31 December 2012**

| | 2012 | 2011 |
|---|---|---|
| | $000 | $000 |
| **Non-current assets** | | |
| Property plant and equipment | 5,350 | 4,164 |
| Website development | 150 | 0 |
| | 5,500 | 4,164 |
| **Current assets** | | |
| Inventory | 2,109 | 1,555 |
| Trade receivables | 2,040 | 1,520 |
| Cash and cash equivalents | 48 | 49 |
| | 4,197 | 3,124 |
| | 9,697 | 7,288 |

| | | |
|---|---|---|
| **Equity** | | |
| Share capital (50c shares) | 2,100 | 2,100 |
| Retained earnings | 2,959 | 2,156 |
| | 5,059 | 4,256 |
| **Non-current liabilities** | | |
| Long term loan | 2,800 | 1,500 |
| **Current liabilities** | | |
| Provisions | 240 | 195 |
| Trade and other payables | 1,400 | 1,205 |
| Accruals | 18 | 12 |
| Bank overdraft | 180 | 120 |
| | 1,838 | 1,532 |
| | 9,697 | 7,288 |

**Draft Statement of Profit or Loss for the year ended 31 December 2012**

| | 2012<br>$000 | 2011<br>$000 |
|---|---|---|
| Revenue | 21,960 | 19,580 |
| Cost of sales | (18,560) | (17,080) |
| Gross profit | 3,400 | 2,500 |
| Operating expenses | (2,012) | (2,012) |
| Finance cost | (340) | (240) |
| Profit before tax | 1,048 | 248 |
| Taxation | (245) | (24) |
| Profit for the period | 803 | 224 |

**Exercise:**

**Using the information provided about Murray Co, perform analytical procedures on the draft financial statements above, and explain the audit risks that arise.**

**Solution: Murray Co analytical procedures**

**Audit risks identified using analytical procedures:**

| Calculation | Explanation of risk |
|---|---|
| Revenue has increased by 12%. | Retailer sales at Murray Co have fallen dramatically in the last two years. The increase in revenue is not consistent with this. Although Murray Co has begun selling directly to consumers for the first time this year, it is unlikely that these sales will have compensated for the loss in retailer sales at this early stage. In addition, revenue may be deliberately overstated by Murray Co in order to increase the chances of a successful listing. There is a risk that revenue is overstated. |
| Gross profit margin has increased from 13% to 14%. | The margins for direct consumer sales are likely to be higher than retailer sales, which may explain this increase. However, the increase could also be caused by overstatement of revenue, as explained above, or understatement of cost of sales. |
| Operating expenses has no movement. | This is unusual given the increase in revenue and cost of sales. There is a risk that the prior year figure has been incorrectly presented in the 2012 column. |
| Net margin has increased from 1% to 4%. | Net margin has increased at a greater rate than gross profit margin. Given that this is the first year of direct consumer sales, the net margin would not be expected to increase significantly as the level of operating expenses would normally be higher at this early stage. This indicates potential overstatement of revenue and understatement of operating expenses. |

| | |
|---|---|
| Inventory days has increased from 33 (1,555/17,080×365) to 41 (2,109/18,560×365) days. | As sales have increased, this could be because of an increase in demand and therefore the need to hold more inventory. However, as retailer sales at Murray Co have fallen dramatically, there is a risk that some of the inventory is bespoke, and may therefore be obsolete. There is a risk that inventory is overstated. |
| Trade receivables days has increased from 28 (1,520/19,580×365) to 34 (2,040/21,960×365) days. | Given that website customers pay on ordering, trade receivables days would be expected to fall. However, some of Murray Co's retail customers are struggling to pay their outstanding balances. Trade receivables may be overstated, and the allowance for doubtful debts understated. |
| Trade payables days has increased from 26 (1,205/17,080×365) to 28 (1,400/18,560×365) days. | The increase in trade payables days is consistent with the increase of 9% in cost of sales. However, an increase in trade payables days could be caused by understatement of cost of sales. The increase in gross profit margin also highlighted this as a potential risk. |
| Current ratio has improved from 2:1 to 2.3:1. | Murray Co appears to be managing its working capital effectively. However, given the plans to list on the stock exchange next year, this may be indicative of manipulation of the financial statements in order to increase the chances of a successful listing. In addition, Murray Co has increased its long and short-term finance during the year. |

**Test your understanding 1**

You are an audit senior at JPR Edwards & Co and you are currently planning the statutory audit of Hook Co for the year ending 30 June 2013. Your firm was appointed as auditor in January 2013 after a successful tender to provide audit and tax services. JPR Edward & Co were asked to tender after the lead partner, Neisha Selvaratalm, met Hook Co's CEO, Pete Tucker, at a charity cricket match. Neisha explained that they were unhappy with the previous auditors as Pete Tucker felt their audit didn't add much value to Hook Co.

Hook Co was established in 1985 and manufacturers electrical goods such as MP3 players, smart phones and personal computers for the entertainment market. They do not retail their goods under their own name but manufacture for larger companies with established brands. Their key client, who represents 70% of their revenue, was the market leader in smart phones and MP3 players in 2012 with 60% market share.

Hook Co uses a number of suppliers to source components for their products. Most suppliers are based in the UK however Hook Co imports microchips, a key component in all their goods, from a number of suppliers based in San Jose, Costa Rica. The suppliers invoice Hook Co in US$ (the UK currency is the £). They assemble their goods in their one factory in Staines, UK, and package their products for their customers before distribution across the UK.

During the year Hook Co started developing applications which can be downloaded onto their smart phones. They have spent $1million on an application called "snore-o-meter" which allows the users to record the sounds they make while they are asleep. There was a technical difficulty in production which meant the launch of "snore-o-meter" was delayed from the 31 March 2012 to its anticipated release on the 31 July 2013.

To fund their expansion into Smartphone applications Hook is seeking a listing on the London Stock Exchange in the fourth quarter of 2013. In preparation Pete Tucker has read the 'UK Corporate Governance Code' and understands the need and benefit of many of its principles however he is unsure how the formation of an audit committee will benefit Hook Co.

**Required:**

**Using the information provided, describe FIVE audit risks and explain the auditor's response to each risk in planning the audit of Hook Co.**

**(10 marks)**

**Test your understanding 2**

Nepco is a European company that manufactures high quality computer components and assembles computer parts. It has existed for some years and is part of a vertical supply chain for a well-known brand of computer hardware. Profits are coming under increasing pressure from manufacturers in the Far East and Asia with lower labour costs, and from rising raw material costs. Nepco is listed on a stock exchange. There is pressure from institutional investors for better returns in the form of dividends and the main institutional investors are considering selling a proportion of their shares in the company. The directors of Nepco are considering whether to move into new market areas.

Nepco has good accounting and internal control systems. Inventory is material to the accounts, and there is a good set of permanent inventory records. No year-end inventory count is conducted. Operational compliance issues are important to Nepco as many countries have inflexible quality standards and some projects are being held up because of difficulties in obtaining approval from regulators for new components. All staff and directors of Nepco are remunerated (at least in part) on a performance-related basis, some with share options. Staff are generally highly qualified and well-paid.

This is your first year as auditors. Your firm has very little experience in this industry. External audit costs are tightly controlled and your firm has agreed to a budget that will allow very little flexibility.

**Required:**

(a) **Describe the risks relating to Nepco under the headings of inherent risk, control risk and detection risk.**

**(12 marks)**

(b) **In the light of the risks identified in (a) above, list the matters to which you will pay particular attention during the audit of Nepco and explain the work you will perform in relation to them.**

**(8 marks)**

**(Total: 20 marks)**

**Test your understanding 3**

(a) **With reference to ISA 520 *Analytical Procedures* explain**

(i) **what is meant by the term 'analytical procedures';**

**(1 marks)**

(ii) **the different types of analytical procedures available to the auditor; and**

**(3 marks)**

(iii) **the situations in the audit when analytical procedures are used.**

**(3 marks)**

Tribe Co sells bathrooms from 15 retail outlets. Sales are made to individuals, with income being in the form of cash and debit cards. All items purchased are delivered to the customer using Tribe's own delivery vans; most bathrooms are too big for individual's to transport in their own motor vehicles. The directors of Tribe indicate that the company has had a difficult year, but are pleased to present some acceptable results to the members.

The statement of profit or loss for the last two financial years are shown below:

**Statement of profit or loss**

| | *31 March 2013* | *31 March 2012* |
|---|---|---|
| | $000 | $000 |
| Revenue | 11,223 | 9,546 |
| Cost of sales | (5,280) | (6,380) |
| | 5,943 | 3,166 |
| Operating expenses | | |
| Administration | (1,853) | (1,980) |
| Selling and distribution | (1,472) | (1,034) |
| Interest payable | (152) | (158) |
| Investment income | 218 | – |
| | 2,684 | (6) |

**Financial statement extract**

| | | |
|---|---|---|
| Cash and bank | 380 | (1,425) |

**Required:**

(b) **As part of your risk assessment procedures for Tribe Co, identify and provide a possible explanation for unusual changes in the statement of profit or loss.**

**(9 marks)**

## 5 Chapter summary

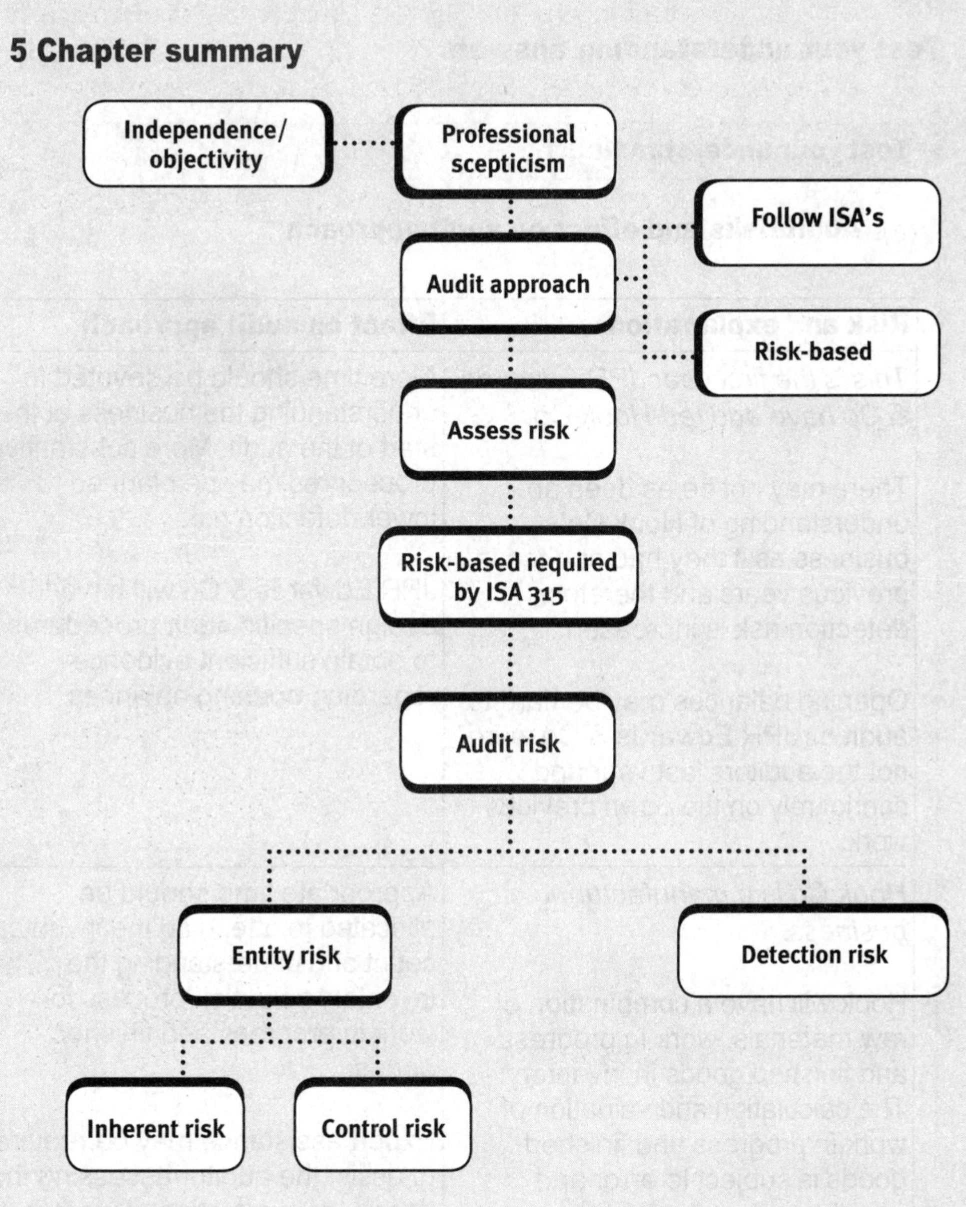

## Test your understanding answers

### Test your understanding 1

(a) **Audit risks and effect on audit approach**

| Risk and explanation | Effect on audit approach |
|---|---|
| *This is the first year JPR Edwards & Co have audited Hook Co.*<br><br>There may not be as deep an understanding of Hook Co's business as if they had audited in previous years and therefore detection risk is increased.<br><br>Opening balances may be hard to audit as JPR Edwards & Co were not the auditors last year and cannot rely on their own previous work. | More time should be devoted to understanding the business at the start of the audit. More substantive procedures may be planned to lower detection risk.<br><br>JPR Edwards & Co will have to design specific audit procedures to obtain sufficient evidence regarding opening balances. |
| *Hook Co is a manufacturing business.*<br><br>Hook will have a combination of raw materials, work in progress and finished goods in inventory. The calculation and valuation of work in progress and finished goods is subject to error and possible overstatement. | Appropriate time should be allocated to attending the inventory count and understanding the inventory valuation process for work in progress and finished goods.<br><br>Expert assistance may be required to assist the auditor assessing the degree of completion of work in progress. |
| *Hook Co manufactures electrical goods for the entertainment market.*<br><br>This is a rapidly changing market and goods can become obsolete quickly and therefore be valued incorrectly in the financial statements. | Hook Co's process for identifying obsolete items should be reviewed thoroughly as changes in technology are likely to render items obsolete quicker than in a more stable market.<br><br>The nature and extent of audit procedures may be increased to ensure inventory is valued appropriately at the lower of cost and NRV. |

| | |
|---|---|
| *Their key client represents 70% of their revenue.*<br><br>Hook Co may be over reliant on this client which could threaten its going concern status if this key client was lost. There is a risk that disclosures of material uncertainties relating to going concern are inadequate. | Procedures should be designed at the planning stage to allow the auditor to assess the going concern risk faced by Hook Co.<br><br>Contracts and other correspondence from the key customer should be reviewed to identify any specific risks that the client may be lost. Analytical procedures should be designed to assess the impact on Hook Co's financial position if the contract was not renewed. |
| *One of Hook Co's key suppliers is based in Costa Rica.*<br><br>Hook Co will translate foreign currency transactions into their reporting currency. There is an increased risk of simple arithmetical error or the wrong exchange rate being used in calculations. | Procedures should be designed to test the arithmetical accuracy of a sample of translations against the published exchange rate from an external source, for example the Financial Times. |
| *Hook Co spent $1m on developing a new product.*<br><br>There is a risk that Hook Co have capitalised development expenditure which should have been expensed through the statement of profit or loss as research costs.<br><br>If the application does not meet the criteria required to classify as development costs they should be expensed to the statement of profit or loss in the year they were incurred. There is a risk over overstatement of intangible assets. | Enquiries should be made as to how Hook Co identifies whether the criteria for capitalisation has been met in accordance with accounting standards (IAS 38).<br><br>Where amounts have been capitalised further procedures should be designed, for example, to assess how Hook Co measures whether the project would be profitable. |

| | |
|---|---|
| *Hook Co is aiming to list on the London Stock Exchange this year.*<br><br>The directors may have greater incentive to 'window dress' the accounts to show a more favourable position in order to increase the proceeds generated from flotation. | Procedures should be planned to ensure areas of judgement and estimates exercised by the directors are reasonable and can be justified.<br><br>Special consideration should be given to sales cut-off testing |

**Test your understanding 2**

(a) **Risks**

(i) Inherent risks include:

- The competition from Asian and Far Eastern companies, and rising raw material prices. This means that there is pressure on profits and the ability to reward employees and pay dividends to institutional shareholders which increases the pressure to manipulate the financial statements to show good returns.
- The potentially volatile market (computer components) in which new technology can render hardware obsolete in a very short time. This means that there is an ongoing risk to the business as a whole (a potential going concern risk) – the company must be adaptable.
- The risk that regulators may reject a product which has taken many months or years to develop.
- The pressures for returns from institutional investors which means that there may be a temptation to manipulate the financial statements.
- The possible sale of shares, increasing the pressure for returns in order to get the best possible price, which increases the pressure to manipulate the financial statements.
- The inherent risks in diversification into unknown areas (the supply of other customers) – but these are not current risks.

(ii) Control risks: there are apparently very few except for the performance-related payment, including share options, which provides an incentive to produce 'acceptable' figures.

(iii) Detection risk: this is the firm's first year as auditors and there are tight controls on audit costs, which may lead to inadequate audit evidence unless the audit is properly directed, supervised and reviewed. This is compounded by the firm's lack of experience in this area. It is important that those with experience are employed on this audit, at least in a review capacity.

(b) **Matters to which attention should be paid and work to be performed**

(i) The good accounting records and internal control combined with the need to keep audit costs down means that a compliance approach, rather than a substantive approach will be necessary wherever possible.

(ii) Audit work will need to be directed towards inventory (despite the fact that it is well controlled) because it is material to the accounts. There is no year-end inventory count, and inventory is relatively easy to manipulate. It is likely that there will be a substantial amount of work-in-progress and its valuation will need to be reviewed carefully. It may be possible to rely on any interim or cyclical inventory counting.

(iii) The projects on which compliance problems have arisen should be examined carefully as the costs may be significant and there may be a temptation to understate them.

(iv) Overall profits and any unadjusted errors should be examined carefully because of the inherent risks noted above and the performance-related pay.

(v) The company's going concern status should be reviewed by examining its financial status, financial support and likely future developments in high risk areas.

**Test your understanding 3**

(a) (i) Explanation of analytical procedures

Analytical procedures are used in obtaining an understanding of an entity and its environment and in the overall review at the end of the audit. They can also be used as a substantive procedure.

'Analytical procedures' means the evaluation of financial and other information and the review of plausible relationships in that information. The review also includes identifying fluctuations and relationships that do not appear consistent with other relevant information or results.

(ii) Types of analytical procedures

Analytical procedures can be used as:

- Comparison of comparable information to prior periods to identify unusual changes or fluctuations in amounts.
- Comparison of actual or anticipated results of the entity with budgets and/or forecasts, or the expectations of the auditor in order to determine the potential accuracy of those results.
- Comparison to industry information either for the industry as a whole or by comparison to entities of similar size to the client to determine whether receivable days, for example, are reasonable.

(iii) Use of analytical procedures

Risk assessment procedures

Analytical procedures are used at the beginning of the audit to help the auditor obtain an understanding of the entity and assess the risk of material misstatement. Audit procedures can then be directed to these 'risky' areas.

Analytical procedures as substantive procedures.

Analytical procedures can be used as substantive procedures in determining the risk of material misstatement at the assertion level during work on the statement of profit or loss and statement of financial position.

Analytical procedures in the overall review at the end of the audit.

Analytical procedures help the auditor at the end of the audit in forming an overall conclusion as to whether the financial statements as a whole are consistent with the auditor's understanding of the entity.

(b) Net profit

Overall, Tribe's result has changed from a net loss to a net profit. Given that sales have only increased by 17% and that expenses, at least administration expenses, appear low, then there is the possibility that expenditure may be understated.

Sales – increase 17%

According to the directors, Tribe has had a 'difficult year'. Reasons for the increase in sales income must be ascertained as the change does not conform to the directors' comments. it is possible that the industry as a whole, has been growing allowing Tribe to produce this good result.

Cost of sales – fall 17%

A fall in cost of sales in unusual given that sales have increased significantly. This may have been caused by an incorrect inventory valuation and the use of different (cheaper) suppliers which may cause problems with faulty goods in the next year.

Gross profit (GP) – increase 88%

This is significant increase with the GP% changing from 33% last year to 53% in 2013. Identifying reasons for this change will need to focus initially on the change in sales and cost of sales.

Administration – fall 6%

A fall is unusual given that sales are increasing and so an increase in administration to support those sales would be expected. Expenditure may be understated, or there has been a decrease in the number of administration staff.

Selling and distribution – increase 42%

This increase does not appear to be in line with the increase in sales – selling and distribution would be expected to increase in line with sales. There may be mis-allocation of expenses from administration or the age of Tribe's delivery vans is increasing resulting in additional service costs.

Interest payable – small fall

Given that Tribe has a considerable cash surplus this year, continuing to pay interest is surprising. The amount may be overstated – reasons for lack of fall in interest payment e.g. loans that cannot be repaid early, must be determined.

Investment income – new this year

This is expected given cash surplus on the year, although the amount is still very high indicating possible errors in the amount or other income generating assets not disclosed on the statement of financial position extract.

Administration – fall 6%

A fall is unusual given that sales are increasing and so an increase in administration to support those sales would be expected. Expenditure may be understated, or there has been a decrease in the number of administration staff.

Selling and distribution – increase 42%

This increase does not appear to be in line with the increase in sales – selling and distribution would be expected to increase in line with sales. There may be mis-allocation of expenses from administration or the age of Tribe's delivery vans is increasing resulting in additional service costs.

Interest payable – small fall

Given that Tribe has a considerable cash surplus this year, continuing to pay interest is surprising. The amount may be overstated – reasons for lack of fall in interest payment e.g. loans that cannot be repaid early, must be determined.

Investment income – new this year

This is expected given cash surplus on the year, although the amount is still very high indicating possible errors in the amount or other income generating assets not disclosed on the statement of financial position extract.

chapter

# 5

# Planning

## Chapter learning objectives

When you have completed this chapter you will be able to:

- Identify and describe the need to plan and perform audits in accordance with ISAs.
- Identify and describe the contents of the overall audit strategy and audit plan.
- Explain the auditor's responsibility for the prevention and detection of fraud and error.
- Explain the auditor's responsibility to consider laws and regulations.
- Explain the difference between interim and final audit.
- Explain the importance of audit documentation and describe the contents of working papers and supporting documentation.

## 1 Objective of the Auditor

'The objective of the auditor is to plan the audit so that it will be performed in an effective manner.' (ISA 300 *Planning an Audit of Financial Statements).*

Audits are potentially complex, risky and expensive processes. Although firms have internal manuals and standardised procedures it is vital that engagements are planned to ensure that the auditor:

- devotes appropriate attention to important areas of the audit
- identifies and resolves potential problems on a timely basis
- organises and manages the audit so that it is performed in an effective and efficient manner
- selects team members with appropriate capabilities and competencies
- directs and supervises the team and reviews their work
- effectively coordinates the work of others, such as experts and internal audit.

Planning ensures that the risk of performing a poor quality audit (and ultimately giving an inappropriate audit opinion) is reduced to an acceptable level.

In order to achieve the overall objectives of the auditor, **the audit must be conducted in accordance with ISAs**.

Conducting the audit in accordance with ISAs:

- ensures that the auditor is fulfilling all of their responsibilities.
- allows a user to have as much confidence in one auditor's opinion as another's and therefore to rely on one audited set of financial statements to the same extent that they rely on another.
- ensures that the quality of audits internationally, is maintained to a high standard (thereby upholding the reputation of the profession).
- provides a measure to assess the standard of an auditor's work (necessary when determining their suitability as an authorised practitioner).

Auditors are also required to perform audits with an attitude of professional scepticism. Having an enquiring mind in itself is not sufficient to comply with a risk based method of auditing. In order to fulfil this responsibility auditors must also use **professional judgement**. This means the application of relevant training, knowledge and experience in making informed decisions about the courses of action that are appropriate to the unique circumstances of the audit engagement.

Therefore the use of a risk based approach requires skill, knowledge, experience and an inquisitive, open mind; something that is neither gained quickly nor easily.

Although risk assessment is a fundamental element of the planning process, risks can be uncovered at any stage of the audit and procedures must be adapted in light of revelations that indicate further risks of material misstatement. It is, ultimately, the responsibility of the most senior reviewer (usually the engagement partner) to confirm that the risk of material misstatement has been reduced to an acceptable level.

## The planning process

Planning consists of a number of elements. They can be summarised as:

- Preliminary engagement activities:
  - evaluating compliance with ethical requirements
  - establishing the terms of the engagement.

- Planning activities:
  - developing the audit strategy
  - developing an audit plan.

## 2 The audit strategy

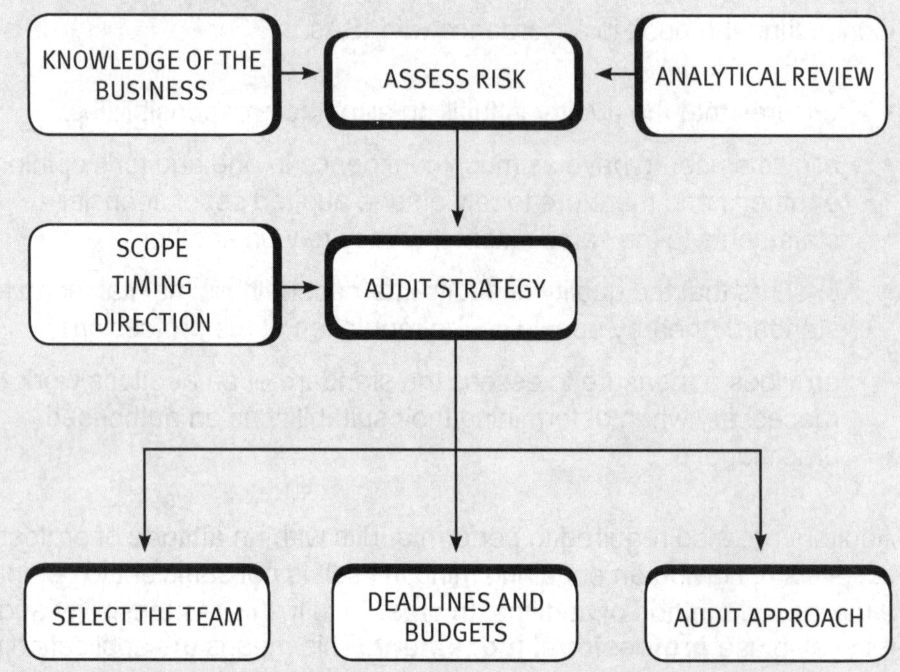


### Considerations in establishing the overall strategy

In determining the audit strategy the auditor should:

(i) Identify the characteristics of the engagement.

(ii) Ascertain the reporting objectives to plan the timing of the audit and the nature of communications.

(iii) Consider the significant factors that will direct the team's efforts.

(iv) Consider the results of preliminary engagement activities.

(v) Ascertain the nature, timing and extent of resources necessary to perform the engagement.

The audit strategy sets the scope, timing and direction of the audit. It allows the auditor to determine the following:

- the resources to deploy for specific audit areas (e.g. experience level, external experts)
- the amount of resources to allocate (i.e. number of team members)
- when the resources are to be deployed
- how the resources are managed, directed and supervised, including the timings of meetings, debriefs and reviews.

## Audit strategy in detail

### Characteristics of the engagement

- The financial reporting framework for the financial statements
- Industry specific requirements, e.g. listed companies and charities
- The number and locations of premises, branches, subsidiaries, etc
- The nature of the client and the need for specialised knowledge
- The reporting currency
- The effect of IT on audit procedures, including availability of data.

### Reporting objectives, timing of the audit, and nature of communication

- The timetable for interim and final reporting
- The organisation of meetings with management
- The expected types and timings of auditor's reports/communications
- The expected nature and timing of communication amongst team members
- Whether there are any expected communications with third parties.

### Significant factors and preliminary engagement activities

- Materiality
- Results of risk assessment
- Professional scepticism
- Results of previous audits
- Evidence of management's commitment to internal controls
- Volume of transactions
- Significant business developments/changes
- Significant industry developments
- Significant financial reporting changes.

### Nature, timing and extent of resources

- The selection of and assignment of work to the engagement team
- Budgets.

## 3 The audit plan

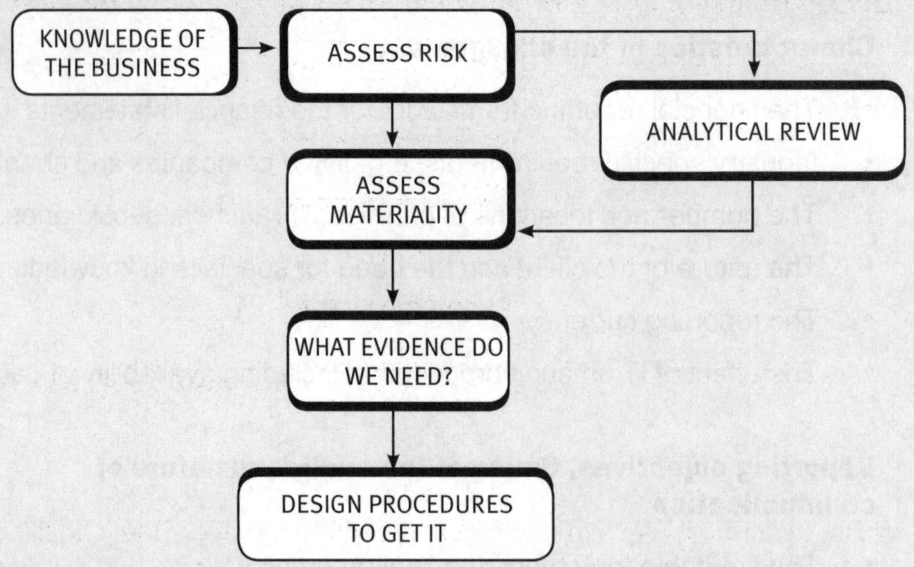


Once the audit strategy has been established, the next stage is to develop a specific, detailed plan to address how the various matters identified in the overall strategy will be applied.

The audit plan is much more detailed than the overall strategy because it includes details of the **nature, timing and extent** of the specific **audit procedures** to be performed. Planning these procedures depends, largely, on the outcomes of the risk assessment process, which was discussed earlier.

### The plan itself

The audit plan should include specific descriptions of:

- the nature, timing and extent of risk assessment procedures.
- the nature, timing and extent of further audit procedures, including:
  - **what** audit procedures are to be carried out
  - **who** should do them
  - **how much** work should be done (sample sizes, etc)
  - **when** the work should be done (interim vs. final).
- any other procedures necessary to conform to ISA's.

**The relationship between the audit strategy and the audit plan**

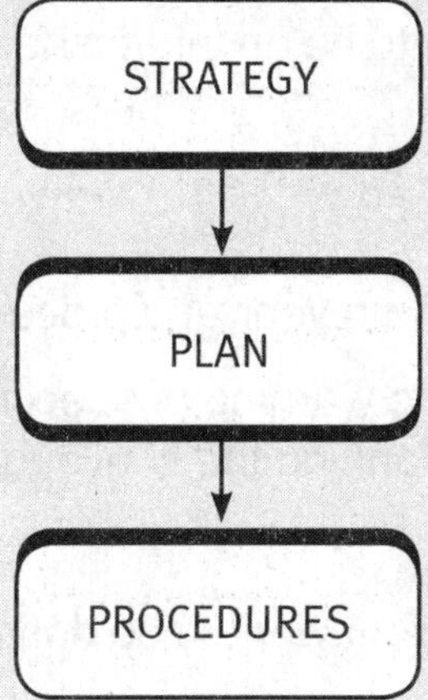


Whilst the strategy sets the overall approach to the audit, the plan fills in the operational details of how the strategy is to be achieved.

It is vital that both the strategy and the plan - and any consequent updates to them – are fully documented as part of audit working papers.

## 4 Interim versus final

The auditor must consider the timing of audit procedures: whether to carry out an interim audit and a final audit, or just a final audit, or alternatively whether to audit the entity throughout the year using Computer Assisted Audit Techniques (CAATs).

**Interim audits** can be completed part way through a client's accounting year (i.e. before the year end). This allows the auditor to spread out their procedures and enables more effective planning for the final stage of the audit. Interim audits normally focus on:

- documenting systems and
- evaluating controls.

It may be possible to:

- test specific and complete material transactions, e.g. purchasing new non-current assets
- attend interim inventory counts
- carry out an interim receivables circularisation.

The **final audit** takes place after the year-end and focuses on the remaining tests and areas that pose significant risk of material misstatement. This usually involves concentration on year-end valuations and areas where there is significant subjectivity.

For an interim audit to be justified the client normally needs to be of a sufficient size because this may increase costs. In argument to this, an interim audit should improve risk assessment and make final procedures more efficient. If there is to be an interim as well as a final audit the timing has to be:

- Early enough:
  - not to interfere with year-end procedures at the client and
  - to give adequate warning of specific problems that need to be addressed in planning the final audit.
- Late enough:
  - to enable sufficient work to be done to ease the pressure on the final audit.

## 5 The impact of fraud

### What is fraud?

ISA 240 t*he Auditor's Responsibilities Relating to Fraud in an Audit of Financial Statements* recognises that misstatement in the financial statements can arise from either fraud or error. The distinguishing factor is whether the underlying action that resulted in the misstatement was intentional or unintentional

**Fraud** is an **intentional** act by one or more individuals among management, those charged with governance, employees or third parties, involving the use of **deception** to obtain an unjust or illegal advantage.

Fraud is a broad legal concept; it is a criminal activity. It is not the responsibility of the auditor to prove whether fraud has actually occured, that is the role of the country's legal system. The auditor's role is to determine whether there is a material misstatement in the financial statements as a result of fraud.

Fraud can be split into two types:

- fraudulent financial reporting – deliberately misstating the accounts to make the company look better/worse than it actually is.
- misappropriation – the theft of the company's assets such as cash or inventory.

### The external auditor's responsibilities

**The external auditor is responsible for obtaining reasonable assurance that the financial statements, taken as a whole, are free from material misstatement, whether caused by fraud or error.** Therefore, the external auditor has some responsibility for considering the risk of material misstatement due to fraud.

In order to achieve this the auditor must:

- Maintain an attitude of **professional scepticism**. This means that the auditor must recognise the possibility that a material misstatement due to fraud could occur, regardless of the auditor's prior experience of the client's integrity and honesty.
- **Discuss** among the engagement team, the **client's susceptibility to fraud** (ISA 315 *Identifying and Assessing the Risks of Material Misstatement Through Understanding the Entity and Its Environment* requires that).
- **Identify and assess the risks of material misstatement due to fraud**.
- Identify, through enquiry, how management assesses and responds to the risk of fraud.
- Enquire of management, internal auditors and those charged with governance if they are aware of any actual or suspected fraudulent activity.
- Obtain sufficient appropriate evidence regarding the assessed risks of material misstatement due to fraud by designing and performing audit procedures that respond to the assessed risks.

**Note**: owing to the inherent limitations of an audit, there is an unavoidable risk that some material misstatements may not be detected, even when the audit is planned and performed in accordance with ISAs. The risks in respect of fraud are higher than those for error because fraud may involve sophisticated and carefully organised schemes designed to conceal it.

## Reporting of fraud

If the auditor identifies a fraud they must communicate the matter on a timely basis to the appropriate level of management (i.e. those with the primary responsibility for prevention and detection of fraud).

If the suspected fraud involves management the auditor must communicate the matter to those charged with governance. If the auditor has doubts about the integrity of those charged with governance they should seek legal advice regarding an appropriate course of action.

In addition to these responsibilities the auditor must also consider whether they have a responsibility to report the occurrence of a suspicion to a party outside the entity. Whilst the auditor does have an ethical duty to maintain confidentiality, it is likely that any legal responsibility will take precedence. In these circumstances it is advisable to seek legal advice.

**The directors' responsibilities**

The primary responsibility for the prevention and detection of fraud rests with those charged with governance and the management of an entity. This is achieved by:

- implementing an **effective system of internal control**, reducing opportunities for fraud to take place and increasing the likelihood of detection (and punishment).
- creating a **culture** of honesty, ethical behaviour, and active oversight by those charged with governance.

The directors should be aware of the potential for fraud and this should feature as an element of their risk assessment and corporate governance procedures. The audit committee should review these procedures to ensure that they are in place and working effectively. This will normally be done in conjunction with the internal auditors.

**Internal auditors** may be given an assignment:

- to assess the likelihood of fraud, or if a fraud has been discovered
- to assess its consequences and
- to make recommendations for prevention in the future.

## 6 Laws and Regulations

**Responsibilities of management**

Management are responsible for ensuring the entity complies with relevant laws and regulations.

This requires management to **monitor legal requirements**, develop **systems of internal control** to ensure compliance with those legal requirements and **monitor** the **effectiveness** of those **control systems**.

**Examples of laws and regulations**

- Company law, e.g. the UK Companies Act 2006
- Corporate Governance law, e.g. the US Sarbanes Oxley Act 2002
- Health and safety law
- Employment law
- Stock exchange rules
- Financial reporting regulations.

## Responsibilities of the auditor

- The auditor must **obtain sufficient, appropriate evidence** of **compliance** with those **laws and regulations** generally recognised to have a **direct effect** on the determination of material amounts and disclosures in the financial statements.
- The auditor must also **perform specified audit procedures** to help **identify** instances of **non-compliance** with **other laws and regulations** that may have a **material impact** on the financial statements. If non-compliance is identified (or suspected) the auditor must then respond appropriately.

### Effect of laws and regulations

ISA 250 distinguishes between two types of laws and regulations: those which are generally recognised to have a **direct effect** on the determination of material amounts and disclosures in the financial statements; and **other laws and regulations**.

Examples of laws and regulations with a **direct effect** include:

- company law (e.g. the Companies Act in the UK)
- taxation legislation.

Examples of **other laws and regulations** include:

- environmental legislation
- employment laws.

Non-compliance with other laws and regulations can impact the financial statements because companies in breach of the law may need to make provisions for future legal costs and fines. In the worst case scenario this could affect the ability of the company to continue as a going concern.

In addition, the auditor may need to report identified non-compliance with laws and regulations either to management or to a regulatory body, if the issue requires such action. An example of the latter would be when the client is in breach of money laundering regulations.

## Specified procedures

ISA 250 *Consideration of Laws and Regulations in an Audit of Financial Statements* requires an auditor to:

- Obtain a general understanding of the client's legal and regulatory environment.

- Inspect correspondence with relevant licensing and regulatory authorities.
- Enquire of management and those charged with governance as to whether the entity is compliant with laws and regulation.
- Remain alert to possible instances of non-compliance.
- Obtain written representations that the directors have disclosed all instances of known and possible non-compliance to the auditor.

## 7 Audit documentation

ISA 230 *Audit Documentation,* requires auditors to prepare and retain written documentation that:

- Provides a sufficient appropriate record of the auditor's basis for the audit report.
- Provides evidence that the audit was planned and performed in accordance with ISAs and applicable legal and regulatory requirements.
- Assists the engagement team to plan and perform the audit.
- Assists members of the engagement team responsible for supervision to direct, supervise and review the audit work.
- Enables the engagement team to be accountable for its work.
- Retains a record of matters of continuing significance to future audits.

Documentation should be sufficient to enable an experienced auditor, with no previous connection to the audit, to understand:

- the nature, timing and extent of audit procedures performed
- the results of the procedures performed and the evidence obtained
- the significant matters arising during the course of the audit and the conclusions reached thereon, and significant professional judgements made in reaching those conclusions.

It is vital that documentation is retained in an audit file, which should be completed in a timely fashion after the date of the audit report (normally not more than 60 days after) and retained for the period required by national regulatory requirements (this is normally five years from the date of the audit report).

**Illustration 1: Wimble & Co working paper**

**Wimble & Co Audit and Accounting Practitioners: Working Paper**

| | | | |
|---|---|---|---|
| Client: | Murray Co | Reference: | RA1 |
| Period end: | 31/12/12 | Prepared by: | Rob Cash |
| Subject: | Risk Assessment | Date prepared: | Dec 1 2012 |

| | |
|---|---|
| Objective: | To identify the risks of material misstatement in the financial statements of Murray Co for the year ended 31 December 2012, in order to provide a basis for designing and performing audit procedures that respond to the assessed risks. |
| Work performed: | Discussion among the engagement team of the susceptibility of the financial statements to material misstatement: **RA1/1**<br><br>A summary of the understanding of the entity and its environment obtained, detailing the key elements including internal control components, sources of information and risk assessment procedures performed: **RA/2**<br><br>Analytical procedures performed: **RA/3** |
| Results: | The identified and assessed risks of material misstatement: **RA/4** |
| Conclusions: | The overall responses to address the risks of material misstatement: **RA/5** |
| Reviewed by: | An Audit Manager |
| Date reviewed: | December 5 2012 |

**Wimble & Co working paper**

**Features of Wimble & Co working paper**

**Name of client**: identifies the client being audited.

**Period-end date**: identifies the period to which the audit work relates.

**Subject**: identifies the topic of the working paper such as the area of the financial statements being audited, or the overall purpose of the work.

**Working paper reference**: provides a clear reference to identify the working paper; RA1 is the first working paper in the risk assessment section.

**Preparer**: identifies the name of the audit team member who prepared the working paper; to enable any queries to be directed to the relevant person.

**Date prepared**: the date the audit work was performed; the end of time period to which issues were considered.

**Objective**: the aim of the work; explains the relevance of the work being performed (in relation to Financial Statement assertions where appropriate).

**Work performed**: the work done cross-referenced to supporting working papers, including details of the sources of information, and items selected for testing (where relevant).

**Results of work performed**: any significant issues identified, exceptions or other significant observations including whether further audit work is necessary.

**Conclusions**: key points (including whether the area is true and fair where relevant).

**Reviewer**: the name of the audit team member who reviewed the work; evidences review as required by the ISAs.

**Date of review**: this must be before the audit opinion is signed

**Types of audit documentation**

Audit documentation includes:

- Planning documentation:
  - overall audit strategy
  - audit plan
  - risk analysis
- Audit programmes
- Summary of significant matters
- Letter of confirmation and representation
- Checklists
- Correspondence
- Abstracts/copies of client records.

For large audits much of the knowledge of the business information may be kept on a permanent file and the audit plan may contain a summary or simply cross refer to the **permanent file**. Typical information on a permanent file includes:

- Names of management, those charged with governance, shareholders
- Systems information
- Background to the industry and the client's business
- Title deeds
- Directors' service agreements
- Copies of contract and agreements.

**Example contents of a current audit file**

The audit work for a specific period is kept on a **current file**.

Typically, there are at least three sections, as follows:

- planning
- performance
- completion.

**Planning**

The main element of this section is likely to be the Audit Planning Memorandum.

This document is the written audit plan and will be read by all members of the audit team before work starts. Its contents are likely to include:

- background information about the client, including recent performance
- changes since last year's audit (for recurring clients)
- key accounting policies
- important laws and regulations affecting the company
- client's trial balance (or draft Financial Statements)
- preliminary analytical review
- key audit risks
- overall audit strategy
- materiality assessment
- timetable of procedures
- deadlines
- staffing and a budget (hours to be worked x charge-out rates)
- locations to be visited.

**Performance**

Working papers are likely to consist of:

- Lead Schedule – showing total figures, which agree to the financial statements
- Back-up schedules – breakdowns of totals into relevant sub-totals
- Audit work programme detailing:
  - the objectives being tested
  - work completed
  - how sampled items selected
  - conclusions drawn
  - who did the work
  - date work completed
  - who reviewed it.

### Completion

The completion (also known as review) stage of an audit has a number of standard components:

- Going concern review
- Subsequent events review
- Final analytical review
- Accounting standards (disclosure) checklist
- Letter of representation
- Summary of adjustments made since trial balance produced
- Summary of unadjusted errors
- Draft final financial statements
- Draft report to those charged with governance (management letter).

### Security and retention of working papers

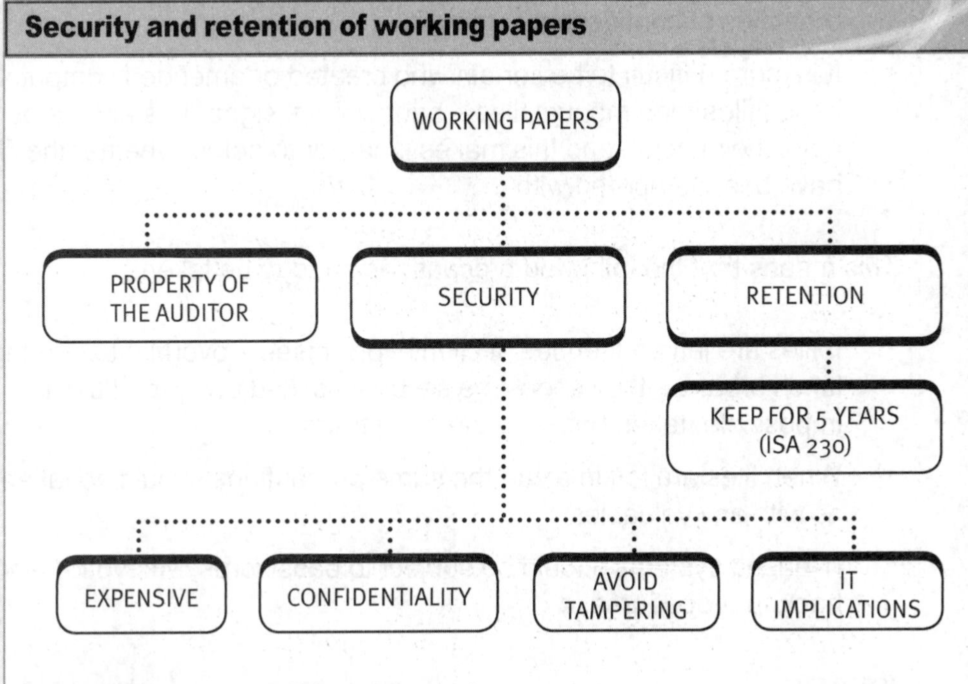


### Who owns the working papers?

The auditor does. This is important because:

- Access to the working papers is controlled by the auditor, not the client, which is an element in preserving the auditor's independence.
- In some circumstances care may need to be taken when copies of client generated schedules are incorporated into the file.

**Security**

Working papers must be kept secure.

- Audits are expensive. If the files are lost or stolen, the evidence they contain will need to be recreated, so the work will need to be done again. The auditors may be able to recover the costs from their insurers, but otherwise it will simply represent a loss to the firm.
- By its nature, audit evidence will comprise confidential, sensitive information. If the files are lost or stolen, the auditor's duty of confidentiality will be compromised.
- There have been cases of unscrupulous clients altering auditors' working papers to conceal frauds.

The implications of IT-based audit systems are also far reaching.

- By their nature, laptops are susceptible to theft, even though the thief may have no interest in the contents of the audit file. Nevertheless, all the problems associated with re-performing the audit and breaches of confidentiality remain.
- It is more difficult to be certain who created or amended computer based files than manual files – handwriting, signatures and dates have their uses – and this makes it harder to detect whether the files have been tampered with.

This means that the following precautions need to be taken.

- If files are left unattended at clients' premises – overnight or during lunch breaks – they should be securely locked away, or if this is impossible, taken home by the audit team.
- When files are left in a car, the same precautions should be taken as with any valuables.
- IT-based systems should be subject to passwords, encryption and backup procedures.

**Retention**

Audit files should be assembled in a timely fashion. This is, ordinarily, no longer than 60 days after the date of the auditor's report.

Once complete the files should be retained as long as required by national law. However, ISA 230 *Audit Documentation,* states that this period is, ordinarily, no shorter than five years from the date of the auditor's report. This should therefore be considered the minimum retention period.

All of this means that firms need to make arrangements for:

- secure storage of recent files
- archiving older files
- archiving and backup of IT based files.

**Test your understanding 1**

ISA 320 *Materiality in Planning and Performing an Audit* provides guidance on the concept of materiality in planning and performing an audit.

**Required:**

**Define materiality and explain how the level of materiality is assessed.**

*Real exam question: June 2011*

**(5 marks)**

**Test your understanding 2**

You are an audit senior responsible for understanding the entity and its environment and assessing the risk of material misstatements for the audit of Rock Co for the year ending 31 December 2012. Rock Co is a company listed on a stock exchange. Rock Co is engaged in the wholesale import, manufacture and distribution of basic cosmetics and toiletries for sale to a wide range of stores, under a variety of different brand names. You have worked on the audit of this client for several years as an audit junior.

**Required:**

(a) **Describe the information you will seek, and procedures you will perform in order to understand the entity and its environment and assess risk for the audit of Rock Co for the year ending 31 December 2012.**

**(10 marks)**

(b) You are now nearing the completion of the audit of Rock Co for the year ending 31 December 2012. Draft financial statements have been produced. You have been given the responsibility of performing a review of the audit files before they are passed to the audit manager and the audit partner for their review. You have been asked to concentrate on the proper completion of the audit working papers. Some of the audit working papers have been produced electronically but all of them have been printed out for you.

**Required:**

**Describe the types of audit working papers you should expect to see in the audit files and the features of those working papers that show that they have been properly completed.**

**(10 marks)**

**(Total: 20 marks)**

# 8 Chapter summary

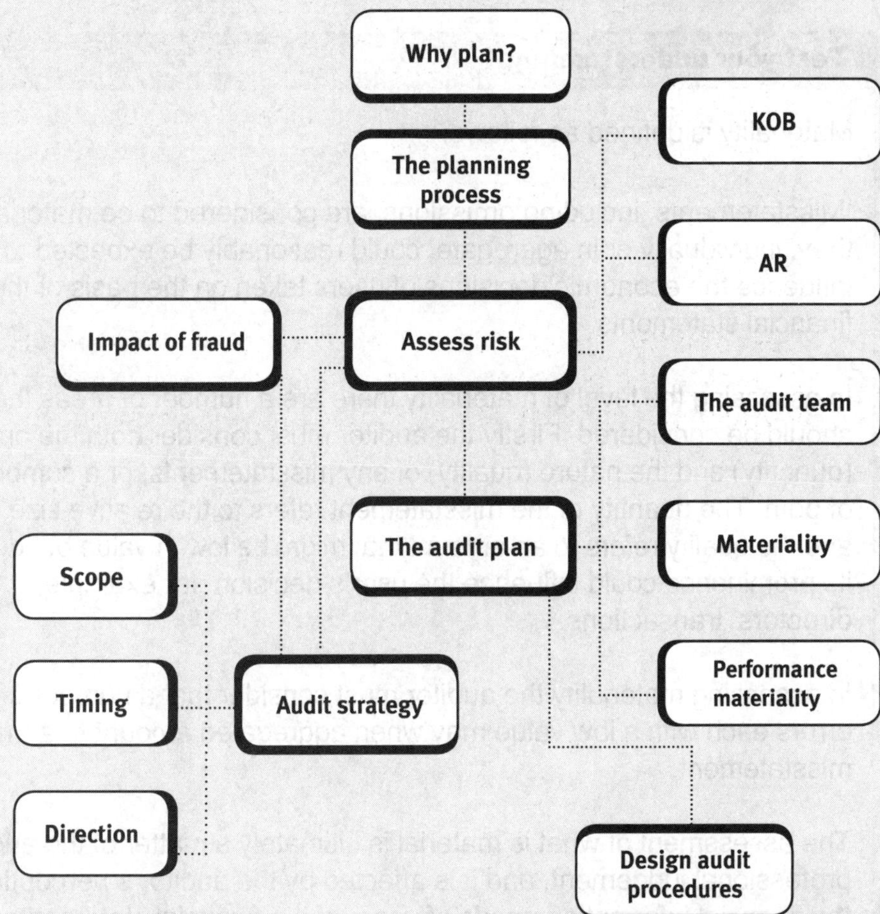

## Test your understanding answers

### Test your understanding 1

Materiality is defined as follows:

'Misstatements, including omissions, are considered to be material if they, individually or in aggregate, could reasonably be expected to influence the economic decisions of users taken on the basis of the financial statements.'

In assessing the level of materiality there are a number of areas that should be considered. Firstly the auditor must consider both the amount (quantity) and the nature (quality) of any misstatements, or a combination of both. The quantity of the misstatement refers to the relative size of it and the quality refers to an amount that might be low in value but due to its prominence could influence the user's decision, for example, directors' transactions.

In assessing materiality the auditor must consider that a number of errors each with a low value may when aggregated amount to a material misstatement.

The assessment of what is material is ultimately a matter of the auditors' professional judgement, and it is affected by the auditor's perception of the financial information needs of users of the financial statements.

In calculating materiality the auditor should also consider setting the performance materiality level. This is the amount set by the auditor, it is below materiality, and is used for particular transactions, account balances and disclosures.

As per ISA 320 materiality is often calculated using benchmarks such as 5% of profit before tax or 1% of gross revenue. These values are useful as a starting point for assessing materiality.

**Test your understanding 2**

(a) **Information and procedures: understanding the entity and its environment and risk assessment for Rock Co**

(i) Understanding the entity and risk assessment is likely to involve a review of prior year risk assessments as a starting point and the identification of changes during the year from the information gathered that may alter that assessment.

(ii) Risk assessment procedures involve enquiries of management and others, analytical procedures and observation and inspection. Members of the engagement team should discuss the susceptibility of the financial statements to material misstatements.

(iii) Risk assessment also involves obtaining an understanding of the relevant industry, regulatory and other matters including the financial reporting framework, the nature of the entity, the application of accounting policies, the entity's objectives and related business risks, and its financial performance. This may involve:

(1) a review of prior year working papers noting any particular issues that arose warranting attention in the current year.

(2) discussions with the audit senior or manager working on Rock in prior years to establish any particular problem areas.

(3) discussions with Rock (and their other advisors such as banks and lawyers) to establish any particular problem areas.

(4) review of any third party information on the client such as press reports.

(5) a review of management accounts, any financial information provided to the stock exchange or draft financial statements that may be available to establish trends in the business.

(6) a review of any changes in stock exchange requirements.

(7) a review of systems documentation (either generated by Rock Co or held by the firm) to see if it needs updating.

(iv) Auditors should obtain an understanding of the control environment, the entity's process for identifying and dealing with business risk, information systems, control activities and monitoring of contents.

(v) Risks should be assessed at the financial statements level, and at the assertion level, and identify significant risks that require special audit consideration, and risks for which substantive procedures alone do not provide sufficient, appropriate audit evidence.

(vi) Analytical procedures are often used to highlight areas warranting particular audit attention. In the case of Rock Co, they are likely to focus on inventory which is likely to have a significant effect on profit (there may be slow moving or obsolete inventory that needs to be written down) and on property, plant and equipment which (as a manufacturer and distributor) is likely to be a significant item on the statement of financial position.

(vii) Risk assessment will facilitate the determination of materiality and tolerable error (calculations are normally based on sales, profit and assets) that will be used in determining the sample sizes and in the evaluation of errors.

(b) **Types and features of audit working papers**

(i) Types of audit working papers include:

(1) systems documentation (flowcharts, systems manuals, narrative notes, checklists and questionnaires, etc.)

(2) constitutional documents

(3) agreements with banks and other providers of finance

(4) details of other advisors used by the entity such as lawyers

(5) regulatory documentation relating to the stock exchange listing

(6) audit planning documentation

(7) audit work programs

(8) working papers showing the work performed

(9) lead schedules showing summaries of work performed and conclusions on individual account areas and the amounts to be included in the financial statements

(10) trial balances, management accounts and financial statements

(11) standard working papers relating to the calculation of sample sizes, for example

(12) schedules of unadjusted differences

(13) schedules of review points

(14) letters of deficiency and management representation letters.

(ii) Features of audit working papers:

(1) All working papers (without exception) should show by whom they were prepared and when, and when they were reviewed and/or updated, and by whom, by means of signatures and dates – these may be electronic in the case of electronic working papers.

(2) Audit planning documentation should include the risk assessment which should be cross referenced to the audit program, and the audit program should be cross referenced to the audit working papers and vice versa.

(3) Working papers showing the work performed should be cross referenced to the audit program and the lead schedule on that particular section of the audit file, and should describe the nature of the work performed, the evidence obtained, and the conclusions reached.

(4) Each section of the audit file should have a lead schedule which should be cross referenced back to the relevant working papers.

(5) Trial balances should be cross referenced back to the relevant section of the audit file, and cross referenced forward to the financial statements.

(6) The financial statements should be cross referenced to the trial balance.

(7) Schedules of unadjusted differences should be cross referenced to the sections of the file to which they relate.

(8) Schedules of review points should all be 'cleared' to show that all outstanding matters have been dealt with.

chapter

# 6

# Evidence

## Chapter learning objectives

When you have completed this chapter you will be able to:

- Discuss the quality and quantity of audit evidence.
- Explain the assertions contained in the financial statements.
- Explain the purpose of substantive procedures and tests of controls.
- Discuss the procedures for obtaining audit evidence.
- Define, discuss and provide examples of audit sampling and explain the need for sampling.
- Explain the use of computer-assisted audit techniques.
- Discuss the extent to which auditors are able to rely on the work of others.

## 1 Audit evidence

In order for the auditor's opinion to be considered trustworthy auditors must come to their conclusions having completed a thorough examination of the books and records of their clients and they must document the procedures performed and evidence obtained, to support the conclusions reached.

The objective of the auditor, in terms of gathering evidence, is described in ISA 500 *Audit Evidence as:*

'to design and perform audit procedures in such a way to enable the auditor to obtain **sufficient appropriate audit evidence** to be able to draw reasonable conclusions on which to base the auditor's opinion.'

- **Sufficiency** relates to the **quantity** of evidence.
- **Appropriateness** relates to the **quality** or relevance and reliability of evidence.

### Sufficient evidence

There needs to be 'enough' evidence to support the auditor's conclusion. This is a matter of professional judgement. When determining whether there is enough evidence the auditor must consider:

- the risk of material misstatement
- the materiality of the item
- the nature of accounting and internal control systems
- the auditor's knowledge and experience of the business
- the results of controls tests
- the size of a population being tested
- the size of the sample selected to test
- the reliability of the evidence obtained.

**Sufficient evidence**

Consider, for example, the audit of a bank balance:

Auditors will confirm year-end bank balances directly with the bank. This is a good source of evidence but on its own is not sufficient to give assurance regarding the completeness and final valuation of bank and cash amounts. The key reason is timing differences. The client may have received cash amounts or cheques before the end of the year, or may have paid out cheques before the end of the year, that have not yet cleared the bank account.

For this reason the auditor should also review and reperform the client's year-end bank reconciliation.

In combination these two pieces of evidence will be sufficient to give assurance over the bank balances.

## Appropriate evidence

Appropriateness of evidence breaks down into two important concepts:

- reliability
- relevance.

### Reliability

Auditors should always attempt to obtain evidence from the most trustworthy and dependable source possible. Evidence is considered more reliable when it is:

- obtained from an independent external source
- generated internally but subject to effective control
- obtained directly by the auditor
- in documentary form
- in original form.

Broadly speaking, the more reliable the evidence the less of it the auditor will need. However, if evidence is unreliable it will never be appropriate for the audit, no matter how much is gathered.

### Relevance

To be relevant audit evidence has to address the objective/purpose of a procedure. For example:

**Attendance at an inventory count**

During counting the auditor will:

- select a sample of items from physical inventory and trace them to inventory records to confirm the **completeness** of accounting records
- select a sample of items from inventory records and trace them to physical inventories to confirm the **existence** of inventory assets.

Whilst the procedures are perhaps similar in nature their purpose (and relevance) is to test different **assertions** regarding inventory balances.

## 2 Financial statements assertions

The objective of audit testing is to assist the auditor in coming to a conclusion as to whether the financial statements are free from material misstatement.

For example:

**Inventory**

There are many ways inventory could be materially misstated:

- items could be missed out of inventory
- items from the next accounting period could be accidentally included
- it might not be valued at the lower of cost and net realisable value
- damaged or obsolete stock might not be identified
- purchase cost may not be recorded accurately
- the stock count may not be performed thoroughly.

For this reason auditors perform a range of tests on the significant classes of transaction, account balances and disclosures. These tests focus on what are known as **financial statements assertions**:

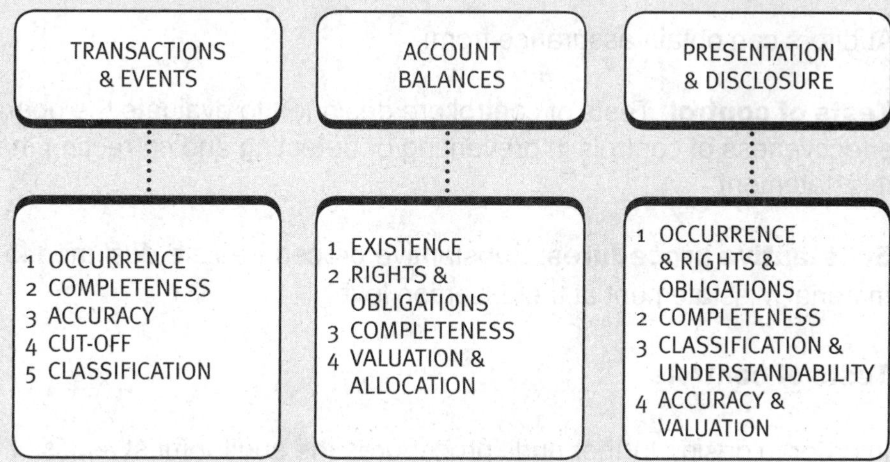


**Occurrence** – the transactions and events recorded actually occured and pertain to the entity.

**Completeness** – all transactions, assets, liabilities and equity interests have been recorded that should have been recorded.

**Accuracy** – amounts, data and other information have been recorded and disclosed appropriately.

**Cut-off** – transactions and events have been recorded in the correct accounting period.

**Classification and understandability** – transactions and events have been recorded in the proper accounts, and described and disclosed clearly.

**Existence** – assets, liabilities and equity interests exist.

**Rights and obligations** – the entity holds or controls the rights to assets and liabilities are the obligations of the entity.

**Valuation and allocation** – assets, liabilities and equity interests are included in the financial statements at appropriate values.

## 3 Sources of audit evidence

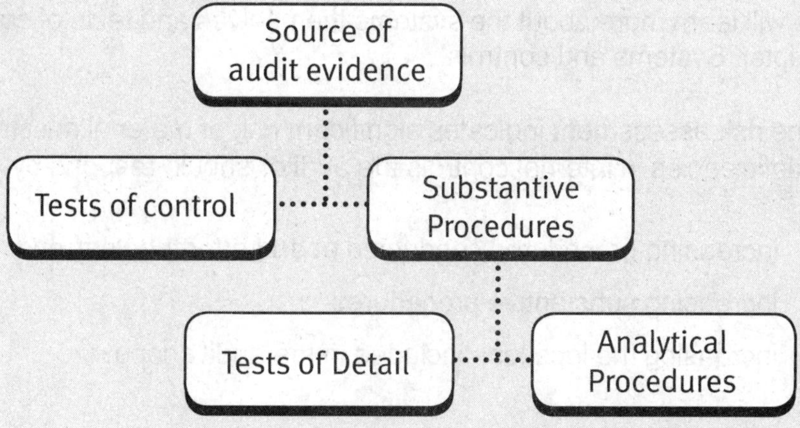

Auditors can obtain assurance from:

**Tests of control**: Tests of control are designed to evaluate the operating effectiveness of controls in preventing or detecting and correcting material misstatement.

**Substantive procedures**: Substantive procedures are designed to detect material misstatement at the assertion level.

## Tests of controls

In order to design further audit procedures the auditor must assess the risk of material misstatement in the financial statements.

Remember: audit risk = inherent risk x **control risk** x detection risk

Internal controls are a vital component of this risk model; they are the mechanisms that clients design in an attempt to prevent, detect and correct misstatement. This is not only necessary for good financial reporting it is necessary to safeguard the assets of the shareholders and is a requirement of corporate governance.

The stronger the control system the lower the risk of material misstatement in the financial statements.

Therefore auditors can seek to **place some reliance on internal control systems** and, as a result, reduce the substantive testing performed. In order to be able to do this they need to:

- ascertain how the system operates
- document the system in audit working papers
- test the operation of the system
- assess the design and operating effectiveness of the control system
- determine the impact on the audit approach for specific classes of transactions, account balances and disclosures.

We will learn more about the systems themselves and tests of controls in the chapter 'Systems and controls'.

If the risk assessment indicates significant risk of material misstatement due to deficiencies in internal controls the auditor should respond by:

- increasing procedures conducted at and after the year-end
- increasing substantive procedures
- increasing the locations included in the audit scope.

An effective control environment may allow the auditor to place more reliance on internal controls and evidence generated internally within the entity. Typically this increases the appropriateness of interim testing and allows the auditor to reduce the quantity of detailed substantive procedures performed.

However, the auditor can never eliminate the need for substantive procedures entirely because there are inherent limitations to the reliance that can be placed on internal control due to:

- human error in the use of judgement
- simple processing errors and mistakes
- collusion of staff in circumventing controls
- systems designed for routine transactions, processing one-off or unusual transactions
- the abuse of power by those with ultimate controlling responsibility (i.e. management override).

The extent of substantive testing to be carried out will depend on the auditor's assessment of the internal control system and the auditor's assessment of the risk of material misstatement. 

**Substantive procedures**

Substantive procedures consist of:

- **Tests of detail**: tests of detail verify specific transactions and balances
- **Substantive analytical procedures**: analytical procedures (as seen in the chapter 'Risk') involve the evaluation of financial information through analysis of plausible relationships among both financial and non-financial data.

**Substantive analytical procedures**

**Analytical procedures as substantive tests**

We have already come across analytical procedures as a significant component of risk assessment at the planning phase of an audit. Later in the text we will also see that they are a critical component of the completion of an audit. Here we consider their use as substantive procedures, i.e. procedures designed to detect misstatement.

Analytical procedures are used to identify trends and understand relationships between sets of data. This in itself will not detect misstatement but will identify possible sources. As such, analytical procedures cannot be used in isolation and should be coupled with other, corroborative, forms of testing, such as enquiry of management.

In order to perform a thorough analytical review auditors do not simply look at current figures in comparison to last year. Auditors may consider other points of comparison, such as budgets and industry data. Other techniques are also available, including:

- ratio analysis
- trend analysis
- proof in total, for example: an auditor might create an expectation of payroll costs for the year by taking last year's cost and inflating for pay rises and changes in staff numbers.

Analytical procedures are useful for assessing several assertions at once as the auditor is effectively auditing a whole accounting balance or class of transaction to see if it is reasonable.

They can be used to corroborate other audit evidence obtained, such as statements by management about changes in cost structures, such as energy savings.

By using analytical procedures the auditor may identify unusual items that can then be further investigated to ensure that a misstatement doesn't exist in the balance.

However, in order to use analytical procedures effectively the auditor needs to be able to create an expectation. It would be difficult to do this if operations changed significantly from the prior year. If the changes were planned, the auditor could use forecasts as a point of comparison. Although these are inherently unreliable due to the amount of estimates involved. In this circumstance it would be pointless comparing to prior years as the business would be too different to be able to conduct effective comparison.

It would also be difficult to use analytical procedures if a business had experienced a number of significant one-off events in the year as these would distort the year's figures making comparison to both prior years and budgets meaningless.

**The suitability of analytical procedures as substantive tests**

The suitability of this approach depends on four factors:

- the assertion/s under scrutiny
- the reliability of the data
- the degree of precision possible
- the amount of variation which is acceptable.

For example.

(1) Assertions

- Analytical procedures are clearly unsuitable for testing the existence of inventories.
- They are, however, suitable for assessing the value of inventory in terms of the need for provisions against old inventories, identified using the inventory holding period ratio.

(2) Reliability

- If controls over financial data are weak then it is likely to contain misstatement and is therefore not suitable as a basis for assessment. This may be true of manually prepared forecasts and industry data from unknown sources.

(3) Precision

- There is likely to be greater consistency over time in information such as gross margins than in discretionary expenditure that is subject to change, like advertising or R&D.

(4) Acceptable variation

- Variations that could have a minor impact on the results for the year (such as cleaning costs, utility accruals) will be regarded differently from variations in balances such as receivables, which could significantly affect the need for bad debt provisions.

In some circumstances the auditor may rely solely on substantive testing:

- The auditor may choose to rely solely on substantive testing where it is considered to be a more efficient or more effective way of obtaining audit evidence, e.g. for smaller organisations.
- The auditor may have to rely solely on substantive testing where the client's internal control system cannot be relied on.

The auditor must always carry out some substantive procedures on material items, and also carry out specific substantive procedures required by ISA 330 *The auditor's response to assessed risks.*

**Required minimum substantive procedures**

ISA 330 *The Auditor's Response to Assessed Risks* requires the auditor to carry out the following substantive procedures:

- Agreeing the financial statements to the underlying accounting records.
- Examination of material journals.
- Examination of other adjustments made in preparing the financial statements.

## 4 Types of audit procedures

ISA 500 identifies eight types of procedures that the auditor can adopt to obtain audit evidence.

In the chapter 'Procedures' we will look in detail at how these procedures are applied in specific circumstances.

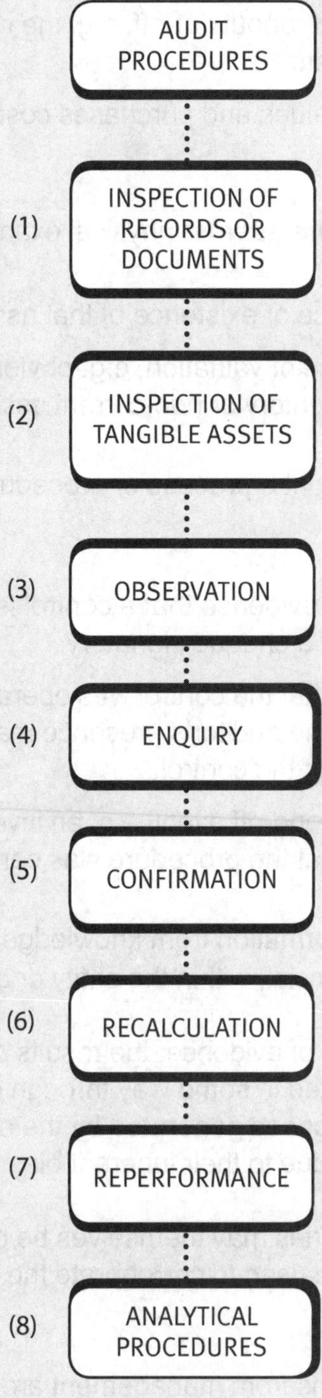

**Explanation of techniques**

**Inspection of documents and records**: examining records or documents, in paper or electronic form.

- May give evidence of rights and obligations, e.g. title deeds
- May give evidence that a control is operating, e.g. invoices stamped paid or authorised for payment by an appropriate signature.
- May give evidence about cut-off, e.g. the dates on invoices, despatch notes, etc.
- Confirms sales values and purchases costs (i.e. by inspecting the invoice)

**Inspection of tangible assets**: physical examination of an asset.

- To obtain evidence of existence of that asset.
- May give evidence of valuation, e.g. obvious evidence of impairment of inventory or non-current assets.

**Observation**: looking at a process or procedure being performed by others.

- May well provide evidence that a control is being operated, e.g. double staffing or a cheque signatory.
- Is only evidence that the control was operating properly at the time of the observation; the auditor's presence may have had an influence on the operation of the control.
- Observation of a one-off event, e.g. an inventory count, may well give good evidence that the procedure was carried out effectively.

**Enquiry**: seeking information from knowledgeable persons, both financial and non-financial, within the entity or outside.

Whilst a major source of evidence, the results of enquiries will usually need to be corroborated in some way through other audit procedures. This is because responses generated by the audit client are considered to be of a low quality due to their inherent bias.

The answers to enquiries may themselves be corroborative evidence. In particular they may be used to corroborate the results of analytical procedures.

Written representations from management are part of overall enquiries. These involve obtaining written statements from management to confirm oral enquiries. These are considered further in the chapter 'Completion and review'.

**Confirmation**: obtaining a direct response (usually written) from an external, third party.

- Examples include:
  - circularisation of receivables
  - confirmation of bank balances in a bank letter
  - confirmation of actual/potential penalties from legal advisers
  - confirmation of inventories held by third parties.
- May give good evidence of existence of balances, e.g. receivables confirmation.
- May not necessarily give reliable evidence of valuation, e.g. customers may confirm receivable amounts but, ultimately, be unable to pay in the future.

**Recalculation**: manually or electronically checking the arithmetical accuracy of documents, records, or the client's calculations, e.g. recalculation of the translation of a foreign currency transaction.

**Reperformance**: the auditor's independent execution of procedures or controls that were originally performed as part of the entity's internal control system, e.g. reperformance of a bank reconciliation.

## 5 Sampling

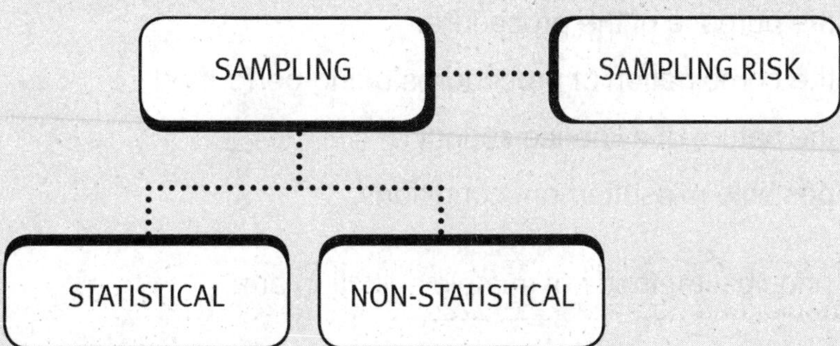


### The need for sampling

It will usually be impossible to test every item in an accounting population because of the costs involved. Consider a manufacturer of fasteners (i.e. nuts, bolts, nails and screws); they will have many thousands, maybe millions, of items of inventory. It would simply be impossible to test the valuation of every single one.

It is also important to remember that auditors give reasonable **not** absolute assurance and are therefore not certifying that the financial statements are 100% accurate.

Audit evidence is gathered on a test basis. Auditors therefore need to understand the implications and effective use of **sampling**.

The definition of sampling, as described in ISA 530 *Audit Sampling* is:

'The application of audit procedures to less than 100% of items within a population of audit relevance such that all sampling units have a chance of selection in order to provide the auditor with a reasonable basis on which to draw conclusions about the entire population.'

**Statistical or non-statistical sampling**

Statistical sampling means any approach to sampling that uses:

- random selection of samples and
- probability theory to evaluate sample results.

Any approach that does not have both these characteristics is considered to be non-statistical sampling.

The approach taken is a matter of auditor judgement.

**Designing a sample**

When designing a sample the auditor has to consider:

- the purpose of the procedure
- the combination of procedures being performed
- the nature of evidence sought
- possible misstatement conditions.

The principal methods of sample selection are:

- **Random selection** – this can be achieved through the use of random number generators or tables.
- **Systematic selection** – where a constant sampling interval is used (e.g. every 50th balance) and the first item is selected randomly.
- **Monetary unit selection** – selecting items based upon monetary values (usually focusing on higher value items).
- **Haphazard selection** – auditor does not follow a structured technique but avoids bias or predictability.
- **Block selection** – this involves selecting a block of contiguous (i.e. next to each other) items from the population. This technique is rarely appropriate.

When non-statistical methods (haphazard and block) are used the auditor uses judgement to select the items to be tested. Whilst this lends itself to auditor bias it does support the risk based approach, where the auditor focuses on those areas most susceptible to material misstatement.

**Illustration 1: Murray Co sampling**

**Sampling**

Murray Co deals with large retail customers, and therefore has a low number of large receivables balances on the receivables ledger. Given the low number of customers with a balance on Murray Co's receivables ledger, all balances would probably be selected for testing. However, for illustrative purposes the following shows how a sample of balances would be selected using systematic and Monetary Unit Sampling.

Credit and zero balances on the receivables ledger have been removed. The number of items to be sampled has been determined as 6. The customer list has been alphabetised.

**Systematic Sampling**

There are 19 customers with balances in the receivables ledger. The sampling interval is calculated by taking the total number of balances and dividing it by the sample size. The sampling interval (to the nearest whole number) is therefore 3.

The first item is chosen randomly; in this case item 10. Every third item after that is then also selected for testing until 6 items have been chosen.

| Customer Ref | Customer Name | Balance $000 | Item number | Sampling Item |
|---|---|---|---|---|
| A001 | Anfield United Shop | 176 | 1 | |
| B002 | The Beautiful Game | 84 | 2 | |
| B003 | Beckham's | 42 | 3 | (5) |
| C001 | Cheryl & Coleen Co | 12 | 4 | |
| D001 | Dream Team | 45 | 5 | |
| E001 | Escot Supermarket | 235 | 6 | (6) |
| G001 | Golf is Us | 211 | 7 | |
| G002 | Green Green Grass | 61 | 8 | |
| H001 | HHA Sports | 59 | 9 | |
| J001 | Jilberts | 21 | 10 | (1) |
| J002 | James Smit Partnership | 256 | 11 | |
| J003 | Jockeys | 419 | 12 | |
| O001 | The Oval | 92 | 13 | (2) |
| P001 | Pole Vaulters | 76 | 14 | |
| S001 | Stayrose Supermarket | 97 | 15 | |
| T001 | Trainers and More | 93 | 16 | (3) |
| W001 | Wanderers | 89 | 17 | |
| W003 | Walk Hike Run | 4 | 18 | |
| W004 | Winners | 31 | 19 | (4) |

**Monetary Unit Sampling**

*Monetary Unit Sampling can utilise either the random or systematic selection method. This example illustrates the systematic selection method.*

The cumulative balance is calculated using the alphabetised list of receivables balances.

The sampling interval is calculated by taking the total value on the ledger of $2,103,000 (to the nearest $000) and dividing by the sample size, 6. The sampling interval is therefore $351,000.

The first item is chosen randomly (a number between 1 and 2,103,000), in this case 233. Each item after that is selected by adding the sampling interval to the last value, until six items have been selected.

**$000**

| Customer Ref | Customer Name | Balance | Cumulative | Sampling Item |
|---|---|---|---|---|
| A001 | Anfield United Shop | 176 | 176 | |
| B002 | The Beautiful Game | 84 | 260 | (1) $233 |
| B003 | Beckham's | 42 | 302 | |
| C001 | Cheryl & Coleen Co | 12 | 314 | |
| D001 | Dream Team | 45 | 359 | |
| E001 | Escot Supermarket | 235 | 594 | (2) $584 |
| G001 | Golf is Us | 211 | 805 | |
| G002 | Green Green Grass | 61 | 866 | |
| H001 | HHA Sports | 59 | 925 | |
| J001 | Jilberts | 21 | 946 | (3) $935 |
| J002 | James Smit Partnership | 256 | 1,202 | |
| J003 | Jockeys | 419 | 1,621 | (4) $1,286 |
| O001 | The Oval | 92 | 1,713 | (5) $1,637 |
| P001 | Pole Vaulters | 76 | 1,789 | |
| S001 | Stayrose Supermarket | 97 | 1,886 | |
| T001 | Trainers and More | 93 | 1,979 | |
| W001 | Wanderers | 89 | 2,068 | (6) $1,988 |
| W003 | Walk Hike Run | 4 | 2,072 | |
| W004 | Winners | 31 | **2,103** | |

The sample size depends upon the level of sampling risk that the auditor is willing to accept.

## Sampling risk

We saw in the chapter 'Risk' that sampling risk is a component of detection risk, the other component being non-sampling risk, and that sampling risk arises from the possibility that the auditors' conclusion, based on a sample, may be different from the conclusion that would be reached if the entire population were subjected to the same audit procedure.

Auditors are faced with sampling risk in tests of controls and in substantive procedures. Sampling risk is essentially the risk that the auditor's sample from a population will not be representative. In other words it will, by chance, include too many or too few errors to give a realistic impression of the population as a whole.

In order to reduce sampling risk the auditor needs to increase the size of the sample selected.

## Evaluating misstatements in a sample

For tests of details the auditor will project misstatements found in the sample to the population as a whole, and evaluate the results of the sample by considering tolerable misstatement.

**Tolerable Misstatement** is defined in ISA 530 *Audit Sampling as:*

"A monetary amount set by the auditor in respect of which the auditor seeks to obtain an appropriate level of assurance that the monetary amount set by the auditor is not exceeded by the actual misstatement in the population."

Tolerable misstatement is the practical application of performance materiality to an audit sample:

- If the total of errors in the sample selected exceeds tolerable misstatement the auditor will extend the sample in order to determine the total misstatement in the population.
- If the total of errors in the sample is less than tolerable misstatement then the auditor may be reasonably confident that the risk of material misstatement in the whole population is low and no further testing will be required.

## 6 Computer assisted audit techniques (CAATs)

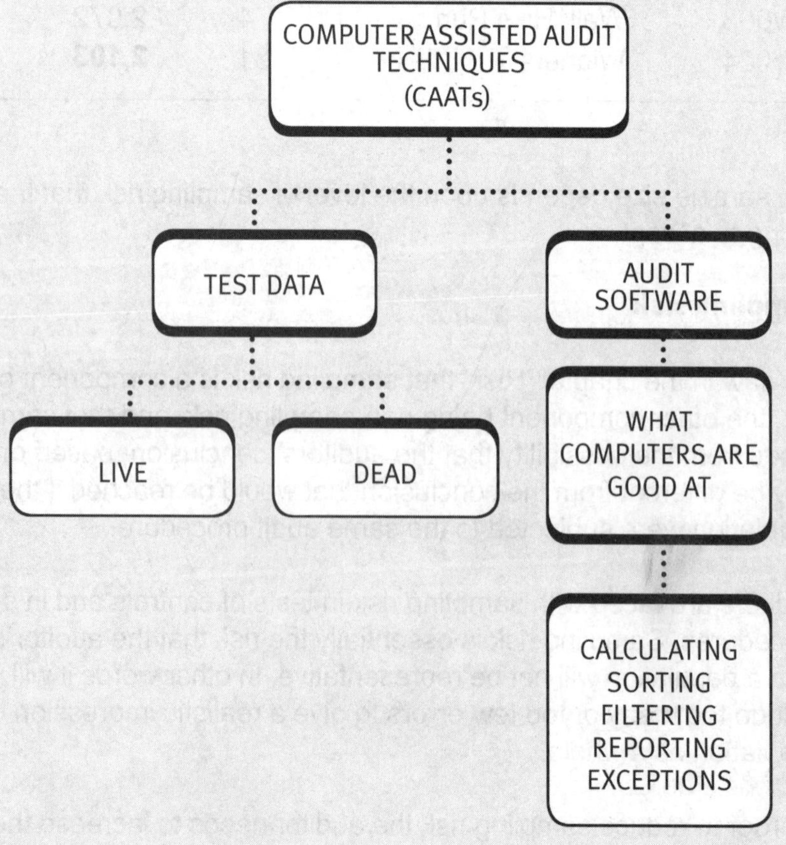

The use of computers as a tool to perform audit procedures is often referred to as a 'computer assisted audit techniques' or CAAT for short.

There are two broad categories of CAAT:

(1) Audit software

(2) Test data

**Audit software**

Audit software is used to interrogate a client's system. It can be either packaged, off-the-shelf software or it can be purpose written to work on a client's system. The main advantage of these programs is that they can be used to scrutinise large volumes of data, which it would be inefficient to do manually. The programs can then present the results so that they can be investigated further.

Specific procedures they can perform include:

- extracting samples according to specified criteria, such as:
  - random
  - over a certain amount
  - below a certain amount
  - at certain dates
- calculating ratios and select indicators that fail to meet certain pre-defined criteria (i.e. benchmarking)
- check arithmetical accuracy (for example additions)
- preparing reports (budget vs actual)
- stratification of data (such as invoices by customer or age)
- produce letters to send out to customers and suppliers
- tracing transactions through the computerised system.

These procedures can simplify the auditor's task by selecting samples for testing, identifying risk areas and by performing certain substantive procedures. The software does not, however, replace the need for the auditor's own procedures.

**Test data**

Test data involves the auditor submitting 'dummy' data into the client's system to ensure that the system correctly processes it and that it prevents or detects and corrects misstatements. The objective of this is to test the operation of application controls within the system.

To be successful test data should include both data with errors built into it and data without errors. Examples of errors include:

- codes that do not exist, e.g. customer, supplier and employee
- transactions above pre-determined limits, e.g. salaries above contracted amounts, credit above limits agreed with customer
- invoices with arithmetical errors
- submitting data with incorrect batch control totals.

Data maybe processed during a normal operational cycle ('live' test data) or during a special run at a point in time outside the normal operational cycle ('dead' test data). Both have their advantages and disadvantages, for example:

- Live tests could interfere with the operation of the system or corrupt master files/standing data.
- Dead testing avoids this scenario but only gives assurance that the system works when not operating live. This may not be reflective of the strains the system is put under in normal conditions.

**Advantages and disadvantages of CAATs**

**Advantages of CAATs**

CAATs allow the auditor to:

- Independently access the data stored on a computer system without dependence on the client.
- Test the reliability of client software, i.e. the IT application controls (the results of which can then be used to assess control risk and design further audit procedures).
- Increase the accuracy of audit tests.
- Perform audit tests more efficiently, which in the long-term will result in a more cost effective audit.

**Disadvantages of CAATs**

- CAATs can be expensive and time consuming to set up, the software must either be purchased or designed (in which case specialist IT staff will be needed).
- Client permission and cooperation may be difficult to obtain.
- Potential incompatibility with the client's computer system.
- The audit team may not have sufficient IT skills and knowledge to create the complex data extracts and programming required.

- The audit team may not have the knowledge or training needed to understand the results of the CAATs.
- Data may be corrupted or lost during the application of CAATs.

**Other techniques**

There are other forms of CAAT that are becoming increasingly common as computer technology develops, although the cost and sophistication involved currently limits their use to the larger accountancy firms with greater resources. These include:

**Integrated test facilities** - this involves the creation of dummy ledgers and records to which test data can be sent. This enables more frequent and efficient test data procedures to be performed live and the information can simply be ignored by the client when printing out their internal records; and

**Embedded audit software** - this requires a purpose written audit program to be embedded into the client's accounting system. The program will be designed to perform certain tasks (similar to audit software) with the advantage that it can be turned on and off at the auditor's wish throughout the accounting year. This will allow the auditor to gather information on certain transactions (perhaps material ones) for later testing and will also identify peculiarities that require attention during the final audit.

### Auditing around the computer

This term means that the 'internal' software of the computer is not documented or audited by the auditor, but the inputs to the computer are agreed to the expected outputs to the computer.

Audit outcome

Increase the AUDIT RISK Why?

The actual computer files and programs are NOT TESTED.

Therefore no DIRECT evidence that the programs are working as documented

Where errors are found it maybe difficult or even impossible to determine why those errors have occurred.

If amendments cannot be made, there is an increased likelihood of audit qualifications.

Since controls are being tested, all discrepancies between predicted and actual results must be fully resolved and documented, irrespective of financial amounts involved.

### The practical implications of CAAT's

**Further audit procedures**

As previously mentioned CAAT's will be extremely useful for assisting with sample selections through stratification and other techniques. For example, identification of:

- receivable, payable or inventory balances over a certain age;
- individually material assets and liabilities;
- transactions over agreed limits (e.g. customer's credit limits);
- changes to standing data, e.g. authorised supplier lists;
- credit balances within receivables and debit balances in payables;

- non-current asset purchases over a certain amount;

CAAT's can also be used to perform certain substantive procedures, such as:

- ratio calculations;
- recalculation of non-current asset depreciation;
- recalculation of employee taxes, state pension schemes and employment pension scheme balances;
- confirmation of batch totals to individual records, e.g. wages and salary payments to payroll records;
- casting of all ledger balances.

## 7 Relying on the work of others

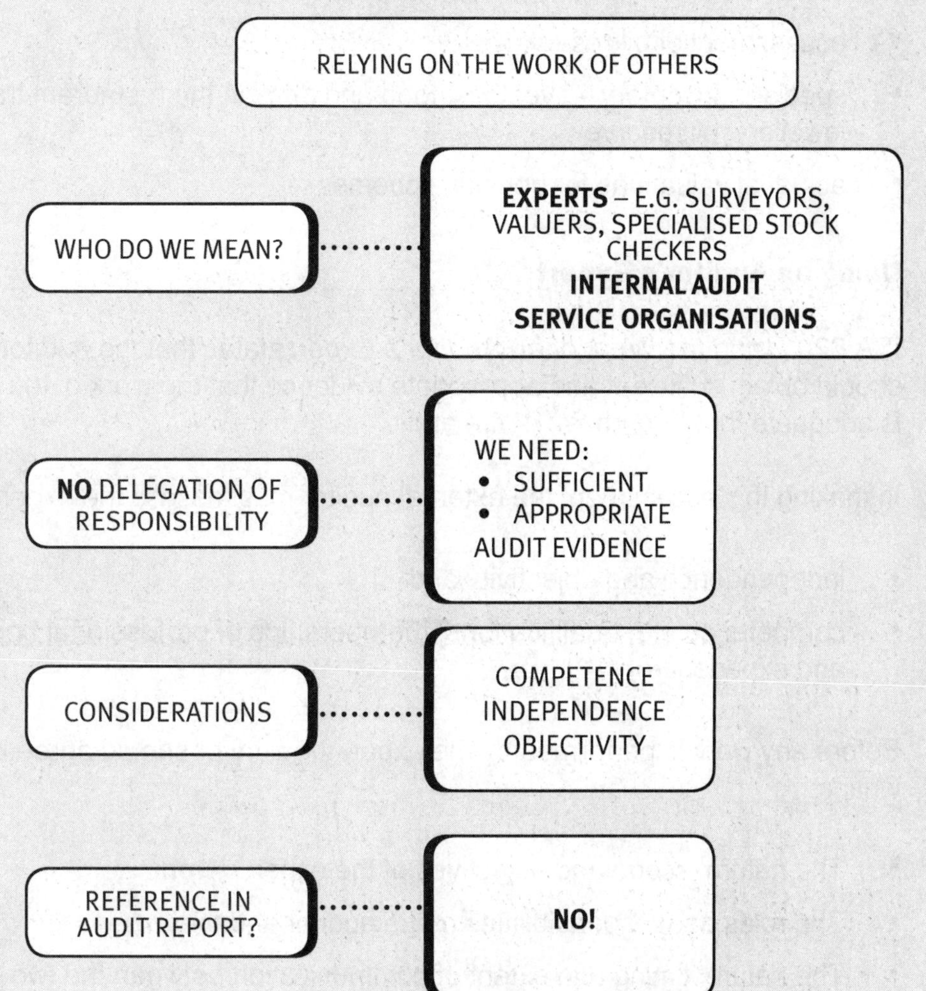
RELYING ON THE WORK OF OTHERS
WHO DO WE MEAN?
EXPERTS – E.G. SURVEYORS, VALUERS, SPECIALISED STOCK CHECKERS
INTERNAL AUDIT
SERVICE ORGANISATIONS
NO DELEGATION OF RESPONSIBILITY
WE NEED:
• SUFFICIENT
• APPROPRIATE
AUDIT EVIDENCE
CONSIDERATIONS
COMPETENCE
INDEPENDENCE
OBJECTIVITY
REFERENCE IN AUDIT REPORT?
NO!

**Why rely on the work of other people?**

- In certain circumstances auditors may need to rely on the work of, or consult parties not involved in the audit process.
- Auditors may also choose to rely on the work of others because they find it effective and efficient to do so.

**The need to consult others**

Auditors do not need to be experts in all aspects of their clients' businesses. Where they lack the technical knowledge and skills to gather evidence about transactions, balances and disclosures they should seek the assistance of an expert. For example:

- property valuation
- construction work in progress
- assessment of oil reserves
- specialist inventory – livestock, food and drink in the restaurant trade, jewellery; oil reserves
- actuarial valuations for pension schemes.

**Using an Auditor's Expert**

ISA 620 *Using the Work of an Auditor's Expert* states that the auditor should obtain sufficient and appropriate evidence that the work of the expert is adequate for the purpose of the audit.

In making this assessment the external auditor must assess the expert's:

- independence and objectivity and
- competence (i.e. qualifications, memberships of professional bodies and experience)

Before any work is performed by the expert the auditor should agree in writing:

- The nature, scope and objectives of the expert's work.
- The roles and responsibilities of the auditor and the expert.
- The nature, timing and extent of communication between the two parties.
- The need for the expert to observe confidentiality.

Once the work has been completed the auditor must then assess it to ensure it is appropriate for the purposes of the audit. This involves consideration of:

- the consistency of the findings with other evidence
- the significant assumptions made
- the use and accuracy of source data.

**Relying on internal audit**

An internal audit department forms part of the client's system of internal control. If this is an effective element of the control system it may well reduce control risk, and therefore reduce the need for the auditor to perform detailed substantive testing. This will need to be taken into account during the planning phase of the audit.

Additionally, auditors may be able to co-operate with a client's internal audit department and place reliance on their procedures in place of performing their own.

ISA 610 (Revised) Using the Work of Internal Auditors (issued March 2012, effective for audits of financial statements for periods ending on or after December 15, 2013) states that before relying on the work of internal auditors, the external auditor must determine whether the work of internal audit can be used and whether that work is adequate for the purposes of the audit.

This involves an evaluation of:

- the extent to which the internal audit function's **organisational status** and relevant policies and procedures support the **objectivity** of the internal auditors)
- the **competence** of the internal audit function
- whether the internal audit function applies a systematic and disciplined **approach**, including quality control.

If the auditor considers it appropriate to use the work of the internal auditors they then have to determine the areas and extent to which the work of the internal audit function can be used (by considering the nature and scope of work) and incorporate this into their planning to assess the impact on the nature, timing and extent of further audit procedures.

They also have to plan adequate time to review the work of the internal audit function to evaluate whether:

- the work was properly planned, performed, supervised, reviewed and documented
- sufficient appropriate evidence has been obtained

- the conclusions reached are appropriate in the circumstances
- the reports prepared are consistent with the work performed.

**Objectivity, competence and approach**

When evaluating the competence of the internal audit function, the external auditor will consider:

- whether the resources of the internal audit function are appropriate and adequate for the size of the organisation and nature of its operations
- whether there are established policies for hiring, training and assigning internal auditors to internal audit engagements
- whether internal auditors have adequate technical training and proficiency, including relevant professional qualifications and experience
- whether the internal auditors have the required knowledge of the entity's financial reporting and the applicable financial reporting framework
- whether the internal audit function possesses the necessary skills (e.g. industry-specific knowledge) to perform work related to the entity's financial statements
- whether the internal auditors are members of relevant professional bodies that oblige them to comply with the relevant professional standards including continuing professional development.

When evaluating whether the internal audit function applies a systematic and disciplined approach, the external auditor will consider:

- whether there are adequate documented internal audit procedures or guidance
- whether the internal audit function has appropriate quality control procedures.

(ISA 610 (Revised) Using the Work of Internal Auditors)

Examples of work of the internal audit function that can be used by the external auditor include:

- Testing of the operating effectiveness of controls.
- Substantive procedures involving limited judgement.
- Observations of inventory counts.

- Tracing transactions through the information system relevant to financial reporting.
- Testing of compliance with regulatory requirements.

Note that the auditor is not required to rely on the work of internal audit. In some jurisdictions, the external auditor may be prohibited or restricted from using the work of the internal auditor by law.

## Service organisations

ISA 402 *Audit considerations relating to an entity using a service organisation* deals with the auditor's responsibility to obtain sufficient appropriate evidence when a client outsources functions to service organisations.

The client may outsource certain functions to another company – a service organisation, e.g.

- payroll
- receivables collection
- the entire finance function
- internal audit.

### Advantages from the auditor's point of view

- The independence of the service organisation may give increased reliability to the evidence obtained.
- Their specialist skills tend to make them more reliable at processing information.
- The auditor may be able to place a high degree of reliance on the reports they produce as a result (reduced control risk).

### Disadvantages

- The auditor may not be able to obtain information from the service provider.
- The auditor may not be allowed to test controls at the service provider.
- This would lead to difficulties in assessing the accuracy and reliability of the information produced by the service provider.
- Ultimately this could lead to a lack of sufficient appropriate evidence and a modified audit report.

**References to the work of others in the audit report**

It is the auditors' responsibility to obtain sufficient and appropriate audit evidence in order to arrive at their audit opinion. Therefore, no reference should be made in the audit report regarding the use of others during the audit.

**Test your understanding 1**

ISA 500 Audit Evidence requires audit evidence to be reliable.

**Required:**

**List FOUR factors that influence the reliability of audit evidence.**

*Real exam: December 2009* **(4 marks)**

**Test your understanding 2**

**List and explain FOUR methods of selecting a sample of items to test from a population in accordance with ISA 530 Audit Sampling.**

*Real exam question: June 2009* **(4 marks)**

**Test your understanding 3**

**List and explain FOUR factors that will influence the auditor's judgement regarding the sufficiency of the evidence obtained.**

*Real exam question: June 2008* **(4 marks)**

**Test your understanding 4**

ISA 620 Using the Work of an Auditor's Expert explains how an auditor may use an expert to obtain audit evidence.

**Required:**

**Explain THREE factors that the external auditor should consider when assessing the competence and objectivity of the expert.**

*Real exam question: December 2008* **(3 marks)**

## 8 Chapter summary

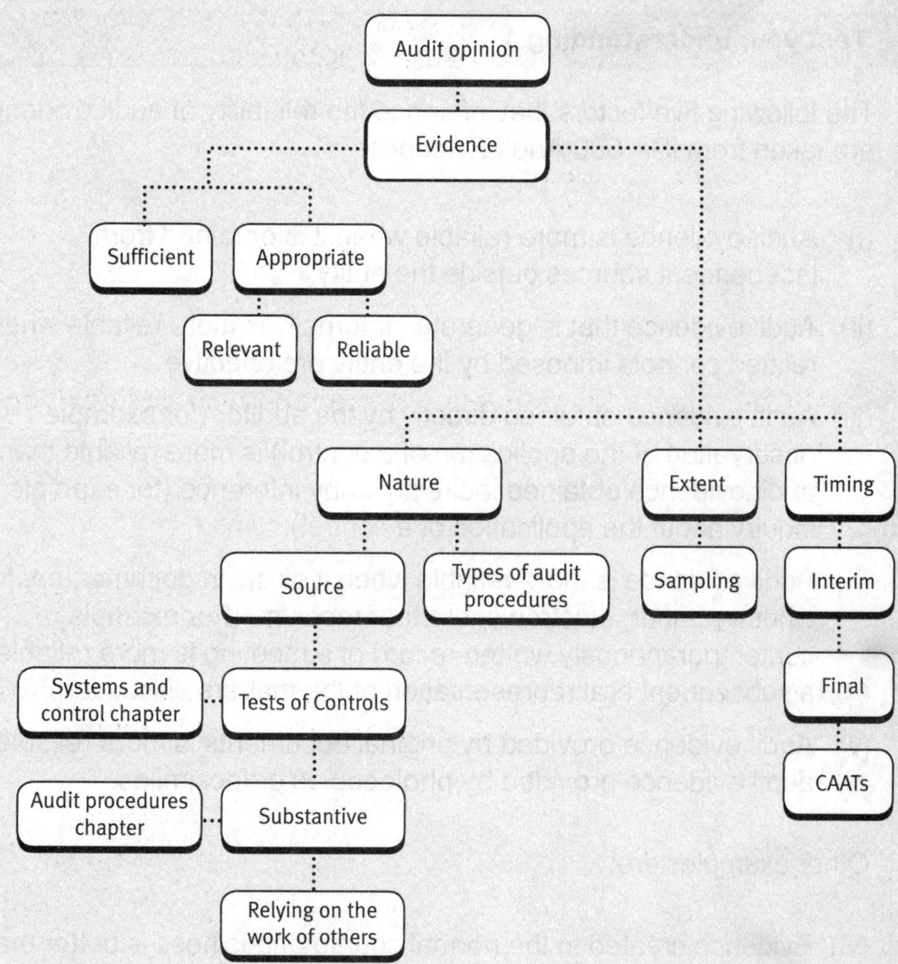

## Test your understanding answers

### Test your understanding 1

The following five factors that influence the reliability of audit evidence are taken from ISA 500 Audit Evidence:

(i) Audit evidence is more reliable when it is obtained from independent sources outside the entity.

(ii) Audit evidence that is generated internally is more reliable when the related controls imposed by the entity are effective.

(iii) Audit evidence obtained directly by the auditor (for example, observation of the application of a control) is more reliable than audit evidence obtained indirectly or by inference (for example, inquiry about the application of a control).

(iv) Audit evidence is more reliable when it exists in documentary form, whether paper, electronic, or other medium. (For example, a contemporaneously written record of a meeting is more reliable than a subsequent oral representation of the matters discussed.)

(v) Audit evidence provided by original documents is more reliable than audit evidence provided by photocopies or facsimiles.

Other examples are:

(vi) Evidence created in the normal course of business is better than evidence specially created to satisfy the auditor.

(vii) The best-informed source of audit evidence will normally be management of the company (although management's lack of independence may reduce its value as a source of such evidence).

(viii) Evidence about the future is particularly difficult to obtain and is less reliable than evidence about past events.

Only four examples are required.

**Test your understanding 2**

**Sampling methods**

Methods of sampling in accordance with ISA 530 Audit Sampling and Other Means of Testing:

- **Random** selection. Ensures each item in a population has an equal chance of selection, for example by using random number tables.
- **Systematic** selection. In which a number of sampling units in the population is divided by the sample size to give a sampling interval.
- **Haphazard** selection. The auditor selects the sample without following a structured technique – the auditor would avoid any conscious bias or predictability.
- **Sequence or block**. Involves selecting a block(s) of contiguous items from within a population.

**Note:** Only four sampling methods were asked for. Another method of sampling is:

- **Monetary Unit Sampling**. This selection method ensures that each individual $1 in the population has an equal chance of being selected.

**Test your understanding 3**

**Sufficiency of evidence**

- Assessment of risk at the financial statement level and/or the individual transaction level. As risk increases then more evidence is required.
- The materiality of the item. More evidence will normally be collected on material items whereas immaterial items may simply be reviewed to ensure they appear correct.
- The nature of the accounting and internal control systems. The auditor will place more reliance on good accounting and internal control systems limiting the amount of audit evidence required.
- The auditor's knowledge and experience of the business. Where the auditor has good past knowledge of the business and trusts the integrity of staff then less evidence will be required.
- The findings of audit procedures. Where findings from related audit procedures are satisfactory (e.g. tests of controls over receivables) then substantive evidence will be collected.
- The source and reliability of the information. Where evidence is obtained from reliable sources (e.g. written evidence) then less evidence is required than if the source was unreliable (e.g. verbal evidence).

**Test your understanding 4**

**Competence and objectivity of experts**

The expert's professional qualification. The expert should be a member of a relevant professional body or have the necessary licence to perform the work.

The experience and reputation of the expert in the area in which the auditor is seeking audit evidence.

The objectivity of the expert from the client company. The expert should not normally be employed by the client.

chapter

# 7

# Systems and controls

## Chapter learning objectives

When you have completed this chapter you will be able to:

- Describe and explain the five key components of an internal control system.
- Explain how auditors record internal control systems.
- Explain how auditors identify deficiencies and significant deficiencies in internal control systems.
- Explain, analyse and provide examples of internal controls.
- List examples of application controls and general IT controls.
- Discuss and provide examples of how to report internal control deficiencies to management.

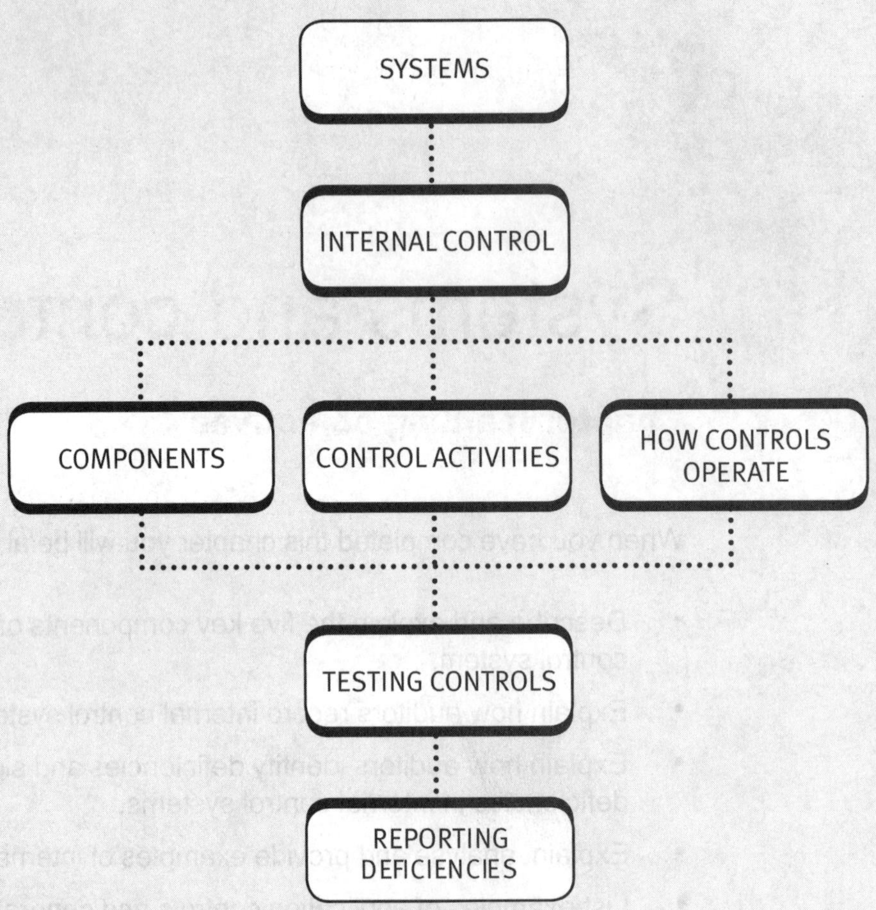


We dealt with the importance of internal control systems to the auditor in an earlier chapter.

This chapter considers the basic components of control systems and how the auditor fulfils their objectives for assessing control risk.

## 1 The components of an internal control system

This is further developed by ISA 315 (Revised) *Identifying and Assessing the Risks of Material Misstatement Through Understanding the Entity and its Environment* (issued March 2012, effective for audits of financial statements for periods ending on or after December 15, 2013) states that auditors need to understand an entity's internal controls. To assist this process it identifies five components of an internal control system:

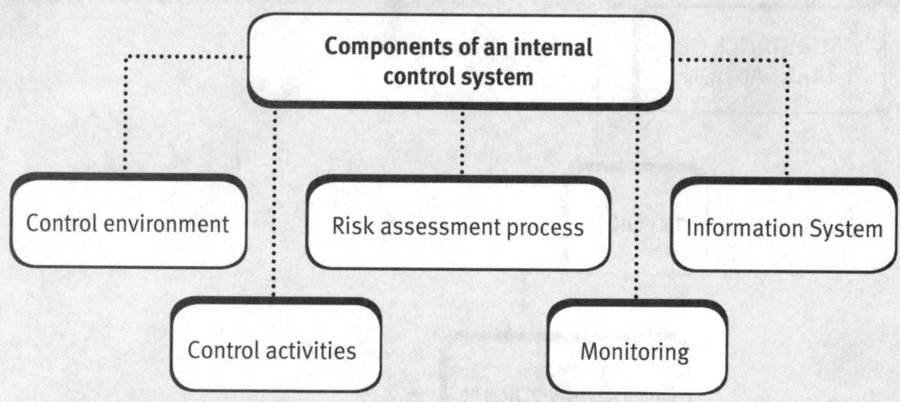

**Control systems – basic principles**

The auditor's main focus is on those systems relevant to the financial statements and, therefore, the audit. The basic objectives of these systems are to:

- measure the effects of transactions and other relevant issues
- record those transactions and effects
- summarise them into a useable form
- publish those summaries to the relevant users of the information to assist decision making.

A simple system can be illustrated as follows:

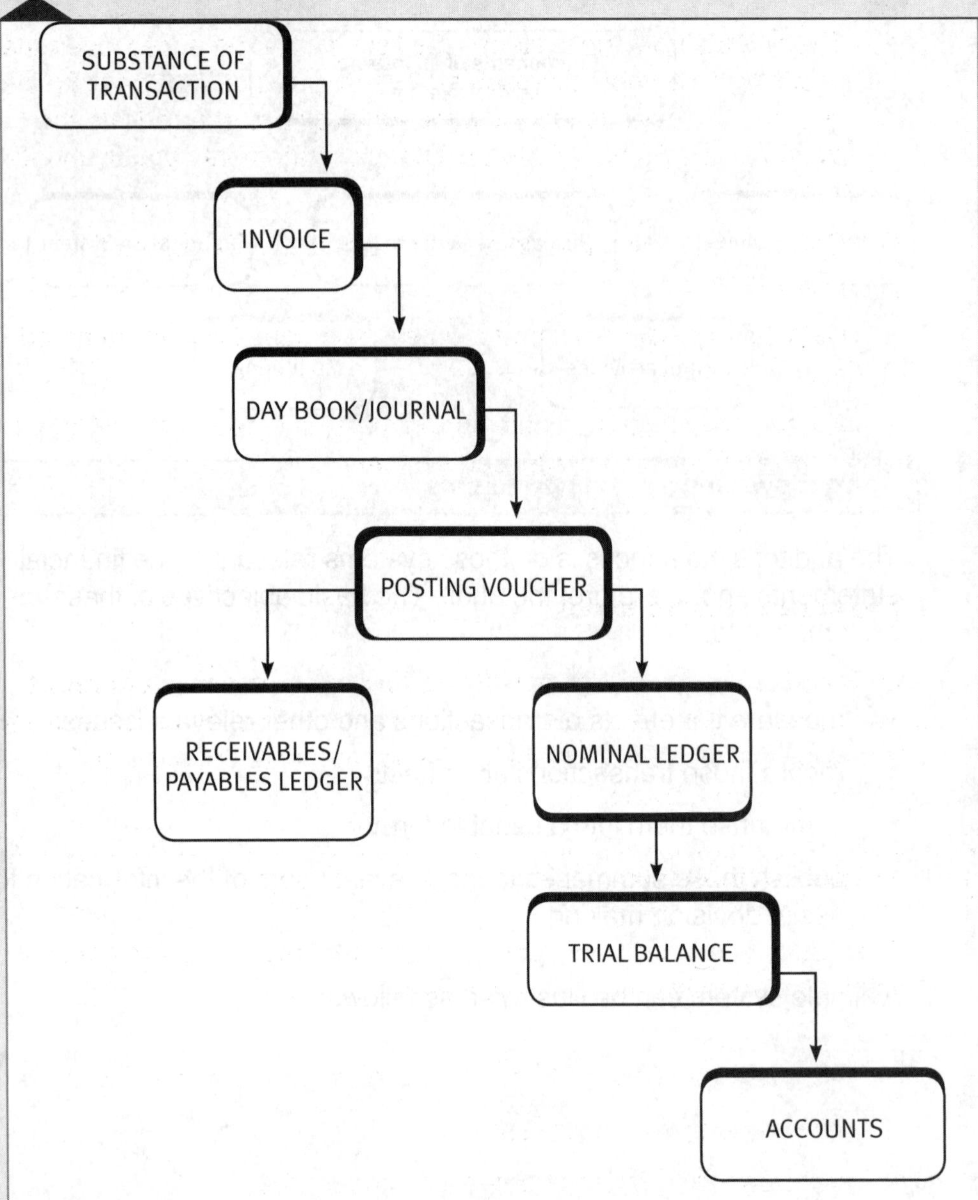


It should be noted that the above illustration represents a typical manual accounting system. These are rare nowadays due to the use of readily available (and cheap) accounting software. However, the basic principles of those systems are still the same and it is worth understanding how the flow of information in a system works.

**Computerised systems**

There are a number of things to understand about the impact of computerised accounting systems:

- The need to transfer information from one piece of paper to another is greatly reduced.

- The outputs from the system – the listings, trial balances, even the financial statements themselves – usually do not form part of a strict chronological sequence. So once an invoice is entered into the system, the TB, the ledger, the financial statements are all updated instantly.
- Once a transaction is entered into the system it is automatically processed.
- Calculations will be accurate (unless someone has programmed them otherwise).
- Human error (inputting data for example) and fraud can still lead to misstatement in computerised systems.

### i. The control environment

The control environment includes the **governance and management** function of an organisation. It focuses largely on the **attitude, awareness and actions** of those responsible for designing, implementing and monitoring internal controls.

**Control environment**

Elements of the control environment that are relevant when the auditor obtains an understanding include the following:

- communication and enforcement of integrity and ethical values
- commitment to competence
- participation by those charged with governance
- management's philosophy and operating style
- organisational structure
- assignment of authority and responsibility
- human resource policies and practices.

The revised ISA 315 states that when assessing the control environment the auditor may also consider how management has responded to the findings and recommendations of the internal audit function regarding identified deficiencies in internal control relevant to the audit, including whether and how such responses have been implemented, and whether they have been subsequently evaluated by the internal audit function.

Evidence regarding the control environment is usually obtained through a mixture of enquiry and observation, although inspection of key internal documents (e.g. codes of conduct and organisation charts) is possible.

### ii. The risk assessment process

The risk assessment process forms the basis for how management determines the business risks to be managed, i.e. threats to the achievement of ongoing business objectives. These processes will vary hugely depending upon the nature, size and complexity of the organisation.

Threats to business objectives can lead to misstatement in the financial statements, e.g. non-compliance with laws and regulations may lead to fines and penalties, which require disclosure or provision in the financial statements.

If the client has robust procedures for assessing the business risks it faces, the risk of misstatement overall, will be lower.

### iii. The information system

The information system is all of the business processes relevant to financial reporting and communication. It includes the procedures within both information technology and manual systems.

**Information system**

The information system includes all of the procedures and records which are designed to:

- initiate, record, process and report transactions
- maintain accountability for assets, liabilities and equity
- resolve incorrect processing of transactions
- process and account for system overrides
- transfer information to the general/nominal ledger
- capture information relevant to financial reporting for other events and conditions
- ensure information required to be disclosed is appropriately reported.

### iv. Control activities

The control activities include all policies and procedures designed to ensure that management directives are carried out throughout the organisation. Examples of specific control activities include those relating to:

- authorisation
- performance review

- information processing
- physical controls
- segregation of duties.

IT affects the way in which control activities are implemented. It is important that auditors assess how controls over IT maintain the integrity and security of information held. Such controls are normally divided into two categories:

- Application
- General

**Application controls**

Application controls are either manual or automated and typically operate at the business process level and apply to the processing of transactions. Examples include:

- batch total checks (e.g. when entering batches of invoices onto the accounts system)
- sequence checks
- matching master files to transaction records (e.g. sales invoice discounts)
- arithmetic checks
- range checks (to ensure that data stays within reasonable ranges)
- existence checks (e.g. to check employees exist)
- authorisation of transaction entries
- exception reporting.

**General controls**

General IT controls are policies and procedures that relate to many applications and support the effective functioning of application controls by helping to ensure the continued proper operation of information systems, e.g. controls over:

- data centre and network operations
- system software acquisition
- program change and maintenance
- access security – passwords, door locks, swipe cards
- backup procedures.

A healthy IT system should include both application and general control procedures.

**A changing world**

Rapid developments in IT have implications for systems and controls. Examples of such issues include:

- transactions automatically triggered by predetermined system criteria, e.g. stock purchases, automated utility billing
- high volume transactions enabled through the use of barcodes and scanning, e.g. supermarkets
- on-line purchasing
- on-line account management
- automated goods delivery, e.g. Amazon
- automated cash collection, e.g. Amazon
- on-line/virtual products, e.g. on-line gambling.

All of these modern business issues require systems that operate effectively and use the most up to date information available. Without excellence in IT systems and controls these businesses would simply not be possible.

### v. Monitoring of controls

This is the process of **assessing the effectiveness of controls** over time and taking necessary remedial action. Clearly if a control is not implemented properly or is simply considered ineffective then misstatements may pass undetected into the financial statements.

Monitoring can be either ongoing or performed on a separate evaluation basis (or a combination of both). Either way, it needs to be effective for the system to work. Monitoring of internal controls is often the key role of internal auditors.

## 2 Ascertaining the systems

Procedures used to obtain evidence regarding the design and implementation of controls include:

- enquiries of relevant personnel
- observing the application of controls
- tracing a transaction through the systems; a **walkthrough**
- inspecting documents, such as internal procedure manuals.

It should also be noted that ISA 315 specifies that enquiry alone is not sufficient to understand the nature and extent of controls.

**Prior knowledge of client systems**

In addition to this, auditors can also use their prior knowledge of the client and the operation of the systems in prior years. However, it must be noted, that auditors cannot simply rely on their systems knowledge from the prior year's audit; much can happen in a year and systems knowledge must be updated and the systems tested once more.

## 3 Documenting client systems

Possible ways of documenting systems include:

- **Narrative notes**, which are simple to record but can be cumbersome if systems are large or complex and do not identify control exceptions clearly.
- **Flowcharts**, which can make a complex system easier to follow.
- **Organisation charts**, which show roles, responsibilities, and reporting lines but not the function of the system.
- **Internal Control Questionnaires** (**ICQs**), which are quick to prepare, simple to complete, easy to understand and clearly highlight deficiencies in the system.
- **Internal Control Evaluation Questionnaires** (**ICEs**), like ICQs these are a cost effective method of recording the system and any member of the team can complete them.

ISA 315 states that the method adopted is a matter of auditor judgement.

**ICQs**

An **ICQ** is a list of possible controls for each area of the Financial Statements. The client is asked to review the list and confirm which are applicable to their system.

**ICEs**

In contrast to ICQ's an **ICE** lists control objectives. Client's are then asked to confirm how they meet that objective.

For example; an ICQ might ask a client: "does a supervisor authorise all weekly timesheets?" An ICE would ask "how does the company ensure that only hours worked are recorded on timesheets?"

There is a risk with ICQs that the client will overstate the level of controls present and unusual controls may be overlooked.

## 4 Testing the system

Having documented the systems the auditor needs to assess whether controls are:

- actually implemented and
- effective.

In order to assess the operating effectiveness of controls in preventing and detecting material misstatement the auditor performs tests of controls. These are designed to gather evidence concerning:

- how controls were applied during the period
- the consistency of application and
- who (or what) they were applied by.

Typical methods of controls testing include:

- observation of control activities, e.g. the inventory count
- inspection of documents recording performance of the control, e.g inspecting an order for evidence of authorisation
- computer aided audit techniques (as seen in the 'Evidence' chapter).

## 5 Sales system

| | |
|---|---|
| **Stage 1** | Order received |
| **Stage 2** | Goods despatched |
| **Stage 3** | Invoice received |
| **Stage 4** | Transactions recorded in books |
| **Stage 5** | Cash received |

### Objectives

The objectives of controls in the sales system are to ensure that:

- goods are only supplied to customers who pay promptly and in full
- orders are despatched promptly and in full to the correct customer
- only valid sales are recorded
- all sales and related receivables are recorded
- revenue is recorded in the period to which it relates
- sales are recorded accurately and related receivables are recorded at an appropriate value.

**Illustration 1: Murray Co sales system**

**Ordering**

For all new customers, a sales manager completes a credit application which is checked with a credit agency and a credit limit is entered onto the sales system by the credit controller. The sales system prompts sales managers to complete an annual credit check for existing customers, and the credit controller amends or approves existing credit limits for these customers. Approved customers are assigned with a unique customer account number.

Orders are placed with the sales team. The orders are entered onto the sales system by a sales assistant. The system automatically checks that the goods are available and that the order will not take the customer over their credit limit. The system generates two order confirmations, one of which is sent to the customer by mail/email confirming the goods ordered and likely despatch date, the other is retained on file.

**Goods despatch**

The warehouse receives the order electronically and goods despatch notes (GDNs) are generated automatically. A member of the warehouse team packs the goods from the GDN and a second member of the team double checks the goods packed to the GDN, signing the GDN to evidence the check.

Two copies of the GDN are sent with the goods ordered; one copy is retained by the customer and the other is signed by the customer and returned to Murray Co to confirm receipt of the goods and retained by the warehouse.

A copy of the GDN is sent to the sales team who update the system, confirming despatch of the goods. A weekly report is sent automatically to the sales manager, who follows-up any incomplete orders with the warehouse manager.

**Invoicing**

Once despatched, a copy of the GDN is sent to the accounts team at head office and a sequentially numbered sales invoice is raised from the GDN. Periodically a computer sequence check is performed for any missing sales invoice numbers.

When the invoice is sent to the customer, the system GDN is marked as 'invoiced'. A system report is reviewed by the senior accountant on a fortnightly basis for any GDNs that have not been invoiced. The report is printed and signed as evidence of review.

The system generates customer invoices using the company price list, which is updated quarterly. Discounts must be requested by a sales manager and authorised by the sales director to allow the accounts team to raise an invoice.

**Recording transaction**

The receivables ledger is reviewed for credit balances by the senior accountant on a monthly basis and the receivables ledger is reconciled with the receivables ledger control account on a monthly basis by the sales ledger manager and reviewed by the company accountant.

Monthly customer statements are sent to customers.

**Cash receipt**

Receipts are counted by the office assistant, recorded by the cashier in the cash book, and the sales ledger clerk is notified of the receipt. The sales ledger clerk agrees the amount received to the amount invoiced and marks the invoice as paid.

The credit controller reviews the aged receivables analysis on a fortnightly basis and investigates any old balances. Overdue debts are chased with a telephone call initially, followed by a copy invoice, and then a warning letter before the debt is passed to a debt collection agency.

**Exercise:**

**Explain the objectives of the controls described in Murray Co's sales cycle.**

**Case Study: Murray Co sales system**

**Ordering**

*Credit checks, setting of credit limits, and checks that an order will not take a customer over their credit limit:* ensures that sales are only made to customers that are likely to make a full and prompt payment.

*Checking that the goods are available:* ensures that orders can be honoured and despatched promptly.

*Written confirmation of the order:* ensures that orders are recorded accurately and that customers receive the goods they ordered.

*Approved customers are assigned with a unique customer account number:* to ensure that sales are only made to customers that have been approved for credit, therefore minimising bad debts.

**Goods despatch**

*Order received electronically by warehouse and automatic generation of GDN:* eliminates risk of human error/oversight ensuring that all orders are fulfilled.

*Second member of warehouse team checks the goods packed, signing the GDN to evidence the check:* segregation of duties reduces the risk of misappropriation of assets.

*Customers sign GDN and return to Murray Co:* helps to ensure that customers pay in full as proof of delivery and acceptance of goods is obtained.

*Sales team confirm despatch of goods:* segregation of duties reduces the risk that goods are recorded as despatched erroneously.

*Weekly report to sales manager:* monitors despatch of goods to ensure that all orders are fulfilled.

**Invoicing**

*A copy of the GDN is sent to the accounts team:* ensures that all goods despatched are invoiced.

*The invoice is checked to the GDN:* the invoice is raised from the GDN and not the original order, as there may have been a problem meaning that the order was not fulfilled.

*Sequentially numbered sales invoice and computer sequence check:* to ensure that all invoices are processed - if any invoice in the sequence is missing it can be traced.

*System GDN marked as 'invoiced':* to prevent the customer being invoiced twice.

*System report reviewed by the senior accountant:* to ensure that all goods are invoiced.

*Company price list:* to ensure that customers are charged the correct price.

*Discounts must be requested by a sales manager and authorised by the sales director:* segregation of duties and authorisation prevents fraud and unauthorised discounts.

**Recording transaction**

*Review of receivables ledger for credit balances:* identifies overpayments which may be caused by goods invoiced where no sale was recorded.

*Receivables ledger reconciliation:* ensures that debts and receipts recorded in individual customer ledgers have also been recorded in the accounts (and visa versa). Segregation of duties monitors performance of controls and prevents fraud.

*Monthly customer statements sent to customers:* enables customers to identify misrecorded invoices and receipts.

**Cash receipt**

*Receipts are counted by the office assistant, recorded by the cashier, and the sales ledger clerk agrees the amount received to the amount invoiced*: Segregation of duties prevents fraud.

*The invoice is marked as paid:* ensures that customers are not chased for debts they have paid.

*The credit controller reviews the aged receivables and investigates any old balances, and credit control procedures are then followed:* to ensure full and prompt payment by customers.

**Illustration 2: Testing Murray Co's sales system**

**Ordering**

- With the client's permission, attempt to enter an order for a fictitious customer account number. The system should reject the order.
- With the client's permission, attempt to enter an order for goods that are known to be out of stock. The system should reject the order.
- Select a sample of sales made and inspect a copy of the order retained on file to ensure the order was confirmed in writing.
- Observe the sales order clerk processing orders and assess whether the order acceptance is automatically generated.
- Inspect a sample of new and existing customer's files to ensure a (recent) satisfactory credit check has been obtained.

**Goods despatch**

- Visit a warehouse and observe the goods despatch process to assess whether all goods are double checked against the goods despatch note (GDN) prior to signing and sending out.
- Inspect a sample of GDNs retained by the warehouse to ensure they are signed as evidence of checking the goods.

**Invoicing**

- Inspect a sample of GDNs and agree to the sales invoice.
- Review the last system generated sequence check of sales invoices to identify any omissions.
- Inspect the file of GDNs with no invoice system reports for evidence of completion on a fortnightly basis.
- Obtain a copy of the current price list and agree for a sample of invoices that relevant/current prices have been used
- With the client's permission, attempt to process an invoice with a sales discount without authorisation from the sales director. The system should reject the invoice.

**Recording transaction**

- Inspect the receivables ledger for evidence of monthly review.
- Inspect the receivables ledger reconciliations for evidence of performance and review on a monthly basis.
- For a sample of customers with outstanding balances, inspect monthly statements sent out.

**Cash receipts**

- Observe the cash receipt process to assess the adequacy of segregation of duties.
- For a sample of cash receipts, inspect the relevant invoice to ensure it has been marked as paid.
- Inspect the aged receivables analysis for evidence of fortnightly review.
- Inspect records of contact made with customers who have overdue debts, to ensure compliance with credit control procedures.

## Illustration 3: Murray Co goods despatch note

The key document in the sales cycle is the goods despatch note:

Murray Co

**Goods Despatch Note**

"*Supplying Equipment to the Sporting Nation*"

**Ref: AB123456MC**

www.murraysports.com

**Murray Company**

1 Murray Mound,
Wimbledon, London
WN1 2LN

**Destination**

**Customer Ref:** W004

**Order Number:** ZY987654WS

**Customer Name:** Winners Co

**Customer Address:** 2 Edinburgh St, Dunblaine, Scotland DL2 2ES

| Line | Product Number | Description | Quantity | Quality and quantity of goods checked and agreed |
|---|---|---|---|---|
| 001 | 4378493729 | Tennis racket | 24 | Yes |
| 002 | 3257845743 | Tennis balls (packs of 6) | 6 | Yes |
| 003 | 4357849574 | Tennis court net | 3 | Yes |
| 004 | 3473895789 | Tennis scoreboard | 3 | Yes |
| 005 | 4574895743 | Winner's trophy | 1 | Yes |
| 006 | 3457435437 | Runner-up trophy | 1 | Yes |
| 007 | 4830998543 | Participant's medal | 24 | Yes |

Signed:

A Warehouse Packer

## 6 Purchase system

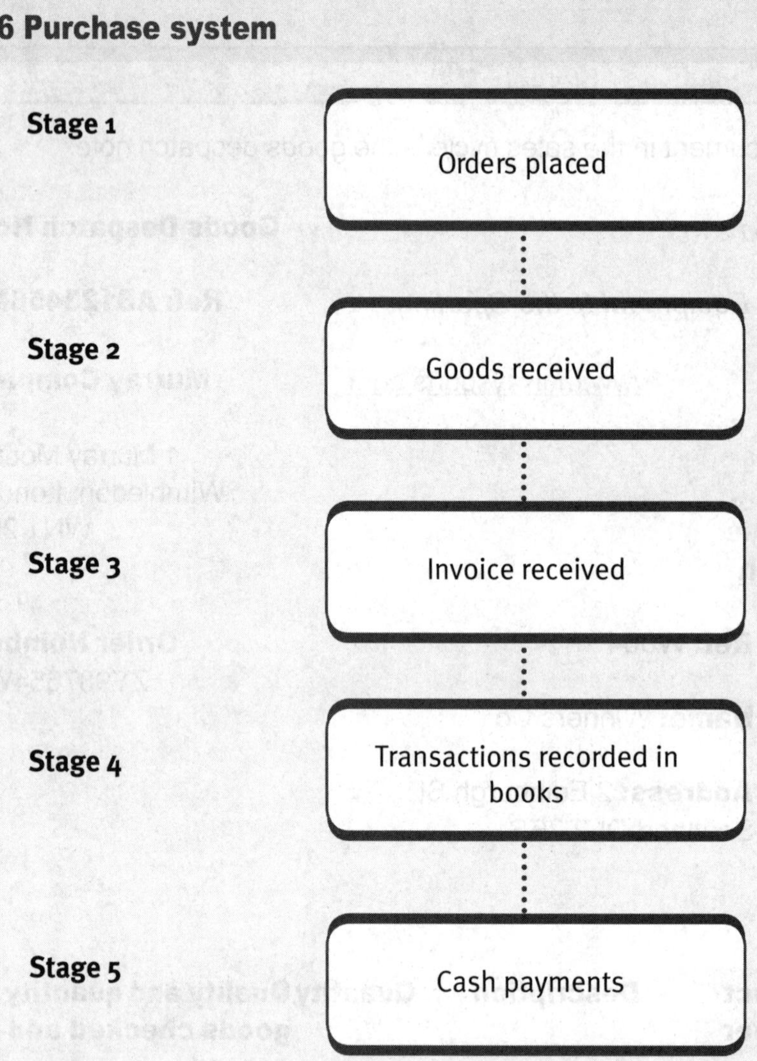


**Objectives**

The objectives of controls in the purchase system are to ensure that:

- all purchases are made with approved suppliers
- all purchases are properly authorised to ensure only necessary goods/services are procured
- all purchases and related payables are recorded
- expenditure is recorded in the period to which it relates
- expenditure is recorded accurately and related payables are recorded at an appropriate value.

## Illustration 4: Murray Co purchase system

### Ordering

Goods or services are obtained by placing a purchase requisition with the centralised purchasing department. Requisitions are sequentially prenumbered, and the purchasing department perform a weekly sequence check. All requisitions must be authorised by an appropriate manager.

On receipt of a purchase requisition, a purchase officer agrees the manager's signature to the signatory list held on file and checks inventory levels where appropriate. Orders are placed with suppliers using sequentially prenumbered purchase orders.

Orders can only be placed with suppliers from the approved suppliers list. Suppliers can only be added to the approved suppliers list by the procurement team once the terms of the contract have been agreed, and references obtained. Written confirmation is requested for all orders placed, and the purchase officer agrees the quoted price against the agreed price list and ensures any bulk discounts to which Murray Co is entitled, have been honoured.

### Goods receipt

Goods are received into the central warehouse. Goods are inspected for condition and quantity by a warehouse operative, and agreed to the purchase order before the supplier's delivery note is signed to accept the goods.

A sequentially pre-numbered goods received note (GRN) is prepared by the warehouse team manager, and grid-stamped. The grid stamp is signed by the warehouse operative to confirm that the goods have been inspected for condition and quantity and agreed to the purchase order.

The warehouse manager updates the inventory system on a daily basis from the prepared GRNs. The warehouse manager checks the sequence of purchase orders received on a weekly basis and informs the purchasing department of any missing orders so that they can be followed-up.

### Invoicing

On receipt of an invoice by the head office accounts team, the invoice is matched to and filed with the relevant GRN, using the purchase order number marked on the invoice (if there is no purchase order number marked on the invoice, this must be obtained from the supplier). The invoice number is noted on the GRN grid-stamp. The invoice is also checked to the original purchase order to ensure the agreed prices and discounts have been honoured.

A monthly check of GRNs is made by the purchases ledger manager, to identify any GRNs for which no invoice has been received.

**Recording transaction**

The purchases ledger clerk enters invoices onto the system in batches. A batch control sheet is used, which details the number of invoices and the total value. These details are checked to the system batch report.

Each invoice is stamped as "recorded" once the details have been entered onto the system. The purchase ledger manager inspects the file of invoices on a monthly basis to ensure that all invoices have been recorded.

Suppliers are required to submit monthly supplier statements, which are reconciled to the suppliers ledger account by the purchases ledger manager. The purchase ledger is reconciled to the purchase ledger control account on a monthly basis by the purchase ledger manager, and reviewed by the company accountant.

**Cash payment**

The list of payments is sent to the company accountant, who agrees the details of each payment to the relevant invoice and signs each invoice to authorise payment and evidence the check. The list of payments is signed by the accountant once all invoices have been checked, and sent to the cashier's office for payment.

If any individual payment is for more than $25,000 or total payments are for more than $250,000 a second signatory is required. These payments must also be checked and signed by either the financial controller, or finance director.

Payments are made by the cashier's office by bank transfer. Invoices are stamped as "paid", and returned to the purchases ledger team who record the payment and file the invoices (separately from invoices not yet paid).

The purchase ledger manager checks GRNs on a monthly basis to ensure that invoices have been received and paid on a timely basis.

**Exercise:**

**Explain the objectives of the controls described in Murray Co's purchases cycle.**

**Case Study: Murray Co purchases system**

**Ordering**

*Centralised purchasing department*: ensures that purchasing is cost effective and only necessary goods and services are procured.

*Sequentially prenumbered requistions and sequence check:* ensures that all requistions are fulfilled, preventing stock outs/manufacturing delays.

*Requisitions authorised and manager's signature agreed, and inventory levels checked:* ensures only necessary goods and services are procured.

*Sequentially prenumbered purchase orders and weekly check by warehouse manager:* to ensure that all goods and services ordered are received as any missing purchase orders can be followed-up.

*Approved suppliers list:* gives assurance about the quality of goods and services and reliability of the suppliers.

*Written confirmation for all orders:* ensures all and only necessary goods and services are received.

*Price agreed to price list and for discounts:* ensures that purchasing is cost effective.

**Goods receipt**

*Goods received into the central warehouse:* having one, secure delivery area prevents goods received being lost or stolen.

*Goods are inspected for condition and quantity and agreed to the purchase order:* prevents Murray Co from having to pay for unnecessary, or poor quality goods.

*Sequentially pre-numbered goods received note (GRN) prepared by the warehouse team manager:* the GRN is a key control in the purchase cycle and must be prepared by someone of appropriate seniority and expertise; sequential pre-numbering ensures that all GRNs are actioned.

*Grid-stamp:* a grid stamp, is a grid that can be ink-stamped onto any document, with boxes for recording different information. It is often used for key-documents in an accounts cycle, to keep track of the progress of that 'transaction'.

*Inventory system updated on a daily basis by the warehouse manager:* prevents unnecessary goods being ordered, ensures inventory levels are up-to-date when checked before accepatance of customer orders.

**Invoicing**

*The invoice is matched to the GRN:* the invoice is matched to the GRN and not the original order, as there may have been a problem meaning that the order was not fulfilled; it ensures that only goods that have been received are paid for.

*Using the purchase order number marked on the invoice*: when placing an order, the supplier will be given the purchase order number. This allows the purchase to be matched to the relevant GRN and requisition.

*The invoice number is noted on the GRN grid stamp, and a monthly check of GRNs with no invoice:* this prevents the goods received being invoiced twice, and ensures that all liabilities are recorded.

**Recording transaction**

*Batch controls:* enable data entry errors to be identified and corrected.

*Invoice stamped as "recorded" and checks to ensure all invoices recorded:* Prevents under or overstatement of trade payables.

*Supplier statement reconciliations:* enables misrecorded purchases, payments and liabilities to be identified and corrected.

*Control account reconciliation:* ensures that credits and payments recorded in individual supplier ledgers have also been recorded in the accounts (and vice versa). Segregation of duties monitors performance of controls and prevents fraud.

**Cash payment**

*The company accountant checks and authorises payments:* payments should only be authorised by a senior member of the finance department to prevent error or fraud.

*Individual payments of more than $25,000, or total payments of more than $250,000 require a second signatory*: a second signatory prevents fraud on unusual transactions.

*Payments are made by the cashier's office and recorded by the purchases ledger team:* segregation of duties prevents fraud.

*Invoices are stamped as "paid" and filed separately from invoices not yet paid:* this prevents invoices being paid twice.

*GRNs are checked on a monthly basis:* to ensure that suppliers are paid on a timely basis, which ensures that early settlement discounts available are obtained, and supplier goodwill is maintained.

**Illustration 5: Testing Murray Co's purchases system**

**Ordering**

- For a sample of purchase orders, ensure a requisition was received.
- Inspect a sample of requisitions for the signature of an appropriate manager.
- Review evidence of the purchasing department's weekly sequence check.
- Inspect the signatory list to ensure it is up-to-date.
- Inspect a sample of requisitions for evidence of inventory levels having been checked first.
- For a sample of purchase orders placed, ensure the supplier appears on the approved suppliers list.
- For a sample of purchase requisitions, inspect the purchase order and written confirmation from the supplier.
- Inspect a sample of purchase orders for evidence of prices having been agreed to price list.

**Goods receipt**

- Visit a warehouse and inspect the delivery area for security of goods.
- Observe the goods receipt process to ensure goods are inspected for condition and quantity before the supplier's delivery note is signed.
- Inspect a sample of GRNs to ensure grid-stamped and signed by the warehouse operative.
- Inspect a sample of recent GRNs to ensure the inventory system has been updated.

**Invoicing**

- Inspect a sample of invoices and ensure filed with the relevant GRN, and the invoice number is written on the GRN.
- Inspect a sample of invoices for evidence of confirmation that the invoice agrees to the GRN and prices agree to the original purchase order.
- Review evidence of the monthly check of GRNs by the purchases ledger manager.

**Recording transaction**

- Inspect a sample of batch control sheets for evidence of completion and agreement to the batch system report.
- Select a sample of invoices recorded on the system and inspect them to ensure they are marked as "recorded".
- Review evidence of the purchase ledger manager's monthly invoice file review.
- For a sample of suppliers, inspect the monthly supplier statements received for evidence of reconciliation.
- Inspect the purchases ledger reconciliations for evidence of performance and review on a monthly basis.

**Cash payment**

- For a sample of payments made, inspect the payment list for evidence of the company accountant's review and authorisation.
- Inspect a sample of invoices for evidence of the accountant's signature and payment stamp.
- Inspect the file of paid invoices and ensure kept separate from invoices not yet paid.
- Review evidence of the purchase ledger manager's monthly invoice review.

**Illustration 6: Murray Co goods received note**

The key document in the purchases cycle is the goods received note:

**Murray Co**

**Goods Received Note: A2012/123478**

**Purchase Order number: MC/34324832809/RC**

**Date and time of receipt:** 31st August 2012: 12:48pm

| **Description** | **Quantity ordered** | **Quantity received** | **Quality of goods checked** |
|---|---|---|---|
| Vectran | 75kg | 75kg | Yes |

**Sign to confirm quantity and quality of goods checked:** Warehouse Operative

**Invoice number:**

**Problems with fraud**

Fraud is specifically designed to mislead people. Consider the following example:

- A company only deals with suppliers on a list authorised by the Finance Director (FD).
- Payments to suppliers are made after the purchases clerk identifies the monthly payments to be made and prepares the cheques.
- The cheques are signed by the FD, who confirms the amounts paid and supplier names to supporting documentation.
- The cheques are countersigned by the Managing Director, who does not check the details but has a good knowledge of who the suppliers are.

This appears like a sensible combination of authorisation controls and segregation of duties.

However, now consider the implication if one of the suppliers is actually controlled by the FD. The supplier regularly overcharges and the purchases clerk is being bribed by the FD in return for their silence.

Of course, this is a potentially criminal scheme, but that is what a fraud is. The auditor, unfortunately, would place reliance on the control system and reduce substantive testing of purchases. It is for this reason that the auditor must always perform some substantive procedures and must always maintain an attitude of professional scepticism.

**Capital expenditure**

Expenditure on non-current assets should be controlled in a similar way to other purchases.

However, because of the significant amounts involved, additional controls will include:

- authorisation for purchase at a more senior level
- an annual capital expenditure budget for each department
- regular review of revenue expenditure to ensure items of a capital nature have not been written off in error
- annual reconciliation of the asset register to the physical assets held

- use of an asset register, which would include location, responsible employee, insurance details, etc
- adequate insurance
- secure, fire-proof storage of insurance documentation, ownership/purchase documentation, e.g. title deeds, vehicle registration documents, etc.

## 7 Payroll system

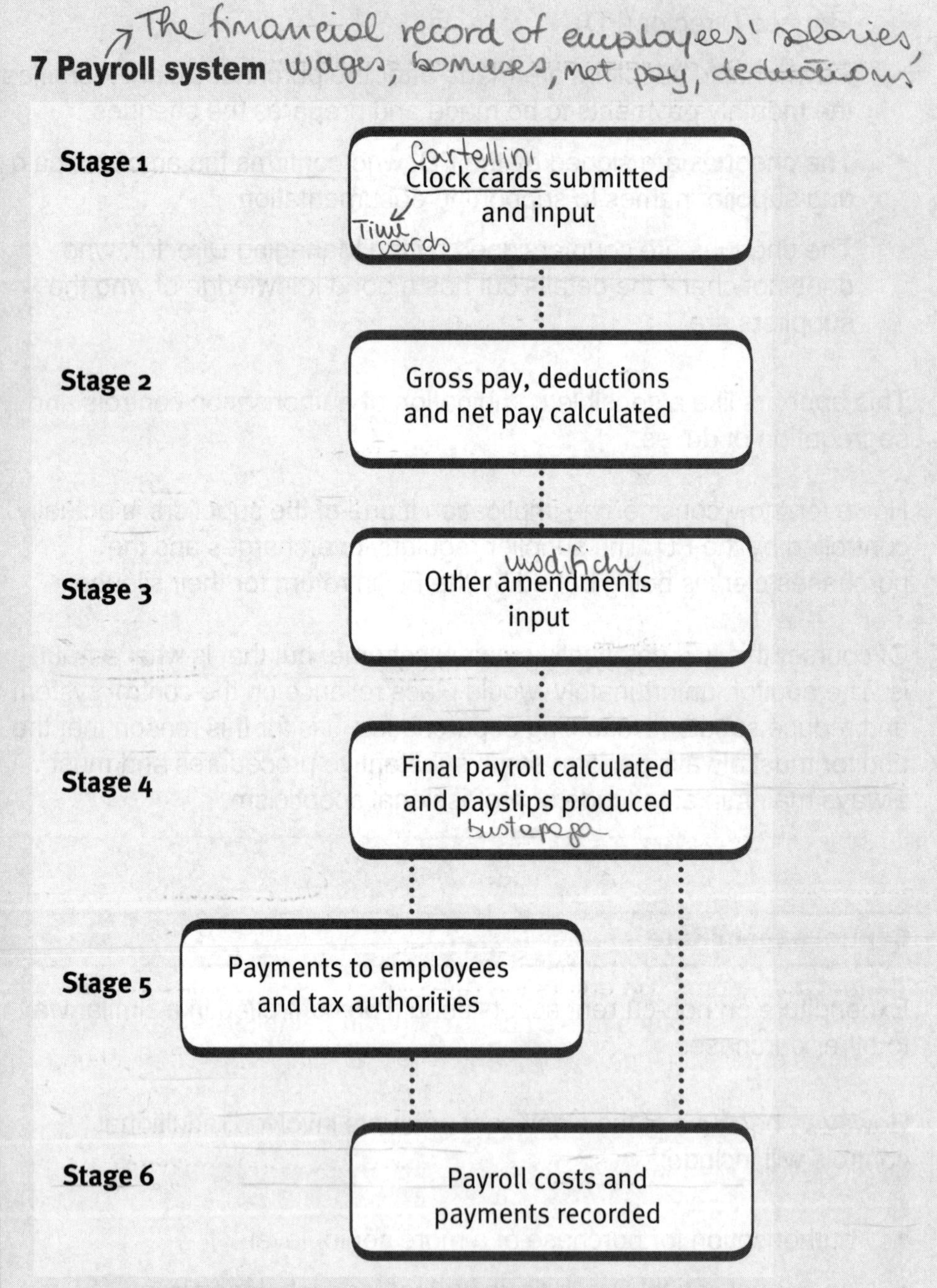

Stage 1
Clock cards submitted and input
Stage 2
Gross pay, deductions and net pay calculated
Stage 3
Other amendments input
Stage 4
Final payroll calculated and payslips produced
Stage 5
Payments to employees and tax authorities
Stage 6
Payroll costs and payments recorded

**Objectives**

The objectives of controls in the payroll system are to ensure that:

- only genuine employees are paid
- employees are only paid for work done
- employees are paid at authorised rates of pay
- gross pay is calculated and recorded accurately
- net pay is calculated and recorded accurately; and
- correct amounts owed are recorded and paid to the taxation authorities.

**Illustration 7: Murray Co payroll cycle**

**Clock cards submitted and input**

Murray Co employs a total of 300 people, 200 of these being workers who are paid weekly in cash. All workers are required to record their times of arrival and departure using a clock card which is inserted in a time recording clock. Use of the time recording clock is supervised by the relevant factory manager.

At weekly intervals the cards are collected and passed to the works office where the clerks total up the hours worked on each card and list the total hours worked (a 'hash' total). The cards and the add list are then passed to the wages clerk who enters the hours worked on the pre-printed payroll sheet (which already has the names printed on it), and agrees the add list total.

**Gross pay, deductions and net pay calculated**

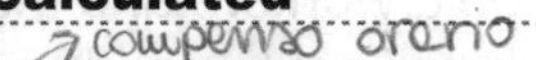

The payroll sheets are then passed to the payroll manager who keeps the payroll records. He enters the rate of pay and calculates the gross pay. He also computes the tax deductions and employer's taxation, which he enters on the payroll along with the salaries and deductions for monthly paid workers. He passes the payrolls back to the wages clerk who calculates the net amount and totals all the columns on the payroll, and raises a payment list for monthly paid employees and payments to the tax authority.

**Other amendments input**

Leaver's and joiner's forms must be completed and authorised by the employee's immediate manager and the finance director at least one month before the amendment is required to the payroll. Other amendments to standing data, e.g. payrises, are completed on a specific form for this purpose, and authorised in the same way.

A monthly report of amendments to standing data is sent to the finance director for review and authorisation.

Standing data files are sent to departmental managers on a quarterly basis for review.

**Final payroll calculated and payslips produced**

The completed payroll is then passed to the company accountant, who scans the payroll, compares the totals with the previous week, and initials the payroll. The company accountant raises a cheque requisition for the weekly paid workers, and signs the payment list for the monthly paid employees, which are then sent to the cashier's department. The payment list also shows payments to be made to the taxation authorities which the company accountant checks to last month's payroll records.

The payroll is returned to the payroll clerk who produces the payslips, and passes these to the cashier's department for processing.

**Payments to employees and tax authorities**

The cashier draws a cheque for the net amount of the payroll which is then signed by two directors. The cheque is given to a secure cash transit company who draw the money from the bank and deliver it under guard to the wages clerk. The cashier then puts the money into pay envelopes along with a pay slip for weekly paid workers.

The sealed envelopes and relevant clock cards are then used for payouts. Each worker obtains his money once he has identified himself and signed his clock card. Unclaimed wages are held for three weeks before being re-banked.

Monthly paid workers and the tax authorities are paid by bank transfer on the last day of each month, as per the payment list authorised by the company accountant.

**Payroll costs and payments recorded**

A copy of the payroll list is sent to the head office accounts team who record the payroll expense and payments made. Any unclaimed wages are notified by the wages office to the head office team on an anomolies list completed once all of the clock cards have been returned. The head office accounts team check the bank statements to ensure that this money has been re-banked.

## Murray Co payroll cycle

### Clock cards submitted and input

*Clock card to record time and supervision of clock card use:* ensures that only genuine employees are paid, for work done.

*Hash total and agreement of the total:* segregation of duties by performing and checking the procedure reduces the risk of human error.

*Pre-printed payroll sheet:* ensures that only genuine employees are paid.

### Gross pay, deductions and net pay calculated

*Payroll sheets:* payroll data is sensitive information; a responsible individual must therefore be responsible for payroll documentation; segregation of duties prevents fraud.

*Calculation of pay and taxation:* it is essential that these calculations are performed correctly; a responsible individual must therefore be responsible for the main calculations; segregation of duties between calculation of gross pay and deductions, and net pay prevents error and fraud.

### Other amendments input

*Completion and authorisation of standing data forms*: ensures that only genuine employees are paid, at authorised rates of pay.

*Use of specific forms:* prevents errors in processing information.

*Monthly review of standing data amendments and quarterly review of standing data files*: ensures that any unauthorised amendments to standing data are identified and resolved.

### Final payroll calculated and payslips produced

*Company accountant's analytical review of payroll*: ensures that any anomolies can be identified and resolved; payroll is a significant cost for most companies and it is important that a responsible individual, independent of preparation of payroll undertakes this role.

*The company accountant raises the cheque requisition and authorises the payment list, the cashier's department makes the relevant payments*: segregation of duties prevents fraud and error.

**Payments to employees and tax authorities**

*Payroll cheque signed by two directors:* this is likely to be a large amount of money and therefore requires authorisation by two senior personnel to prevent fraud and error.

*Cash is delivered by a secure transit company, under guard:* due to the amount of cash likely to be needed to pay the weekly paid workers, it would not be appropriate for Murray Co staff to go to the bank to get the money themselves as this would threaten their personal safety.

*Pay-slip*: allows the workers themselves to check the money received and raise any anomolies.

*Sealed envelopes, identification, and signature on clock-card:* prevents someone other than the worker, fraudulently claiming the money.

*Unclaimed wages are rebanked after three weeks:* prevents misappropriation.

**Payroll costs and payments recorded**

*The head office accounts team record the payroll expense and payments and the wages office notify the team of unclaimed wages:* segregation of duties prevents fraud and error.

*Bank statements checked for deposit of unclaimed wages*: prevents misappropriation.

**Illustration 8: Testing Murray Co's payroll system**

**Clock cards submitted and input**

- Observe the use and supervision of clocking in and out procedures.
- Inspect a sample of payroll sheets to ensure employee's names are pre-printed.
- Inspect a sample of payroll sheets for evidence of the wages clerk's check of the add list total.

**Gross pay, deductions and net pay calculated**

- Review a sample of calculations of gross pay, tax deductions and net pay to ensure the appropriate rates of pay, and tax deductions are being used.

**Other amendments input**

- Select a sample of leaver's and joiner's from human resources records, and ensure that payroll forms have been completed and authorised on a timely basis.
- Select a sample of employees with payrises or other amendments to pay from human resources records, and ensure that the relevant payroll form has been completed and authorised on a timely basis.
- Inspect the monthly report of amendments to standing data for the finance director's authorisation.
- Select a sample of amendments made to standing data and trace to the monthly report authorised by the finance director, and the relevant amendment form.
- Inspect the standing data files sent to departmental managers for evidence of review.
- For any anomolies identified by departmental managers, enquire of and corroborate the reasons for the anomaly and what action was taken to resolve the issue.

**Final payroll calculated and payslips produced**

- Inspect the weekly payroll for the company accountant's initials.
- For a sample of cheques raised for wages, inspect the cheque requisition to ensure completed by the company accountant.
- Inspect the monthly payment list for salaried employees for the company accountant's signature.

**Payments to employees and tax authorities**

- Observe the process of paying employees for compliance with procedures.
- Inspect the bank mandate to ensure it requires the signature of two directors for large cheques.

**Payroll costs and payments recorded**

- Agree the payroll expense and payments made for a sample of months to the payroll list.
- Inspect the unclaimed wages list for evidence that the deposit has been identified on the bank statement by the accounts team.

## 8 The Inventory System

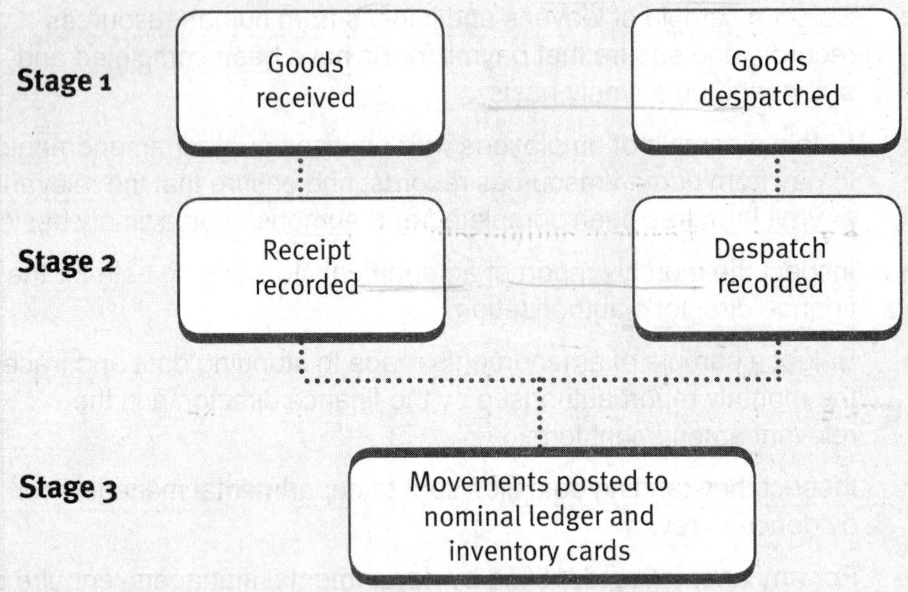


### Objectives

The objectives of controls in the inventory system are to ensure that:

- inventory levels meet the needs of production (raw materials and components) and customer demand (finished goods)
- inventory levels are not excessive, preventing obsolescence and unnecessary storage costs
- inventory is safeguarded from theft, loss or damage
- inventory movements are recorded on a timely basis
- all inventory is recorded.

### The inventory system

The majority of controls within and tests of control for the inventory system appear within the sales system (for goods despatched) and purchases system (for goods received). In addition, there should be adequate controls over the storage of inventory to prevent theft and damage, including:

- sprinklers, fire alarms and temperature monitors.
- valuable inventory stored in a secure, locked location with a single entry/exit point.
- other security measures, e.g. CCTV, security staff.
- inventory adequately insured.

There should also be either annual, or periodic inventory counts.

## 9 The cash cycle

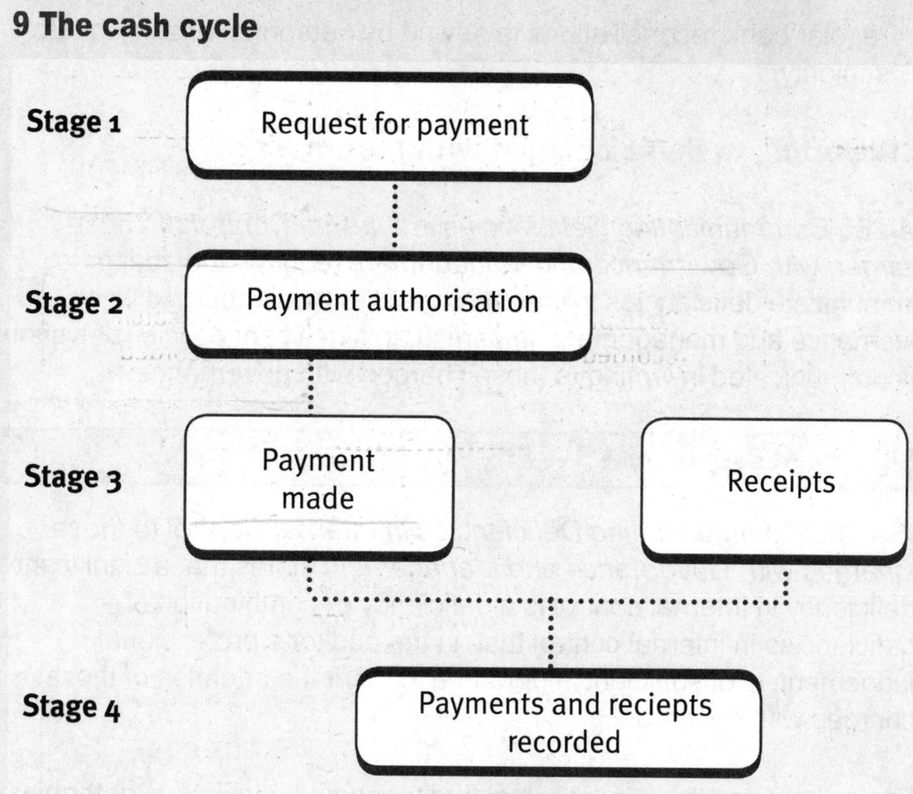


### Objectives

The objectives of controls in the cash cycle are to ensure that:

- petty cash levels are kept to a minimum, preventing theft
- payments can only be made for legitimate business expenditure
- cash can only be withdrawn for authorised purposes
- cash is safeguarded
- receipts are banked on a timely basis
- cash movements are recorded on a timely basis.

### The cash cycle

The majority of controls within and tests of control for the cash cycle appear within the sales system (for cash received) and purchases and payroll systems (for cash payments).

In addition, there should be adequate controls over access to cash and bank records, including:

- cash and cheque books/stationery stored in a locked safe, with restricted access
- frequent banking of cash and cheques received
- controls over bank transfers and online banking, e.g. secure passwords and pin numbers

- regular bank reconciliations reviewed by personnel of appropriate seniority.

## 10 Reporting to those charged with governance

ISA 265 *Communicating Deficiencies in Internal Control to Those Charged with Governance and Management* requires the auditor to communicate deficiencies in internal control to those charged with governance and management. In particular, significant deficiencies should be communicated in writing to those charged with governance.

**Significant deficiencies**

ISA 265 *Communicating Deficiencies in Internal Control to those Charged with Governance and Management* states that a significant deficiency in internal control is a deficiency or combination of deficiencies in internal control that, in the auditor's professional judgement, is of sufficient importance to merit the attention of those charged with governance.

Examples of matters the external auditor should consider in determining whether a deficiency in internal controls is significant include:

- The likelihood of the deficiencies leading to material misstatements in the financial statements in the future.
- The susceptibility to loss or fraud of the related asset or liability.
- The subjectivity and complexity of determining estimated amounts.
- The financial statement amounts exposed to the deficiencies.
- The volume of activity that has occurred or could occur in the account balance or class of transactions exposed to the deficiency or deficiencies.
- The importance of the controls to the financial reporting process.
- The cause and frequency of the exceptions detected as a result of the deficiencies in the controls.
- The interaction of the deficiency with other deficiencies in internal control.

The form, timing and addressees of this communication should be agreed at the start of the audit, as part of the terms of the engagement. This report, traditionally known as a management letter or report to management, is usually sent at the end of the audit process.

If you are asked for a covering letter in the exam, you should include the above matters within it.

You may be required to identify and explain deficiencies from your analysis of the control system described in a scenario. You may also be asked to explain the consequence of the each deficiency and make a recommendation to overcome it:

**Deficiency** Clear description of what is wrong.

**Consequence** What could happen if the deficiency is not corrected. Focus on what matters to the client – the risk of lost profits, stolen assets, extra costs, errors in the accounts.

**Recommendation** This must deal with the specific deficiency you have observed. It must also provide greater benefits than the cost of implementation.

Try to specify exactly how the recommended control would operate including suggesting who should carry out the control procedures, and how frequently it should be performed.

When the auditor reports deficiencies, it should be made clear that:

- the report is not a comprehensive list of deficiencies, but only those that have come to light during normal audit procedures
- the report is for the sole use of the company
- no disclosure should be made to a third party without the written agreement of the auditor
- no responsibility is assumed to any other parties.

**Management letter extract**

| Deficiency | Consequence | Recommendation |
|---|---|---|
| There appear to be purchase invoices missing from the sequentially numbered invoice file. | There is a possibility that purchases and liabilities are not completely recorded. | All invoices should be sequentially filed on receipt by the accounts department. Regular checks should be made to ensure a complete record, with any missing items investigated (and copies requested if necessary). |

**Test your understanding 1**

After performing tests of controls, the auditor is of the opinion that audit evidence is not sufficient to support the audit opinion; in other words many control errors were found.

**Required:**

**Explain THREE actions that the auditor may now take in response to this problem.**

*Real exam question: June 2008* **(3 marks)**

**Test your understanding 2**

Rhapsody Co supplies a wide range of garden and agricultural products to trade and domestic customers. The company has 11 divisions, with each division specialising in the sale of specific products, for example, seeds, garden furniture, agricultural fertilizers. The company has an internal audit department which provides audit reports to the audit committee on each division on a rotational basis.

Products in the seed division are offered for sale to domestic customers via an Internet site. Customers review the product list on the Internet and place orders for packets of seeds using specific product codes, along with their credit card details, onto Rhapsody Co's secure server. Order quantities are normally between one and three packets for each type of seed. Order details are transferred manually onto the company's internal inventory control and sales system and a two part packing list is printed in the seed warehouse. Each order and packing list is given in a random alphabetical code based on the name of the employee inputting the order, the date and the products being ordered.

In the seed warehouse, the packets of seeds for each order are taken from specific bins and despatched to the customer with one copy of the packing list. The second copy of the packing list is sent to the accounts department where the inventory and sales computer is updated to show that the order has been despatched. The customer's credit card is then charged by the inventory control and sales computer. Bad debts in Rhapsody are currently 3% of the total sales.

Finally, the computer system checks that for each charge made to a customer's credit card account, the order details are on file to prove that the charge was made correctly. The order file is marked as completed confirming that the order has been despatched and payment obtained.

**Required:**

In respect of sales in the seeds division of Rhapsody Co:

(i) **identify and explain FOUR deficiencies in the sales system;**

(ii) **explain the possible effect of each deficiency; and**

(iii) **provide a recommendation to alleviate each deficiency.**

**(14 marks)**

**Test your understanding 3**

You are carrying out the audit of the purchases system of Spondon Furniture. The company has a turnover of about $10 million and all the shares are owned by Mr and Mrs Fisher, who are non-executive directors and are not involved in the day-to-day running of the company.

The bookkeeper maintains all the accounting records and prepares the annual financial statements.

The company uses a standard computerised accounting package.

You have determined that the purchases system operates as follows:

- When materials are required for production, the production manager sends a handwritten note to the buying manager. For orders of other items, the department manager or managing director sends handwritten notes to the buying manager. The buying manager finds a suitable supplier and raises a purchase order. The purchase order is signed by the managing director. Purchase orders are not issued for all goods and services received by the company.
- Materials for production are received by the goods received department, who issue a goods received note (GRN), and send a copy to the bookkeeper. There is no system for recording receipt of other goods and services.
- The bookkeeper receives the purchase invoice and matches it with the goods received note and purchase order (if available). The managing director authorises the invoice for posting to the purchase ledger.
- The bookkeeper analyses the invoice into relevant nominal ledger account codes and then posts it.
- At the end of each month, the bookkeeper prepares a list of payables to be paid. This is approved by the managing director.

- The bookkeeper prepares the cheques and remittances and posts the cheques to the purchase ledger and cashbook.
- The managing director signs the cheques and the bookkeeper sends the cheques and remittances to the payables.

Mr and Mrs Fisher are aware that there may be weaknesses in the above system and have asked for advice.

**Identify the deficiencies in controls in Spondon's purchases system, explain what the impact is and suggest improvements.**

**(12 marks)**

**Test your understanding 4**

(a) **Define 'tests of control' and explain why they are an important procedure in the statutory audit of any company.**

**(3 marks)**

You are an audit senior working at a medium sized firm of auditors. One of your clients is an exclusive hotel called 'Numero Uno' situated in the centre of Big City. As part of your audit procedures you are assessing the controls surrounding payroll. You have read last year's audit file and have obtained the following information:

The hotel employs both full and part time staff. Due to the nature of the business most of the work is done in shifts. All staff are paid on a monthly basis.

New members of staff are given an electronic photo identification card on the day they join by the personnel department. This card is used to 'clock in' and 'clock out' at the start and end of the shift to record the hours worked.

At the end of each week the information recorded on the system is sent automatically to the payroll department and also to the head of each of the three main operating divisions: Rooms, Food & Beverage and Corporate Events. Each division head must reply back to the payroll department by email to authorise the hours worked by their staff.

The payroll clerk collates all the authorised information and then inputs the hours worked into a standardised computerised payroll package. This system is password protected using an alphanumerical password that only the payroll clerk and the finance manager know.

Once the hours have been inputted, the calculations of gross pay and taxation are calculated automatically along with any other statutory deductions. At the end of the calculations a payroll report is produced and printed. The finance manager reviews the report and compares the data to last month to identify and follow up any unusual variances. When he is satisfied with the information he authorises the payroll run by signing the payroll report and the payroll clerk submits the data.

Payslips are sent to the home address of each employee and payment is made by bank transfer.

**Required:**

(b) **With reference to the scenario:**

(i) **Identify and explain FOUR STRENGTHS within the hotel's internal control system in respect of payroll.**

**(6 marks)**

(ii) **For each of the identified strengths, state a test of control the auditor could perform to assess if the controls are operating effectively.**

**(4 marks)**

**(Total: 12 marks)**

**Test your understanding 5**

Bassoon Co runs a chain of shops selling electrical goods all of which are located within the same country.

It has a head office that deals with purchasing, distribution and administration. The payroll for the whole company is administered at head office.

There are 20 staff at head office and 200 staff in the company's 20 shops located in high streets and shopping malls all over the country.

Head office staff (including directors) are all salaried and paid by direct transfer to their bank accounts.

The majority of the staff at the company's shops are also paid through the central salary system, monthly in arrears. However, some students and part time staff are paid cash out of the till.

Recruitment of head office staff is initiated by the department needing the staff who generally conduct interviews and agree terms and conditions of employment. Bassoon Co has an HR manager who liaises with recruitment agencies, places job adverts and maintains staff files with contracts of employment, etc.

Shop managers recruit their own staff.

Shop staff receive a basic salary based on the hours worked and commission based on sales made.

The company has a fairly sophisticated EPOS (electronic point of sale) till system at all shops that communicates directly with the head office accounting system.

All staff when making a sale have to log on with a swipe card which identifies them to the system. This means that the sales they are responsible for are analysed by the system and commissions are calculated.

Store managers have a few 'guest cards' for temporary and part time staff, who generally do not receive commissions.

Store managers and regional supervisors are paid commissions based on the performance of their store or region. Directors and other head office staff usually receive a bonus at Christmas, depending on the company's performance. This is decided by the board in consultation with departmental managers and put through the system by the payroll manager.

The payroll manager is responsible for adding joiners to the payroll and deleting leavers as well as implementing changes in pay rates, tax coding and other deductions and for making sure that the list of monthly transfers is communicated to the bank.

The computerised payroll system is a standard proprietary system which is sophisticated enough to incorporate the commission calculations mentioned above, which are fed in directly from the EPOS system.

The company employs an IT manager who is responsible for the maintenance of all IT systems and installing new hardware and software.

**Comment on the strengths and deficiencies of the payroll system at Bassoon Co and recommend any changes which you think are appropriate.**

**(10 marks)**

## 11 Chapter summary

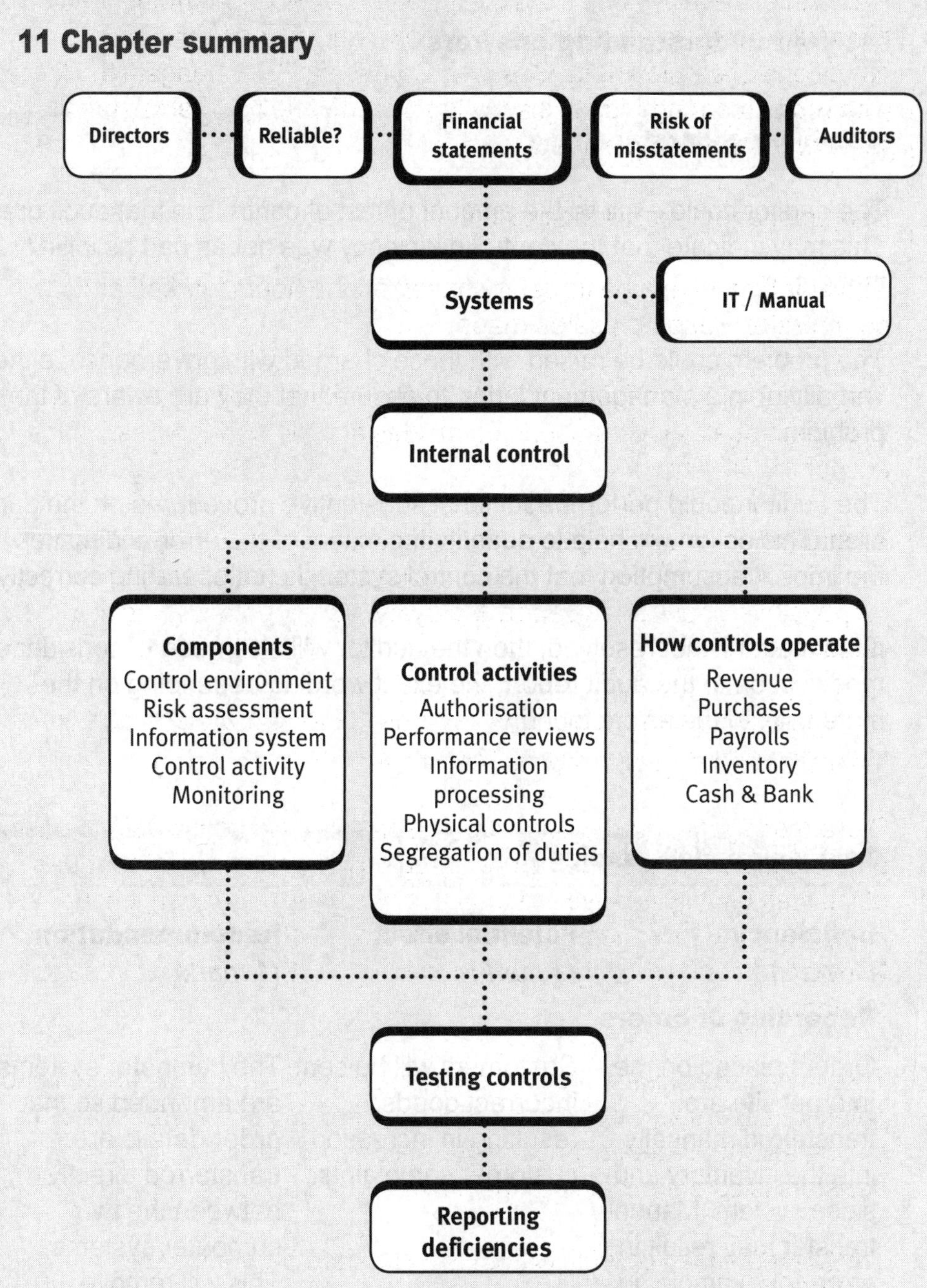

## Test your understanding answers

### Test your understanding 1

The auditor could expand the amount of test of controls in that audit area. This may indicate that the control deficiency was not as bad as initially thought.

The problem could be raised with those charged with governance, either verbally or in a management letter, to ensure that they are aware of the problem.

The auditor could perform additional substantive procedures on the audit area. This action will help to quantify the extent of the error and makes the implicit assumption that the control system is not operating correctly.

If the matter is not resolved, then the auditor will also need to consider a modification to the audit report; the exact wording depending on the materiality of the errors found.

### Test your understanding 2

| **Deficiency** *(1 mark)* | **Potential effect** *(1 mark)* | **Recommendation** *(1 mark)* |
|---|---|---|
| **Recording of orders** | | |
| Orders placed on the Internet site are transferred manually into the inventory and sales system. Manual transfer may result in error, for example, in recording order quantities or product codes. | Customers will be sent incorrect goods resulting in increased customer complaints. | The computer systems are amended so that order details are transferred directly between the two computer systems. This will remove manual transfer of details limiting the possibility of human error. |

| Deficiency (1 mark) | Potential effect (1 mark) | Recommendation (1 mark) |
|---|---|---|
| **Control over orders and packing lists** | | |
| Each order/packing list is given a random alphabetical code. This type of code makes it difficult to check completeness of orders at any stage in the despatch and invoicing process. | Packing lists can be lost resulting either in goods not being despatched to the customer or the customer's credit card not being charged. | Orders/packing lists are controlled with a numeric sequence. At the end of each day, gaps in the sequence of packing lists returned to accounts are investigated. |
| **Obtaining payment** | | |
| The customer's credit card is charged after despatch of goods to the customer, meaning that goods are already sent to the customer before payment is authorised. | Rhapsody Co will not be paid for the goods despatched where the credit company rejects the payment request. Given that customers are unlikely to return seeds, Rhapsody Co will automatically incur a bad debt. | Authorisation to charge the customer's credit card is obtained prior to despatch of goods to ensure Rhapsody Co is paid for all goods despatched. |
| **Completeness of orders** | | |
| There is no overall check that all orders recorded on the inventory and sales system have actually been invoiced. | Entire orders may be overlooked and consequently sales and profit understated. | The computer is programmed to review the order file and orders where there is no corresponding invoice for an order, these should be flagged for subsequent investigation. |

**Test your understanding 3**

| **Deficiency** *(1 mark)* | **Effect** *(1 mark)* | **Recommendation** *(1 mark)* |
|---|---|---|
| (1) Hand written orders are done (with no numbering). | Orders for goods not required and potential orders being missed for action. Therefore over spending or potential shock outs due to orders not being processed. | Have prenumber orders which are authorised by a manager. |
| (2) Purchase orders are not issued for all goods and services. | Goods/services being purchased that are not legitimate or required. | Purchase orders required for all goods. For services a budget should be set and quotes obtained. |
| (3) No system for recording receipt of other goods and services. | Goods received that are of poor quality or incorrect amounts. | Count goods in before they are signed. |
| (4) It doesn't state that the GRN are checked to anything. | Goods received that are of poor quality or incorrect amounts. | Agree GRN back to the purchase order. |
| (5) There is no review done of the bookkeeper posting the invoices into the nominal ledger. | Errors could go undetected, therefore pay suppliers the incorrect amount. | A review by a manager should be done on a regular basis. |
| (6) A list of payables is given to the managing director. | The managing director will not know if payables are valid or correct therefore could be paying incorrect amounts. | The managing director should also review source documents before signing the list. |

| Deficiency (1 mark) | Effect (1 mark) | Recommendation (1 mark) |
|---|---|---|
| (7) Lack of segregation of duties | | |
| The managing director authorises invoices, approves payment and signs cheques. | It is easy to place through a purchase invoice to pay himself and this would go undetected. | Segregate duties by sharing the responsibility with another manager. |

**Test your understanding 4**

(a) **Tests of control**

A test of control tests the operating effectiveness of controls in preventing, detecting or correcting material misstatements.

It is important for the external auditor to test controls to ensure their initial understanding obtained when assessing the control environment and internal controls is appropriate.

This will allow the auditor to identify and assess the risks of material misstatements in the financial statements and to determine to what extent to rely on the internal control system during the audit.

The auditor will then be able to design sufficient and appropriate substantive audit procedures to reduce detection risk, and therefore audit risk, to an acceptable level.

(b) **Payroll system strengths and tests of control**

Strengths in the control environment at the hotel in respect of payroll are set out below including the test of control to be performed by the auditor.

| **Strength (i)** | **Explanation (i)** | **Test of control (ii)** |
|---|---|---|
| All staff are assigned a unique ID card by the personnel department to record hours worked. | Segregation of duties between allocating the cards and processing payroll will reduce the risk of the creation of 'ghost' employees' by the payroll department. | Ask a sample of employees to confirm who provided them with their unique ID card on joining the business. |
| Hours worked are authorised by divisional heads. | There is a reduced risk that hours are overstated as the divisional head is more likely to identify errors or anomalies. | Inspect the email sent by the divisional head for a sample of months and agree to the employees hours recorded on the payroll system. |
| The payroll system is password protected with an alphanumerical password known only to the payroll clerk and finance manager. | The password is difficult to guess and therefore will reduce the risk of unauthorised access. There is a reduced risk that payroll data is manipulated. | The auditor should use test data and enter a 'dummy' password into the payroll system to ensure that access is not granted. |
| Payroll calculations are automatically calculated by the standardised payroll software. | There is a reduced risk of human error as the calculations are automatically generated using a standardised software package. | The auditor should recalculate a sample of employee's monthly pay from across the year and compare to the calculations on the payroll report for those months. |
| The finance manager reviews the payroll report and compares to last month before the final payroll is processed. | The comparison of data to the prior month should highlight any unusual movements that could be errors before the payroll is processed. | For a sample of months, inspect the payroll reports for evidence of the finance manager's signature confirming that the review has been performed. |

| | | |
|---|---|---|
| Payslips are sent to the home address of each employee. | This should reduce the risk that payslips are misplaced or manipulated. It would also reduce the risk of a confidentiality breach. | Ask a sample of employees to confirm how they receive their monthly payslips. |
| Payments are sent by bank transfer to each employee. | This will reduce the risk of payments being stolen or handed to the wrong employee. | Inspect the bank statements to identify payments made to a sample of employees on the payroll report for one month. Inspect the bank statement to ensure the payment has a bank transfer reference as the means of payment. |

**Test your understanding 5**

| **Strength** *(1 mark)* | **Deficiency** *(1 mark)* | **Recommendation** *(1 mark)* |
|---|---|---|
| Salaries are paid by direct transfer to the employees bank accounts (less chance of mis-appropriation of cash). | | |
| | Cash paid to part time staff (easier to misappropriate cash). | Apply the payroll system to all employees. |
| | No control over the appointment of head office staff the HR Manager deals with (may recruit unnecessary staff). | Head office staff should be approved by the board. |
| | No control over shop staff, the shop manager recruits own staff. | Should be approved by head office. |

| Strength (1 mark) | Deficiency (1 mark) | Recommendation (1 mark) |
|---|---|---|
| Having a sophisticated EPOS till system (unlikely for errors to occur). | | |
| Individual swipe cards linked to commission (you know who is doing the transaction and because they receive a commission it encourages the staff to recognise the sale). | | |
| | Guest cards, could be anybody and they could steal a card to access till at a later date to steal money. | A control system to monitor guest cards so management know who has a specific card. |
| | Lack of segregation of duties, the payroll manager is responsible for all processing. | Split the responsibilities up, maybe get a manager to review the payroll managers work. |
| | In the question it states the IT manager is responsible for systems, but doesn't state there is restricted access. | Place passwords on the system and change them on a regular basis. |

chapter

# 8

# Procedures

## Chapter learning objectives

When you have completed this chapter you will be able to:

- Provide examples of procedures used to audit specific balances.
- Discuss and provide examples of how analytical procedures are used as substantive procedures.
- Apply audit techniques to small and not-for-profit organisations.
- Discuss the problems associated with the audit and review of accounting estimates.

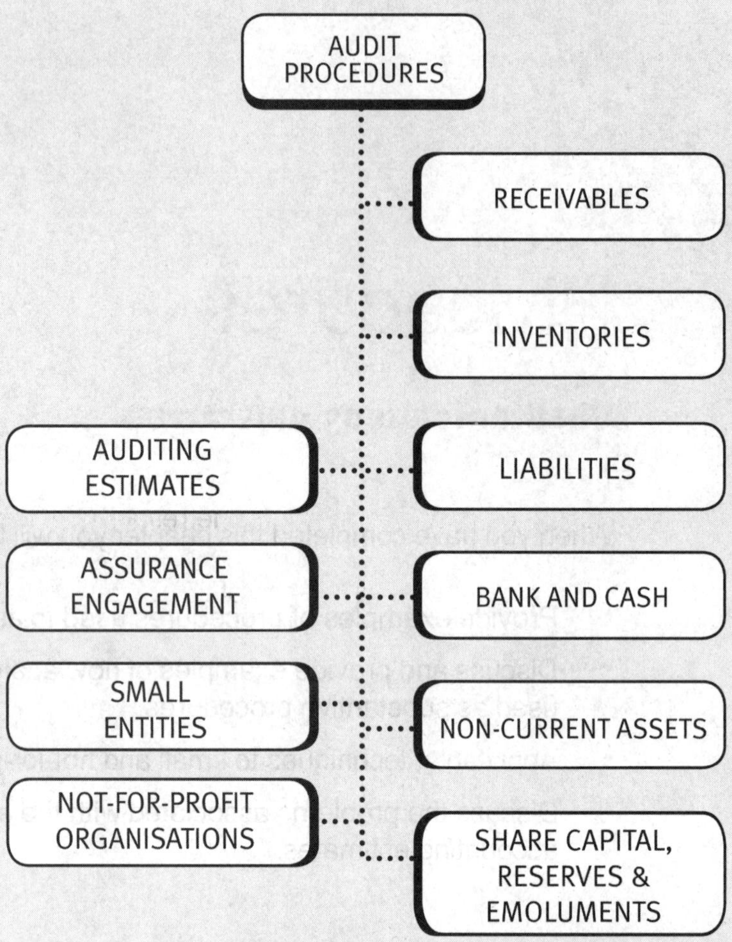


We dealt with the principles of audit evidence in an earlier chapter. This chapter deals with the **application** of those principles.

Audit procedures must be designed to respond to the specific risks of material misstatement identified for each individual client. In the exam, you should make your answers specific to the scenario.

This chapter is a starting point to help you familiarise yourself with the basic auditing techniques to allow you to apply them to questions. It is not an exhaustive summary of all audit procedures.

In addition, this chapter focuses on the audit of the statement of financial position. This is because the statement of financial position is often tested directly, but many areas of the statement of profit or loss are tested indirectly. This is known as **directional testing**.

## 1 Directional testing

The concept of directional testing derives from the principle of double-entry bookkeeping, i.e. for every debit there should be a corresponding credit; therefore any misstatement of a debit entry will also result in a misstatement of a credit entry.

Auditor's primarily test debit entries for overstatement (assets and expenses) and credit entries for understatement (liabilities and income), indirectly testing the corresponding entries at the same time.

- All accounts are then tested for both understatement and overstatement; e.g. directly testing payables for understatement also indirectly tests expenses/cost of sales for understatement.
  - Testing for understatement tests completeness; testing for overstatement tests valuation, existence, rights and obligations, and occurrence.

## 2 Bank and cash

Bank and cash is a good example of where the reliability of the evidence available means that only a small quantity of evidence is needed. The auditor relies mainly on just two key pieces of evidence: the bank confirmation letter and the bank reconciliation.

- Obtain the company's bank reconciliation and cast to ensure arithmetical accuracy.
- Verify the reconciliation's balance per the cash book to the year end cash book.
- Trace all of the outstanding lodgements to the pre year-end cash book, post year-end bank statement and also to paying-in-book pre year-end.
- Trace all unpresented cheques through to a pre year end cash book and post year-end statement. For any unusual amounts or significant delays obtain explanations from management.
- Examine any old unpresented cheques to assess if they need to be written back into the purchase ledger as they are no longer valid to be presented.

**Illustration 1: Murray Co bank reconciliation**

**Bank reconciliation as at 31 December 2012**

| | $ |
|---|---|
| Balance per cash book | 180,345.22 |
| Add Unpresented cheques | 2,223.46 |
| Less Outstanding lodgements | (1,600.34) |
| Difference | 1.34 |
| Balance per bank statement | 180,969.70 |

- Obtain a bank confirmation letter from the company's bankers.
- Verify the balance per the bank statement to an original year end bank statement and also to the bank confirmation letter.
- Agree all balances listed on the bank confirmation letter to the company's bank reconciliations or the trial balance to ensure completeness of bank balances.
- Examine the bank confirmation letter for details of any security provided by the company or any legal right of set-off as this may require disclosure.

**Illustration 2: Murray Co bank confirmation letter**

Wimble & Co
14 The Grove
Kingston
KI4 6AP

Manager (Audit Confirmations)
**National Bank** Anytown Branch
High Street, Anytown, AT1 1HS

14 December 2012

Dear Sir,

**Re: Murray Co**

In accordance with the agreed practice for provision of information to auditors, please forward information on our mutual client as detailed below on behalf of the bank, its branches and subsidiaries. This request and your response will not create any contractual or other duty with us.

Company name: Murray Co

Main account number: 01789311

Sort code: 4-83-12

**Information required**

- Standard **x**
- Trade finance **x**
- Derivative and commodity trading
- Custodian arrangements
- Other information (see attached)

**Audit confirmation date: 31/12/12**

The Authority to Disclose Information signed by your customer is already held by you. This is dated 30/11/11. Please advise us if this Authority is insufficient for you to provide full disclosure of the information requested.

The contact name is: Don Henman (Audit Partner)
Telephone: 01234 123456

Yours Faithfully,

*Wimble & Co*

Wimble & Co

**Murray Co bank confirmation letter**

The bank confirmation letter provides direct confirmation of bank balances from the bank: it is third-party, independent, written evidence and therefore very reliable. The format of the letter is usually standard and agreed between the bank and auditor.

The letter should be sent a minimum of two weeks before the client's year end. The letter should include enough information to allow the bank to trace the client. The bank should then forward on all details on all balances for the client; this will ensure completeness.

Permission must have been given by the client for the bank to release this information to the auditors, as they too have a duty of confidentiality to their clients. In some jurisdictions such disclosures are illegal, and so bank confirmation letters cannot be used as audit evidence.

- Review the cash book and bank statements for any unusual items or large transfers around the year end, as this could be evidence of window dressing.
- Count the petty cash in the cash tin at the year end and agree the total to the balance included in the financial statements.

## Non-current liabilities

The bank confirmation letter will also provide details of loans held, the amounts outstanding, accrued interest and any security provided in relation to those loans. Additional procedures that the auditor will need to perform in relation to loan payables include:

- Review disclosures of interest rates, and the split of the loan between current and non-current.
- Review restrictive covenants (terms) in the loan agreement and determine the effect of any loan covenant breaches.
- Recalculate interest accrual in accordance with terms within the loan agreement, to ensure mathematical accuracy.

## 3 Non-current assets

Auditing tangible non-current assets requires the auditor to obtain sufficient appropriate evidence over many areas:

- existing assets
- additions
- disposals and the related profit/loss in the statement of profit or loss
- depreciation (which of course affects both the statement of financial position and the statement of profit or loss)
- revaluations
- related disclosures (the property, plant and equipment note, depreciation policies, useful economic lives, revaluations and assets held under finance leases).

**Illustration 3: Murray Co property plant and equipment**

**Non-current assets: property, plant and equipment note**

| | Land & buildings | Fixtures, fittings & equipment | Motor vehicles | Total |
|---|---|---|---|---|
| | $000 | $000 | $000 | $000 |
| **Cost at 1 January 2012** | 3,000 | 2,525 | 375 | 5,900 |
| Additions | – | 1,050 | 75 | 1,125 |
| Disposals | – | (300) | – | (300) |
| **Cost at 31 December 2012** | 3,000 | 3,275 | 450 | 6,725 |
| **Accumulated depreciation at 1 January 2012** | 386 | 489 | 125 | 1,000 |
| Charge for the year | 97 | 338 | 56 | 499 |
| Disposals | – | (116) | – | (124) |
| **Accumulated depreciation at 31 December 2012** | 483 | 711 | 181 | 1,375 |
| **Net book value at 31 December 2011** | 2,517 | 2,564 | 269 | 5,350 |
| **Net book value at 31 December 2012** | 2,614 | 2,036 | 250 | 4,900 |

**Additions**

- Obtain a breakdown of additions, cast the list and agree to the non-current asset register: verifies **completeness**.
- Select a sample of additions and agree cost to supplier invoice: verifies **valuation**.
- Review the list of additions and confirm that they relate to capital expenditure items rather than repairs and maintenance: verifies **existence**
- Review the repairs and maintenance account in the general ledger for items of a capital nature: verifies **completeness**.

- Inspect supplier invoices (for equipment), title deeds (for property), and registration documents (for motor vehicles) to ensure they are in the name of the client: verifies: **rights and obligations**.
- If assets have been constructed by the client, obtain an analysis of the costs incurred, cast for arithmetical accuracy and agree a sample of costs to supporting documentation (e.g. payroll, material invoices): verifies **valuation**.

**Disposals**

- Obtain a breakdown of disposals, cast the list and agree all assets removed from the non-current asset register: verifies **existence**.
- Select a sample of disposals and agree sale proceeds to supporting documentation such as sundry sales invoices: verifies **accuracy of profit on disposal**.
- Recalculate the profit/loss on disposal and agree to the statement of profit or loss: verifies **accuracy of profit on disposal**.

**Existing assets**

- Select a sample of assets from the non-current asset register and physically inspect them: verifies **existence**.
- Select a sample of assets visible at the client's premises and inspect the asset register to ensure they are included: verifies **completeness**.
- Cast the non-current asset register totals and sub-totals to ensure arithmetical accuracy: verifies **valuation**.
- Inspect assets for condition and usage to identify signs of impairment: verifies **valuation** and **allocation**.
- For leased assets, inspect the lease document to assess whether the lease is an operating or finance lease and appropriately treated (finance lease assets should be capitalised and a corresponding liability created in accordance with IAS 17 *Leases*): verifies **rights and obligations**.
- For revalued assets, inspect the valuer's report and agree the amount stated to the amount included in the general ledger and the financial statements: verifies **valuation**; and ensure that all assets in the same class have been revalued.

**Depreciation** (audit procedures verify **valuation**, **allocation**, and **accuracy** of the **depreciation charge** in the statement of profit or loss)

- Review the reasonableness of the depreciation rates and compare to industry averages.

- Review the capital expenditure budgets for the next few years to assess the appropriateness of the useful economic lives in light of plans to replace assets.
- Review profits and losses on disposal of assets disposed of in the year, to assess the reasonableness of the depreciation policies (if depreciation policies are reasonable, there should not be a significant profit or loss).
- Recalculate the depreciation charge for a sample of assets.
- Review the disclosure of the depreciation charges and policies in the draft financial statements and compare to the prior year to ensure consistency.
- Reperform depreciation calculation for revalued assets to ensure the charge is based on the new carrying value.
- Perform a proof in total calculation for the depreciation charged for each category of assets, discuss with management if significant fluctuations arise.

**Illustration 4: depreciation proof-in-total**

The depreciation charge for fixtures and fittings for the year ending 31 December 2012 included in the draft financial statements of Murray Co is $338,000 (to the nearest $000).

Murray Co's depreciation policy is to depreciate fixtures and fittings using the straight line method. The useful economic life for fixtures and fittings is ten years.

**Exercise:**

**Create an expectation of what total depreciation for fixtures and fittings should be for year ending 31 December 2012.**

**Solution**

The total cost of fixtures and fittings in the draft financial statements of Murray Co is $3,275,000 (to the nearest $000).

We can set an **expectation for total depereciation for fixtures and fittings for the year ending 31 December 2012** as $3,275,000/10: **$328,000** (to the nearest $000).

The **difference** ($10,000) is only **3%** more than our expectation, and we can therefore conclude that depreciation is true and fair.

## Intangible non-current assets

Remember that the auditor's role is to obtain sufficient appropriate evidence that the financial statements conform in all material respects with the relevant financial reporting framework. For this reason, you will need to have a good understanding of the basic International Financial Reporting Standards.

### Development Costs

Development costs should only be capitalised as an intangible asset if the recognition criteria of IAS 38 *Intangible Assets* have been met. Development costs are capitalised when: the technical feasibility of the asset for sale or use can be demonstrated and the costs can be measured reliably.

- The entity must intend to complete the development and use or sell the asset and have the resources to do so, as well as demonstrate how the asset will generate future economic benefit. If these critera are not satisfied, the costs must be expensed to the statement of profit or loss along with all research expenditure.

**Note:** the audit procedures suggested below focus on obtaining evidence that the treatment of the relevant item conforms with these requirements.

- Obtain a breakdown of costs capitalised, cast for mathematical accuracy and agree to the amount included in the financial statements: verifies **valuation**.
- For a sample of costs, agree to invoices or timesheets: verifies **valuation**.
- Inspect board minutes for any discussions relating to the intended sale or use of the asset: verifies **existence**.
- Discuss the details of the project with management, to evaluate compliance with IAS 38 criteria: verifies **existence**.
- Inspect project plans and other documentation, to evaluate compliance with IAS 38 criteria: verifies **existence**.
- Inspect budgets to confirm financial feasibility: verifies **existence**.

### Other intangible assets

- Inspect purchase documentation for purchased intangible assets: verifies **existence, rights and obligations** and **valuation**.
- Inspect specialist valuer's report and agree the amount stated to the amount included in the general ledger and the financial statements: verifies **valuation.**

**Note:** audit procedures for ammortisation are similar to those for depreciation.

## 4 Inventory

Remember that the inventory balance on the statement of financial position is also the closing inventory figure on the statement of profit or loss. As such, cut-off is also a relevant assertion in addition to the usual assertions for account balances.

The main source of evidence for inventory, is normally the year-end inventory count (although some clients may use continuous inventory counting, throughout the year).

ISA 501 *Audit evidence – specific considerations for selected items* requires the auditor to attend the physical inventory count (unless impracticable), if inventory is material to the financial statements.

The inventory count is the responsibility of the client. The auditor attends the count to help obtain sufficient appropriate evidence to form an opinion as to whether inventory is free from material misstatement.

In order to obtain sufficient appropriate evidence, the auditor must perform procedures before, during and after the inventory count during the final audit.

### Before inventory count

- Contact client to obtain a copy of the inventory count instructions, to understand how the count will be conducted and assess the effectiveness of the count process.

**Illustration 5: Murray Co inventory count instructions**

(1) A finance manager must manage the inventory count.

(2) No goods are to be received or despatched during the inventory count.

(3) Each team will consist of two members of staff from the finance department.

(4) The teams will be allocated a team number and will be provided with a map of the warehouse. Each area of the warehouse is marked on the map with the number of the team that is to count inventory in that area. The warehouse manager will be in attendance to ensure that each team is clear about which area they are counting, before it is counted.

(5) One person must count the items. The second person will record the count and item information on the inventory tag. A description of the item, the inventory reference number (located on the inventory), quantity, unit of measure, location and team number should be noted on the tag.

(6) The tag will be taped to the shelf where the item is located. The tags are sequentially prenumbered; please use them in order.

(7) If you make a mistake on the tab do not use the tab, cross out the information, note the number of the replacement tag on the reverse of the unusable tag and hand to the Finance Manager at the end of the count, so that the sequence can be checked.

(8) Any damaged or obsolete items will be moved to a designated area. After the count, an assessment of the goods will be made by the finance manager with advice from a sales manager and the warehouse manager, to determine the provision appropriate for the condition of the items.

(9) Once the first count is complete, a second count will take place, with each team counting an area that they were not responsible for on the first count (again according to the warehouse map).

(10) One person will count the item. The second person will sign the inventory tag to agree the details completed by the first team, and note the team number on the tag. Any discrepencies should be notified to the Finance Director immediately. The details noted on the inventory tag, including the inventory tag number must then be transfered to the inventory count sheets. The inventory count sheets are pre-printed with a description of the item and the inventory reference number (but not the quantities) and sequentially numbered.

(11) After the count, the inventory count sheets are compared to the inventory records by the finance manager any adjustments investigated and records updated by another finance manager (not involved in the count).

**Exercise:**

**Discuss the reasons for each of the processes described on Murray Co's inventory count instructions.**

**Solution: Murray Co inventory count instructions**

The reasons for each of the processes within the inventory count instructions include:

(1) A suitably trained and senior individual should be responsible for the count to ensure that any issues can be resolved on a timely basis.

(2) Inventory records could be misstated if product lines are missed or double counted due to movements in the warehouse.

(3) Segregation of duties between those who have day-to-day responsibility for inventory and those who are checking it prevents errors and fraud being hidden by the warehouse team.

(4) Providing clear instructions for which team is to count what inventory ensures that all inventory is counted, and prevents double-counting.

(5) Segregation of duties within the team prevents errors and fraud.

(6) Pre-numbering the inventory tags will ensure that all inventory counted is detailed on the inventory count sheet.

(7) A sequence check will ensure that all inventory tags have been accounted for.

(8) Damaged or obsolete goods should be written down or provided against to ensure that they are stated at the lower of cost and NRV. A suitably trained member of the finance team should perform this assessment to ensure the valuation is appropriate.

(9) Counting the lines twice helps to ensure completeness and accuracy of the counts, and that any adjustments made are appropriate.

(10) The inventory count sheets should not have the quantities pre-printed to prevent the count team simply agreeing with the quantities, making counting errors more likely.

(11) The year-end inventory balance of Murray Co will be based on the records maintained. Therefore, the records must be complete, accurate and valid. It is important that an authorised inividual who is independent of the count process and the warehouse can amend records.

- Review prior year working papers to understand the inventory count process and identify any issues that would need to be taken into account this year.
- Book audit staff to attend the inventory counts.
- Ascertain whether any inventory is held by third parties, and if applicable determine how to gather sufficient appropriate evidence.
- Consider the need for using an expert to assist in valuing the inventory being counted.
- Send a letter requesting direct confirmation of inventory balances held at year end from any third party warehouse providers used regarding quantities and condition.

**During inventory count**

- Observe the count to ensure that the instructions are being followed.
- Attend the inventory count (if one is to be performed) at the third party warehouses to review the controls in operation: verifies **completeness** and **existence**.
- Perform a two way test count: Select a sample of items from the inventory count sheets and physically inspect the items in the warehouse: verifies **existence**.
- Select a sample of physical items from the warehouse and trace to the inventory count sheets to ensure that they are recorded accurately: verifies **completeness**.
- Ensure that goods held on behalf of third parties is segregated and recorded separately: verifies **rights and obligations**.
- Inspect the inventory being counted for evidence of damage or obsolescence that may affect the net realisable value: verifies **valuation.**
- Record details of the last deliveries prior to the year end. This information will be used in final audit procedures to ensure that no further amendments have been made thereby overstating or understating inventory: verifies **cut-off**.
- Obtain copies of inventory count sheets at the end of the inventory count, ready for checking against final inventory listing after the inventory count.

**After inventory count; final audit procedures**

- Trace the items counted during the inventory count to the final inventory list to ensure it is the same as the one used at the year-end and to ensure that any errors identified during counting procedures have been rectified: verifies **completeness**.
- Cast the list (showing inventory categorised between finished goods, WIP and raw materials) to ensure arithmetical accuracy and agree totals to financial statement disclosures: verifies **completeness**.
- Inspect purchase invoices for a sample of inventory items to agree their cost and
- Inspect post-year-end sales invoices for a sample of inventory items to determine if the net realisable value is reasonable. This will also assist in determining if inventory is held at the lower of cost and net realisable value has been used: verifies **valuation**.
- Inspect the ageing of inventory items to identify old/slow-moving amounts that may require provision, and discuss these with management: verifies **valuation**.
- Recalculate work-in-progress and finished goods valuations using payroll records for labour costs and utility bills for overhead absorption: verifies **valuation**.
- Calculate inventory turnover/days and compare this to prior year, to assess whether inventory is being held longer and therefore requires greater provision: verifies **valuation**.
- Calculate gross profit margin and compare this to prior year, investigate any significance differences that may highlight an error in costs of sales and closing inventory: verifies **valuation**.
- Trace the goods received immediately prior to the year-end to year-end payables and inventory balances: verifies **cut-off**.
- Trace goods despatched immediately prior to the year-end to the nominal ledgers to ensure the items are removed from inventory and a sale (and receivable where relevant) has been recorded: verifies **cut-off**.
- Inspect any reports produced by the auditors of third party warehouses in relation to the adequacy of controls over inventory.
- Inspect any documentation in respect of third party inventory.

- Inspect the ageing of inventory items to identify old/slow-moving amounts that may require provision, and discuss these with management: verifies **valuation**.
- Recalculate work-in-progress and finished goods valuations using payroll records for labour costs and utility bills for overhead absorption: verifies **valuation**.
- Calculate inventory turnover/days and compare this to prior year, to assess whether inventory is being held longer and therefore requires greater provision: verifies **valuation**.
- Calculate gross profit margin and compare this to prior year, investigate any significance differences that may highlight an error in costs of sales and closing inventory: verifies **valuation**.
- Trace the goods received immediately prior to the year-end to year-end payables and inventory balances: verifies **cut-off**.
- Trace goods despatched immediately prior to the year-end to the nominal ledgers to ensure the items are removed from inventory and a sale (and receivable where relevant) has been recorded: verifies **cut-off**.
- Inspect any reports produced by the auditors of third party warehouses in relation to the adequacy of controls over inventory.
- Inspect any documentation in respect of third party inventory.

**Continuous/perpetual inventory systems**

The procedures suggested above apply to all inventory counts, whether carried out as a one-off year-end count or where inventory is counted on a rolling basis throughout the year. The objective is the same:

- To identify whether the client's inventory system reliably records, measures and reports inventory balances.

Where the client uses a continuous counting system, lines of inventory are counted periodically (say monthly) throughout the year so that by the end of the year all lines have been reviewed.

**Advantages**

- Reduces time constraints for auditor, and enables them to attend counts relating to lines at greater risk of material misstatement.
- Slow moving and damaged inventory is identified and adjusted for in the client's records on a continuous basis; the year-end valuation should therefore be more accurate.

**Disadvantages**

- The auditor will need to obtain sufficient appropriate evidence that the system operates effectively at all times, not just at the time of the count.
- Additional procedures will be necessary to ensure that the amount included for inventory in the financial statements is appropriate, particularly with regard to cut-off and year-end provisions/estimates.

## 5 Receivables

The focus of testing for receivables is valuation. **Note** the effect of directional testing, e.g. directly testing receivables for overstatement also indirectly tests revenue for overstatement (Dr: Receivables, Cr: Revenue).

- Perform a positive receivables circularisation of a representative sample of Murray Co's year-end balances, for any non-replies, with Murray Co's permission, send a reminder letter to follow-up: verifies **existence** and **rights and obligations**.

### Illustration 6: Murray Co positive confirmation letter

***Customer Co***

***Customer's address***

**7 January 2013**

Dear Sirs

As part of their normal audit procedures we have been requested by our auditors, Wimble & Co, to ask you to confirm the balance on your account with us at 31 December 2012, our year end.

The balance on your account, as shown by our records, is shown below. After comparing this with your records will you please be kind enough to sign the confirmation and return a copy to the auditor in the prepaid envelope enclosed. If the balance is not in agreement with your records, will you please note the items making up the difference in the space provided.

Please note that this request is made for audit purposes only and has no further significance.

Your kind co-operation in this matter will be greatly appreciated.

Yours faithfully

*Chief Accountant*

***Wimble & Co***

***Auditor's address***

Dear Sirs

We confirm that, except as noted below[x], a balance of $10,000 was owing by us to Murray & Co at 31 December 2012.

(*space for customer's signature*)

[x]Details of differences:

**Murray Co confirmation letters**

A **positive** receivables circularisation requires customers to respond whether or not the balance is correct. It is possible to perform a negative receivables circularisation instead; this requests customers to respond only if they disagree with the balance and is only suitable if the risk of material misstatement is low.

*"7th January 2013"*: The confirmation letter should be **sent as soon as possible after the year end**, to increase the chance of an accurate and timely response

*"As part of their normal audit procedures, we have been requested by our auditors to confirm the balance on your account with us at 31st December 2013... please be kind enough to sign the confirmation and return a copy to the auditor..."*: It is the **client** who **writes to their customers** requesting the information but the **response** must be **sent directly to the auditors** to reduce the risk of the client inteferring with any response.

"...*in the prepaid envelope enclosed"*: By making it as easy as possible to respond increase the chance that sufficient customers will confirm balances for it to be a valid audit test.

"*If the balance is not in agreement with your records, will you please note the items making up the difference in the space provided*": Requesting the customer to complete the reconciliation increases the reliance the auditor can place on this evidence (although the auditor will review the reconciliation and investigate any unreconciled differences or disagreements).

Positive receivables circularisations are considered to be a reliable source of evidence because they are written and original from a third party external source.

- Review after date cash receipts and follow through to pre-year-end receivable balances: verifies **valuation, rights and obligations** and **existence**.
- Calculate average receivable days and compare this to prior year, investigate any significant differences: verifies **completeness** and **valuation**.
- Review the reconciliation of the sales ledger control account to the sales ledger list of balances: verifies **completeness** and **existence**.
- Select a sample of goods despatched notes (GDN) before and just after the year end and follow through to the sales invoice to ensure they are recorded in the correct accounting period: verifies **completeness** and **existence** (**cut-off** of revenue).

- Review a sample of post year-end credit notes to identify any that relate to pre-year-end transactions to ensure that they have not been included in receivables: verifies **existence** (**occurence** of revenue).
- Select a sample of year-end receivable balances and agree back to valid supporting documentation of GDN and sales order: verifies **existence**.
- Review board minutes of Murray Co to assess whether there are any material disputed receivables that may require write off: verifies **existence** and **rights and obligations**.
- Inspect the **aged receivables report** to identify any slow moving balances, discuss these with the credit control manager to assess whether an allowance or write down is necessary: verifies **valuation** and **allocation**.
- For any slow moving/aged balances review customer correspondence to assess whether there are any invoices in dispute: verifies **existence** and **rights and obligations**.
- Review the sales ledger for any credit balances and discuss with management whether these should be reclassified as payables: verifies **valuation of receivables** and **completeness of payables**.

**Illustration 7: Murray Co aged receivables analysis**

**Aged receivables analysis at 31 December 2012 ($000)**

| Ref | Customer Name | Total | Current | 30-60 days | 60-90 days | 90-120 days | 120 days |
|---|---|---|---|---|---|---|---|
| A001 | Anfield United Shop | **176** | 95 | 76 | 5 | 0 | 0 |
| B001 | Bibs and Balls | **0** | 0 | (24) | 0 | 24 | 0 |
| B002 | The Beautiful Game | **84** | 62 | 0 | 20 | 0 | 2 |
| B003 | Beckham's | **42** | 32 | 10 | 0 | 0 | 0 |
| C001 | Cheryl & Coleen Co | **12** | 12 | 0 | 0 | 0 | 0 |
| D001 | Dream Team | **45** | 0 | 31 | 14 | 0 | 0 |
| E001 | Escot Supermarket | **235** | 97 | 65 | 0 | 0 | 73 |
| G001 | Golf is Us | **211** | 0 | 0 | 0 | 100 | 111 |
| G002 | Green Green Grass | **61** | 50 | 11 | 0 | 0 | 0 |
| H001 | HHA Sports | **59** | 40 | 0 | 19 | 0 | 0 |
| J001 | Jilberts | **21** | 11 | 10 | 0 | 0 | 0 |
| J002 | James Smit Partnership | **256** | 73 | 102 | 34 | 45 | 2 |

| | | | | | | | |
|---|---|---|---|---|---|---|---|
| J003 | Jockeys | **419** | 278 | 120 | 21 | 0 | 0 |
| O001 | The Oval | **92** | 48 | 44 | 0 | 0 | 0 |
| P001 | Pole Vaulters | **76** | 0 | 0 | 76 | 0 | 0 |
| P002 | Polo Polo | **0** | 0 | 0 | 0 | 0 | 0 |
| S001 | Stayrose Supermarket | **97** | 24 | 23 | 23 | 27 | 0 |
| T001 | Trainers and More | **93** | 73 | 20 | 0 | 0 | 0 |
| T002 | Tike Co | **(54)** | 0 | 0 | 0 | 0 | (54) |
| W001 | Wanderers | **89** | 60 | 29 | 0 | 0 | 0 |
| W002 | Whistlers | **(9)** | 645 | (654) | 0 | 0 | 0 |
| W003 | Walk Hike Run | **4** | 0 | 0 | 0 | 0 | 4 |
| W004 | Winners | **31** | 21 | 10 | 0 | 0 | 0 |
| **Total** | | **2,040** | **1,621** | **(127)** | **212** | **196** | **138** |

**Exercise:**

**Identify, with reasons, four trade receivables balances from the aged receivables analysis that should be selected for further testing.**

**Solution: Murray Co aged receivables analysis**

**Jockeys**: the outstanding balance is over 20% of the total receivables balance at the year end and is therefore material.

**Golf is Us**: this large and old balance may require write off, or a specific allowance made if the recoverability of the amount is in doubt (similarly for Escot supermarket)

**Tike & Co**: the large and old credit balance on the listing suggests that an error may have been made. A payment from another customer may have been misallocated to this account or the client may have overpaid an invoice, or paid an invoice twice in error. It may be appropriate to reclassify this balance, along with the balance for Whistlers, as a trade payable.

**Whistlers**: although the amount is small, the credit balance appears to be due to a difference between a recent large payment and the outstanding balance. This error may indicate other potential errors, and requires further investigation.

*There are other balances that could be identified and justified for similar reasons to the above.*

**More on external confirmations**

Note: ISA 505 *External confirmations* requires the auditor to maintain control over external confirmation requests when using external confirmations as a source of audit evidence.

This can be achieved by:

- the auditor preparing the confirmation letters and determing the information to be requested and the information that should be included in the request
- the auditor selecting the sample of external parties to obtain confirmation from
- the auditor sending the requests to the confirming party

**Prepayments**

Prepayments are services or goods for which a company has paid in advance.

- Review the level of prepayments in comparison to prior year: verifies **existence**, **valuation**, and **completeness**.
- For a sample of prepayments, inspect bank statements to ensure payment has been made: verifies **existence**.
- For a sample of prepayments, inspect invoices to ensure payment relates to goods or services not yet received: verifies **existence**.
- For a sample of prepayments, recalculate the amount prepaid to confirm mathematical accuracy: verifies **valuation**.

## 6 Payables and accruals

The focus of testing for liabilities is completeness. Note the effect of directional testing, e.g. directly testing payables for understatement also indirectly tests cost of sales for understatement (Dr: Payables, Cr: Purchases).

- For a sample of trade payables balances, obtain supplier statements and reconcile these to the purchase ledger balances, and investigate any reconciling items: verifies **existence** and **completeness**.

## Illustration 8: Murray Co supplier statement

Murray Co's trade payable balance at 31 December 2012 is $1,400,000 (to the nearest $000). The total balance has already been agreed to the purchase ledger which shows that trade payables consists of fifteen suppliers.

A junior member of the audit team, Rob Cash, has been checking five of these balances by reconciling suppliers' statements to the balances on the purchase ledger. He is unable to reconcile a material balance, relating to Racket Co, who supply Vectran material to Murray Co, for stringing tennis rackets. He has asked for your assistance, and your suggestions on the audit work which should be carried out on the differences.

The balance of Racket Co on Murray Co's purchase ledger is shown below:

**Purchase ledger** Supplier: Racket Co

| Date | Type | Reference | Status | Dr ($) | Cr ($) | Balance ($) |
|---|---|---|---|---|---|---|
| 10.10.12 | Invoice | 6004 | Paid 1 | | 21,300 | |
| 18.10.12 | Invoice | 6042 | Paid 1 | | 15,250 | |
| 23.10.12 | Invoice | 6057 | Paid 1 | | 26,340 | |
| 04.11.12 | Invoice | 6080 | Paid 2 | | 35,720 | |
| 15.11.12 | Invoice | 6107 | Paid 2 | | 16,320 | |
| 26.11.12 | Invoice | 6154 | Paid 2 | | 9,240 | |
| 31.11.12 | Payment | Cheque | Alloc 1 | 61,630 | | |
| | Discount | | Alloc 1 | 1,260 | | |
| 14.12.12 | Invoice | 6285 | | | 21,560 | |
| 21.12.12 | Invoice | 6328 | | | 38,240 | |
| 31.12.12 | Payment | Cheque | Alloc 2 | 60,050 | | |
| | Discount | | Alloc 2 | 1,230 | | |
| **31.12.12** | **Balance** | | | | | **59,800** |

Racket Co have sent the following supplier statement:

| Date | Type | Reference | Status | Dr ($) | Cr ($) | Balance ($) |
|---|---|---|---|---|---|---|
| 07.10.12 | Invoice | 6004 | | 21,300 | | |
| 16.10.12 | Invoice | 6042 | | 15,250 | | |
| 22.10.12 | Invoice | 6057 | | 26,340 | | |
| 02.11.12 | Invoice | 6080 | | 37,520 | | |
| 13.11.12 | Invoice | 6107 | | 16,320 | | |
| 22.11.12 | Invoice | 6154 | | 9,240 | | |
| 10.12.12 | Receipt | Cheque | | | 61,630 | |
| 04.12.12 | Invoice | 6210 | | 47,350 | | |
| 12.12.12 | Invoice | 6285 | | 21,560 | | |
| 18.12.12 | Invoice | 6328 | | 38,240 | | |
| 28.12.12 | Invoice | 6355 | | 62,980 | | |
| **31.12.12** | **Balance** | | | | | **234,470** |

Racket Co's terms of trade with Murray Co allow a 2% cash discount on invoices where Racket Co receives a cheque from the customer by the end of the month following the date of the invoice (i.e. a 2% discount will be given on November invoices paid and received by 31 December).

On Murray Co's purchase ledger, under 'Status' the cash and discount marked 'Alloc 1' pay invoices marked 'Paid 1' (similarly for 'Alloc 2' and 'Paid 2').

Murray Co's goods received department checks the goods when they arrive and issues a goods received note (GRN). A copy of the GRN and the supplier's advice note is sent to the purchases accounting department.

**Exercise:**

(a) **Prepare a statement reconciling the balance on Murray Co's purchase ledger to the balance on Racket Co's supplier's statement.**

(b) **Describe the audit work you will carry out on each of the reconciling items you have determined in your answer to part (a) above, in order to determine the balance which should be included in the financial statements.**

**Case Study Solution: Murray Co supplier statement**

Many companies send out monthly statements of account as part of their credit control procedures. It is likely that audit clients will receive a number of these statements from suppliers at the year-end. These can be reconciled to their own payables control account to ensure that their records are correct. This is known as a supplier statement reconciliation and is an important source of audit evidence.

There are a two reasons why there may be a variance, including:

- **Timing differences**, e.g. invoices sent by the supplier but not yet received by the customer; payments sent by the customer but not yet received by the supplier; returns and credit notes not yet appearing on the supplier's statement; or
- **Errors**.

(a) **Reconciliation of purchase ledger balance to balance on supplier's statement:**

| | $ | $ |
|---|---|---|
| **Balance per purchase ledger:** | | **59,800** |
| Differences: | | |
| (i) 31.11: Discount not allowed by supplier | 1,260 | |
| (ii) 04.11: Transposition error, invoice 6080 | 1,800 | |
| (iii) 04.12: Invoice 6210 not on purchase ledger | 47,350 | |
| (iv) 28.12: Invoice 6355 not on purchase ledger | 62,980 | |
| (v) 31.12: Cash in transit | 60,050 | |
| (vi) Discount not allowed | 1,230 | |
| | | 174,670 |
| **Balance per supplier's statement:** | | **234,470** |

(b) **Audit work**

(i) The date of the cash payment for the October invoices suggests that Racket Co will not have received the cheque for $61,630 until after the 30 November and so Murray Co may not be entitled to the 2% cash discount. The entry in Murray Co's ledger suggest the cheque was posted on 30 November however this is not conclusive evidence that the cheque was actually sent to Racket Co on this date.

- The auditor should enquire with Murray Co's purchase ledger controller about this item, and inspect correspondence with Racket Co to establish entitlement to the discount.
- If Murray Co is obliged to pay the 2% disallowed discount, this should be added to the purchase ledger balance.
- If Racket Co will allow the discount, there is no need to make any adjustments to the purchase ledger balance.

(ii) The apparent transposition error on invoice 6080 would be checked by inspecting the invoice.

- If the invoice shows $37,520, then an additional payable of $1,800 should be added at the year-end to correct this error.
- No adjustment will be necessary if Murray Co's figure is correct.

(iii) It appears that invoice 6210 for $47,350 has not been included on Murray Co's purchase ledger.

- The auditor should enquire with the warehouse manager whether these goods have been received;
- inspect the GRNs around the expected delivery date in order to identify the relevant GRN; and
- inspect correspondence with Racket Co for discussions relating to a dispute regarding these goods (if relevant).
- If the goods have been received, the purchase invoices file should be inspected to identify if there is a related purchase invoice.
- If there is a purchase invoice, enquire with the purchases department why the invoice has not been posted to the purchase ledger. This may be because of a dispute (e.g. an incorrect price, the wrong quantity or a fault with the goods).
- If the goods relating to this invoice are in inventory (or have been sold) a purchase accrual should be made for this item (note that the actual quantity of goods received should be accrued for) and correspondence relating to this invoice with Racket Co should be inspected to assess what payment has been agreed.

- If the goods have not been received, no adjustment needs to be made (but a copy of correspondence disputing the delivery/invoice should be placed on file as evidence).

(iv) The appropriate treatment of invoice 6355 depends on whether or not Murray Co received the goods before the year-end. The auditor should:

- Inspect the GRN for the date to determine if the goods were received before the year-end.
- If the date is before the year-end, then Murray Co should include a purchase accrual at the year-end for this invoice.

(v) The cheque on 31 December appears to be cash in transit. The auditor should:

- Inspect Murray Co's bank statement to confirm that the cheque was cleared by the bank after the year-end.
- If the cheque cleared within one week of the year-end (with most other cheques issued immediately before the year-end) then this is validly cash in transit.
- If most cheques issued immediately before the year-end take more than a week to clear, this indicates window-dressing of the financial statements (i.e. the cheques were actually sent out after the year-end), in which case the amounts should Cr back to trade payables and Dr back to cash

(vi) If, as appears likely, the cheque for $60,050 is not received by Racket Co until some time after the year-end, then the discount of $1,230 may be disallowed. If this discount is disallowed, it should be added to payables at the year-end (see (i) above).

- Obtain a listing of trade payables from the purchase ledger and agree to the general ledger and the financial statements: verifies **completeness** and **classification and understandibility**.
- Obtain the list of accruals from the client, cast it to confirm mathematical accuracy and agree to the general ledger and the financial statements: verifies **completeness** and **classification and understandability**.
- Ensure payables and accruals are included in financial statements as current liabilities: verifies **classification**.
- Reconcile the total of purchase ledger accounts with the purchase ledger control account, and cast the list of balances and the purchase ledger control account: verifies **completeness**.

- Review the list of trade payables and accruals against prior years to identify any significant omissions: verifies **completeness**.
- Review after date payments, if they relate to the current year then follow through to the purchase ledger or accrual listing: verifies **completeness**.
- Review after date invoices to ensure no further items need to be accrued: verifies **completeness**.
- Enquire of management their process for identifying goods received but not invoiced or logged in the purchase ledger and ensure that it is reasonable: verifies **completeness**.
- Select a sample of goods received notes before the year-end and follow through to inclusion in the year-end payables balance: verifies **completeness of payables** and **cut-off of purchases**.
- Calculate the trade payable days and compare to prior years, investigate any significant differences: verifies **completeness** and **valuation**.
- Select a sample of payable balances and perform a trade payables' circularisation, follow up any non-replies and any reconciling items between balance confirmed and trade payables' balance: verifies **completeness** and **existence**.
- Review the purchase ledger for any debit balances, for any significant amounts discuss with management and consider reclassification as current assets: verifies **valuation** of payables and **completeness of receivables**.
- Recalculate a sample of accrued costs by reference to contracts and payment schedules (e.g. loan interest): verifies **valuation** (**accuracy** of purchases and other expenses).

## 7 Provisions

IAS 37 *Provisions, Contingent Liabilities and Contingent Assets* requires an entity to recognise a provision if: a present obligation has arisen as a result of a past event; payment is probable ('more likely than not'); and the amount can be estimated reliably. If payment is only possible, a contingent liability must be disclosed in the notes to the financial statements.

Note that the audit procedures suggested below focus on obtaining evidence that the treatment of the relevant item conforms with these requirements.

- Enquire with the directors or inspect relevant supporting documentation to **confirm** that a **present obligation** exists at the year end.
- Inspect relevant board minutes to ascertain whether **payment is probable**.
- Obtain a breakdown of the items to be provided for and cast it: verifies **completeness**.
- Recalculate the provision and agree components of the calculation to supporting documentation: verifies **completeness**.
- Review the post year-end period to identify whether any payments have been made, compare actual payments to the amounts provided to assess whether the provision is reasonable: verifies **valuation**.
- Obtain a written representation from management to confirm the **completeness** of the provision.
- If applicable, enquire with the client's solicitors about the likely outcome and chances of payment.
- Review the disclosure of the provision to ensure compliance with IAS 37 *Provisions, Contingent Liabilities and Contingent Assets*: verifies **classification and understandibility**.

**Illustration 9: Murray Co provision**

The statement of financial position shows that Murray Co has $240,000 provisions for the year ended 31 December 2012. The majority of the provision relates to provisions for warranties ($200,000). However, $40,000 of the provision relates to a claim made by an ex-employee of Murray Co who is claiming for unfair dismissal.

The audit plan includes the following audit procedures in relation to this provision:

- Enquire with the directors when the employee was dismissed in order to confirm that a present obligation exists at the year end.
- Review correspondence with the employee to verify that the employee was dismissed before the year end.
- Inspect relevant board minutes to ascertain whether it is probable that the payment will be made to the employee.
- Enquire with the solicitors on the merits of the unfair dismissal case and the likely payment.
- Obtain a breakdown of the costs to be provided for and cast it to ensure completeness.
- Recalculate the provision to confirm completeness and agree components of the calculation to supporting documentation, e.g. fee estimate from Murray Co's solicitors, claim received from ex-employee.

- Review the post year-end period to identify whether any payments have been made to the solicitors or ex-employee, compare actual payments to the amounts provided to assess whether the provision is reasonable.
- Obtain a written representation from management to confirm the completeness of the provision.
- Review the disclosure of the provision to ensure compliance with IAS 37 *Provisions, Contingent Liabilities and Contingent Assets.*

Note: ISA 501 *Audit evidence - special considerations for selected items* requires the auditor to design and perform audit procedures in order to identify litigation and claims involving their client which may give rise to a risk of material misstatement.

## 8 Share capital, reserves & director's remuneration

Director's remuneration is a key audit area as it is invariably material by nature.

### Share capital

- Agree authorised share capital and nominal value disclosures to underlying shareholding agreements/statutory constitution documents.
- Inspect cash book for evidence of cash receipts from share issues and ensure amounts not yet received are correctly disclosed as share capital called-up not paid in the financial statements.
- Inspect board minutes to verify issue of share capital during the year.

### Dividends

- Inspect board minutes to agree dividends proposed before the year-end.
- Inspect bank statements to agree dividends paid before the year-end.
- Inspect dividend warrants to agree dividend payment.

### Directors remuneration

- Obtain and cast a schedule of director's remuneration split between wages, bonuses, benefits, pension contributions and other remuneration, and agree to financial statement disclosures.
- Inspect payroll records and agree wages, bonuses, and pension contributions.
- Inspect bank statements to verify the amounts actually paid to directors.

- Inspect board minutes for discussion and approval of directors' bonus announcements or other additional remuneration.
- Obtain a written representation from directors that they have disclosed all related party transactions and director remuneration to the auditor.

**Reserves**

- Agree opening reserves to prior-year closing reserves and reconcile movements.
- Agree movements in reserves to supporting documentation (e.g. revaluation reserve movements independently valuers report).

## 9 Statement of profit or loss

Remember directional testing. The majority of transactions and events in the statement of profit or loss are audited indirectly through the direct tests performed on the corresponding debits or credits in the statement of financial position. However, the auditor will normally perform **substantive analytical procedures** on these areas and some specific additional procedures, such as those suggested below.

In the exam, if you are asked for substantive procedures in relation to statement of profit or loss assertions, include those procedures from the relevant corresponding part of the statement of financial position.

**Payroll** (audit procedures verify **completeness** and **accuracy**)

- Agree the total wages and salaries expense per the payroll system to the general ledger and the financial statements.
- Cast a sample of payroll records to verify the accuracy of the payroll expense.
- Recalculate the gross and net pay for a sample of employees, and agree to the payroll records.
- Re-perform calculation of statutory deductions to confirm whether correct deductions for this year have been included within the payroll expense.
- Select a sample of joiners and leavers, agree their start/leaving date to supporting documentation, recalculate that their first/last pay packet was accurately calculated and recorded.
- For salaries, agree the total net pay per the payroll records to the bank transfer listing of payments and to the cashbook.
- For wages, agree the total cash withdrawn for wage payments equates to the weekly wages paid plus any surplus cash subsequently banked.
- Agree the year-end tax liabilities to the payroll records, and subsequent payment to the post year-end cash book.

- Agree the individual wages and salaries per the payroll to the personnel records and records of hours worked per clocking in cards.
- Perform a proof in total of total wages and salaries, incorporating joiners and leavers and the pay increase. Compare this to the actual wages and salaries in the financial statements and investigate any significant differences.

**Case study: Murray Co payroll proof in total**

Total payroll for the year ending 31 December 2011 was $1,220,000 (to the nearest $000). At this time Murray Co had 34 employees.

Total payroll for the year ending 31 December 2012 included in the draft financial statements of Murray Co is $1,312,000 (to the nearest $000). Murray Co now has 37 employees.

All employees received a 5% payrise on 31 March 2012.

**Exercise:**

**Create an expectation of what total payroll will be for year ending 31 December 2012.**

**Solution**

The average salary per employee in 2011 was $35,882 ($1,220,000/34). We know that all employees received a payrise for 9 months of 2012 of 5%. The average value of this payrise is therefore $150 per employee in 2012 (5%×9/12×$35,882).

The average salary for 2012 should therefore equal $36,032 ($35,882+$150).

We can set an **expectation for total payroll for the year ending 31 December 2012** as 37×$36032: **$1,333,000** (to the nearest $000).

The **difference** ($21,000) is **less than 2%** more than our expectation, and we can therefore conclude that the payroll cost is true and fair.

**Revenue**

- Recalculate discounts and sales tax applied for a sample of large sales invoices: verifies **accuracy**.
- Select a sample of customer orders and agree these to the despatch notes and sales invoices through to inclusion in the sales ledger: verifies **completeness**.

**Purchases and other expenses**

- Recalculate discounts and sales tax applied for a sample of large purchase invoices: verifies **accuracy**.
- Select a sample of purchase orders and agree these to the GRNs and purchase invoices through to inclusion in the purchases ledger: verifies **completeness**.

## 10 Accounting estimates

There are many accounting estimates in the financial statements, e.g. allowances for receivables, expected life of property, plant and equipment, valuation of provisions etc. Accounting estimates are inherently risky because they are about the future, cannot be 'right', and are often not supported by documentary evidence.

ISA 540 *Auditing Accounting Estimates* requires the auditor to:

- Obtain an understanding of how management identify those transactions, events or conditions that give rise to the need for an estimate.

For each estimate in the financial statements, the auditor must also:

- Enquire of management how the accounting estimate is made and the data on which it is based.
- Determine whether events occurring up to the date of the auditor's report (after the reporting period) provide audit evidence regarding the accounting estimate.
- Review the method of measurement used and assess the reasonableness of assumptions made.
- Test the operating effectiveness of the controls over how management made the accounting estimate.
- Develop an expectation of the possible estimate (point estimate) or a range of amounts to evaluate management's estimate.
- Review the judgements and decisions made by management in the making of accounting estimates to identify whether there are indicators of possible management bias.
- Evaluate overall whether the accounting estimates in the financial statements are either reasonable or misstated.
- Obtain sufficient appropriate audit evidence about whether the disclosures in the financial statements related to accounting estimates and estimation uncertainty (e.g. contingent liabilities) are reasonable.

- Obtain written representations from management and, where appropriate, those charged with governance whether they believe significant assumptions used in making accounting estimates are reasonable.

**Related party transactions**

A related party is defined by ISA 550 *Related Parties* as 'a person or entity that has control or significant influence, directly or indirectly...over the reporting entity'.

There may be related party transactions in any area of the financial statements, for any company.

Related party transactions are a difficult area for the auditor because:

- The relationship between the parties may be very complicated.
- Related party transactions may not be on normal commercial terms.
- Related party transactions may not have documentation to support them.
- Related party transactions are material by nature (i.e. regardless of the value of a related party transaction, if it is not presented fairly or disclosed adequately, the financial statements will be materially mistated).

**Smaller entities**

The characteristics of smaller commercial entities can lead to both advantages and disadvantages:

- **Lower risk**: Smaller entities may well be engaged in activity that is relatively simple and therefore lower risk. However, this will not be true for small – often one person businesses – where there is a high level of expertise in a particular field, e.g. consultancy businesses, creative businesses, the financial sector.
- **Direct control by owner managers** is a strength because they know what is going on and have the ability to exercise real control. They are also in a strong position to manipulate the figures or put private transactions 'through the books'.
- **Simpler systems**: Smaller entities are less likely to have sophisticated IT systems, but pure, manual systems are becoming increasingly rare. This is good news in that many of the bookkeeping errors associated with smaller entities may now be less prevalent. However, a system is only as good as the person operating it.

**Evidence implications**

- The normal rules concerning the relationship between risk and the quality and quantity of evidence apply irrespective of the size of the entity.
- The quantity of evidence may well be less than for a larger organisation.
- It may be more efficient to carry out 100% testing in a smaller organisation.

**Problems**

- **Management override** – Smaller entities will have a key director or manager who will have significant power and authority. This could mean that controls are lacking in the first place or they are easy to override.
- **No segregation of duties** – Smaller entities tend to have a limited number of accounts clerks who process information. To overcome this the directors should authorise and review all work performed.
- **Less formal approach** – Smaller entities tend to have simple systems and very few controls due to the trust and the lack of complexity. It is therefore difficult to test the reliability of systems and substantive testing tends to be used more.

**Not-for-profit organisations**

'Not for profit' ('NFP') organisations include charities and public sector entities. The most important differences from privately owned companies are that 'NFP' entities:

- do not have profit maximisation as their main objective. These will be either social or philanthropic;
- do not have external shareholders; and
- will not distribute dividends.

**Potential problems auditing a 'NFP' entity**

Some 'NFP' entities, particularly small charities, may have weaker systems due to:

- lack of segregation of duties, as the organisation will be restricted with the amount of staff;
- the use of volunteers, who are likely to be unqualified and have little awareness of the importance of controls;
- the use of less formalised systems and controls.

Significantly, with many charities, much of the income received is by way of donation. These transactions will not be accompanied by invoices, orders or despatch notes.

Assessing the going concern of a 'NFP' entity may also be more difficult, particularly for charities who are reliant on voluntary donations. Many issues, such as the state of the economy, could impact on their ability to generate revenue in the short term.

**Audit implications**

Auditors of not for profit organisations will be required to assess whether the aims of the organisation are being met in an economic, efficient and effective manner. For this reason "value for money" audits are much more appropriate. These are discussed in more detail in the internal audit chapter.

Testing tends to concentrate on substantive procedures where control systems are lacking. In the absence of documentary evidence procedures rely heavily on analytical review, enquiry and management representation.

The volumes of transactions in not for profit organisations may be lower than a private one, therefore auditors may be able to test a larger % of transactions.

Ultimately, if sufficient appropriate evidence is not available the auditor will have to modify their audit report.

## 11 Assurance engagements

A common engagement is a review of a company's cash forecast, in order to provide assurance over the reasonableness of the assumptions used.

The following procedures are typical of those that would be performed in the review of a cash forecast. They are generic procedures. In the exam, remember to tailor the procedures to the scenario.

Procedures in the examination of a cash forecast would include:

- Agree the opening balance of the cash forecast is in agreement with the closing balance of the cash book, to ensure the opening balance of the forecast is accurate.
- Consider how accurate company forecasts have been in the past by comparing past forecasts with actual outcomes. If forecasts have been reasonably accurate in the past, this would make it more likely that the current forecast is reliable.
- Determine the assumptions that have been made in the preparation of the cash flow forecast. For example, if the company is operating in a poor economic climate, you would not expect cash flows from sales and realisation of receivables to increase, but either to decrease or remain stable. If costs are rising you would expect cost increases to be reflected in the cash forecasts.
- Agree the timing of receipts from realisation of receivables and payments to suppliers with credit periods and previous trade receivables and payables payment periods.
- Examine the company's detailed budgets for the forecast period and discuss any specific plans with the directors.
- Examine the assessment of the non-current assets required to meet production needs. Agree cash out flows for non-current assets to supplier quotations.
- For acquisitions of buildings, agree the timing and amount of cash out flows to completion date and consideration in sale and purchase agreement.
- Consider the adequacy of the increased working capital and the working capital cash flows included in the forecast.
- If relevant review the post year end period to compare the actual performance against the forecast figures.
- Recalculate and cast the cash flow forecast balances.
- Review board minutes for any other relevant issues which should be included within the forecast.

**Test your understanding 1**

(a) **List and explain FOUR assertions from ISA 315 Identifying and Assessing the Risk of Material Misstatement Through Understanding the Entity and its Environment that relate to the recording of classes of transactions.**

*Real exam question: June 2009*

(b) **List FOUR assertions relevant to the audit of tangible non-current assets and state one audit procedure which provides appropriate evidence for each assertion.**

*Real exam question: December 2008*

**Test your understanding 2**

You are an audit senior working at a medium sized firm of auditors. One of your clients is an exclusive hotel called 'Numero Uno' situated in the centre of Big City.

'Numero Uno' prides itself on delivering a first class dining experience and is renowned for its standards of service and cooking that few restaurants in the country come close to. Its inventory therefore consists of the very best foods and beverages from across the globe.

Food products held in inventory are mostly fresh as the head chef will only work with the very best ingredients. 'Food' inventory is stored in the kitchens and managed by the head chef himself.

The majority of beverages held at the hotel are expensive wines that have been sourced from exclusive vineyards. The hotel also stocks a wide range of spirits and mixers. All beverages are stored either in the hotel cellar or behind the bar. The cellar can only be accessed by the duty manager who holds the key. As part of your audit procedures you will attend the year end inventory count of the hotel's beverages.

**Required:**

(a) **Describe the audit procedures an auditor would conduct before and whilst attending the inventory count of the beverages in the hotel.**

**(7 marks)**

(b) **Identify and explain THREE financial statement assertions that are most relevant to inventory.**

**(3 marks)**

(c) **Apart from attending the inventory count, describe the substantive procedures an auditor would carry out to confirm the valuation of the wine and spirits held in inventory at the year end.**

**(5 marks)**

**(Total: 15 marks)**

**Test your understanding 3**

(a) **Describe the steps an auditor should take when conducting a trade receivables confirmation (circularisation) test.**

**(4 marks)**

(b) **Explain why a direct confirmation test may not provide sufficient appropriate audit evidence on its own.**

**(3 marks)**

You are the audit manager in charge of the audit of Builders Mate, a limited liability company. The company's year end is 31 March, and Builders Mate has been an audit client for three years. Builders Mate sells small tools, plant and equipment exclusively to the building trade. They have 12 warehouse style shops located throughout the country. Builders Mate does not manufacture any products themselves.

The audit fieldwork is due to commence in 3 weeks time and you are preparing the audit work programme for the trade receivables section of the audit. Extracts from the clients trial balance show the following information.

| | $ |
|---|---|
| Trade receivables control account | 124,500 |
| General trade receivables provision | (2,490) |
| Specific trade receivables provision | 0 |

From your review of last year's audit file you have determined that last year there were 2 specific provisions of $5k and $2k as well as a 3% general provision.

Initial conversations with the client indicate that there are no specific provisions that are to be made this year however they intend to reduce the general provision from 3% to 2%.

You are aware that two of Builders Mate's major customers went into administration during the year and they are likely to be liquidated in the near future. Both of these customers owed material amounts at the year-end.

**Required:**

(c) **Describe substantive procedures the auditor should perform on the year-end trade receivables of Builders Mate.**

**(9 marks)**

(d) **Describe how audit software could facilitate the audit of trade receivables.**

**(4 marks)**

**(Total: 20 marks)**

**Test your understanding 4**

You are the external auditor of Tracey Transporters, a public limited company (TT). The company's year end is 31 March. You have been the auditor since the company was formed 24 years ago to take advantage of the increase in goods being transported by road. Many companies needed to transport their products but did not always have sufficient vehicles to move them. TT therefore purchased ten vehicles and hired these to haulage companies for amounts of time ranging from three days to six months.

The business has grown in size and profitability and now has over 550 vehicles on hire to many different companies. At any one time, between five and 20 vehicles are located at the company premises where they are being repaired; the rest could be anywhere on the extensive road network of the country it operates in. Full details of all vehicles are maintained in a non-current asset register.

Bookings for hire of vehicles are received either over the telephone or via e-mail in TT's offices. A booking clerk checks the customer's credit status on the receivables ledger and then the availability of vehicles using the Vehicle Management System (VMS) software on TT's computer network. E-mails are filed electronically by customer name in the e-mail program used by TT. If the customer's credit rating is acceptable and a vehicle is available, the booking is entered into the VMS and confirmed to the customer using the telephone or e-mail. Booking information is then transferred within the network from the VMS to the receivables ledger program, where a sales invoice is raised. Standard rental amounts are allocated to each booking depending on the amount of time the vehicle is being hired for. Hard copy invoices are sent in the post for telephone orders or via e-mail for e-mail orders.

The main class of asset on TT's statement of financial position is the vehicles. The net book value of the vehicles is $6 million out of total shareholders' funds of $15 million as at 31 March 20X5.

**Required:**

(a) **List and explain the reason for the audit tests you should perform to check the completeness and accuracy of the sales figure in TT's financial statements.**

**(10 marks)**

(b) **List and describe the audit work you should perform on the statement of financial position figure for vehicles in TT's financial statements for the year ended 31 March 20X5.**

**(10 marks)**

**(Total: 20 marks)**

**Test your understanding 5**

You are the auditor of BearsWorld, a limited liability company which manufactures and sells small cuddly toys by mail order. The company is managed by Mr Kyto and two assistants. Mr Kyto authorises important transactions such as wages and large orders, one assistant maintains the payables ledger and orders inventory and pays suppliers, and the other assistant receives customer orders and despatches cuddly toys. Due to other business commitments Mr Kyto only visits the office once per week.

At any time, about 100 different types of cuddly toys are available for sale. All sales are made cash with order – there are no receivables. Customers pay using credit cards and occasionally by sending cash. Turnover is over $5.2 million.

You are planning the audit of BearsWorld and are considering using some of the procedures for gathering audit evidence recommended by ISA 500 as follows:

(i) Analytical Procedures

(ii) Inquiry

(iii) Inspection

(iv) Observation

(v) Re-calculation

**Required:**

(a) **For EACH of the above procedures:**

(i) **Explain its use in gathering audit evidence.**

**(5 marks)**

(ii) **Describe one example for the audit of BearsWorld.**

**(5 marks)**

(b) **Discuss the suitability of each procedure for BearsWorld, explaining the limitations of each.**

**(10 marks)**

(c) **Tabulate FIVE key features of small companies such as BearsWorld and the impact these may have on your audit work.**

**(10 marks)**

**(Total: 30 marks)**

## 12 Chapter summary

AUDIT PROCEDURES

- RECEIVABLES
- INVENTORIES
- LIABILITIES
- BANK AND CASH
- NON-CURRENT ASSETS
- SHARE CAPITAL, RESERVES & EMOLUMENTS
- AUDITING ESTIMATES
- ASSURANCE ENGAGEMENT
- SMALL ENTITIES
- NOT-FOR-PROFIT ORGANISATIONS

## Test your understanding answers

### Test your understanding 1

(a) **Assertions: classes of transactions**

- **Occurrence:** The transactions and events that have been recorded have actually occurred and pertain to the entity.
- **Completeness:** All transactions and events that should have been recorded have been recorded.
- **Accuracy:** The amounts and other data relating to recorded transactions and events have been recorded appropriately.
- **Cut-off.** Transactions and events have been recorded in the correct accounting period.
  Classification. Transactions and events have been recorded in the proper accounts.

(b) **Tangible non-current assets: assertions**

- Completeness: ensure that all non-current assets are recorded in the non-current asset register by agreeing a sample of assets physically verified back to the register.
- Existence: ensure non-current assets exist by taking a sample of assets from the register and physically seeing the asset.
- Valuation and allocation: ensure assets are correctly valued by checking the reasonableness of depreciation calculations.
- Rights and obligations: ensure the company owns the asset by seeing appropriate document of ownership for example, a purchase invoice.
- Presentation and disclosure assertions: ensure all necessary financial statements disclosures have been made by reviewing the financial statements.

**Note:** Only four assertions were required.

**Test your understanding 2**

(a) **Procedures before the count**

- Review prior year working papers to understand the inventory count process and identify any issues that would need to be taken into account this year.
- Contact Numero Uno (client) to obtain stocktaking instructions for this year to understand how the count will be conducted and assess the effectiveness of the count process.
- Book audit staff to attend the inventory count.
- Ascertain whether any inventory is held by third parties and if applicable determine how to gather sufficient audit evidence.
- Consider the need for using an expert to assist in valuing the inventory being counted. There may be some speciality wines and spirits that require expert valuation.

**During the count**

- Observe the count to ensure that the instructions are being followed.
- Inspect the bottles being counted for evidence of damage or obsolescence that may affect the net realisable value and hence overall valuation of inventory.
- Perform a test count. Select a sample of beverages from the inventory count sheets and physically observe the items in the cellar or bar to confirm they exist.
- Perform a test count. Select a sample of physical beverages from the cellar or bar and trace to the inventory count sheets to ensure that they are recorded accurately and therefore that the records are complete.
- Record cut off information by obtaining details of the last deliveries prior to the year end. This information will be used in final audit procedures to ensure that no further amendments have been made thereby overstating or understating inventory.

(b) **Inventory assertions**

| **Identify** | **Explain** |
|---|---|
| Existence | To confirm whether the inventory recorded actually exists. |
| Rights and obligations | To confirm whether the company has the rights of ownership to record the inventories in its financial statements. |
| Completeness | To confirm if all inventory balances have been recorded. |
| Valuation and allocation | To assess whether all inventories are valued appropriately (i.e. at the lower of cost and net realisable value and net of any provisions for damaged and slow moving goods). |
| Cut-off | To ensure that all inventory movements around the year-end are recorded in the correct period. |

(c) **Substantive procedures**

- Trace the items counted during the inventory count to the final inventory list to ensure it is the same as the one used at the year-end and to ensure that any errors identified during counting procedures have been rectified.
- Inspect purchases invoices for a sample of beverages to agree their cost, ensuring that the description of goods on the invoice matches the beverage.
- For beverages sold to customers after the year end, inspect a sample of restaurant bills/invoices back to the final inventory records ensuring that the sales value exceeds the cost. Where sales value is less than cost, ensure that the beverage is stated at the realisable value.
- For high value items such as Champagne, vintage wine and exotic spirits use an expert valuer to review the net realisable value of a sample of items to ensure the value is reasonable.
- Inventory noted during the count as possibly obsolete or damaged should be traced to the inventory records to ensure the valuation has been adjusted to take this into account. The expert valuer may provide assistance with these valuations.

**Test your understanding 3**

(a) **Trade receivables circularisation**

Several steps should be performed by an auditor when performing a trade receivables circularisation audit test:

- Audit client approval should be obtained in advance to perform the direct confirmation test of trade receivables.
- Obtain a list of receivables balances, and cast it.
- Select a suitable sample from the list of receivables balances using an appropriate sampling technique.
- The confirmation letter should be designed and prepared for each receivable ensuring the contact details are correct and return details clearly state that the reply should be made direct to the auditor.
- A business reply envelope, addressed to the auditor, could be included for this purpose.
- The letter should be printed on client-headed paper and signed by the client, and then passed to the auditor.
- The sending of letters, including any follow-up requests, should be controlled and performed by the auditor to ensure the integrity of the test.
- Replies should be matched or reconciled to the audit client's receivables accounting records.
- Alternative audit procedures will be required for all non-responses to the confirmation letter.

(b) **Sufficiency of the evidence from a direct confirmation test.**

Several factors influence the sufficiency of evidence gathered during a direct confirmation of trade receivables and other evidence may be required by an auditor to form an opinion in this area:

- There is often a low response rate from trade receivables meaning that other audit procedures will be required for these balances.
- The type of confirmation letter, whether a positive or negative confirmation request, will influence the sufficiency of evidence gathered. Negative confirmations provide less persuasive audit evidence than positive confirmations and it is unlikely that a negative confirmation will provide sufficient evidence on its own.
- The reliability of the responses to the confirmation requests may be in doubt for example if there is a risk of fraud being perpetrated.

- Mistakes and errors may be present in the accounting records of the trade receivables confirming the balance outstanding.
- Customers may agree with balances containing errors in their favour.

(c) **Substantive procedures for trade receivables.**

- Trace and agree the receivables balances on the trial balance to Builders Mate's accounting system and the draft financial statements.
- Confirm the trade receivables control account balance matches the sum of the individual trade receivables ledger accounts.
- For a sample goods dispatched notes around the year-end trace to the sales invoice and ledger accounts to ensure that the transactions have been recorded in the correct accounting period.
- Cast a sample of trade receivable ledger accounts to confirm arithmetical accuracy.
- Select a sample of individual trade receivables and perform a direct confirmation test using a positive confirmation letter.
- For non-responses to the direct confirmation test confirm cash has been received post year-end for the outstanding amounts.
- Cash receipts recorded in the trade receivables ledger account should be traced and agreed to their remittance advice as well as the cash book and bank statements.
- Recalculate the general provision based on the 2% figure to ensure arithmetical accuracy.
- Discuss with the Builders Mate management why the general provision has reduced from 3% to 2% and assess the reasonableness of the explanations provided.
- Obtain or prepare an aged receivables analysis to identify aged debts that may require a specific provision. Discuss with management any such balances and ensure specific provisions are made if appropriate.
- Trace and confirm that the specific provisions made in the prior year were either written off or the cash was recovered in the current accounting period.
- Discuss with management the reason for not making specific provisions for the two customers in administration who owe material amounts at the year-end.

- Consider and discuss with management the potential implications of failing to make specific provisions on the audit opinion.
- Compare a sample of individual trade receivables to their prior year balance and investigate any unusual or unexpected changes between the balances.

(d) **Audit software**

Audit software can be used to improve the effectiveness and efficiency of the audit process of trade receivables.

- Audit software can be used to prepare an aged receivables analysis and to identify potential irrecoverable debts using a range of criteria set by the auditor.
- It can analyse the receivables ledger for credit balances or negative balances.
- Audit software will be more efficient and accurate at casting and recalculating figures, totals and balances such as the general provision or casting of the receivables ledgers.
- It could also select a sample for testing and prepare direct confirmation letters.

**Test your understanding 4**

(a)

| Audit test | Reason for test |
|---|---|
| Discuss with booking clerk how orders are recorded from the customer. | The main problem with the sales system in TT is the lack of evidence for the receipt of the telephone order. Checks are therefore required to ensure that orders are completely and accurately recorded in the Vehicle Management System (VMS) where no input document is available. |
| Discuss with the directors the recruitment and training of booking clerks. | To check on the personnel controls in TT which will be designed to minimise loss of customer orders.<br><br>To ensure that staff have appropriate skill and training to operate the ordering system without losing customer orders. |
| With client's permission, attempt to enter orders into the VMS from an input terminal. | To confirm the completeness and accuracy of recording of orders by the computer system. |
| For a sample of confirmed e-mail orders held in the e-mail program, trace details onto the VMS ensuring that details of vehicle hire regarding time and dates are accurately recorded. | To check for accuracy of transfer of information from the e-mail to the VMS.<br><br>The method of filing of the e-mails means that completeness of e-mail orders cannot easily be determined. Audit software may be able to re-sort the orders. |
| Review hard copy customer complaint files and e-mail files on computer for evidence of unfilled orders. | To check for evidence of orders being sent by customers but not entered into TT's sales system. |
| For a sample of bookings in the VMS, trace details to the list of sales invoices raised maintained in the receivables ledger program. | To check for completeness of transfer of information between the two programs. The test can be carried out manually or using test data. Manual testing may be difficult where there is no obvious audit trail between the two systems. |

| | |
|---|---|
| For a sample of sales invoices in the VMS, agree the rental amount being charged to standard charges held in the receivables ledger file. | To check for accuracy of charging for each individual vehicle hire.<br><br>Evidence of undercharging would indicate that sales are understated. |
| Cast the list of invoices in the receivables ledger program for one month. Trace total sales to the general ledger program. | To ensure that the total sales for that month are accurate. Transfer of data to the nominal ledger ensures that the total sales amount is recorded correctly in the ledger. |
| Cast the monthly sales figures in the general ledger and agree to the financial statements. Investigate any discrepancies. | The final cast and checking ensures that the financial accounts figure is accurate.<br><br>Casting tests can be carried out manually or using computer audit software |

(b) Audit work on vehicles

- Obtain non-current asset register from client. Cast the cost, depreciation and net book value columns of the register and agree to the financial statements of TT.

For a sample of new additions in the non-current asset register:

- Agree to board minute or similar documentation for evidence of authority to purchase vehicle. (Occurrence assertion).
- Agree to the physical asset to confirm existence of the vehicle. Where the vehicle is on hire during the audit visit, obtain alternative evidence of existence such as payment from customer near year-end for hire. (Existence assertion).
- Check the physical condition of the vehicle to ensure that repairs and renewal expenditure is not being understated. (Existence of repair expenditure).
- Agree details to purchase invoice or similar document for evidence of ownership. (Ownership assertion).
- Test the calculation of depreciation in the non-current asset register, ensuring that the rates used are those disclosed in the financial statements. (Valuation and accuracy assertion).

For a sample of disposals during the year (for occurrence assertion).

- Review profits and losses generated on sale of vehicles and ensure these are not excessive. If they are check the accuracy of the depreciation rates used as this may indicate over or under charge of depreciation. (Valuation and accuracy assertion).
- Compare sales income to sale of similar vehicles with similar mileage and ensure comparable.
- Ensure asset has been removed from the non-current asset register.
- Check calculation of profit or loss on sale.
- Agree receipt on sale to the cash book.

For a sample of vehicles purchased during the year, agree details to purchase invoice and Purchase Day Book (PDB) ensuring details recorded in the correct year (Occurrence assertion).

For a sample of vehicle purchases in the PDB, agree details to the non-current asset register (Completeness assertion).

Agree totals in non-current asset register to the financial statements, ensuring vehicles are disclosed separately in the non-current assets note (material item). (Classification and understandability assertion).

Ensure that the accounting policy for depreciation is clearly stated in the financial statements and is the same as last year. (Classification and understandability assertion).

**Test your understanding 5**

(a) Audit procedures

(i) *Analytical procedures* consist of evaluations of financial information made by a study of plausible relationships among both financial and non-financial data.

*Inquiry* means to seek relevant information from sources, both financial and non-financial, either inside or outside the company being audited. Evidence may be obtained orally or in writing.

*Inspection* is the physical review or examination of records, documents and tangible assets. It may include examination of records for evidence of controls in the form of a compliance test.

*Observation* involves looking at a process or procedure as it is being performed to ensure that the process actually works as documented.

*Re-calculation* means the checking of the mathematical accuracy of documents or records.

(ii) *Analytical procedures*

Review of sales income year on year to try to identify whether income has been understated, possibly by cash being taken prior to banking. There is no control over the opening of post so cash could be withdrawn by one assistant, and the deficit made up by a fraud on customers.

*Inquiry*

Obtain statements from suppliers to check the completeness of liabilities at the end of the year. As there is no control over purchases, invoices could have been misplaced resulting in a lower purchases and trade payables figure.

*Inspection*

The assets of the company, namely cuddly toys in inventory at the end of the year, can be inspected to ensure all inventory is recorded and that the toys are saleable in their current condition.

*Observation*

Procedures such as the opening of the post and recording of customer orders can be observed to ensure that the administrator is recording all orders in the sales day book and cash book.

*Re-calculation*

Checking additions in the cash book to confirm that the total amount of cash recorded is accurate and can be included in the sales figure (cash receipts normally equal sales because there are no receivables).

(b) *Analytical procedures*

This method of collecting evidence will be useful in BearsWorld because it will help to identify unusual changes in income and expenditure. As BearsWorld is a relatively small company, monitoring gross profit will show relatively small changes in sales margin or purchasing costs. Decisions by Mr Kyto to amend margins can therefore be traced into the actual sales made.

However, the technique may be limited in its application because it will not detect errors or omissions made consistently year on year. If either assistant is defrauding the company (for example by removing cash) each year, then analytical procedures will not detect this.

*Enquiry*

Enquiry evidence will be very useful in the audit of BearsWorld, especially where this is derived from third parties. Third party evidence is generally more reliable than client originated evidence as there is a decreased likelihood of bias. Trade payables can therefore be verified using supplier statement reconciliations. A review of any customer complaints file (if these letters are kept) will also help to identify any orders that have not been despatched.

External inquiry evidence will be less useful in the audit of sales and receivables because goods are paid for prior to despatch – there are no receivables. Internal evidence will be available from Mr Kyto and the assistant; however the lack of segregation of duties means that this will not be so reliable.

*Inspection*

Inspection of documents within BearsWorld will be useful, particularly regarding checking whether expenses are bona fide. All purchase invoices, for example, should be addressed to BearsWorld and relate to purchases expected from that company, e.g. cuddly toys for resale, office expenses, etc.

Inspection of documents can take a long time; however, given the poor internal control system within BearsWorld, the auditor may have no choice but to use this method of gathering evidence.

The fact that an invoice is addressed to the company does not confirm completeness of recording so inspection of the cash book for unusual payments verified by checking the purchase invoice will also be required. Additional substantive testing would also be required due to poor controls.

*Observation*

Observation may be useful because it will show how the assistants check documents. However, no information is provided on any internal controls within BearsWorld so simply viewing how documents are checked without any evidence of checking has limited benefit.

Observation tests will be of limited usefulness because the assistants may act differently when an auditor is present. The same problem will apply to any observation checking carried out by Mr Kyto.

*Re-calculation*

Re-calculation evidence is very useful for checking additions on invoices, balancing of control accounts, etc. This means that the arithmetical accuracy of the books and records in BearsWorld can be confirmed.

The main weakness of re-calculation checking is that calculations can only be carried out on figures that have been recorded. If there are any omissions then checks cannot be carried out.

(c) **Features of small companies**

| Feature | Effect on audit |
|---|---|
| Concentration of ownership and management in one/few people. | There is likely to be more supervision, since the owner will want to protect his investment. But there is an increased risk of fraud by the owner as he may not distinguish between personal/business assets. |
| Less complicated business activities. | Easier for auditor to gain an understanding of the business and assess risk. |
| Less sophisticated accounting systems. | Auditor unlikely to use CAATs. |
| Limited internal controls as less segregation of duties and management can override. | Unlikely to reply on controls. Likely to perform extensive substantive testing. |
| Unlikely to have a qualified accountant. | Audit firm is likely to prepare the financial statements prior to the audit. This means they should be prepared with due care, but the auditor must be careful to check just as thoroughly as if the accounts had been prepared by someone else. |

chapter

# 9

# Completion and review

## Chapter learning objectives

When you have completed this chapter you will be able to:

- Explain the purpose of, auditor's responsibilities regarding, and procedures involved in a subsequent events review.
- Explain the responsibilities of auditors and management regarding going concern, and the procedures to be applied in performing going concern reviews.
- Discuss the purpose of, quality of and procedure for obtaining written representations.
- Explain the significance of uncorrected misstatements, and describe auditor's procedures in the overall review of the financial statements.
- Explain the auditor's responsibilities in relation to opening balances and comparative information.

## 1 Introduction

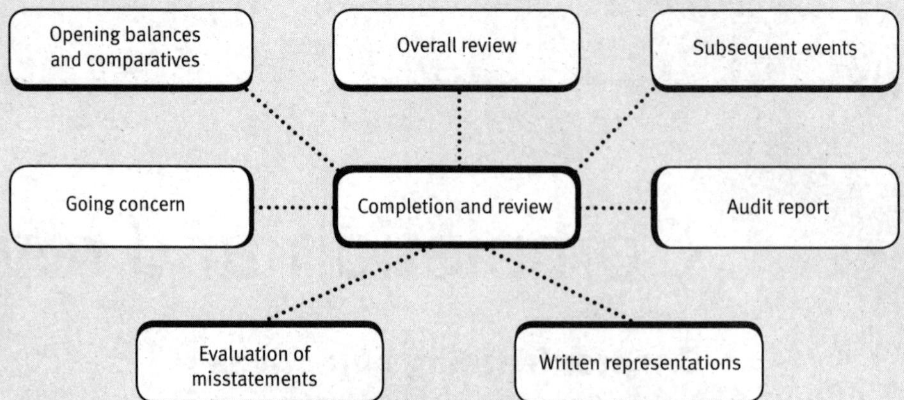


After the auditor has completed their substantive testing there are still many procedures that need to be performed before they can sign the audit report. These include:

- the consideration of opening balances and comparatives
- a subsequent events review
- a going concern review
- obtaining written representations
- consideration of misstatements
- the audit file review.

**Opening balances**

ISA 510 *Initial Engagements – Opening Balances* requires that when auditors take on a new client, they must ensure that:

- opening balances do not contain material misstatements
- prior period closing balances have been correctly brought forward or, where appropriate, restated
- appropriate accounting policies have been consistently applied, or changes adequately disclosed.

Considerations:

- Were the previous financial statements audited?
- If the previous financial statements were audited, was the opinion modified?
- If the previous opinion was modified, has the matter been resolved since then?

- Were any adjustments made as a result of the audit? If so, has the client adjusted their accounting ledgers as well as the financial statements?

If auditors are unable to satisfy themselves with regard to the preceding period, they will have to consider modifying the current audit report.

**Audit procedures**

Where the prior period was audited by another auditor or unaudited, the auditors will need to perform additional work in order to satisfy themselves regarding the opening position. Such work would include:

- Consulting the client's management.
- Reviewing records and accounting and control procedures in the preceding period.
- Consulting with the previous auditor and reviewing (with their permission) their working papers and relevant representation letters.
- Substantive testing of any opening balances where the above procedures are unsatisfactory.

Some evidence of the opening position will also usually be gained from the audit work performed in the current period.

**Comparatives**

ISA 710 *Comparative Information – Corresponding Figures and Comparative Financial Statements* requires that comparative figures comply with the identified financial reporting framework and that they are free from material misstatement.

The IASB's Framework for the Preparation and Presentation of Financial Statements and IAS 1 Presentation of Financial Statements both require that financial statements show comparatives.

Two categories of comparatives exist:

- corresponding figures where preceding period figures are included as an integral part of the current period financial statements; and
- comparative financial statements where preceding period amounts are included for comparison with the current period.

**Corresponding figures**

Audit procedures in respect of corresponding figures should be significantly less than for the current period and are limited to ensuring that corresponding figures have been correctly reported and appropriately classified. This involves evaluating whether:

- accounting policies are consistently applied; and
- corresponding figures agree to the prior period financial statements.

**Comparative financial statements**

Sufficient appropriate evidence should be gathered to ensure that comparative financial statements meet the requirements of an applicable financial reporting framework. This involves evaluating whether:

- accounting policies are consistently applied; and
- comparative figures agree to the prior period financial statements.

## 2 Subsequent events review

**Subsequent events**

**Definition:** Subsequent events are events occurring between the date of the financial statements and the date of the auditor's report, and facts that become known to the auditor after the date of the auditor's report

**Auditors responsibility**

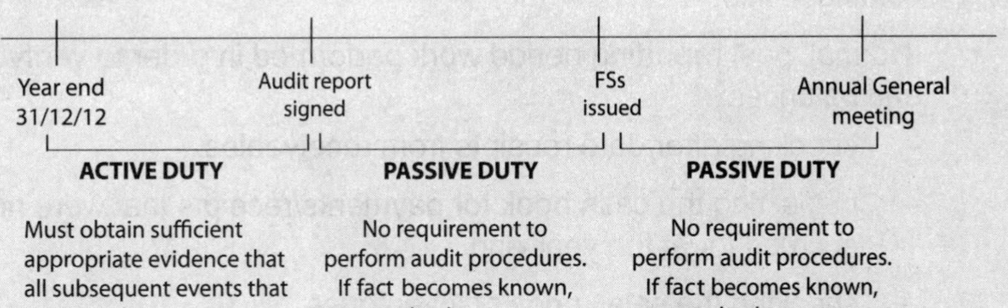


Must obtain sufficient appropriate evidence that all subsequent events that require adjustment or disclosure have been identified.

No requirement to perform audit procedures. If fact becomes known, must take the necessary action.

No requirement to perform audit procedures. If fact becomes known, must take the necessary action.

**ACTIONS**

- ✓ Discuss with management
- ✓ Review the financial statements to ensure revised
- ✓ If client refuses
  - seek legal advice and
  - speak at Annual General Meeting or
  - resign if more expeditious
- ✓ Extend subsequent events testing to date of new audit report and provide new audit report on amended financial statements (note if FSs already issued, they will need to be recalled)

ISA 560 *Subsequent Events* details the responsibilities of the auditors with respect to subsequent events and suggests audit procedures to perform.

### Audit procedures

The nature of procedures performed in a subsequent events review depends on many variables, such as the nature of transactions and events and the availability of data and reports. However, the following procedures are typical:

- Enquiring of directors if they are aware of any subsequent events that require adjustment in the financial statements.
- Enquiring into management's procedures/systems for the identification of subsequent events.
- Inspection of minutes of members' and directors' meetings.
- Reviewing accounting records including budgets, forecasts and interim information.

- Obtaining, from management, a letter of representation that all subsequent events have been considered in the preparation of the financial statements.
- Inspection of correspondence with legal advisors.
- Enquiring of the progress with regards to reported provisions and contingencies.
- 'Normal' post reporting period work performed in order to verify year-end balances:
  - checking after date receipts from receivables
  - inspecting the cash book for payments/receipts that were not accrued for at the year-end
  - checking the sales price of inventories.

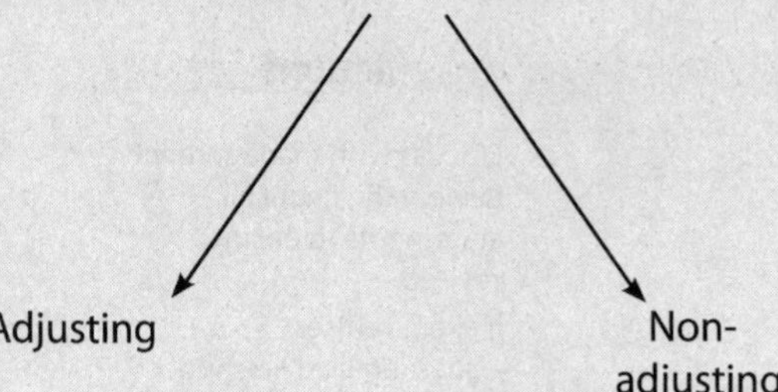
There are two types of subsequent events
Adjusting
Non-adjusting

- **Adjusting** – events providing additional evidence relating to conditions existing at the reporting date they require **adjustment** in the financial statements.

- **Non-adjusting** – events concerning conditions which arose after the reporting date, but which may be of such materiality that **disclosure** is required to ensure that the financial statements are not misleading.

**Examples**

✓ Trade receivables going bad
✓ Credit notes relating to sales made before the reporting date
✓ Inventory at the year end sold lower than cost

**Examples**

✓ Take over
✓ Legal issues after the year end
✓ A fire after the year end

**Illustration 1: Murray Co subsequent events review**

**Murray Co subsequent events review for the year ended 31 December 2012**

(1) On 2 January 2013, Golf is Us, a major customer of Murray Co, was placed into administration owing $211,000.

(2) On 3 January 2013, the sales director left the company. The sales director is suing Murray Co for constructive dismissal. If successful, the claim amounts to $280,000.

(3) On 5 Febuary 2013 there was a fire at the premises of the third party warehouse provider, which destroyed all inventory held there. Approximately one quarter of Murray Co's inventory was stored in these premises. The total value of inventory stored at the premises was $1,054,000.

(4) The financial statements include a $40,000 provision for an unfair dismissal case brought by an ex-employee of Murray Co. On 7 February 2013 a letter was received from the claimant's solicitors stating that they would be willing to settle out-of-court for $25,000. It is likely the company will agree to this.

$000

| **Financial Statement Extracts** | 31 December 2012 | 31 December 2011 |
|---|---|---|
| Revenue | 21,960 | 19,580 |
| Total assets | 9,697 | 7,288 |
| Profit before tax | 1,048 | 248 |

**Exercise:**

**For each of the events above:**

**Discuss whether the financial statements require amendment.**

**Solution: Subsequent events review**

To determine whether or not the financial statements should be adjusted in respect of each of the events described, IAS 10 *Events After the Reporting Period* needs to be applied. If the event provides evidence of conditions that existed at the reporting date (an adjusting event), then an adjustment should be made. If the event provides evidence of conditions that arose after the reporting date (a non-adjusting event), no adjustment is required but a disclosure may be necessary if the event is material and non-disclosure would render the financial statements misleading.

The auditor will only compel the directors' to amend the financial statements for adjusting events if the adjustment is material. When assessing materiality in the exam, it is sufficient to calculate materiality in relation to each measure individually, using the lower end of the thresholds for prudence. If the item is material to one or more of the measures then it requires adjustment.

(1) Gold is Us was placed into administration after the year-end, which provides evidence of the recoverability of the receivables balance at the year end. Therefore this is an **adjusting event**. The total value of the balance is $211,000 which is 1% of revenue, 2% of total assets and 26% of profit, and is therefore **material**. The receivables balance should be written-off or an allowance for receivables created.

(2) The sales director left the company after the year-end and is suing for constructive dismissal, which is an event that arose after the reporting date. Therefore this is a **non-adjusting event**. The total value of the claim is $50,000, which is less than 0.5% of revenue, less than 1% of assets and 5% of profit before tax and is therefore not material by size. However, as this is a director's transaction, it is **material by nature** and the nature of the event and any estimates of the financial impact should therefore be **disclosed**.

(3) A fire destroyed inventory after the year-end, which is therefore a **non-adjusting event** (as the inventory was not damaged at the year-end). The total value of inventory stored at the premises is $1,054,000, which is 5% of revenue, 11% of total assets and 101% of profit and is therefore **material** and the nature of the event and any estimates of the financial impact should be **disclosed**.

(4) After the year-end a letter was received offering to settle a claim for unfair dismissal out-of-court. This is an event that provides evidence of the valuation of the provision at the year-end and is therefore an **adjusting event**. The current provision is for $40,000 and the adjustment would therefore be $15,000. This is **not material** (being less than 0.5% revenue, 1% total assets and less than 5% profit before tax) and therefore **no adjustment** is necessary.

## 3 Going concern

ASSUMING THAT:
An enterprise will continue in operational existence for the foreseeable future
THEN
PREPARE FINANCIAL STATEMENTS ON A GOING CONCERN BASIS

### The going concern concept

According to IAS1 financial statements should be prepared on the basis that the company is a going concern unless it is inappropriate to do so.

**Going concern** is defined in IAS1 as the assumption that the enterprise will continue in operational existence for the foreseeable future.

The period that management (and therefore the auditor) is required to consider is the period required by the applicable financial reporting framework or by law or regulation if longer. Generally the period is a minimum of twelve months from the year-end; in some jurisdictions (e.g. the United Kingdom) the period is a minimum of twelve months from the date the financial statements are approved.

- Consideration of the 'foreseeable future' involves making a judgement about future events, which are inherently uncertain.
- Uncertainty increases with time and judgements can only be made on the basis of information available at any point – subsequent events can overturn that judgement.
- There may be circumstances in which it is appropriate to look further ahead. This depends on the nature of the business and their associated risks.

**UK syllabus focus**

ISA 570 (UK & Ireland) *Going Concern* requires management to assess going concern for a period of at least one year from the (expected) date of approval of the financial statements (rather than 12 months from the reporting date).

## The going concern concept – significance

Whether or not a company can be classed as a going concern affects how its financial statements are prepared.

- Financial statements are prepared on the basis that the reporting entity is a going concern.
- IAS1 states that 'an entity should prepare its financial statements on a going concern basis, unless
  - management intends to liquidate the entity or to cease trading or
  - the directors have no realistic alternative but to do so.'
- Where the assumption is made that the company will cease trading, the financial statements are prepared using the **break-up basis** under which:
  - the basis of preparation and the reason why the entity is not regarded as a going concern are disclosed
  - assets are recorded at likely sale values
  - inventory and receivables are likely to require more provisions
  - additional liabilities may arise (severance costs for staff, the costs of closing down facilities, etc.).

**Going concern responsibilities**

Both directors and auditors of an entity have responsibilities regarding going concern.

**Directors**

- It is the directors' responsibility to assess the company's ability to continue as a going concern when they are preparing the financial statements.
- If they are aware of any material uncertainties which may affect this assessment, then IAS 1 requires them to disclose such uncertainties in the financial statements.
- When the directors are performing their assessment they should take into account a number of relevant factors such as:
  - current and expected profitability
  - debt repayment
  - sources (and potential sources) of financing.

**Auditors**

- ISA 570 Going Concern states that the auditor needs to consider the appropriateness of management's use of the going concern assumption.
- The auditors need to assess the risk that the company may not be a going concern.
- The auditor will also need to obtain sufficient appropriate evidence that the company is a going concern.
- The auditor must conclude whether there are any material uncertainties regarding going concern.
- Where there are material uncertainties, the auditor must ensure that the directors have made sufficient disclosure of such matters in the notes to the financial statements.

## Audit procedures

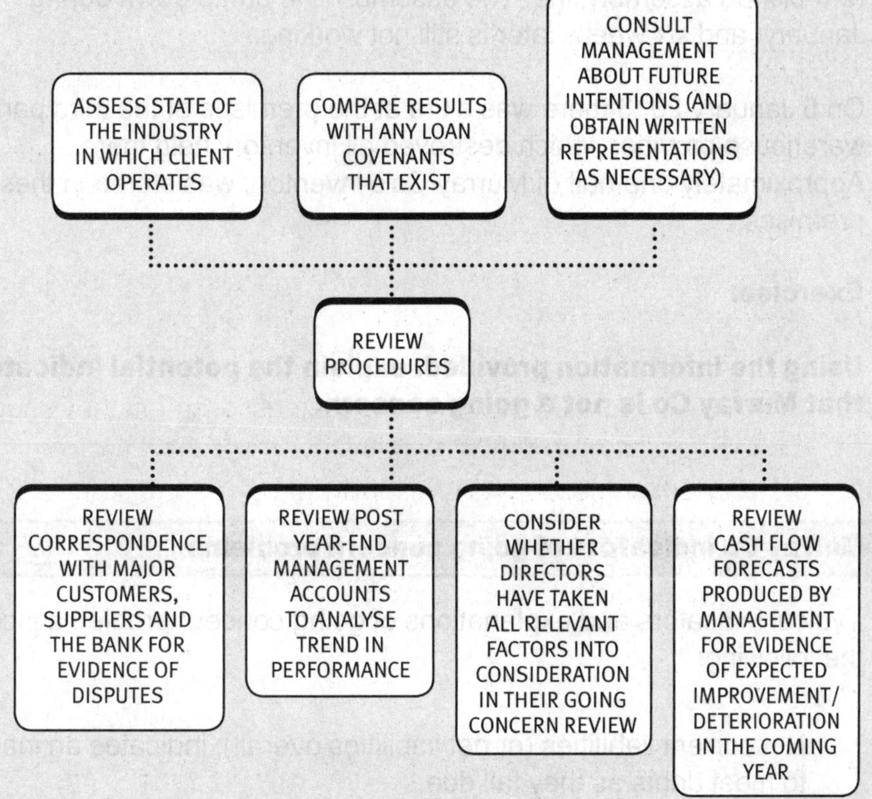

### Murray Co going concern review

**Murray Co going concern review for the year ended 31 December 2012**

On 2 January 2013, Golf is Us, a major customer of Murray Co, was placed into administration owing $211,000. On 3 January 2013, the sales director left the company and has yet to be replaced. The sales director is suing Murray Co for constructive dismissal.

The company is seeking new funding through an initial public offering of shares in the company (i.e. listing on the stock exchange). In the event that the initial public offering does not proceed, this will require Murray Co's existing banking arrangements to be renegotiated and additional funding to be raised from either existing or new investors.

The financial statements of Murray Co show an overdraft at 31 December 2012 of $180,000 (2011: $120,000). The overdraft limit is $250,000. The cash flow forecast shows negative monthly cash flows for the next twelve months. As a result of cash shortages in February 2013, a number of suppliers were paid late.

The assembly line for ergometers (rowing machines) was refurbished during the year at a cost of $1m. The additional $1.5m loan facility provided to Murray Co during the year is secured, in part, on the refurbished assembly line. The assembly line broke down during January, and six weeks later is still not working.

On 5 January 2013 there was a fire at the premises of the third party warehouse provider, which destroyed all inventory held there. Approximately one half of Murray Co's inventory was stored in these premises.

**Exercise:**

**Using the information provided, explain the potential indicators that Murray Co is not a going concern.**

**Murray Co indicators of going concern problems**

Typical indicators and explanations of going concern problems include the following:

- Net current liabilities (or net liabilities overall); indicates an inability to meet debts as they fall due.
- Borrowing facilities not agreed or close to expiry of current agreement; lack of access to cash may make it difficult for a company to manage its operating cycle.
- Defaulted loan agreements; loans normally become repayable on default, company may find it difficult to repay loan.
- Unplanned sales of non-current assets; indicates an inability to generate cash from other means and as non-current assets generate income, will cause a decline in income and therefore profits.
- Missing tax payments; results in fines and penalties, companies normally prioritise tax payments indicating a lack of working capital.
- Failure to pay staff; indicates a significant lack of working capital.
- Negative cash flow; indicates overtrading.
- Inability to obtain credit from suppliers; suggests failure to pay suppliers on time and working capital problems.
- Major technology changes; inability or insufficient funds to keep up with changes in technology will result in loss of custom and obsolescence of inventory.
- Legal claims; successful legal claims may result in significant cash payments that can only be settled with liquidation.
- Loss of key staff; may result inability to trade.

- Over-reliance on a small number of products, staff , suppliers or customers; loss may result in inability to trade.

The following table explains the potential going concern indicators at Murray Co:

| **Indicator** | **Explanation** |
|---|---|
| A major customer has been put into administration | Unless the customer can be replaced, this will result in significant loss of future revenues and profit. |
| The sales director left the company and has yet to be replaced. | Loss of a key director will impact on the company's sales. As Murray Co has already lost a major customer, without an experienced sales director to generate new sales the company will face significantly reduced sales and cash flows. |
| The sales director is suing Murray Co for constructive dismissal. | Murray Co will need to pay expensive legal costs in order to defend this litigation, pressurising cash flows further. In addition, this may damage their reputation and make it difficult to recruit a suitable replacement or other key staff. |
| Murray Co is seeking new funding through an initial public offering of shares in the company. | If Murray Co does obtain new funding through listing, alternative finance will need to be obtained in order to continue to operate. |
| Murray Co is operating close to it's overdraft limit. | Murray Co is heavily dependent on a short-term source of finance, that is repayable on demand. It may be difficult to obtain further sources of finance if the overdraft reaches it limit. |
| The cash flow forecast shows negative monthly cash flows for the next twelve months. | If the company continues to have cash outflows then the overdraft will increase further and there may be no cash available to pay debts as they fall due. |
| A number of suppliers have been paid late. | If suppliers are paid late they may refuse to supply Murray Co with goods/components or impose 'cash on delivery' terms which will disrupt production, and delay sales to customers. |
| The loan facility is secured, in part, on the refurbished assembly line which has broken down. | The bank may withdraw the loan facility if the asset on which it is secured is significantly impaired. Murray Co do not have sufficient cash to repay the loan. Unless Murray Co can negotiate with the bank or raise alternative finance (or sell non-current assets), they will have no realistic alternative but to liquidate. |

| The assembly line broke down during January, and six weeks later is still not working. | If Murray Co cannot meet customer orders due to manufacturing problems, refunds may have to be given, customer goodwill may be lost along with future revenue, which will put further pressure on cash flows. |
|---|---|
| A fire at the premises of the third party warehouse provider, destroyed approximately one half of Murray Co's inventory. | If Murray Co cannot meet customer orders due to this lost revenue, refunds may have to be given, customer goodwill may be lost along with future revenue, which will put further pressure on cash flows. If the losses are not covered by insurance, this will significantly impact profit. |

**Disclosures**

Where there is any significant doubt over the future of a company, the directors should include disclosures in the financial statements explaining:

- the nature of and circumstances surrounding the doubts
- the possible effect on the company.

Where the directors have been unable to assess going concern in the usual way (e.g. for less than one year beyond the date on which they sign the financial statements), this fact should be disclosed.

Where the financial statements are prepared on a basis other than the going concern basis, the basis used should be disclosed.

## Reporting implications

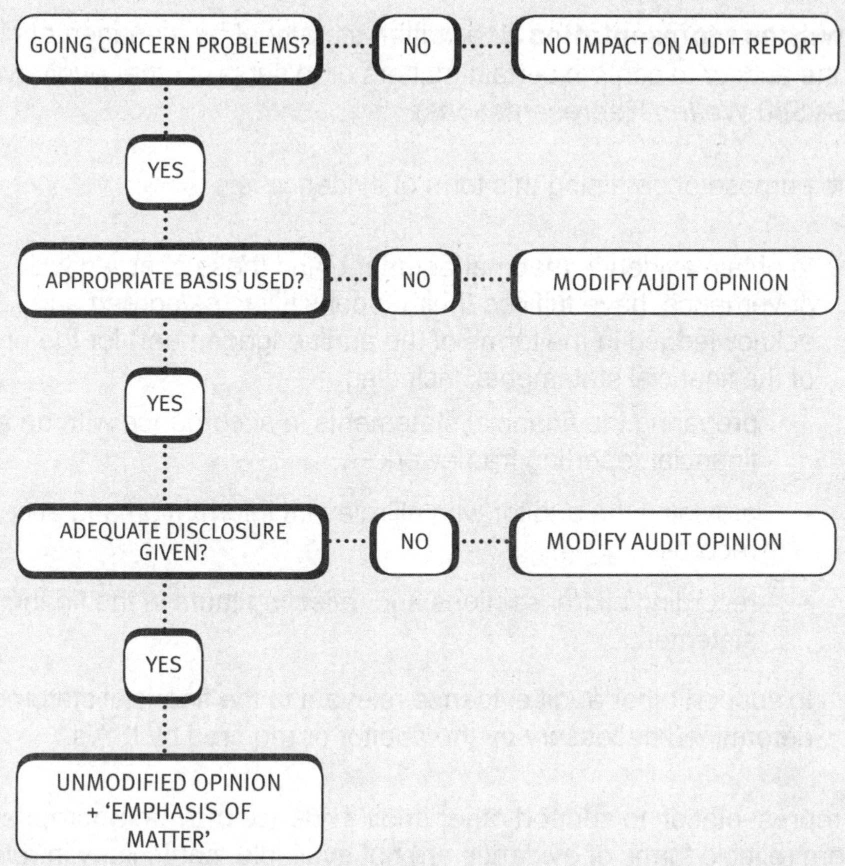


In relation to going concern it is important to understand the following:

- Financial statements are normally prepared on the going concern basis.
- Where the going concern basis is used and is appropriate, the auditors do not need to mention the fact in their report.
- If the auditor believes that the **going concern basis used** in the financial statements is **inappropriate** they will **modify the audit opinion**.
- If the directors appropriately **disclose** an **uncertainty** with regard to going concern the auditor (without modifying their opinion) will refer to this in the audit report in an **'emphasis of matter'** paragraph.
- If the directors prepare the financial statements on another basis (i.e. not going concern) and this is appropriate the auditor will also refer to this in an emphasis of matter paragraph.
- If the period assessed by management is less than twelve months from the statement of financial position date and management is unwilling to extend the assessment, the auditor will modify the audit opinion, due to an inability to obtain sufficient appropriate audit evidence regarding the use of the going concern assumption.

## 4 Written representation letter

A **written representation** is: a written statement by management provided to the auditor to confirm certain matters or to support other audit evidence (ISA 580 *Written Representations*).

The purpose of obtaining this form of evidence is:

- to obtain evidence that management, and those charged with governance, have fulfilled their responsibility (as agreed and acknowledged in the terms of the audit engagement) for the preparation of the financial statements, including:
  - preparing the financial statements in accordance with an applicable financial reporting framework;
  - providing the auditor with all relevant information and access to records
  - recording all transactions and reflecting them in the financial statements.
- to support other audit evidence relevant to the financial statements if determined necessary by the auditor or required by ISA's.

A representation to support other audit evidence may be appropriate where more reliable forms of evidence are not available, particularly in relation to matters requiring management judgement or knowledge restricted to management. Examples include:

- plans or intentions that may affect the carrying value of assets or liabilities
- confirmation of values where there is a significant degree of estimation or judgement involved, e.g. provisions and contingent liabilities
- formal confirmation of the directors' judgement on contentious issues, e.g. the value of assets where there is a risk of impairment
- aspects of laws and regulations that may affect the financial statements, including compliance.

ISA 580 requires written representations to be in the form of a representation letter addressed to the auditor.

Note that written representations cannot substitute for more reliable evidence that should be available and do not constitute sufficient appropriate evidence on their own, about any of the matters with which they deal.

Written representations should only be sought to support other audit evidence.

e.g

**Illustration 2: Murray Co written representation letter**

**Murray Co**
**1 Murray Mound, Wimbledon**
**London WN1 2LN**

**Wimble & Co**
**2 Court Lane, Wimbledon**
**London WN1 2LN**

18 February 2013

Dear Wimble & Co,

This representation letter is provided in connection with your audit of the financial statements of Murray Company for the year ended December 31, 2012 for the purpose of expressing an opinion as to whether the financial statements give a true and fair view in accordance with International Financial Reporting Standards.

We confirm that:

*Financial Statements*

- We have fulfilled our responsibilities, as set out in the terms of the audit engagement dated November 25, 2011, for the preparation of the financial statements in accordance with International Financial Reporting Standards; in particular the financial statements give a true and fair view in accordance therewith.
- Significant assumptions used by us in making accounting estimates, including those measured at fair value, are reasonable. (ISA 540)
- Related party relationships and transactions have been appropriately accounted for and disclosed in accordance with the requirements of International Financial Reporting Standards. (ISA 550)
- All events subsequent to the date of the financial statements and for which International Financial Reporting Standards require adjustment or disclosure have been adjusted or disclosed. (ISA 560)
- The effects of uncorrected misstatements are immaterial, both individually and in the aggregate, to the financial statements as a whole. A list of the uncorrected misstatements is attached to the representation letter. (ISA 450)
- The basis and amount of the warranty provision are reasonable. (specific matter)

*Information Provided*

- We have provided you with:
  - Access to all information of which we are aware that is relevant to the preparation of the financial statements, such as records, documentation and other matters;
  - Additional information that you have requested from us for the purpose of the audit; and
  - Unrestricted access to persons within the entity from whom you determined it necessary to obtain audit evidence.
- All transactions have been recorded in the accounting records and are reflected in the financial statements.
- We have disclosed to you the results of our assessment of the risk that the financial statements may be materially misstated as a result of fraud. (ISA 240)
- We have disclosed to you all information in relation to fraud or suspected fraud that we are aware of and that affects the entity and involves:
  - Management;
  - Employees who have significant roles in internal control; or
  - Others where the fraud could have a material effect on the financial statements. (ISA 240)
- We have disclosed to you all information in relation to allegations of fraud, or suspected fraud, affecting the entity's financial statements communicated by employees, former employees, analysts, regulators or others. (ISA 240)
- We have disclosed to you all known instances of non-compliance or suspected non-compliance with laws and regulations whose effects should be considered when preparing financial statements. (ISA 250)
- We have disclosed to you the identity of the entity's related parties and all the related party relationships and transactions of which we are aware. (ISA 550)
- We have disclosed to your all information in relation to settlement of the unfair dismissal, including our intentions thereon. (specific matter)
- We have disclosed to you all information in relation to the constructive dismissal brought by the previous Sales Director, including our intention thereon. (specific matter)

*Ed Perry*

Edward Perry

Finance Director, Murray Co

*Maria Williams*

Maria Williams
Managing Director, Murray Co

**Murray Co written representation letter**

In practice, the auditor will often draft the written representations letter but it must be printed on client headed paper and signed by the client.

The letter must be signed by an appropriate senior member of client management, with appropriate responsibilities for the financial statements and knowledge of the matters concerned. This would normally be the chief executive and chief financial officer.

The date of the written representation letter should be the same as the date the financial statements are authorised. It must be obtained (and signed) before the audit report is finalised.

## Reliability of written representations

Written representations are client generated, and may be subject to bias. It is therefore a potentially unreliable form of audit evidence.

The auditor must consider the reliability of written representations in terms of:

- inconsistencies with other forms of evidence
- concerns about the competence, integrity, ethical values or diligence of management.

If written representations are inconsistent with other evidence, the auditor must:

- consider the reliability of representations in general
- reconsider their initial risk assessment
- consider the need to perform further audit procedures.

If there are concerns about the competence, integrity, ethical values or diligence of management the auditor must:

- Consider whether the engagement can be conducted effectively.
- If they conclude that it cannot then they should withdraw from the engagement, where permitted by laws and regulations.
- If they are not permitted to withdraw they should consider the impact on the audit report - it is likely that this would lead to them disclaiming their opinion.

**Need for written representations**

Although possibly unreliable, written representations are a necessary and important source of evidence.

If management refuse to provide requested written representations, the auditor should:

- discuss the matter with management to understand why they are refusing
- re-evaluate the integrity of management and consider the effect that this may have on the reliability of other representations (oral or written) and audit evidence in general
- determine the possible effect on the audit opinion.

If management refuses to provide written representations about their responsibilities, the auditor must disclaim their opinion.

## Overall review of evidence

**What happens in the final review?**

The overall review stage of the audit is the point at which the final decisions are taken:

OVERALL REVIEW

**Financial statements ok?**

- **Do the financial statements comply with the relevant reporting framework?**
  - Law.
  - Applicable accounting standards.
  - GAAP.
  - Other regulations (e.g. Stock Exchange listing requirements).
  - Does other information published with the financial statements (e.g. Directors' report, – Chairman's review) conflict with them in any way?

**Audit evidence ok?**

- **Does the evidence gathered in the course of the audit support the audit opinion?**
  - Was the audit plan followed?
  - Has sufficient, appropriate audit evidence been gathered?
  - Has the work been performed in accordance with professional standards and legal requirements?
  - What issues arose? What errors were found?
  - Have the matters been raised for future consideration?
  - Was the plan suitably modified to allow for changing circumstances?
  - Have necessary consultations taken place both within the firm and with outside experts?
  - Has the file been adequately reviewed at lower levels within the firm (e.g. by the senior and the manager)?
  - Have the necessary checklists been completed?
  - Work supports conclusions reached and is appropriately documented

**Other completion procedures**

- **Have the necessary completion procedures been carried out?**
  - Final analytical review.
  - Consideration of the firm's continued independence.
  - Second partner review (if appropriate).
  - Subsequent events review.
  - Going concern review.
  - Management representations obtained.
  - Objectives of the engagement procedures have been achieved.

The review is carried out by the engagement partner who has ultimate responsibility for committing the audit firm when signing the audit report.

### What is the purpose of a final review?

It is the responsibility of the engagement partner to perform a review of audit documentation (including a discussion with the engagement team) in order to satisfy themselves that sufficient appropriate evidence has been obtained to support any conclusions reached and, ultimately, the audit opinion. Considerations include, for example:

- has work been performed in accordance with professional standards?
- have the significant risks identified during planning been addressed?
- are there any critical areas of judgement relating to difficult or contentious matters?
- are there any significant matters for further consideration?
- have appropriate consultations taken place or are more needed?
- have the objectives of the engagement procedures been achieved?
- does the work documented support the conclusions made?

- is there a need to revise the nature, timing and extent of procedures?
- is the evidence sufficient to support an opinion?

Reviews are also significant for a firm's appraisal system and development of staff. Additionally they are an important element of any monitoring system, implemented to identify and rectify deficiencies that could lead to poor quality work.

Appropriate review procedures are an integral part of an audit and are a requirement of ISA 220 *Quality Control for an Audit of Financial Statements.*

**Evaluation of misstatements**

In accordance with ISA 450 *Evaluation of Misstatements Identified During the Audit* all misstatements should be communicated to management on a timely basis, unless they are clearly trivial. Management should be asked to correct **all** misstatements identified during the audit. Auditors should try and obtain an understanding of management's reasons for refusing to adjust any of the misstatements. The auditor should determine whether uncorrected misstatements are material in aggregate or individually, and if material should consider the potential impact on their audit report.

Prior to evaluating the significance of uncorrected misstatements the auditor should reassess materiality to confirm whether it remains appropriate to the financial statements. Then the auditor must assess whether uncorrected misstatements are, individually or in aggregate, material. To do this they should consider the size and nature of the misstatements, both in relation to the financial statements as a whole and to particular classes of transaction, account balances and disclosures.

Finally, the auditor should obtain a written representation from management and those charged with governance that they believe the effect of the uncorrected misstatements is immaterial, individually and in aggregate.

Once these procedures have been completed the auditor should then consider the impact of uncorrected misstatements on their reporting. The impact on the audit report is considered in the next chapter. Other reports are considered below.

**Other reports**

ISA 260 *Communication with Those Charged with Governance* requires the auditor to make additional communications to managers, directors and those charged with governance at the conclusion of the audit of matters significant to the oversight of the financial reporting process.

One of the matters requiring communication is 'significant findings from the audit.' The existence of errors may indicate that a client's accounting policies and practices contravene financial reporting requirements or that the internal control systems are deficient. Either way these matters should be communicated to the client.

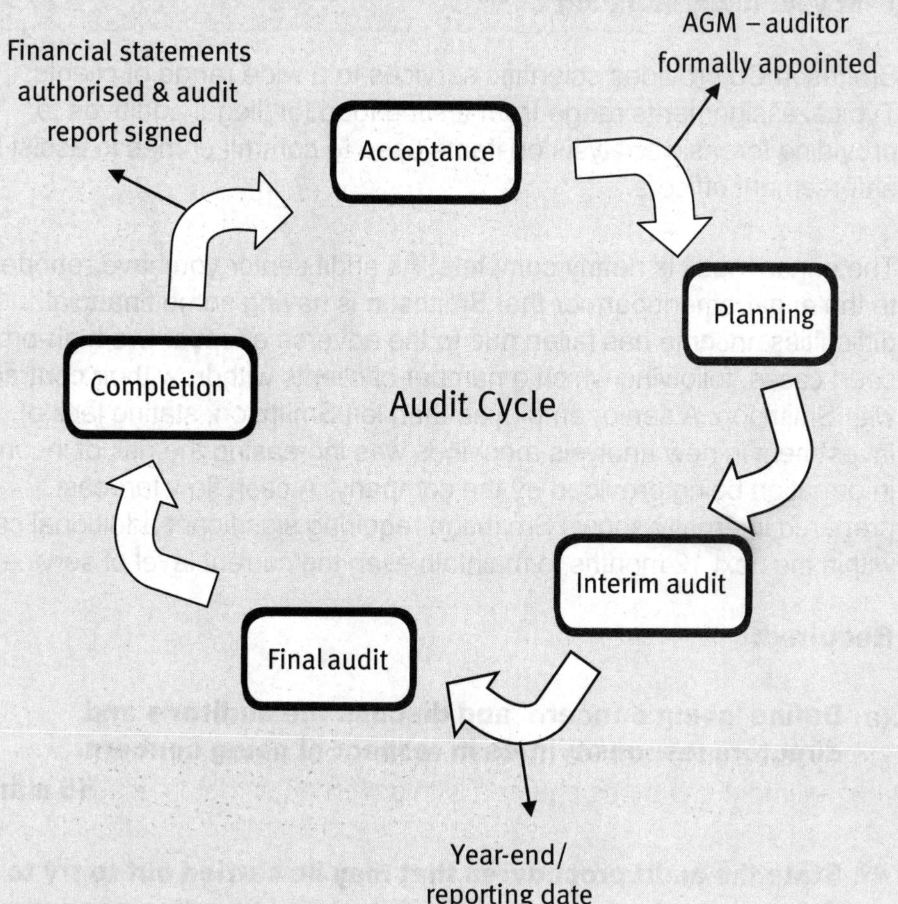

### Test your understanding 1

ISA 570 Going Concern provides guidance to auditors in respect of ensuring that an entity can continue as a going concern.

**Required:**

**Explain the actions that an auditor should carry out to try and ascertain whether an entity is a going concern.**
*Real exam question: December 2007*

**(5 marks)**

### Test your understanding 2

Smithson Co provides scientific services to a wide range of clients. Typical assignments range from testing food for illegal additives to providing forensic analysis on items used to commit crimes to assist law enforcement officers.

The annual audit is nearly complete. As audit senior you have reported to the engagement partner that Smithson is having some financial difficulties. Income has fallen due to the adverse effect of two high-profile court cases, following which a number of clients withdrew their contracts with Smithson. A senior employee then left Smithson, stating lack of investment in new analysis machines was increasing the risk of incorrect information being provided by the company. A cash flow forecast prepared internally shows Smithson requiring significant additional cash within the next 12 months to maintain even the current level of services.

**Required:**

(a) **Define 'going concern' and discuss the auditor's and directors responsibilities in respect of going concern.**

**(5 marks)**

(b) **State the audit procedures that may be carried out to try to determine whether or not Smithson Co is a going concern.**

**(10 marks)**

(c) **Explain the audit procedures the auditor may take where the auditor has decided that Smithson Co is unlikely to be a going concern.**

**(5 marks)**

**Test your understanding 3**

Potterton is a listed company that manufactures body lotions under the 'ReallyCool' brand. The company's year end is 31 March 2011, and today's date is 1 June 2011. Draft profit before taxation is $4 million.

The audit is nearing completion, but two issues remain outstanding:

(1) On 27 May 2011 a legal claim was made against the company on behalf of a teenager who suffered severe burns after using 'ReallyCool ExtraZingy Lotion' in July 2010. Potterton is considering an out-of-court settlement of $100,000 per year for the remaining life of the claimant. However, no adjustment or disclosure has been made in the financial statements.

(2) At a Board Meeting on 30 April 2011, the directors of Potterton proposed a dividend of $2 million. It is highly likely that the shareholders will approve the dividend at the Annual General Meeting on 3 September 2011. The directors have recorded the dividend in the draft Statement of Changes in Equity for the year ended 31 March 2011.

**Required:**

(a) **Explain whether the two outstanding issues are adjusting or non-adjusting events, in accordance with IAS 10, Events after the Reporting Period.**

**(8 marks)**

(b) **Explain appropriate audit procedures in order to reach a conclusion on the two outstanding issues.**

**(5 marks)**

(c) **Explain the likely impact on the audit opinion if the directors refuse to make any further adjustments or disclosures in the financial statements.**

**(4 marks)**

**(Total: 17 marks)**

**Test your understanding 4**

ISA 580 Written Representations provides guidance on the use of management representations as audit evidence.

**Required:**

(a) **List SIX items that could be included in a management representation letter.**

*Real exam question: June 2008*

(b) **List THREE reasons why auditors obtain written representations.**

**Test your understanding 5**

(a) **Explain the purpose of a management representation letter.**

**(5 marks)**

(b) You are the manager in charge of the audit of Crighton-Ward, a public limited liability company which manufactures specialist cars and other motor vehicles for use in films. Audited turnover is $140 million with profit before tax of $7.5 million.

All audit work up to, but not including, the obtaining of management representations has been completed. A review of the audit file has disclosed the following outstanding points:

*Lion's Roar*

The company is facing a potential legal claim from the Lion's Roar company in respect of a defective vehicle that was supplied for one of their films. Lion's Roar maintains that the vehicle was not built strongly enough while the directors of Crighton-Ward argue that the specification was not sufficiently detailed. Dropping a vehicle 50 metres into a river and expecting it to continue to remain in working condition would be unusual, but this is what Lion's Roar expected. Solicitors are unable to determine liability at the present time. A claim for $4 million being the cost of a replacement vehicle and lost production time has been received by Crighton-Ward from Lions' Roar. The directors' opinion is that the claim is not justified.

*Depreciation*

Depreciation of specialist production equipment has been included in the financial statements at the amount of 10% pa based on reducing balance. The treatment is consistent with prior accounting periods (which received an unmodified auditor's report) and other companies in the same industry and sales of old equipment show negligible profit or loss on sale. The audit senior, who is new to the audit, feels that depreciation is being undercharged in the financial statements.

**Required:**

**For each of the above matters:**

(i) **discuss whether or not a paragraph is required in the representation letter; and**

(ii) **if appropriate, draft the paragraph for inclusion in the representation letter.**

**(10 marks)**

(c) A suggested format for the letter of representation has been sent by the auditors to the directors of Crighton-Ward. The directors have stated that they will not sign the letter of representation this year on the grounds that they believe the additional evidence that it provides is not required by the auditor.

**Required:**

**Discuss the actions the auditor may take as a result of the decision made by the directors not to sign the letter of representation.**

**(5 marks)**

**(Total: 20 marks)**

# 5 Chapter summary

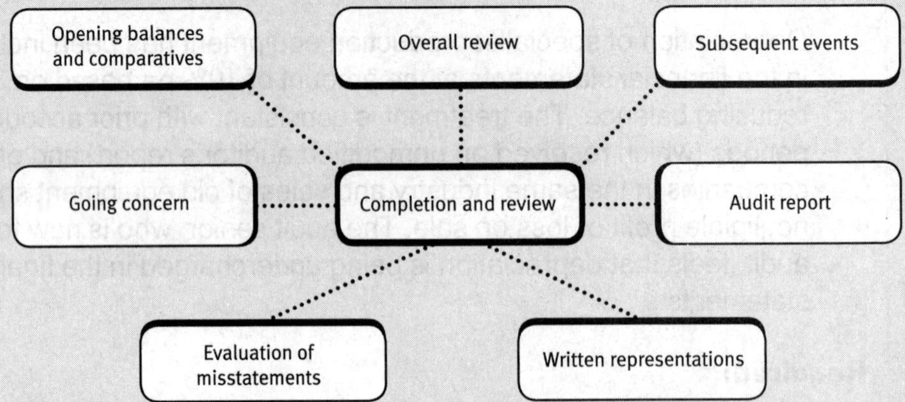

## Test your understanding answers

### Test your understanding 1

**Audit work: going concern**

- Review management's plans for future actions based on its going concern assessment.
- Gather additional sufficient and appropriate audit evidence to confirm or dispel whether or not a material uncertainty exists regarding the going concern concept.
- Seek written representations from management regarding its plans for future action.
- Obtain information from company bankers regarding continuance of loan facilities.
- Review receivables ageing analysis to determine whether there is an increase in days, which may also indicate cashflow problems.

### Test your understanding 2

(a) Going Concern

"Going concern" means that the entity will continue in operational existence for the foreseeable future without the intention or the necessity of liquidation or otherwise ceasing trade. It is one of the fundamental accounting concepts used by auditors and stated in IAS 1 presentation of financial statements.

The auditor's responsibility in respect of going concern is explained in ISA 570 Going Concern.

The ISA states: "When planning and performing audit procedures and in evaluating the results thereof, the auditor should consider the appropriateness of management's use of the going concern assumption in the preparation of the financial statements."

The auditor's responsibilities are:

(i) To carry out appropriate audit procedures that will identify whether or not an organisation can continue as a going concern;

(ii) To ensure that the organisation's management have been realistic in their use of the going concern assumption when preparing the financial statements; and

(iii) To report to the members where they consider that the going concern assumption has been used inappropriately, for example; when the financial statements indicate that the organisation is a going concern but audit procedures indicate this may not be the case.

It is the directors' responsibility to prepare the financial statements on an appropriate basis, be that either the going concern or the break-up basis.

(b) Audit Procedures Regarding Going Concern

- Obtain a copy of the cash flow forecast and discuss the results of this with directors.
- Discuss with the directors their view of whether Smithson can continue as a going concern. Ask for their reasons and try and determine whether these are accurate.
- Enquire of the directors whether they have considered any other forms of finance for Smithson to make up the cash shortfall identified in the cash flow forecast.
- Obtain a copy of any interim financial statements of Smithson to determine the level of sales/income after the year-end and whether this matches the cash flow forecast.
- Enquire about the possible lack of capital investment within Smithson identified by the employee leaving. Review current levels of non-current assets with similar companies and review purchase policy with the directors.
- Consider the extent to which Smithson rely on the senior employee who recently left the company. Ask the HR department whether the employee will be replaced and, if so, how soon
- Obtain a solicitor's letter and review to identify any legal claims against Smithson related to below standard services being provided to clients. Where possible, consider the financial impact on Smithson and whether insurance is available to mitigate any claims.

- Review Smithson's order book and client lists to try and determine the value of future orders compared to previous years.
- Review the bank letter to determine the extent of any bank loans and whether repayments due in the next 12 months can be made without further borrowing.
- Review other events after the end of the financial year and determine whether these have an impact on Smithson.
- Obtain a letter of representation point confirming the directors' opinion that Smithson is a going concern.

(c) Audit Procedures if Smithson is not considered to be a Going Concern

- Discuss the situation again with directors. Consider whether additional disclosures are required in the financial statements or whether the financial statements should be prepared on the break-up basis.
- Explain to the directors that if additional disclosure or restatement of the financial statements is not made then the auditor will have to modify the audit report.
- Consider how the audit report should be modified. Where the directors provide adequate disclosure of the going concern situation of Smithson, then an emphasis of matter paragraph is likely to be appropriate to draw attention to the going concern disclosures.
- Where the directors do not make adequate disclosure of the going concern situation then modify the audit report making reference to the going concern problem.
- The modification will be an "except for" qualification or an adverse opinion depending upon the auditor's opinion of the situation.

**Test your understanding 3**

(a) **Analysis of events**

**Legal claim:** The legal claim is within the scope of IAS 10, because it was received on 27 May 2011. This date is after the reporting date (31 March 2011) but before the date that the financial statements will be authorised for issue. The legal claim is an adjusting event because it provides evidence of conditions existing at the end of the reporting period. As at 31 March 2011, the claimant had purchased and used the product, and the damage to the claimant's skin had already occurred.

The legal claim is material, because, if the claimant lived for, say, another 40 years, the company would owe him/her $4 million. This is 100% of the current year draft profit before taxation.

Therefore profit should be reduced and liabilities increased by the expected value of the claim.

**Proposed dividend:** The proposed dividend is within the scope of IAS 10, because it was proposed after the reporting date (31 March 2011) but before the date that the financial statements will be authorised for issue. The proposed dividend is a non-adjusting event because it is indicative of a condition that arose after the end of the reporting period. No liability for the dividend can exist until the shareholders approve the dividend at the Annual General Meeting.

The proposed dividend is material because it constitutes 50% ($2m/$4m x 100) of the company's profit before tax.

Therefore the dividend should not be recognised in the financial statements for the year ended 31 March 2011. However, the proposed dividend should be disclosed in a note to the financial statements.

(b) **Audit procedures**

**Legal claim:**

- Review legal correspondence in order to understand the likely outcome of the legal claim.
- Review customer correspondence/legal files in order to identify other similar claims which could give rise to additional liabilities.

- Discuss with Production Director the likely cause of the burns (e.g. allergy in user or inadequate printed instructions on product use) to determine the likelihood of any claim being successful in court.
- Review trade/consumer press to identify whether the claim might damage Reallycool's reputation which could impact future revenues or even create a going concern threat.
- Propose adjustment of the financial statements to the directors.

**Proposed dividend:**

- Inspect Board Minutes in order to confirm the amount of the proposed dividend.
- Propose an adjustment to the financial statements to remove the dividend from being recognised in the Statement of Changes in Equity but ensure that the dividend proposal is disclosed within the notes.

(c) **Impact on audit opinion.**

The auditor must modify the audit opinion on the financial statements if the directors refuse to make the relevant adjustments in the financial statements requested by the auditors.

Both the legal claim (which should have been recognised) and the proposed dividend (which should have been disclosed rather than recognised) are materially misstated.

The auditor must express a qualified ('except for') opinion if they conclude that the misstatements are material, but not pervasive, to the financial statements.

The auditor must express an adverse opinion if they conclude that misstatements are both material and pervasive to the financial statements.

Given the size of the amounts involved, an adverse opinion may be appropriate in these circumstances.

**Test your understanding 4**

| | | |
|---|---|---|
| (a) | No irregularities involving management or employees that could have a material effect on the financial statements. | ½ mark |
| | All books of account and supporting documentation have been made available to the auditors. | ½ mark |
| | Information and disclosures with reference to related parties is complete. | ½ mark |
| | Financial statements are free from material misstatements including omissions. | ½ mark |
| | No non-compliance with any statute or regulatory authority. | ½ mark |
| | No plans that will materially alter the carrying value or classification of assets or liabilities in the financial statements. | ½ mark |
| | No plans to abandon any product lines that will result in any excess or obsolete inventory. | ½ mark |
| | No events, unless already disclosed, after the end of the reporting period that need disclosure in the financial statements. | ½ mark |
| (b) | Formal confirmation by management of their responsibilities. | 1 mark |
| | Contentious matter where no other, better quality, evidence is available. | 1 mark |
| | Required by ISA 580 and other ISAs. | 1 mark |

**Test your understanding 5**

(a) Written representations are a form of audit evidence. They are contained in a letter, written by the company's directors and sent to the auditor, just prior to the completion of audit work and before the audit report is signed.

Representations are required for two reasons:

- First, so the directors can acknowledge their collective responsibility for the preparation of the financial statements and to confirm that they have approved those statements.
- Second, to confirm any matters, which are material to the financial statements where representations are crucial to obtaining sufficient and appropriate audit evidence.

In the latter situation, other forms of audit evidence are normally unavailable because knowledge of the facts is confined to management and the matter is one of judgement or opinion.

Obtaining representations does not mean that other evidence does not have to be obtained. Audit evidence will still be collected and the representation will support that evidence. Any contradiction between sources of evidence should, as always, be investigated.

(b) *Lion's Roar*

The amount of the claim is material being 50% of profit before taxation.

There is also a lack of definitive supporting evidence for the claim. The two main pieces of evidence available are the claim from Lion's Roar itself and the legal advice from Crighton Ward's solicitors. However, any claim amount cannot be accurately determined because the dispute has not been settled.

The directors have stated that they believe the claim not to be justified, which is one possible outcome of the dispute. However, in order to obtain sufficient evidence to show how the treatment of the potential claim was decided for the financial statements, the auditor must obtain this opinion in writing. Reference must therefore be made to the claim in the representation letter.

Paragraph for inclusion in representation letter: 'A legal claim against Crighton-Ward by Lion's Roar has been estimated at $4 million by Lion's Roar. However, the directors are of the opinion that the claim is not justified on the grounds of breach of product specification.

No provision has been made in the financial statements, although disclosure of the situation is adequate. No similar claims have been received or are expected to be received.'

*Depreciation*

This matter is unlikely to be included in the letter of representation because the auditor appears to have obtained sufficient evidence to confirm the accounting treatment. The lack of profit or loss on sale confirms that the depreciation charge is appropriate – large profits would indicate over-depreciation and large losses, under-depreciation. The amount also meets industry standards confirming that Crighton-Ward's accounting policy is acceptable. Including the point in the representation letter is inappropriate because the matter is not crucial and does not appear to be based on judgment or opinion. The only opinion here appears to be that of the auditor – unless the 'feelings' can be turned into some appropriate audit evidence, the matter should be closed.

(c) Lack of representation letter

The auditor may take the following actions:

- Discuss the situation with the directors to try and resolve the issue that the directors have raised.
- The auditor will need to explain the need for the representation letter again (and note that the signing of the letter was mentioned in the engagement letter).
- Ascertain exact reasons why the directors will not sign the letter.
- Consider whether amendments can be made to the letter to incorporate the directors' concerns that will still provide the auditor with appropriate and sufficient audit evidence.
- The discussion must clearly explain the fact that if the auditor does not receive sufficient and appropriate audit evidence, then the audit report will have to be modified.

The reason for the modification will be the auditor's inability to obtain sufficient appropriate evidence regarding the amounts and disclosures in the financial statements. An 'except for' qualification for the material uncertainty is likely, although a disclaimer may be required, especially if the legal claim is thought to require a provision.

Even if the letter is subsequently signed, the auditor must still evaluate the reliability of the evidence. If, in the auditor's opinion, the letter no longer provides sufficient or reliable evidence, then a qualification may still be required.

chapter

# 10

# Reporting

## Chapter learning objectives

When you have completed this chapter you will be able to:

- Discuss the need for auditors to communicate with those charged with governance.
- Describe and analyse the format and content of unmodified audit reports.
- Describe and analyse the format and content of modified audit reports.
- Describe the format and content of emphasis of matter and other matter paragraphs.
- Identify and explain the contents of other reports made to management.

## 1 The audit report

The objectives of an auditor, in accordance with ISA 700 *Forming an Opinion and Reporting on Financial Statements,* are:

- to form an opinion on the financial statements based upon an evaluation of their conclusions drawn from audit evidence
- to express clearly that opinion through a written report.

The auditor forms an opinion on whether the financial statements are prepared, in all material respects, in accordance with the applicable financial reporting framework. In order to do that they must conclude whether they have obtained reasonable assurance about whether the financial statements as a whole are free from material misstatement (whether due to fraud or error).

In particular the auditor should evaluate whether:

- the financial statements adequately disclose the significant accounting policies
- the accounting policies selected are consistently applied and appropriate
- accounting estimates are reasonable
- information is relevant, reliable, comparable and understandable
- the financial statements provide adequate disclosures to enable the users to understand the effects of material transactions and events
- the terminology used is appropriate.

When the auditor concludes that the financial statements are prepared, in all material respects, in accordance with the applicable financial reporting framework they issue an **unmodified opinion** in the audit report.

If there are no other matters which the auditor wishes to draw to the attention of the users, they will issue an **unmodified report**.

## 2 Contents of the audit report

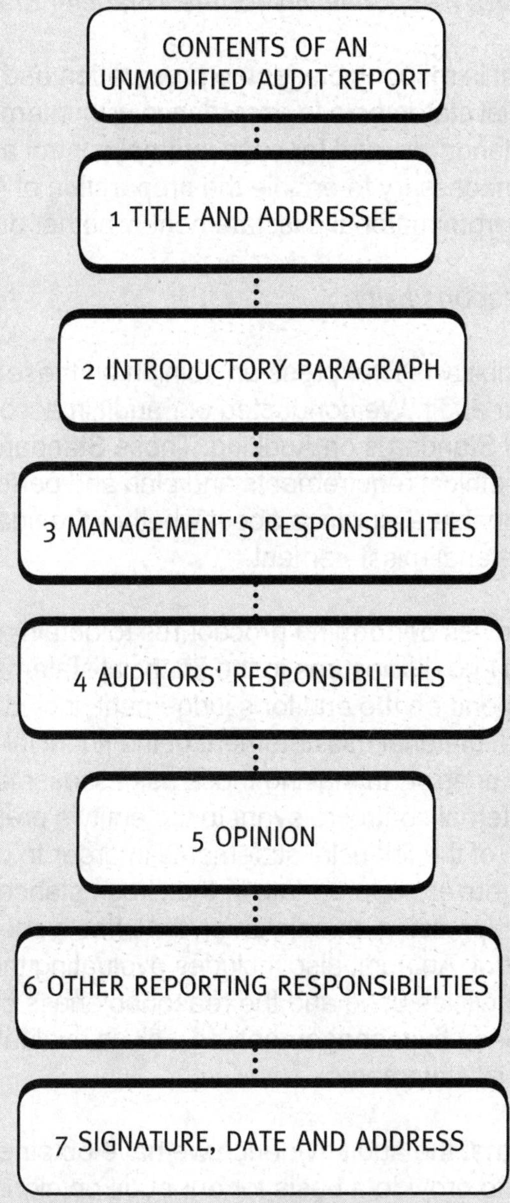

**Illustration 1: Unmodified audit report**

**INDEPENDENT AUDITOR'S REPORT to the members of Murray Company**

**Report on the Financial Statements**

We have audited the accompanying financial statements of the Murray Company, which comprise the statement of financial position as at 31 December, 2012, and the statement of profit or loss and comprehensive income, statement of changes in equity and cash flow statement for the year then ended, and a summary of significant accounting policies and other explanatory information.

*Management's Responsibility for the Financial Statements*

Management is responsible for the preparation and fair presentation of these financial statements in accordance with International Financial Reporting Standards, and for such internal control as management determines necessary to enable the preparation of financial statements that are free from material misstatement, whether due to fraud or error.

*Auditor's Responsibility*

Our responsibility is to express an opinion on these financial statements based on our audit. We conducted our audit in accordance with International Standards on Auditing. Those Standards require that we comply with ethical requirements and plan and perform the audit to obtain reasonable assurance about whether the financial statements are free from material misstatement.

An audit involves performing procedures to obtain audit evidence about the amounts and disclosures in the financial statements. The procedures selected depend on the auditor's judgement, including the assessment of the risks of material misstatement of the financial statements, whether due to fraud or error. In making those risk assessments, the auditor considers internal control relevant to the entity's preparation and fair presentation of the financial statements in order to design audit procedures that are appropriate in the circumstances, but not for the purpose of expressing an opinion on the effectiveness of the entity's internal control. An audit also includes evaluating the appropriateness of accounting policies used and the reasonableness of accounting estimates made by management, as well as evaluating the presentation of the financial statements.

We believe that the audit evidence we have obtained is sufficient and appropriate to provide a basis for our audit opinion.

*Opinion* (UK & Ireland: *Opinion on Financial Statements)*

In our opinion, the financial statements give a true and fair view of the financial position of Murray Company as at December 31 2012, and of its financial performance and its cash flows for the year then ended in accordance with International Financial Reporting Standards.

*Wimble & Co*

18 February 2012

Wimble & Co, London

**Murray Co unmodified audit report**

ISA 700 provides guidance as to the nature and wording of the audit report. Most importantly the report must be in writing.

In addition it recommends that the audit report be broken into distinct sections that explain the purpose, nature and scope of an audit. The main reason for this is to ensure that the users of the audit report understand the nature of audit procedures and that only reasonable assurance is being offered. One of the primary purposes of this is to reduce the 'expectations gap.'

The recommended elements of the report are as follows:

**Title**

- The title should clearly indicate that it is the report of an independent auditor. "Independent auditor's report" distinguishes the report from other reports issued by management or other types of assurance report.

**Addressee**

- The report should be addressed to the intended user of the report which is usually the shareholders, or other parties as required by the circumstances of the engagement.

**Introductory paragraph**

- Identifies the entity whose financial statements have been audited;
- States that the financial statements have been audited;
- Identifies the title of each of the financial statements;
- Refers to the accounting policies applied to the financial statements; and
- Specifies the date or period covered by the financial statements.

**Responsibilities of management**

A description of management's responsibility for

- the preperation and fair presentation of the financial statements; and
- designing and implementing an effective internal control system necessary for the preparation and fair presentation of the financial statements.

**Responsibilities of the auditor**

- Express an opinion on the financial statements.
- The audit was conducted in accordance with ISA's;
- Requirement to comply with ethical standards;
- The fact that the audit was planned and performed to obtain reasonable assurance about whether the financial statements are free from material misstatement.
- Audit involves procedures designed to obtain evidence about amounts and disclosures in the financial statements;
- The procedures are based upon auditor judgement, including a risk assessment and consideration of internal controls;
- Obtain sufficient, appropriate audit evidence on which to base the opinion.

**Auditor's opinion (headed 'Opinion')**

- When expressing an unmodified opinion the auditor (unless otherwise required by relevant laws or regulations) uses one of the following phrases:
  - "the financial statements present fairly, in all material respects........"; or
  - "the financial statements show a true and fair view of .......................".

**Other reporting responsibilities**

- The auditor may have other reporting responsibilities under local legislation or regulations. For example, in the UK the auditor must express an opinion on whether the Director's report is consistent with the financial statements.

**Auditor's signature**

- The report may be signed in the name of the firm, or the personal name of the auditor, as appropriate for the particular jurisdiction.
- There may also be a requirement to state the auditor's professional accountancy designation or that the firm is recognised by the appropriate licensing authority (i.e. that the firm/partner is a member of a body such as ACCA and is registered to audit).

### Date of report

- The audit report should be dated no earlier than the date on which the auditor has obtained sufficient appropriate evidence upon which to base their opinion.
- This requires that all the statements and notes/disclosure that comprise the financial statements are finalised and that those with responsibility for preparation of the financial statements have acknowledged their role.
- Practically this means that the auditor should sign their report **after** the directors have approved the financial statements.

### Auditor's address

- The audit report should name a specific location, which is normally the city where the auditor maintains the office that has responsibility for the audit.

**UK Syllabus Focus**

### ISA 700 (UK & Ireland) The Auditor's Report on Financial Statements

In the UK & Ireland, the auditor's responsibilities are not required to include the scope of the audit. Instead, the auditor's report must:

- cross reference to a "Statement of the Scope of an Audit" on the FRC's website,
- cross reference to a "Statement of the Scope of an Audit" elsewhere within the annual report, or
- include a description of the scope of an audit in the auditor's report.

## 3 Modifications to the audit report

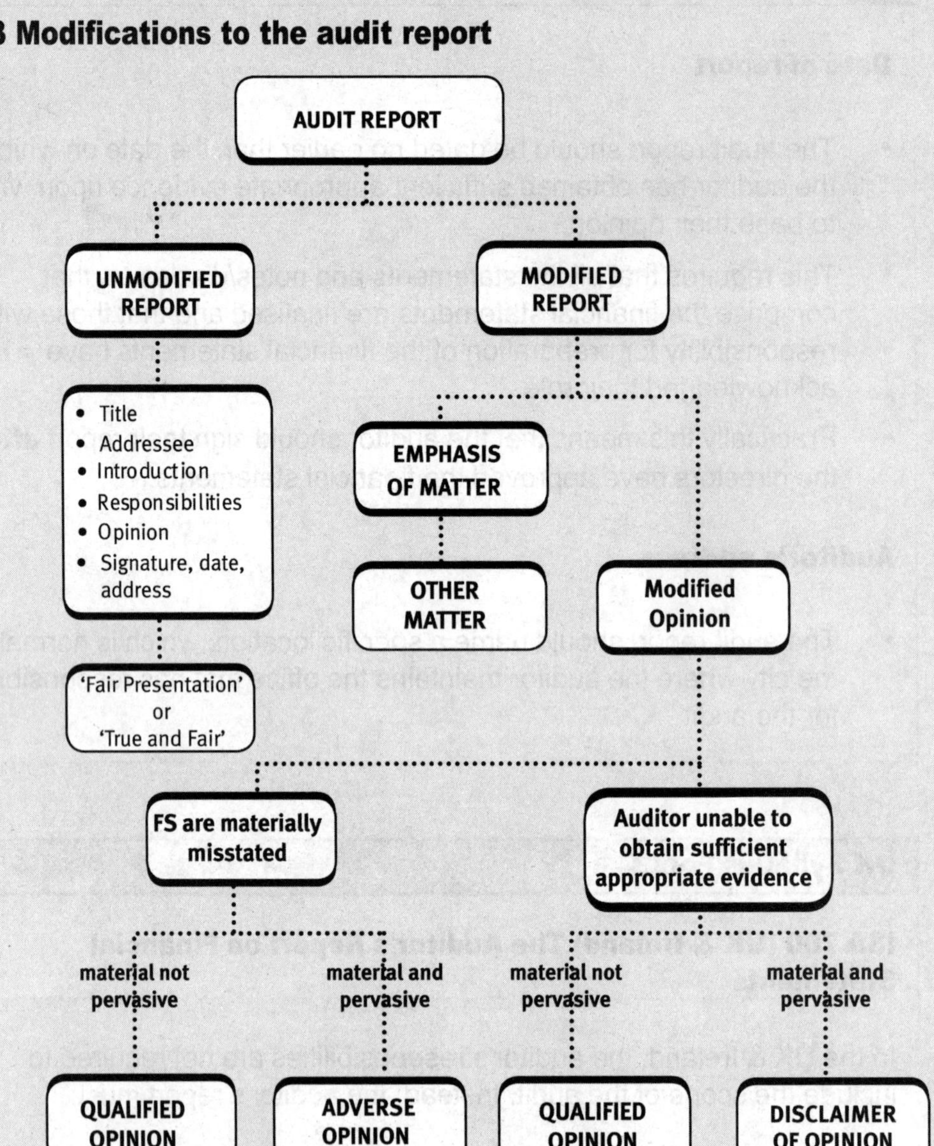


There are two ways that the audit report can be modified:

- by modifying the audit opinion
- through inclusion of additional paragraphs.

### Modifying the audit opinion

There are two reasons why an auditor would need to modify the audit opinion:

- they conclude that the financial statements as a whole are not free from material misstatements

- they have been unable to obtain sufficient appropriate evidence to conclude that the financial statements as a whole are free from material misstatement.

In order to determine the appropriate audit opinion, the auditor must evaluate the significance of the matter, and determine whether it is material or material and pervasive.

Pervasive means that the matter is:

- not confined to specific elements of the financial statements
- if confined represents a substantial proportion of the financial statements or
- is fundamental to users understanding of the financial statements.

The appropriate audit opinion is then determined as follows:

| | **Auditor's Judgement Regarding the Pervasiveness of the Matter** | |
|---|---|---|
| **Nature of Matter** | **Material but Not Pervasive** | **Material and Pervasive** |
| Financial statements are materially misstated | Qualified opinion | Adverse opinion |
| Inability to obtain sufficient appropriate evidence | Qualified opinion | Disclaimer of opinion |

If the matter is not material then the auditor's opinion will not be modified and a 'true and fair' or 'present fairly' wording will be used.

- If the auditor gives either of the two qualified opinions, assurance is provided on the financial statements except for the element where an actual or potential misstatement was identified.
- If the auditor concludes that the matter is pervasive, giving an adverse or disclaimer of opinion, they do not provide any assurance.

When the auditor modifies their opinion on the financial statements, they must include a 'Basis for Modification Paragraph' in the audit report that describes the matter giving rise to the modification.

This paragraph should be placed immediately before the opinion paragraph.

**Illustration 2: Murray Co qualified opinion 1**

*Example where the auditor concludes that the financial statements are materially (but not pervasively) misstated:*

*Basis for Qualified Opinion (*UK & Ireland: *Basis for Qualified Opinion on Financial Statements)*

No allowance has been provided in the financial statements for a receivable for which recoverability is in doubt, which, in our opinion, is not in accordance with International Financial Reporting Standards. The allowance for the year ended 31 December 2012 should be $211,000 based on the value of the receivable in current assets and the likely recoverability of the amount. Accordingly, current assets should be reduced by an allowance of $211,000 and the profit for the year and accumulated profit should be decreased by the same amount.

*Opinion*

In our opinion, **except for the effect on the financial statements of the matter referred to in the Basis for Qualified Opinion paragraph, the financial statements present a true and fair view** of the financial position of Murray Company..................(remainder of wording as per an unmodified report).

**Illustration 3: Murray Co Adverse opinion**

*Example where the auditor concludes that the financial statements are materially and pervasively misstated:*

*Basis for Adverse Opinion (UK & Ireland: Basis for Adverse Opinion on Financial Statements)*

As explained in note 12 to the financial statements, the financial statements have been prepared on the going concern basis. However, in our opinion, due to the number and significance of the material uncertainties, Murray Co is not a going concern in accordance with IAS 1 *Presentation of Financial Statements* and therefore the financial statements should not be prepared on the going concern basis.... [explanation of the various effects on the amounts presented in the financial statements].

*Adverse Opinion*

In our opinion, **because of the significance of the matter discussed in the Basis for Adverse Opinion paragraph , the financial statements do not give a true and fair view** of the financial position......

**Illustration 4: Murray Co qualified opinion 2**

*Example where the auditor concludes that they have been unable to gather sufficient appropriate evidence and the possible effects are deemed to be material but not pervasive:*

*Basis for Qualified Opinion (UK & Ireland:* Basis for Qualified Opinion on Financial Statements)

As described in note 8 to the financial statements, Murray Company is the defendant in a lawsuit alleging constructive dismissal. The Company has filed a counter action, and preliminary hearings and discovery proceedings on both actions are in progress. The liability has been disclosed as contingent in accordance IAS 37 *Provisions and Contingent Liabilities.* We have been unable to obtain a response to our request for information from the solicitors representing Murray Company in the case. We were unable to confirm or verify by alternative means the likely success of the lawsuit and therefore unable to determine whether disclosure of a contingent liability is appropriate, or whether a provision for the value of the claim of $280,000 should be included in the statement of financial position as at 31 December 2012 and an associated expense included in the statement of profit or loss for the year ended 31 December 2012.

As a result, we were unable to determine whether any adjustments to the financial statements might have been necessary in respect of an unrecorded provision and associate expense, and the associated elements of the statement of changes in equity and cash flow statement.

*Opinion*

In our opinion, **except for the potential effect on the financial statements of the matter referred to in the Basis for Qualified Opinion paragraph, the financial statements present a true and fair view** of the financial position of Murray Company.................. (remainder of wording as per an unmodified report).

**Illustration 5: Murray Co Disclaimer of opinion**

*Example where the auditor concludes that they have been unable to gather sufficient appropriate evidence and the possible effects are deemed to be both material and pervasive.*

*Basis for Disclaimer of Opinion (*UK & Ireland: *Basis for Disclaimer of Opinion on Financial Statements)*

Due to a fire at a third party warehouse provider's premises, the records relating to inventory held there were destroyed. We were unable to confirm or verify by alternative means closing inventory of $1,054,000 deducted from cost of sales included in the statement of profit or loss for the year ended 31 December 2012, and the inventory balance of $1,054,000 included in the statement of financial position as at 31 December 2012.

As a result, we were unable to determine whether any adjustments to the financial statements might have been necessary in respect of recorded or unrecorded inventory or cost of sales, and the associated elements of the statement of changes in equity and cash flow statement.

*Disclaimer of Opinion*

Because of the significance of the matter described in the Basis of Disclaimer of Opinion paragraph, **we have not been able to obtain sufficient appropriate evidence to provide a basis for an audit opinion. Accordingly, we do not express an opinion on the financial statements**.

## 4 Additional paragraphs

In specific circumstances, the auditor can draw the users' attention to matters that are significant to their understanding of the financial statements by way of an additional paragraph in the audit report. These circumstances are:

(i) Matters already presented/disclosed in the financial statements that are fundamental to understanding the financial statements. These are highlighted in **Emphasis of Matter** paragraphs

(ii) Other matters relevant to understanding the audit, the auditor's responsibilities or the audit report. These are presented in **Other Matter** paragraphs.

### Emphasis of Matter paragraphs

These are presented immediately after the opinion paragraph. It is important to note that they have **do not affect the audit opinion**, nor are they a substitute for one.

These paragraphs simply draw the readers' attention to a note already disclosed in the financial statements. The matters referred to must be **fundamental** to the users' understanding of the financial statements. Widespread use of them would diminish their effectiveness.

Examples of where it may be necessary to add an Emphasis of Matter paragraph include:

- an uncertainty relating to the future outcome of exceptional litigation or regulatory action
- early application of a new accounting standards that has a pervasive effect on the financial statements
- a major catastrophe that has had, or continues to have, a significant effect on the entity's financial position.

**Illustration 6: Emphasis of Matter Paragraph**

*Emphasis of Matter*

In forming our opinion on the financial statements, which is not modified in respect of this matter, we have considered the adequacy of the disclosure made in note 12(b) to the financial statements concerning the uncertainty of Murray Company's future funding. The Company is seeking new funding through an initial public offering of shares. In the event that the initial public offering does not proceed, this will require the Company's existing banking arrangements to be renegotiated and additional funding to be raised from either existing or new investors. This condition indicates the existence of a material uncertainty which may cast significant doubt on the Company's ability to continue as a going concern. The financial statements do not include any adjustments that would result if the Company was unable to continue as a going concern.

**Other Matter paragraphs**

Circumstances where these may be necessary include if there is a material inconsistency between the audited financial statements and the 'other information' contained in the annual report (such as the Chairman's Report).

An Other Matter paragraph would not be used where the material misstatement in the 'other information' does not contradict the financial statements, e.g. a company materially mistating the volume of carbon dioxide emissions. This would be described as a material misstatement of fact. The auditor would need to seek legal advice on an appropriate course of action if management refuse to amend the mistatement. (Note the UK difference in the UK syllabus focus below).

**Other matter paragraph**

Other circumstances where an Other Matter paragraph may be necessary include:

- to explain why the auditor has not resigned, when a pervasive inability to obtain sufficient appropriate evidence is imposed by management (e.g. denying the auditor access to books and records) but the auditor is unable to withdraw from the engagement due to legal restrictions;
- when national laws/regulations require, or permit, the auditor to elaborate on their responsibilities;
- when the client issues another set of financial statements (e.g. one according to IFRS and one according to UK GAAP) and the auditor has also issued a report on those financial statements; and
- when a set of financial statements is prepared for a specific purpose and user group and the users have determined that a general purpose framework meets their financial information needs.

## 5 Reporting to those charged with Governance

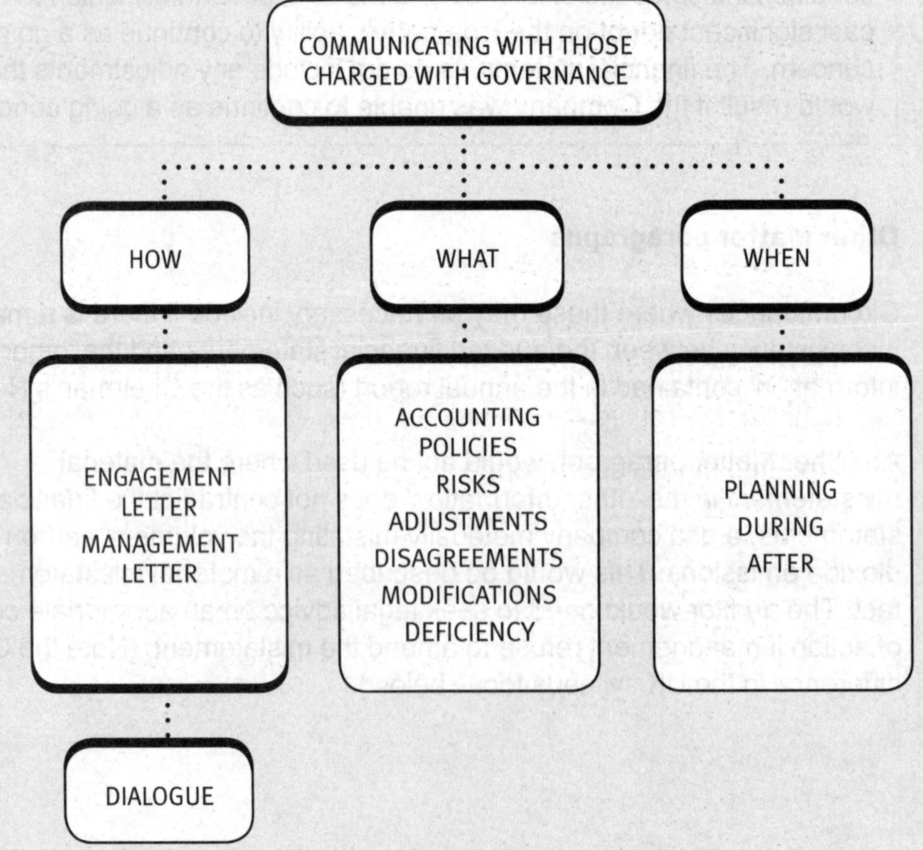

ISAs, in particular ISA 260 *Communication with Those Charged with Governance* and ISA 265 *Communicating Deficiencies in Internal Control to Those Charged with Governance and Management*, require the external auditors to engage in communications with management.

The main forms of formal communication between the auditors and management are: the engagement letter (see 'Ethics and Acceptance' chapter); and another written communication, usually sent at the end of the audit, which is often referred to as 'the management letter.'

The objectives of these communications are:

- to communicate the responsibilities of the auditor and an overview of the scope and timing of the audit
- to obtain, from those charged with governance, information relevant to the audit
- to provide timely observations arising from the audit that are significant to the responsibilities of those charged with governance
- to promote effective two-way communication between the auditor and those charged with governance.

Whilst a formal communication is usually sent at the conclusion of the audit there may be a need to communicate particular matters at other times to help meet the third objective, for example; if a fraud is discovered.

Audit matters of governance interest include:

- auditor independence
- effects of significant accounting policies and changes to them
- potential financial effect of risks/uncertainties
- material audit adjustments
- disagreements with management concerning the financial statements
- significant difficulties encountered during the audit
- expected modifications to the audit report
- significant internal control deficiencies, including fraud.

**Communication with those charged with governance**

**Timing of communications**

| **Stage of audit** | **Communication required** |
|---|---|
| Planning | Practical matters concerning forthcoming audit.<br>Independence of auditor.<br>Expected fees.<br>Nature and scope of audit work.<br>Ensure letter of engagement is up to date. |
| During the audit | If any situation occurs and it would not be appropriate to delay communication until the audit is concluded. |
| Conclusion of audit | Major findings from audit work.<br>Uncorrected misstatements.<br>Qualitative aspects of accounting/reporting pp.<br>Final draft of letter of representation.<br>Expected modifications to audit report.<br>Significant internal control deficiencies. |

**UK Syllabus Focus**

**ISA 260 *Communication with those charged with governance* (UK & Ireland) Revised:**

- Clarifies that those charged with governance are both executive and non-executive directors (or equivalent), including members of the audit committee, whereas management would not normally included non-executive directors.
- Sets out additional information that the auditors are required to report to those charged with governance:
  - information relevant to compliance with the UK Corporate Governance Code for relevant entities
  - business risks relevant to financial reporting
  - significant accounting policies
  - management's valuation of material assets and liabilities and related disclosures

- effectiveness of internal controls relevant to financial reporting
- other business risks and effectiveness of other internal controls where the auditor has obtained an understanding of these matters.

**UK Syllabus Focus**

**ISA 720A (UK & Ireland) The Auditor's Responsibilities Relating to Other Information in Documents Containing Audited Financial Statements**

In the UK & Ireland the auditor is also required to identify any information contained within any of the financial or non-financial information in the annual report that is apparently materially incorrect based on, or materially inconsistent with, the knowledge acquired by the auditor in the course of performing the audit.

If on reading the other information, the auditor becomes aware of a material misstatement of fact that management refuses to correct, they may include a description of this misstatement of fact in an Other Matters paragraph.

**ISA 720(b) (UK & Ireland) The Auditor's Statutory Reporting Responsibility in Relation to Directors' Reports**

In the United Kingdom legislation (i.e. the Companies Act 2006) requires the auditor of a company to state in the auditor's report whether, in the auditor's opinion, the information given in the directors' report is consistent with the financial statements.

**Objectives**

The objective of the auditor is to form an opinion on whether the information given in the directors' report is consistent with the financial statements and to respond appropriately if it is not consistent.

This would appear in an "Opinion on Other Matters" paragraph, directly below the "Opinion on the Financial Statements".

**Requirements**

The auditor shall read the information in the directors' report and assess whether it is consistent with the financial statements.

The auditor is not required to verify, or report on, the completeness of the information in the directors' report. If, however, the auditor becomes aware that information that is required by law or regulations to be in the directors' report has been omitted the auditor communicates the matter to those charged with governance.

If the auditor identifies any inconsistencies between the information in the directors' report and the financial statements the auditor shall seek to resolve them.

If the auditor is of the opinion that the information in the directors' report is materially inconsistent with the financial statements, and has been unable to resolve the inconsistency, the auditor shall state that opinion and describe the inconsistency in the auditor's report.

If an amendment is necessary to the financial statements and management and those charged with governance refuse to make the amendment, the auditor shall express a qualified or adverse opinion on the financial statements.

**Test your understanding 1**

**In terms of audit reports, explain the term 'modified'.**

*Real exam question: June 2009* **(2 marks)**

**Test your understanding 2**

ISA 260 (Revised and Redrafted) Communication with Those Charged with Governance deals with the auditor's responsibility to communicate with those charged with governance in relation to an audit of financial statements.

**Required:**

(i) **Describe TWO specific responsibilities of those charged with governance; and**

**(2 marks)**

(ii) **Explain FOUR examples of matters that might be communicated to them by the auditor.**
*Real exam question: December 2009*

**(4 marks)**

**Test your understanding 3**

**Henry**

(a) Aragon Co made a very poor attempt to conduct their inventory count. You attended, however there was insufficient evidence that the inventory valuation at $4 million is accurate. Sales revenue was $50 million and profit for the year was $15 million.

(b) Boleyn Co did not provide for a bad debt of $50,000 despite the fact that the customer went bankrupt just after the year end. Profit for the year was $500,000 and trade receivables $200,000.

(c) Seymour Co is being sued by a competitor company for the theft of intellectual property. The amount that Seymour is being sued for is material, but not a substantial amount, and the case could go either way. However, this is not mentioned anywhere in the financial statements.

(d) Howard Co is a cash retailer. There is no system to confirm the accuracy of cash sales.

(e) Cleves Co has neglected to include a statement of profit or loss in its financial statements.

(f) Parr Co is undergoing a major court case that would bankrupt the company if lost. The directors assess and disclose the case as a contingent liability in the accounts. The auditors agree with the treatment and disclosure.

**Required:**

**For each of the above situations state what type of audit report should be issued and explain your choice.**

**(18 marks)**

**Test your understanding 4**

You are the audit manager of Brakes Co and you are undertaking an overall review of the evidence obtained as part of the audit finalisation. Brakes Co is a global manufacturer of braking systems for use in domestic and commercial motor vehicles. $250,000 was raised through a new share issue in the year. Draft profit before tax is $9m and total assets are $37m.

(a) Explain the importance of the overall review of evidence obtained.

**(3 marks)**

(b) During your review you notice that one section of the file remains incomplete; that relating to share capital and reserves.

**Required:**

**Describe audit procedures that should be performed in respect of Brake's share capital and reserves:**

**(4 marks)**

(c) The following matters arising during the audit of Brakes Co have been noted on file for your attention:

(i) A customer of Brakes Co had to withdraw one of their family car models this year due to concerns over the safety of the braking system. The customer has lodged a legal claim against Brakes Co for $10m for the negligent supply of 'faulty' braking systems. The company's lawyers believe that there is an 80% chance that Brakes Co will lose the case but the directors believe that their quality control procedures have always been robust and that the braking systems will be proven to have been safe. They have however decided to disclose the matter in the accounts to provide additional information to shareholders.

**(5 marks)**

(ii) Brakes Co also produces and sells brake fluid. Another customer has recently returned a small batch of brake fluid because the fluid appeared to be contaminated with oil. Brakes Co issued the customer with a credit note for the full value ($137,500) and correctly accounted for this in the draft financial statements. As the brake fluid was returned before the year end, Brakes Co has included it in the year end inventory listing at cost ($125,000). Brakes Co may be able to re-filter and re-sell the brake fluid at the original price, but filtering will cost a further $62,500.

**(4 marks)**

(iii) Four months ago, Brakes Co began renting some additional warehouse space from a third party storage provider, Wheels Co. At the year end, a number of items of raw material belonging to Brakes were stored by Wheels Co. The directors of Brakes Co did not make you aware of the new third party storage facility. Consequently, no audit procedures were included in the audit plan to verify the quantity of raw material owned by Brakes Co but held by Wheels at the year end. $3.2m is included in inventory in Brakes Co draft financial statements, in respect of this raw material.

**(4 marks)**

**Required:**

**Discuss each of these issues and describe the impact on the audit report if the above issues remain unresolved.**

Note: The mark allocation is shown against each of the three issues above. Audit report extracts are NOT required.

**(13 marks)**

**(Total: 20 marks)**

## 6 Chapter summary

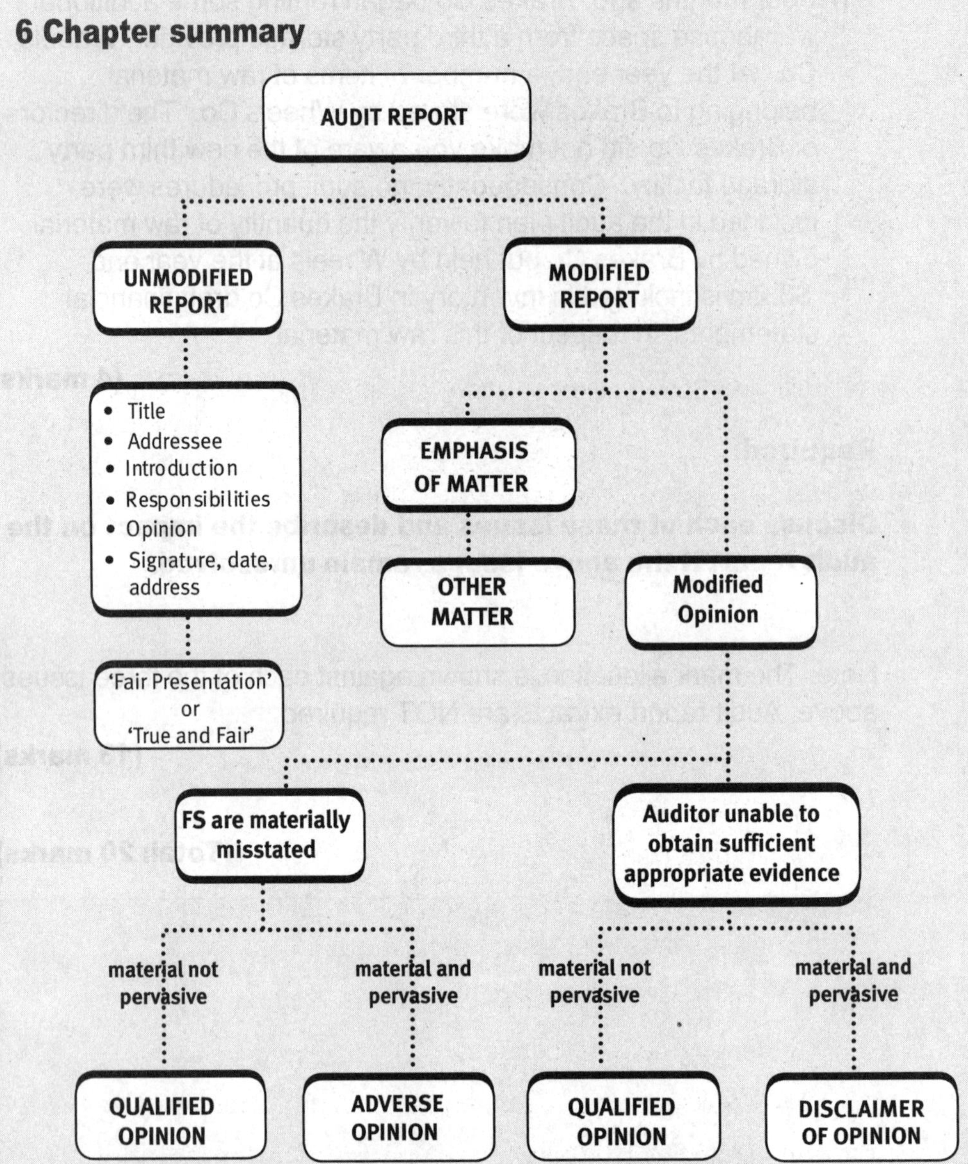

## Test your understanding answers

### Test your understanding 1

**Audit report term**

**Modified.** An auditor modifies an audit report in any situation where it is inappropriate to provide an unmodified report.

For example, the auditor may provide additional information in an emphasis of matter (which does not affect the auditor's opinion) or modify the audit opinion because the financial statements as a whole are not free from material misstatement or the auditor is unable to obtain sufficient appropriate evidence to conclude.

### Test your understanding 2

(i) Those charged with governance are responsible for overseeing:

- the strategic direction of the entity
- obligations related to the accountability of the entity. This includes overseeing the financial reporting process;
- promotion of good corporate governance;
- risk assessment processes;
- the establishment and monitoring of internal controls;
- compliance with applicable law and regulations; and
- implementation of controls to prevent and detect fraud and errors.

(ii) General audit matters that might be communicated to those charged with governance are:

(1) The auditor's responsibilities in relation to financial statement audit. This would include:

- A statement that the auditor is responsible for forming and expressing an opinion on the financial statements.
- That the auditor's work is carried out in accordance with ISAs and in accordance with local laws and regulations.

(2) Planned scope and timing of the audit. This would include:

– The audit approach to assessing the risk of serious misstatement, whether arising from fraud or error.

– The audit approach to the internal control system and whether reliance will be placed on it.

– The timing of interim and final audits, including reporting deadlines.

(3) Significant findings from the audit. This could include:

– Significant difficulties encountered during the audit, including delays in obtaining information from management.

– Material deficiencies in internal control and recommendations for improvement.

– Audit adjustments, whether or not recorded by the entity, that have, or could have, a material effect on the entity's financial statements. For example, the bankruptcy of a material receivable shortly after the year-end that should result in an adjusting entry.

(4) A statement on independence issues affecting the audit. This would include:

– That the audit firm has ensured that all members of the audit team have complied with the ethical standards of ACCA.

– That appropriate safeguards are in place where a potential threat to independence has been identified.

**Test your understanding 3**

(a) There is a lack of sufficient appropriate audit evidence, specifically relating to the valuation of inventory. Inventory is a material amount since it is 8% of sales revenue and 27% of profit. A modified report with a qualified opinion will be issued (using the 'except for' wording) due an inability to obtain sufficient appropriate audit evidence.

(b) The financial statements are materially misstated as the event after the reporting date is an adjusting event in accordance with IAS 10 and therefore the debt should be written off. The debt of $50,000 is material since it is 10% of profit and 25% of the total receivables. A report with a qualified opinion will be issued (using the 'except for' wording) due to a material misstatement.

(c) The financial statements are materially misstated since this is a contingent liability in accordance with IAS 37 and so should be disclosed by note. The matter is material. A modified report with a qualified opinion will be issued (using the 'except for' wording) due to a material omission.

(d) There is a lack of sufficient appropriate audit evidence if there is no method available to confirm cash sales. The matter would be material and pervasive since if cash sales cannot be confirmed, it may also not be possible to verify other figures in the financial statements. A modified report with a disclaimer of opinion will be issued.

(e) The financial statements are materially misstated since legislation requires companies to publish a statement of profit or loss. The matter would material and pervasive. A modified report with an adverse opinion will be issued.

(f) An unmodified opinion would be issued since the auditors agree with the treatment and disclosure of the contingent liability. However, there is a fundamental uncertainty (the outcome of the court case will be determined in the future). An modified report with an emphasis of matter paragraph would be issued.

**Test your understanding 4**

(a) Reasons why the overall review of evidence obtained is important:

- It enables the auditor to satisfy themselves that sufficient appropriate evidence has been obtained.
- It enables the auditor to satisfy themselves that the evidence supports any conclusions reached, and is appropriately documented.
- It enables the auditor to ensure work has been performed in accordance with professional standards and applicable legal and regulatory requirements (quality control monitoring).
- For the appraisal and development of staff.

(b) Audit procedures regarding share capital and reserves

Share capital

- Agree authorised share capital and nominal value disclosures to underlying shareholding agreements/statutory constitution documents.
- Inspect cash book for evidence of cash receipts from share issues and ensure amounts not yet received are correctly disclosed as share capital called-up not paid in the financial statements.
- Inspect board minutes to verify issue of share capital during the year.

Reserves

- Agree opening reserves to prior-year closing reserves and reconcile movements.
- Agree movements in reserves to supporting documentation (e.g. revaluation reserve movements independently valuers report).

(c) Impact on audit report:

(i) Faulty brake systems

According to IAS 37 Provisions, Contingent Liabilities and Contingent Assets, if there is a present obligation, a probable outflow of resources to settle the obligation and a reliable estimate can be made of the obligation then a provision should be recognised. If the obligation is only possible, then a contingent liability should be disclosed.

It is probable that Brakes Co will lose the legal case and therefore the claim of $10m should be provided for in the financial statements. The amount of $10m is 111% ($10m/ $9m) of profit before tax and is therefore material. The $10m provision would turn a profit of $9m into a loss of $1m and is also therefore pervasive.

Refusal to provide would change the whole view given by the financial statements and as a result an adverse opinion would be necessary.

A 'basis for adverse opinion' paragraph would need to be included before the opinion, describing the matter giving rise to the modification.

(ii) Contaminated brake fluid

Inventory should be stated at the lower of cost and net realisable value, in accordance with IAS 2 Inventories.

The contaminated brake fluid cost $125,000. If sold at the original price charged of $137,500, the net realisable value will be $75,000 ($137,500 less $62,500 re-filtering costs). Inventory is therefore overstated by $50,000.

$50,000 is not material at 0.6% of profit ($50,000/$9m) and 0.1% of total assets ($50,000/$37m).

The misstatement should be brought to the attention of management and they should be asked to correct it.

However, as the misstatement is not material, the audit opinion would not be modified in this respect and no reference to the misstatement would be made in the audit report.

(iii) Inventory held at third party premises

The auditor has not obtained sufficient appropriate evidence over the inventory held at third party premises.

The inventory is material to the statement of profit or loss at 36% of profit ($3.2m/$9m) and the statement of financial position at 8.6% of total assets ($3.2m/$37m)).

If alternative sources of evidence cannot be obtained, it will be necessary to modify the audit opinion due to lack of sufficient appropriate evidence.

A qualified opinion using the 'except for' wording would be necessary.

A 'basis for qualified opinion' paragraph would need to be included before the opinion, describing the matter giving rise to the qualification.

(ii) Contaminated brake fluid

Inventory should be stated at the lower of cost and net realisable value, in accordance with IAS 2 Inventories.

The contaminated brake fluid cost $125,000. If sold at the original price charged of $137,500, the net realisable value will be $75,000 ($137,500 less $62,500 re-filtering costs). Inventory is therefore overstated by $50,000.

$50,000 is not material at 0.6% of profit ($50,000/$9m) and 0.1% of total assets ($50,000/$87m).

The misstatement should be brought to the attention of management and they should be asked to correct it.

However, as the misstatement is not material, the audit opinion would not be modified in this respect and no reference to the misstatement would be made in the audit report.

(iii) Inventory held at third party premises

The auditor has not obtained sufficient appropriate evidence over the inventory held at third party premises.

The inventory is material to the statement of profit or loss at 36% of profit ($3.2m/$9m) and the statement of financial position at 3.6% of total assets ($3.2m/$87m).

If alternative sources of evidence cannot be obtained, it will be necessary to modify the audit opinion due to lack of sufficient appropriate evidence.

A qualified opinion using the 'except for' wording would be necessary.

A 'basis for qualified opinion' paragraph would need to be included before the opinion, describing the matter giving rise to the qualification.

chapter

# 11

# Corporate governance

## Chapter learning objectives

When you have completed this chapter you will be able to:

- Discuss the objective, relevance and importance of corporate governance.
- Discuss the provisions of international codes of corporate governance that are most relevant to auditors.
- Analyse the structure and roles of audit committees and discuss their benefits and limitations.
- Explain the importance of internal control and risk management.
- Compare the responsibilities of management and auditors for the design and operation of systems and controls.

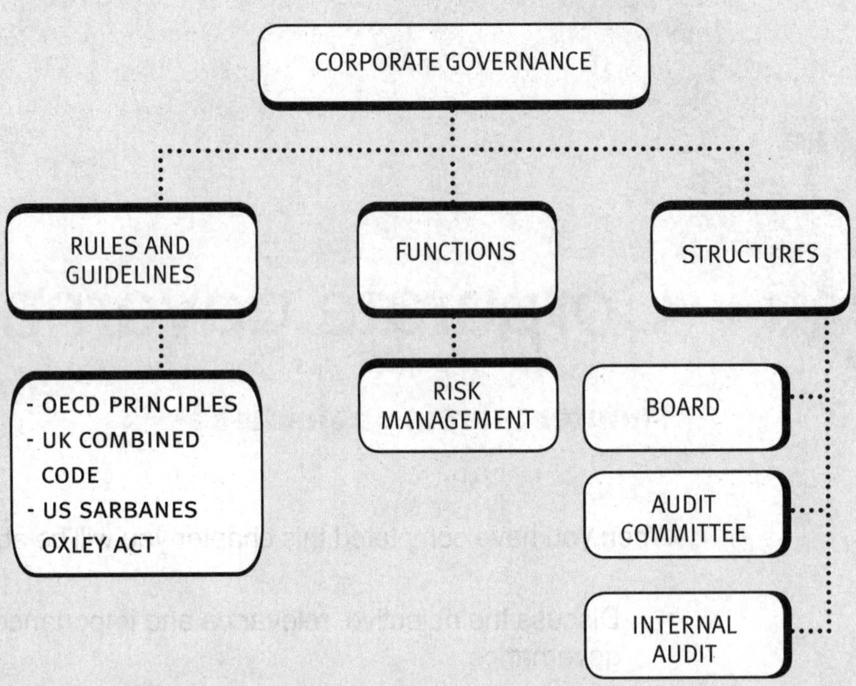


## 1 Introduction

In response to major accounting scandals (e.g. Enron), regulators sought to change the rules surrounding the governance of companies, particularly publically owned ones.

In the US the Sarbanes Oxley Act (2002) introduced a set of rigorous corporate governance laws and at the same time the UK Corporate Governance Code (previously the Combined Code) introduced a set of best practice corporate governance initiatives into the UK.

### What is corporate governance?

**Corporate governance** is the means by which a company is **operated** and **controlled**.

The aim of corporate governance initiatives is to ensure that companies are run well in the interests of their shareholders and the wider community. It concerns such matters as:

- the responsibilities of directors
- the appropriate composition of the board of directors
- the necessity for good internal control
- the necessity for an audit committee
- relationships with the external auditors.

It is particularly important for publicly traded companies because large amounts of money are invested in them, either by 'small' shareholders, or from pension schemes and other financial institutions. The wealth of these companies significantly affects the health of the economies where their shares are traded.

**Enron**

In the year 2000 Enron, a US based energy company, employed 22,000 people and reported revenues of $101 billion. In late 2001 they filed for bankruptcy protection. After a lengthy investigation it was revealed that Enron's financial statements were sustained substantially by systematic, and creatively planned, accounting fraud.

In the wake of the fraud case the shares of Enron fell from over $90 each to just a few cents each, a number of directors were prosecuted and jailed and their auditors, Arthur Andersen, were accused of obstruction of justice and forced to stop auditing public companies. This ruling against Arthur Andersen was overturned at a later date but the damage was done and the firm ceased trading soon after.

This was just one of a number of high profile frauds to occur at the turn of the millennium.

The Enron scandal is an example of the abuse of the trust placed in the management of publicly traded companies by investors. This abuse of trust usually takes one of two forms:

- the direct extraction from the company of excessive benefits by management, e.g. large salaries, pension entitlements, share options, use of company assets (jets, apartments etc.)
- manipulation of the share price by misrepresenting the company's profitability, usually so that shares in the company can be sold or options 'cashed in'.

In response regulators sought to change the rules surrounding the governance of companies, particularly publically owned ones. In the US the Sarbanes Oxley Act (2002) introduced a set of rigorous corporate governance laws and at the same time the Combined Code introduced a set of best practice corporate governance initiatives into the UK.

**The OECD Principles of Corporate Governance**

Although there have always been well run companies as well as those where scandals have occurred, the fact that scandals do occur has led to the development of codes of practice for good corporate governance.

Often this is due to pressures exerted by stock exchanges. In 1999 the Organisation for Economic Co-operation and Development, OECD, assisted with the development of their 'Principles of Corporate Governance.' These were intended to:

- assist member and non-member governments in their efforts to evaluate and improve the legal, institutional and regulatory framework for corporate governance in their countries.
- provide guidance and suggestions for stock exchanges, investors, corporations, and other parties that have a role in the process of developing good corporate governance.

The OECD principles were first published in 1999 and were revised in 2004. Their focus is on publicly traded companies. However, to the extent they are deemed applicable, they are a useful tool to improve corporate governance in non-traded companies.

There are six principles, each backed up by a number of sub principles. The principles, and those sub-principles relevant to the auditor, are reproduced below.

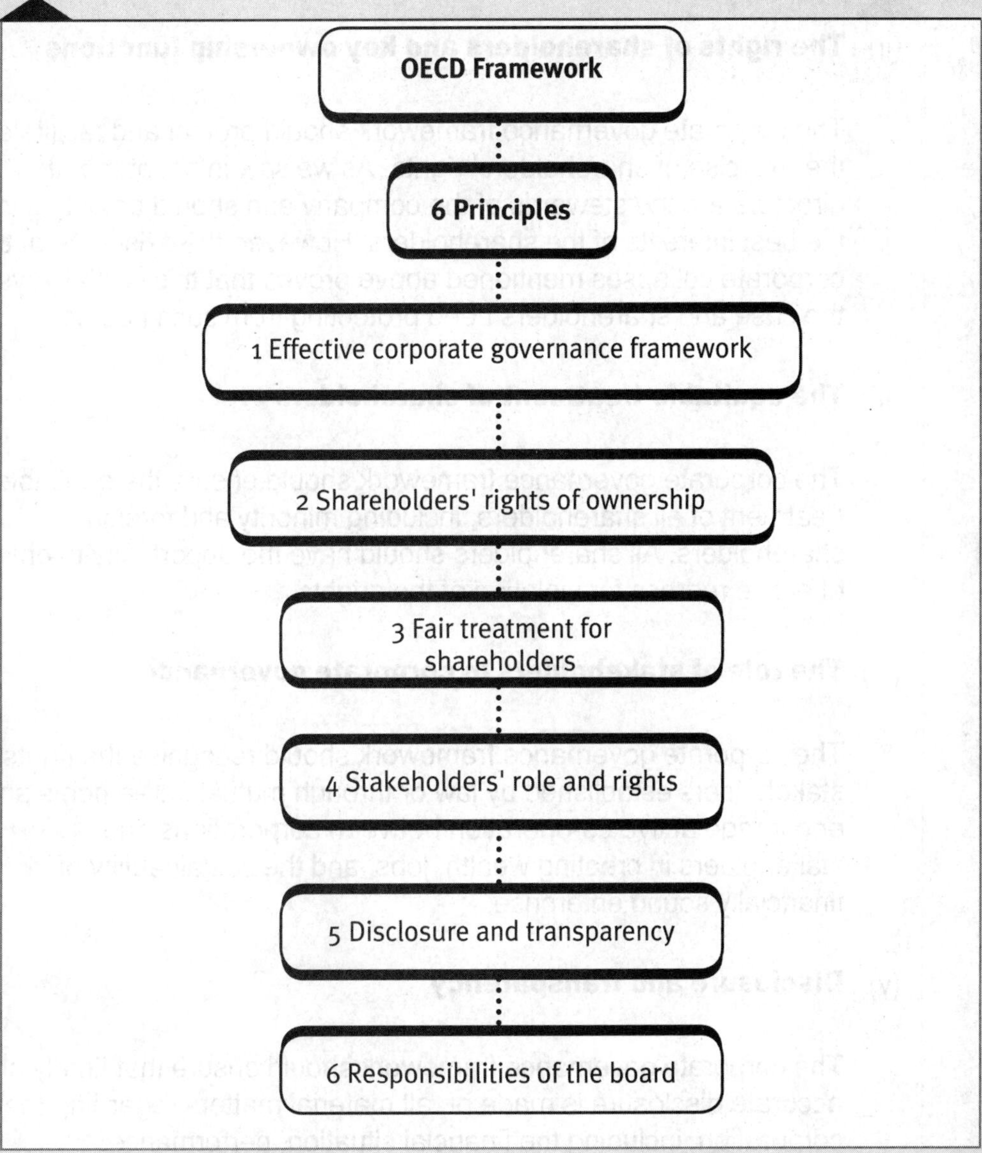


**The principles in detail**

**Structure of the Principles**

**The six Principles:**

(i) **Ensuring the basis for an effective corporate governance framework**

The corporate governance framework should promote transparent and efficient markets, be consistent with the rule of law and clearly articulate the division of responsibilities among different supervisory, regulatory and enforcement authorities. In other words, making sure everyone involved is aware of their individual responsibilities so no party is in doubt as to what they are accountable for.

(ii) **The rights of shareholders and key ownership functions**

The corporate governance framework should protect and facilitate the exercise of shareholders' rights. As we saw in chapter 1, the directors are the stewards of the company and should be acting in the best interests of the shareholders. However, the existence of the corporate collapses mentioned above proves that this isn't always the case and shareholders need protecting from such people.

(iii) **The equitable treatment of shareholders**

The corporate governance framework should ensure the equitable treatment of all shareholders, including minority and foreign shareholders. All shareholders should have the opportunity to obtain effective redress for violation of their rights.

(iv) **The role of stakeholders in corporate governance**

The corporate governance framework should recognise the rights of stakeholders established by law or through mutual agreements and encourage active co-operation between corporations and stakeholders in creating wealth, jobs, and the sustainability of financially sound enterprise.

(v) **Disclosure and transparency**

The corporate governance framework should ensure that timely and accurate disclosure is made on all material matters regarding the corporation, including the financial situation, performance, ownership and governance of the company. Therefore, the annual financial statements should be produced on a timely basis and include all matters of interest to the shareholders. For any matters of significance arising during the year, these should be communicated to the shareholders as appropriate.

(vi) **The responsibilities of the board**

The corporate governance framework should ensure the strategic guidance of the company, the effective monitoring of management by the board, and the board's accountability to the company and the shareholders. The introduction of audit committees and non executive directors on the board is the usual way for monitoring management. Non executive directors are not involved in the day to day running of the company and are therefore more independent. They can evaluate the effectiveness of the executive board on its merits and make sure they are carrying out their duties properly.

### The OECD principles and the audit

**Sub principle VC**

'An annual audit should be conducted by an independent, competent and qualified auditor in order to provide an external and objective assurance to the board and shareholders that the financial statements fairly represent the financial position and performance of the company in all material respects.'

**Sub principle VD**

'External auditors should be accountable to the shareholders and owe a duty to the company to exercise due professional care in the conduct of the audit.'

### The OECD principles and the board

- **Reviewing and guiding corporate strategy**, major plans of action, risk policy, annual budgets and business plans; setting performance objectives; monitoring implementation and corporate performance, and overseeing major capital expenditures, acquisitions and divestitures.
- **Monitoring the effectiveness of the company's governance** and making changes as needed.
- **Selecting, compensating, monitoring and, when necessary, replacing key executives** and overseeing succession planning.
- **Aligning key executive and board remuneration** with the longer term interests of the company and its shareholders ensuring a formal and transparent board nomination and election process.
- Monitoring and managing **potential conflicts of interest of management, board members and shareholders**, including misuse of corporate assets and abuse in related party transactions.
- Ensuring the **integrity of the corporation's accounting and financial reporting systems**, including the independent audit, and that appropriate systems of control are in place, in particular, systems for risk management, financial and operational control, and compliance with the law and relevant standards.
- Overseeing the process of **disclosure and communications**.

**The status of the OECD principles**

- The Principles represent a common basis that OECD Member countries consider essential for the development of good governance practice.
- They are intended to be concise, understandable and accessible to the international community.
- They are not intended to be a substitute for government or private sector initiatives to develop more detailed 'best practice' in governance.

## 2 Corporate governance in action

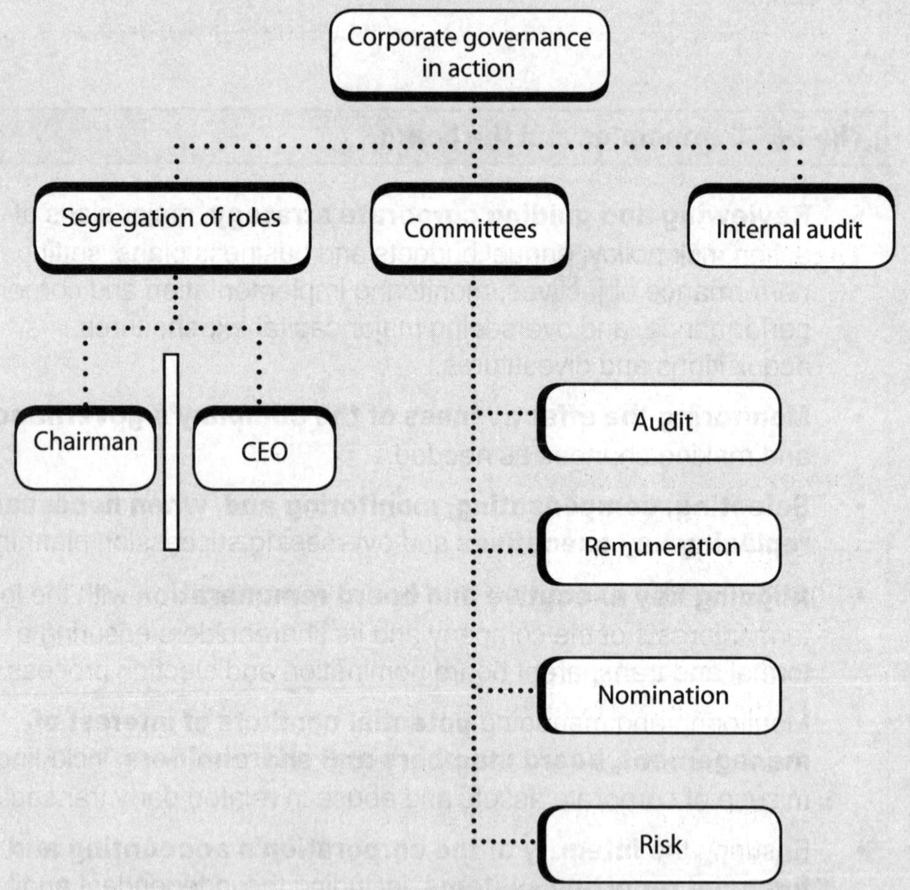


There are a number of principles of corporate governance that are globally accepted as essential to the effective management of companies, particularly publically owned ones. These are:

- Segregation between the roles of chairman and chief executive officer (CEO)
- Non-executive directors
- Audit (and other) committee

- Risk management
- Internal audit

**The roles of the board members**

**Segregation of Roles**

Best practice recommends that the roles of Chairman and Chief Executive Officer should be held be different people to reduce the power of prominent board members.

**The chairman's role**

- Head of the non-executive directors.
- Enables flow of information and discussion at board meetings.
- Ensures satisfactory channels of communication with the external auditors.
- Ensures the effective operation of sub-committees of the board.

**The Chief executive's role**

- Ensures the effective operation of the company.
- Head of the executive directors.

**Non-executive directors**

Non-executive directors are usually employed on a part-time basis and do not take part in the routine executive management of the company. Their role is as follows.

- Participation at board meetings.
- Provision of experience, insight and contacts to assist the board.
- Membership of sub-committees as independent, knowledgeable parties.

**Advantages of participation by non-executive directors**

- Oversight of the whole board.
- Often act as a 'corporate conscience'.
- They bring external expertise to the company.

**Disadvantages**

- They, and the sub-committees, may not be sufficiently well-informed or have time to fulfil the role competently.
- They are subject to the accusation that they are staffed by an 'old boy' network and may fail to report significant problems and approve unjustified pay rises.

Enron provides a cautionary note as its audit committee proved incapable of preventing the wrongdoing of the executive directors.

**Audit Committees**

The audit committee

- Composition
  - Minimum of 3 non-execs
  - At least 1 with financial expertise
- Objectives
  - Increase public confidence
  - Financial awareness of non-execs
  - Liaison with external auditors
- Function
  - Financial statements
  - Controls
  - Internal audit
  - External audit
  - Whistleblowing

An audit committee is a committee consisting of non-executive directors which is able to view a company's affairs in a detached and independent way and liaise effectively between the main board of directors and the external auditors.

**Best practice for listed companies:**

- The company should have an audit committee of at least three non-executive directors (or, in the case of smaller companies, two).
- At least one member of the audit committee should have recent and relevant financial experience.

**The objectives of the audit committee**

- Increasing public confidence in the credibility and objectivity of published financial information (including unaudited interim statements).
- Assisting directors (particularly executive directors) in meeting their responsibilities in respect of financial reporting.
- Strengthening the independent position of a company's external auditor by providing an additional channel of communication.

**The function of the audit committee**

- Monitoring the integrity of the financial statements.
- Reviewing the company's internal financial controls.
- Monitoring and reviewing the effectiveness of the internal audit function.
- Making recommendations in relation to the appointment and removal of the external auditor and their remuneration.
- Reviewing and monitoring the external auditor's independence and objectivity and the effectiveness of the audit process.
- Developing and implementing policy on the engagement of the external auditor to supply non-audit services.
- Reviewing arrangements for confidential reporting by employees and investigation of possible improprieties ('whistleblowing').

**Benefits:**

- Improved credibility of the financial statements, through an impartial review of the financial statements, and discussion of significant issues with the external auditors.
- Increased public confidence in the audit opinion, as the audit committee will monitor the independence of the external auditors.
- Stronger control environment, as the audit committee help to create a culture of compliance and control.

- The internal audit function will report to the audit committee increasing their independence and adding weight to their recommendations.
- The skills, knowledge and experience (and independence) of the audit committee members can be an invaluable resource for a business.
- It may be easier and cheaper to arrange finance, as the presence of an audit committee can give a perception of good corporate governance.
- It would be less burdensome to meet listing requirements if an audit committee (which is usually a listing requirement) is already established.

**Problems:**

- Difficulties recruiting the right non-executive directors who have relevant skills, experience and sufficient time to become effective members of the committee.
- The cost. Non-executive directors are normally remunerated, and their fees can be quite expensive.

**The audit committee and internal audit**

The audit committee should:

- Ensure that the internal auditor has direct access to the board chairman and to the audit committee and is accountable to the audit committee.
- Review and assess the annual internal audit work plan.
- Receive periodic reports on the results of internal audit work.
- Review and monitor management's responsiveness to the internal auditor's findings and recommendations.
- Meet with the head of internal audit at least once a year without the presence of management.
- Monitor and assess the effectiveness of internal audit in the overall context of the company's risk management system.

## 3 Risk management

### Risk management

Companies face many risks, for example:

- The risk that products may become technologically obsolete.
- The risk of losing key staff.
- The risk of a catastrophic failure of IT systems.
- The risk of changes in government policy.
- The risk of fire or natural disaster.

Companies therefore need to:

- Identify potential risks and
- Decide on appropriate ways to minimise those risks.

**Risk management in practice**

Risks can arise from many sources and be of various natures, e.g. operational, financial, legal.

Companies need mechanisms in place to identify and then assess those risks. In so doing companies can rank risks in terms of their relative importance by scoring them with regard to their likelihood and potential impact. This could take the form of a 'risk map':

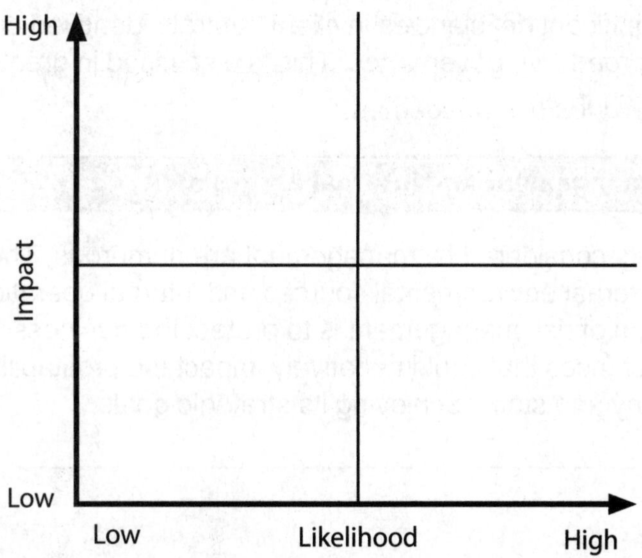

A risk that ranked as highly likely to occur and high potential impact on the business would be prioritised as requiring immediate action. A risk that was considered both low likelihood and low impact might simply be ignored or, simply insured against.

Ways of managing exposure to risk include:

- insuring against it;
- implementing internal procedures and controls (e.g. training) to minimise the risk of occurrence;
- discontinuing especially risky activities; and
- simply accepting the risk as inevitable but trivial.

**Internal controls and risk management**

One way of minimising risk is to incorporate internal controls into a company's systems and procedures.

It is the director's responsibility to implement internal controls and monitor their application and effectiveness.

Auditors are not responsible for the design and implementation of their clients' control systems. Auditors have to assess the effectiveness of controls for reducing the risk of material misstatement of the financial statements. They incorporate this into their overall risk assessment, which allows them to design their further audit procedures. This concept of **audit risk** assessment is considered in detail in later chapters.

In addition to this auditors are required, in accordance with ISA 265, to report significant deficiencies in client controls identified during the audit to those charged with governance. This is discussed in greater detail in the reporting chapter.

**Risk management and internal controls**

The risks considered by management are numerous. They come from both external environmental sources and internal operational ones. The main aim of risk management is to protect the business from unforeseen circumstances that could negatively impact the profitability of the company and stop it achieving its strategic goals.

However, the main controls considered throughout this text and those in relation to the financial frauds discussed earlier are financial ones. The main aims of financial controls are to:

- reduce the risk that the financial statements contain misstatement, whether due to fraud or error; and
- reduce the risk of theft, or misuse, of the company's assets.

**UK Syllabus Focus**

**FSA Listing Rules**

The 'UK Corporate Governance Code' (formerly "the Combined Code" and last updated in June 2010) adopts what is commonly referred to as the ''comply or explain'' approach. It is not a rigid (or enforced) set of rules. Instead it consists of principles (main and supporting) and provisions.

In the UK all companies quoted on the stock exchange have to comply with the FSA listing rules. These include a requirement that all companies include in their annual report:

- a statement of how the company has applied the main principles set out in the Code; and
- a statement as to whether the company has complied with all relevant provisions set out in the Code.

The main provisions of the Code are:

**Leadership**

- Every company should be headed by an effective board with collective responsibility;
- There should be a clear division of responsibilities between the Chairman and the Chief Executive;
- No one individual should have unfettered powers of decision; and
- Non-executive directors should constructively challenge and help develop proposals on strategy.

**Effectiveness**

- The board should have the appropriate balance of skills, experience, independence and knowledge;
- There should be a formal, rigorous and transparent procedure for the appointment of new directors;
- All directors should receive induction and should regularly update and refresh their skills and knowledge;
- The board should be supplied with quality and timely information to enable it to discharge its duties;
- The board and individuals should be subject to a formal and rigorous annual evaluation of performance; and
- All directors should be submitted for re-election at regular intervals.

**Accountability**

- The board should present a balanced and understandable assessment of the company's position and prospects;
- The board is responsible for determining the nature and extent of the significant risks it is willing to take in achieving its strategic objectives;
- The board should maintain sound risk management and internal control systems; and
- The board should establish formal and transparent arrangements for corporate reporting and risk management and internal control principles and for maintaining an appropriate relationship with the company's auditor.

**Remuneration**

- This should be sufficient to attract, retain and motivate directors of the quality required to run the company successfully, but should not be excessive;
- A significant proportion this should be structured so as to link rewards to corporate and individual performance;
- There should be a formal and transparent procedure for developing policy on executive remuneration; and
- No director should be involved in deciding his or her own remuneration.

**Relations with Shareholders**

- There should be a dialogue with shareholders based on the mutual understanding of objectives;
- The board as a whole has responsibility for ensuring that a satisfactory dialogue with shareholders takes place; and
- The board should use the AGM to communicate with investors and to encourage their participation.

**Test your understanding 1**

(1) **What is meant by corporate governance?**

**(3 marks)**

(2) **Why are external auditors interested in corporate governance?**

**(3 marks)**

(3) **What are the key things the OECD principles are intended to deliver?**

**(5 marks)**

(4) **Explain the difference between a unitary board of directors and a two-tier board.**

**(2 marks)**

(5) **Who should make up a typical audit committee?**

**(1 mark)**

(6) **What is the committee's role?**

**(2 marks)**

(7) **Why would a company need an audit committee if it has a good relationship with its external auditors?**

**(4 marks)**

(8) **A company has identified one of its major risks as loss of key staff. Explain:**

(a) **what they should do as a result of this?**

(b) **how they might reduce or even eliminate the risk?**

(c) **why the auditor is interested in this, given that it is not a direct financial risk?**

**(5 marks)**

**(Total: 25 marks)**

## 4 Chapter summary

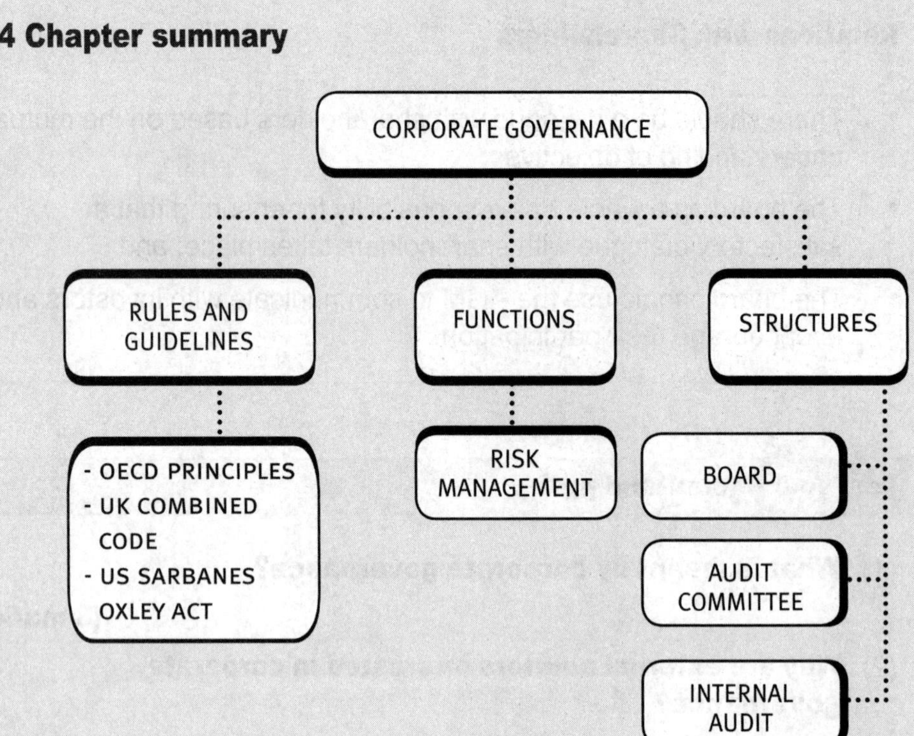

## Test your understanding answers

### Test your understanding 1

| | |
|---|---|
| (1) What is meant by corporate governance? | The term corporate governance refers to the means by which a company is managed in the interests of all stakeholders. It will include consideration of:<br>(1) directors' responsibilities — 1 mark<br>(2) composition of the board of directors — 1 mark<br>(3) audit requirements (internal and external) — 1 mark |
| (2) Why are the external auditors interested in corporate governance? | Corporate governance is the responsibility of the company's management and not its external auditors. — 1 mark<br>However, it is the responsibility of the external auditors to form an opinion on the truth and fairness of the company's financial statements. — 1 mark<br>If a company has good standards of corporate governance and is therefore managed well in the interests of all stakeholders, the auditors are likely to conclude that the risk of material misstatement in the financial statements is reduced. — 1 mark<br>As a result of this they may well be able to reduce the extent of the audit procedures they carry out. — 1 mark |

| | | | |
|---|---|---|---|
| 3 | What are the key things the OECD principles are intended to deliver? | A framework so that companies are governed well which should be beneficial to financial markets. | 1 mark |
| | | Fair treatment of all shareholders | 1 mark |
| | | Companies to be run in the interests of all stakeholders. | 1 mark |
| | | Transparency of disclosure about the company's performance and state of affairs. | 1 mark |
| | | The management of the company should carry out its role in the interest of all stakeholders. | 1 mark |
| (4) | Explain the difference between a unitary board of directors and a two-tier board? | **Unitary board**<br><br>Single board of directors. Monitored by sub-committees and non-executive directors. | 1 mark |
| | | **Two-tier board**<br><br>Two boards: Executive board (decision-makers) Monitored by supervisory board consisting of employees, investors etc | 1 mark |
| (5) | Who should make up a typical audit committee? | The audit committee should be made up of non-executive directors and include someone with relevant financial experience. | 1 mark |
| (6) | What is the committee's role? | The audit committee provides a channel of communication between the internal workings of the company and the external auditor. | 1 mark |
| | | It also provides a channel of communication for employees who have concerns about the way the company is run. | 1 mark |

| | | |
|---|---|---|
| 7 Why would a company need an audit committee if it has a good relationship with its external auditors? | A good relationship with external auditors is of immense help and support to an entity in complying with regulations, optimising controls and generally ensuring good corporate governance.<br><br>However, the existence of an audit committee will enhance the company's corporate governance profile by:<br><br>1 improving public confidence<br>2 providing further support to directors<br>3 strengthening the independence of the external auditor<br>4 improving internal procedures e.g. management accounting, & communication generally. | 1 mark<br><br>1 mark<br><br>1 mark<br>1 mark<br><br>1 mark<br><br>1 mark |
| (8) A company has identified one of its major risks as loss of key staff. Explain<br>• what they should do as a result of this?<br>• how they might reduce or even eliminate the risk?<br>• why the auditor is interested in this, given that it is not a direct financial risk? | The risk committee should discuss the issue and assess its seriousness in relation to its likelihood and potential impact. They should then decide what action is appropriate in order to manage the risk. This risk might be reduced by:<br><br>• ensuring favourable employment packages for such individuals<br>• ensuring training for other staff assists in case of succession issues<br>• ensure key tasks are not carried out by just one person.<br><br>The auditor must consider the possible impact of all significant risks as any of these could ultimately have financial consequences or going concern issues, hence impacting on the audit opinion. | 1 mark<br><br>1 mark<br><br>1 mark<br><br>1 mark<br><br>1 mark |

chapter

# 12

# Internal audit

## Chapter learning objectives

When you have completed this chapter you will be able to:

- Discuss the nature and purpose of internal audit assignments.
- Discuss the factors to be taken into account when assessing the need for internal audit.
- Discuss the elements of best practice in the structure and operations of internal audit.
- Compare and contrast the role of external and internal audit.
- Discuss the scope and the limitations of the internal audit function.

## 1 The need for internal audit

Corporate Governance is about ensuring that companies are run well in the interest of all stakeholders. In order to achieve this companies must create a strong board of directors, structured according to the principles discussed in the corporate governance chapter, who have clearly defined responsibilities.

However, it is not sufficient to simply have mechanisms in place to manage a business; their effectiveness must be regularly evaluated. All systems need some form of monitoring and feedback. This is the role of internal audit.

### Further discussion of the need for internal audit

Having an internal audit department is generally considered to be 'best practice,' rather than being required by law. This allows flexibility in the way internal audit is established to suit the needs of a business.

In small, or owner managed businesses there is unlikely to be a need for internal audit because the owners are able to exercise more direct control over operations, and are accountable to fewer stakeholders.

The need for internal audit, therefore will depend on:

- scale, diversity and complexity of activities;
- number of employees;
- cost/benefit considerations; and
- the desire of senior management to have assurance and advice on risk and control.

### Regulatory guidance

**The UK Corporate Governance Code**

This sets out the requirements relating to the composition and functions of the audit committee (or equivalent body). As a minimum, they must:

- monitor the financial reporting process;
- monitor the effectiveness of the company's internal control, internal audit, and risk management systems.

Where there is no internal audit function, the audit committee should consider annually whether there is a need for an internal audit function and make a recommendation to the board. Where there is no internal audit function, the reasons for the absence of such a function should be explained in the relevant section of the annual report

**The Sarbanes-Oxley Act (2002)**

Section 404 of the Act requires companies to document, evaluate, test and monitor their internal controls over financial reporting. This requires the senior management of a company to assess the design, operating effectiveness and adequacy of internal controls over financial reporting. Management often turns to internal audit to support compliance with these requirements.

Management are required to issue an annual report that addresses any material deficiencies in the company's internal controls. Section 404 also requires that the external auditor attests to assertions made by management about the effectiveness of the systems and controls.

## 2 The role of the internal audit function

The role of internal audit can vary depending on the requirements of the business. One of the key activities of the internal audit function is often to provide assurance. They would provide this assurance to internal management on issues such as:

- whether the company is demonstrating best practice in corporate governance
- risk identification and management
- effectiveness of internal controls
- reliability of financial and operating information
- economy, efficiency and effectiveness of operating activities
- compliance with laws and regulations.

In addition to the above, internal audit will carry out ad hoc assignments, as required by management, e.g. detection and/or investigation of fraud.

If the internal audit department is to be effective in providing assurance it needs to be:

- sufficiently resourced, both financially and in terms of qualified, experienced staff
- well organised, so that it has well developed work practices and
- independent and objective.

Internal auditors are (generally) employed by the company they are reporting on and are often managed as part of the finance function. They will therefore have to report upon the effectiveness of financial systems that they form a part of.

It is therefore difficult for internal audit to remain truly objective. However, acceptable levels of independence can be achieved through one, or more, of the following strategies:

- reporting channels separate from the management of the main financial reporting function
- reviews of internal audit work by managers independent of the function under scrutiny
- outsourcing the internal audit function to a professional third party.

**Case Study: Murray Co Internal Audit function**

**Murray Co's internal audit function**

The internal audit function at Murray Co consists of a head of internal audit; two senior internal audit managers; four internal audit managers, seven internal auditors and an internal audit assistant. The head of internal audit has been in post for twelve years, and the other members of the team have varying lengths of service from two to fifteen years.

The head of internal audit is responsible for recruiting staff into the internal audit team. The head of internal audit was appointed by the audit commitee.

The head of internal audit reports to the audit committee and agrees the scope of work for the internal audit function with the audit commitee.

The internal audit staff have no operational responsibility. Where the staff have previously transferred from another department within Murray Co, the head of internal audit ensures that another member of the team carries out the audit of that system.

Murray Co's internal audit function follow the International Standards for the Professional Practice of Internal Auditing issued by the Global Institute of Internal Auditors.

**Case Study: Barker Co Internal Audit function**

**Barker Co's internal audit function**

The internal audit function at Barker Co consists of a chief internal auditor; one senior internal audit managers; one audit manager, one auditor and an audit assistant. The chief internal auditor has been in post for ten years, and the other members of the team have varying lengths of service from five to nine years.

The finance director is responsible for recruiting all staff into the internal audit function. The chief internal auditor reports to the finance director and agrees the scope of work for the internal audit function with the him.

The internal audit team spend 50% of their time carrying out internal audit assignments and 50% of their time working in the finance department. Due to the limited number of staff in the team, this has resulted in the internal auditors reviewing their own work.

Barker Co's internal audit team follow a variety of standards, in accordance with their own professional training.

**Exercise:**

**Compare and contrast the effectiveness of Murray Co and Barker Co's internal audit functions.**

**Murray Co and Barker Co Internal Audit functions**

**Reporting system**

The chief internal auditor at Barker Co reports to the finance director. This limits the effectiveness of the internal audit reports as the finance director will also be responsible for some of the financial systems that the internal audit function is reporting on. Similarly, the chief internal auditor may soften or limit criticism in reports to avoid confrontation with the finance director.

To ensure independence, the chief internal auditor should report to the Audit Committee, as the head of internal audit at Murray Co does.

**Recruitment of staff**

All of the internal audit team at Barker Co are recruited by the finance director. The finance director may appoint personnel who are less likely to criticise his work. To ensure independence, head of internal audit should be appointed by the audit committee, and they should then recruit and appoint the rest of the team, as at Murray Co.

### Scope of work

The scope of work of internal audit at Barker Co is decided by the finance director in discussion with the chief internal auditor. This means that the finance director may try and influence the chief internal auditor regarding the areas that the internal audit department is auditing, possibly directing attention away from any contentious areas that the director does not want auditing.

To ensure independence, the scope of work of the internal audit department should be decided by the chief internal auditor, perhaps with the assistance of an audit committee, as at Murray Co.

### Audit work

The internal audit team at Barker Co review their own work. This limits independence as the auditor may overlook or fail to identify errors or deficiencies in those areas. This is a self-review threat.

If possible, the internal audit team should not have operational responsibility. However, if this is not possible, the internal audit work should be arranged so that no member of the team reviews areas where they have operational responsibility, as Murray Co does.

### Lengths of service of internal audit staff

The internal audit team staff of both companies have been employed for a long time. This may limit their effectiveness as they will be very familiar with the systems being reviewed and therefore may not be sufficiently objective to identify errors in those systems.

However, there are sufficient staff at Murray Co to ensure that the team can be rotated into different areas of internal audit work, and their work can be independently reviewed. Due to the small number of staff in the internal audit team, Barker Co may not be able to achieve this.

Given the extent of limitations, it may be appropriate for Barker Co to outsource its internal audit function.

### Variation of standards

Individual staff at Barker Co follow the auditing standards they are familiar with. Standards of internal audit are not uniform across the profession. This could lead to inconsistency in the way internal audit is performed across different assignments, and it can lead to manipulation of internal audit aims and measurement. Barker Co should follow an agreed, recognised set of professional internal audit standards, such as those followed by Murray Co.

## 3 Outsourcing the internal audit function

In common with other areas of a company's operations, the directors may consider that outsourcing the internal audit function represents better value than an in-house provision. Local government authorities are under particular pressure to ensure that all their services represent 'best value' and this may prompt them to decide to adopt a competitive tender approach.

### Advantages

- Greater focus on cost and efficiency of the internal audit function.
- Staff may be drawn from a broader range of expertise.
- Risk of staff turnover is passed to the outsourcing firm.
- Specialist skills may be more readily available.
- Costs of employing permanent staff are avoided.
- May improve independence.
- Access to new market place technologies, e.g. audit methodology software without associated costs.
- Reduced management time in administering an in-house department.

### Disadvantages

- Possible conflict of interest if provided by the external auditors (In some jurisdictions – e.g. the UK, the ethics rules specifically prohibit the external auditors from providing internal audit services).
- Pressure on the independence of the outsourced function due to, e.g. threat by management not to renew contract.
- Risk of lack of knowledge and understanding of the organisation's objectives, culture or business.
- The decision may be based on cost with the effectiveness of the function being reduced.
- Flexibility and availability may not be as high as with an in-house function.
- Lack of control over standard of service.
- Risk of blurring of roles between internal and external audit, losing credibility for both.

## 4 Internal audit assignments

Internal auditors perform many different types of assignment. Common examples include:

- Value for money assignments
- The audit of IT systems
- Financial audit
- Operational audit

### Value for money

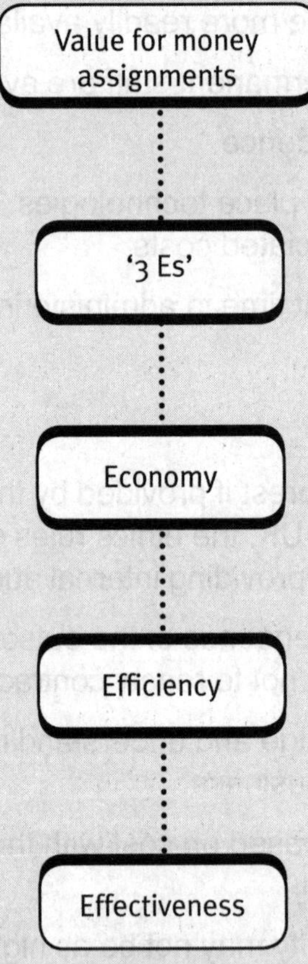


**Value for money (VFM)** is concerned with obtaining the best possible combination of services for the least resources. It is often referred to as a review of the three "E's":

- **Economy** – obtaining the best quality of resources for the minimum cost.
- **Efficiency** – obtaining the maximum departmental/organisational outputs with the minimum use of resources.

- **Effectiveness** – achievement of goals and targets (departmental/organisational etc).

Comparisons of value for money achieved by different organisations (or branches of the same organisation) are often made using performance indicators that provide a measure of economy, efficiency or effectiveness. This is particularly common in the 'not-for-profit' sector (i.e. public services and charities), but it can apply to any company.

e.g

**Value for money: hospital**

Examples of value for money indiciators for a hospital might include:

- Economy – cost of medical supplies per annum;
- Efficiency – number of patients treated per year;
- Effectiveness – recovery rates.

## The audit of IT systems

The external auditor considers IT systems from the perspective of whether they provide a reliable basis for the preparation of financial statements, and whether there are internal controls which are effective in reducing the risk of misstatement.

Internal audit will also consider this. However, their role is much wider in scope and will also consider whether:

- the company is getting value for money
- the procurement process was effective
- the ongoing management/maintenance of the system is appropriate.

Whilst this is an ongoing role project auditing can be used to look at whether the objectives of a specific project, such as commissioning a new factory or implementing new IT systems, were achieved.

## Financial audit

The main aim of a financial reporting system, from a business' perspective; is to create accurate, complete and timely information to be used as a basis for internal decision making and business planning. This information is also needed to satisfy the requirements of actual and potential investors and trading partners.

Typical examples of financial information include:

- annual financial statements
- interim financial statements
- monthly management accounts
- forecasts and projections.

The main aim of internal financial audit is to ensure that the information produced is reliable and produced in an efficient timely manner. If not then executive decisions may be based upon unreliable information or, may not be possible at all.

The other aim of financial audit is to assess the financial health of a business. More importantly it is about ensuring there are mechanisms in place for the early identification of financial risk, such as:

- adverse currency fluctuations
- adverse interest rate fluctuations
- cost price inflation.

In both cases the focus of internal audit will be on the processes and controls that underpin the creation of the various financial reports to ensure that they are as effective as possible for assisting decision making and the risk management processes of the company.

## 5 Operational internal audit assignments

Operational auditing covers:

- examination and review of the whole, or part of, a business' operations
- the effectiveness of operational controls
- identification of areas for improvement in efficiency and performance.

## General approach

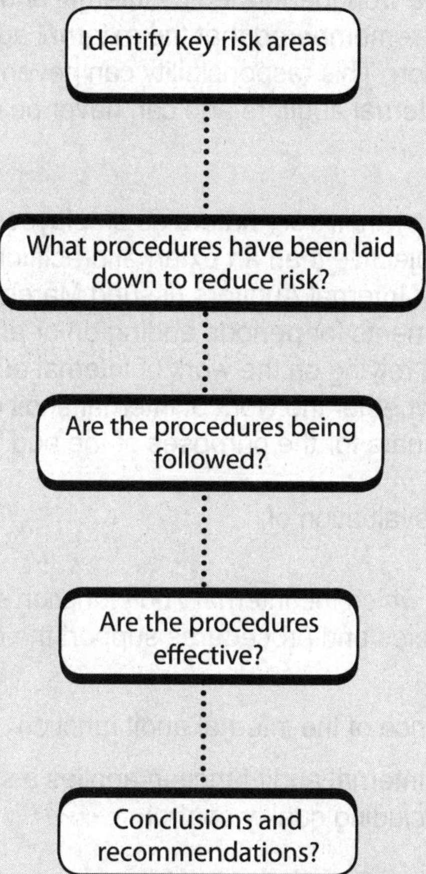


In operational audit a risk based approach should be used that:

- identifies the principal business risks involved which may prevent the organisation achieving its objectives
- assesses the extent to which controls are in place and are operating effectively in order to manage these risks.

The outcome of each assignment should be a report to management which appraises the control systems which are currently in place and which makes appropriate recommendations for improvement.

A common operational audit that internal auditors would be required to carry out, is a review of the procurement activities within an organisation, i.e. evaluating whether the organisation is achieving value for money in its purchases of goods and services. This would require an assessment of:

- the suppliers being used
- the amount being paid for goods and services
- whether the right goods and services are being procured.

## 6 Internal auditors and the statutory audit

Whilst some of the work performed by internal and external auditors may be similar it must be remembered that the external auditor is solely responsible for the audit opinion. This responsibility can never be reduced by the use of the work of the internal auditors and can never be delegated to internal audit.

Internal auditors, by their very nature as employees of the organisation, will always be less objective than an external practitioner. ISA 610 (Revised) Using the Work of Internal Auditors (issued March 2012, effective for audits of financial statements for periods ending on or after December 15, 2013) states that before relying on the work of internal auditors, the external auditor must determine whether the work of internal audit can be used and whether that work is adequate for the purposes of the audit.

This involves an evaluation of:

- the extent to which the internal audit function's organisational status and relevant policies and procedures support the objectivity of the internal auditors)
- the competence of the internal audit function
- whether the internal audit function applies a systematic and disciplined approach, including quality control.

**Contrasting internal and external auditors**

As assurance practitioners, both external and internal auditors will need to plan their work so that they gather sufficient appropriate audit evidence, in keeping with the objectives of the assignment.

**External audit**

The focus of external audit is on ensuring that the financial statements are: free from material misstatement; and properly prepared in accordance with a relevant reporting framework. Therefore the planning of external audit work will be done to achieve this objective.

All statutory audits must be planned in accordance with ISAs and other regulatory requirements.

**Internal audit**

Internal auditors plan their work so that they achieve the objectives of their assignments, as dictated by management.

**Who does the planning?**

As we know, external auditors are **independent** so they must be in control of planning their own work, in accordance with the objectives above.

Internal auditors' work may be programmed for them by management so that they focus on the areas thought to be most important by the board and those charged with governance.

However, it adds to the strength of corporate governance if the internal audit function has a degree of independence in the selection and objectives of its assignments.

**Evidence**

The general rule for assurance engagements is that the practitioner should gather sufficient appropriate evidence to support the opinion in the report which is the outcome of the assignment.

ISA 330 states that under ISAs the auditor gathers evidence which addresses the risk of misstatement as assessed during the planning process and in the light of evidence gathered subsequently.

The external auditor, therefore is always governed by this when deciding what evidence is appropriate.

As we have seen above, the internal auditor may have different objectives, depending on the nature of the assignment. For example, consider the auditor's approach to non-current assets:

- The **external auditor** is concerned with whether the figures for non current assets are materially misstated. So the auditor may check purchase prices against invoices, check depreciation is applied properly and physically inspect some assets, all on a test basis, and may therefore conclude that the figure for non current assets is materially correct.
- The **internal auditor** may have an assignment to ensure that the plant register at a particular factory is up to date, and so will need to check that every item recorded exists and that all machines on the factory floor are recorded. The auditor may or may not be concerned with values, depending on the nature of the assignment.

**Reporting**

The report produced by the internal auditor, is determined by the nature of the assignment.

The external auditor's report on financial statements is determined by statute and by ISAs (700, 705 & 706). The external auditor must also communicate to those charged with governance, as discussed earlier in the text.

**Types of report provided in internal audit assignments**

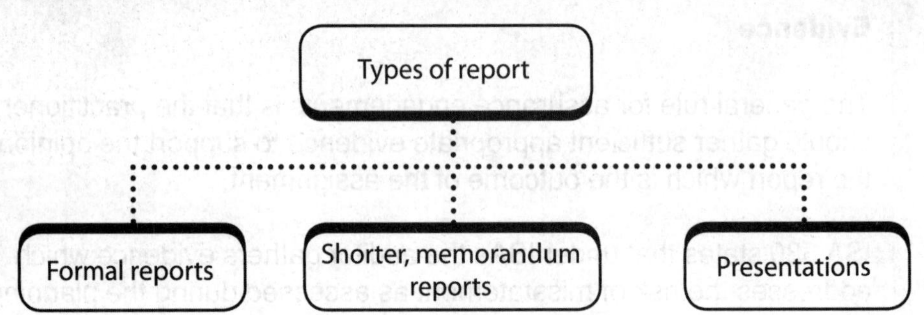


**Formal reports**

A formal written report is the traditional outcome from an internal audit assignment. A recommended structure for the report is set out in the following section.

**Shorter memorandum reports**

For:

- smaller scale assignments
- assignments where less depth is required
- assignments where results are required urgently
- a shorter, less formal report may be required.

Nevertheless, the same care needs to be taken with the contents of the report:

- **Addressees** – make sure it goes to the right people (especially reports delivered by email).
- **Subject matter** – make sure the purpose of the report is clear and that the objective is addressed by the content of the report.

- **Structure** – make sure the report is laid out well so that its message is communicated efficiently. Surprisingly, although this type of report is less formal, it still needs to be properly structured and lack of formality should not be taken as an excuse for sloppy drafting.

**Presentations**

- An oral presentation can have a greater impact than a written document.
- Usually, however, a presentation will be delivered as well as the main report and used to highlight the key findings.
- Although the delivery methods are clearly different, the structure of a presentation has much in common with the structure of a formal written report.

**Structure of a formal report**

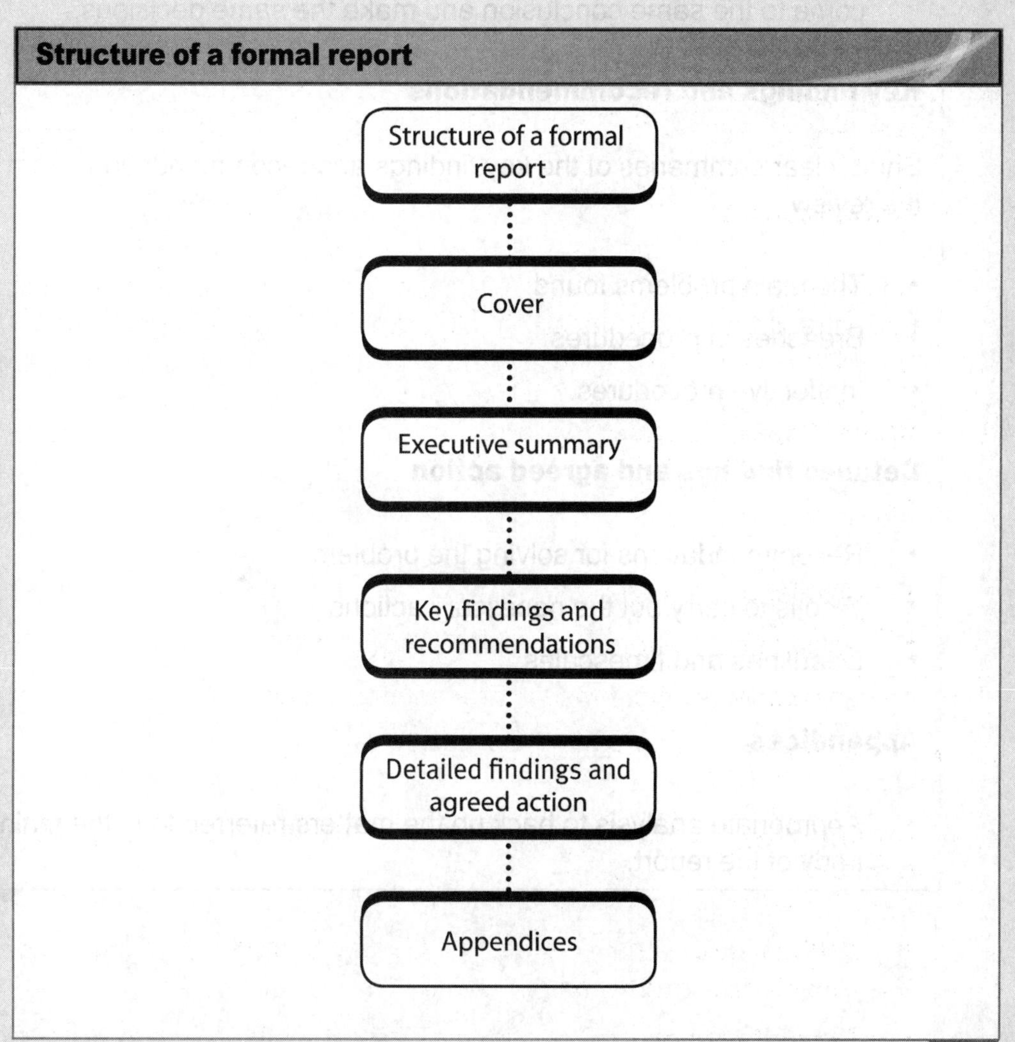

**Cover of report**

- Subject
- Distribution list
- Date of issue
- Any rating/evaluation.

**Executive Summary**

The executive summary is like the whole report in miniature:

- It needs to grab the reader's attention to make sure they read the whole report.
- If the readers were only able to read the executive summary rather than all the detail of the whole report, they should still be able to come to the same conclusion and make the same decisions.

**Key findings and recommendations**

Short, clear summaries of the key findings and recommendations from the review.

- The main problems found.
- Breaches in procedures.
- Ineffective procedures.

**Detailed findings and agreed action**

- Recommendations for solving the problem.
- Who is to carry out the necessary actions.
- Deadlines and timescales.

**Appendices**

- Appropriate analysis to back up the matters referred to in the main body of the report.

**Alternative formats**

The key findings can be set out either in:

- Paragraph format
- Tabular format.

*Tabular format example*

| Ref | Finding | Action: | Action by: | Date |
|---|---|---|---|---|
| 1 | 30 purchase invoices were reviewed: 10 had no evidence of being matched to goods received notes or purchase orders, nor evidence of authorisation for payment.<br><br>**Risk**<br><br>Fraudulent payment. Payment may be made for goods or services not received. Damage to reputation. | All invoices must be supported by a corresponding purchase order and evidence of receipt of goods or service, with a review by the manager being evidenced by signature, prior to processing payment. | DCXX | By end of month |

**Test your understanding 1**

You are the senior manager in the internal audit department of Octball, a limited liability company. You report to the chief internal auditor and have a staff of six junior auditors to supervise, although the budget allows for up to ten junior staff.

In a recent meeting with the chief internal auditor, the difficulty of staff recruitment and retention was discussed. Over the past year, five junior internal audit staff have left the company, but only two have been recruited. Recruitment problems identified include location of Octball's head office in a small town over 150 kilometres from the nearest major city and extensive foreign travel, often to cold climates.

Together with the chief internal auditor you believe that outsourcing the internal audit department may be a way of alleviating the staffing problems. You would monitor the new outsourced department in a part-time role taking on additional responsibilities in other departments, and the chief internal auditor would accept the post of Finance Director (FD) on the board, replacing the retiring FD.

Two firms have been identified as being able to provide the internal audit service:

- The NFA Partnership, a local firm specialising in provision of accountancy and internal audit services. NFA does not audit financial statements or report to members, and
- T&M, Octball's external auditors, who have offices in 75 countries and employ in excess of 65,000 staff.

**Required:**

(a) **Discuss the advantages and disadvantages of appointing NFA as internal auditors for Octball.**

**(8 marks)**

(b) **Discuss the issues T&M need to consider before they could accept appointment as internal auditors for Octball.**

**(7 marks)**

(c) **Assume that an outsourcing company has been chosen to provide internal audit services. Describe the control activities that Octball should apply to ensure that the internal audit service is being maintained to a high standard.**

**(5 marks)**

**(Total: 20 marks)**

## Test your understanding 2

Flylo is an airline. The company owns some of its fleet of aircraft. Other aircraft are leased from third parties. Flylo has an internal audit function that has recently been expanded. Your firm is the external auditor to Flylo. Your firm has been asked to investigate the extent to which it may be able to rely on the work of internal audit in the following areas:

- sales and ticketing;
- fleet acquisition and maintenance;
- trade payables and long-term debt financing (borrowings).

The company outsources its in-flight catering and payroll functions to different service organisations.

**Required:**

(a) **Explain why the work of the internal auditors, in the three areas noted above, is likely to be useful to you as the external auditor.**

**(9 marks)**

(b) **Explain how the quality of the internal audit function is likely to influence the extent of your reliance on internal audit work.**

**(5 marks)**

(c) **Describe the audit evidence you will seek relating to internal controls over the out-sourced functions (in-flight catering and payroll).**

**(6 marks)**

**(Total: 20 marks)**

## 7 Chapter summary

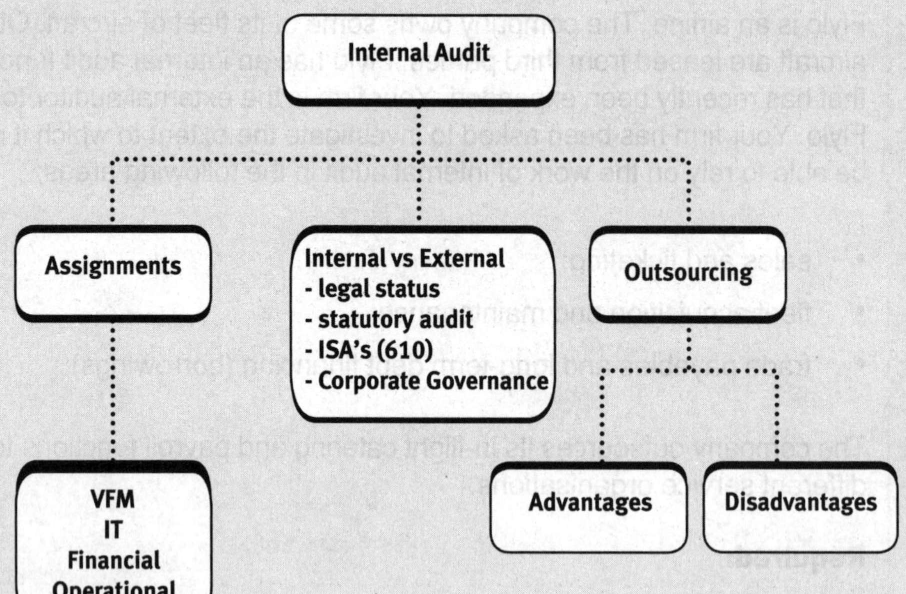
Internal Audit
Assignments
VFM
IT
Financial
Operational
Internal vs External
- legal status
- statutory audit
- ISA's (610)
- Corporate Governance
Outsourcing
Advantages
Disadvantages

## Test your understanding answers

### Test your understanding 1

(a) **Benefits of outsourcing to NFA**

*Expertise available*

The NFA partnership will be able to provide the necessary expertise for internal audit work. They may be able to provide a broader range of expertise as they serve many different clients therefore staff may be available for specialist work that Octball could not afford to employ.

*Buy-in skills as necessary*

If internal audit is only required for specific functions or particular jobs each year then the expertise can be purchased as required. Taking this approach will minimise in-house costs.

*Independence/Qualifications*

No information is provided on the qualification of staff in NFA, although as an independent firm it is likely that care will be taken that staff do remain independent and have the appropriate qualifications in order that they can provide an appropriate high level of service.

*Audit techniques – training*

Outsourcing will remove the need for training internal staff. Effectively training will be provided for 'free' as the outsourcing firm will be responsible for keeping staff up-to-date with new auditing techniques and processes.

**Problems with outsourcing to NFA**

*Fee pressure*

NFA may experience some fee pressure, but only in respect of maintaining cost effectiveness of the internal audit department. The relationship needs to be managed carefully to ensure that NFA do not decrease the quality of their work due to insufficient fees.

*Knowledge*

The NFA partnership will not have any prior knowledge of Octball. This will be a disadvantage as this will mean the partnership will need time to ascertain the accounting systems and controls etc in Octball before commencing work. However, provision of an independent view may identify control deficiencies etc that the current internal audit department have missed.

*Location*

The NFA partnership may not be able to provide this service to Octball as they are a local firm and therefore the issue of travel and working away from home would remain.

*Continuity of service – staffing*

As provision of audit services is the NFA partnership's main activity, they should also be able to budget for client requirements although this cannot be guaranteed as staff may still leave. However, as a larger internal auditing firm, they will be able to offer staff better career progression which should assist staff retention.

(b) Items to be considered by T&M

*Independence*

T&M need to ensure that independence can be maintained in a number of areas:

- Independence regarding recommending systems or preparing working papers and subsequent checking of those systems or working papers. While the internal audit department may need to carry out these functions, T&M must ensure that separate staff are used to provide the internal and external audit functions.
- Staff from T&M will be expected to follow the ethical guidance of ACCA which means that steps will be taken to avoid conflicts of interest or other independence issues such as close personal relationships building up with staff in Octball. Any real or perceived threats to independence will lower the overall trust that can be placed on internal audit reports produced by T&M.

*Training*

As a firm of auditors, T&M will automatically provide training for its staff as part of the in-house compliance with association regulations (e.g. compulsory CPD). T&M will need to ensure that staff providing the internal audit function to Octball are aware of relevant guidance for internal auditors.

*Skills*

T&M must ensure that they have staff with the necessary skills and sufficient time to undertake the internal audit work in Octball. Skills may not be an issue because staff in T&M will already understand audit procedures.

*Fee pressure*

There may be fee pressure on T&M, either to maintain the cost effectiveness of the internal audit department, or to maintain the competitiveness of the audit fee itself in order to keep the internal audit work.

*Knowledge*

As external auditors, T&M will already have knowledge of Octball. This will assist in establishing the internal audit department as systems documentation will already be available and the audit firm will already be aware of potential deficiencies in the control systems.

(c) Controls to maintain the standard of the internal audit department

- If T&M are appointed, ensure that the internal and external audit is managed by different departments in the firm.
- Setting and review of performance measures such as cost, areas reviewed, etc with explanations obtained for any significant variances.
- Use of appropriate audit methodology, including clear documentation of audit work carried out, adequate review, and appropriate conclusions drawn.
- Review of working papers by myself, ensuring adherence to International Standards on Auditing where appropriate and any in-house standards on auditing.
- The work plan for internal audit is agreed prior to work commencing and this is followed by the outsourcing company.

**Test your understanding 2**

(a) **Use of the work of the internal auditors by external auditors**

*Sales and ticketing*

(i) The sales function is likely to be integrated with the accounting and internal control system used to produce the figure in the financial statements for revenue, on which the external auditor reports.

(ii) The internal auditors' work on the ticketing system is less likely to be useful because it relates to an operational area which does not have a direct impact on the financial statements. There are, however, regulatory matters that may need to be considered by the external auditor. Ticketing may also have an indirect effect because it is likely to be integrated with the sales system and there is likely to be some crossover between the controls over ticketing and controls over sales generally. The work of the internal auditors is therefore likely to be of some use to the external auditor.

*Fleet acquisition and maintenance*

(iii) The internal auditors' work on the fleet acquisition system is likely to be very relevant to the external auditors because owned aircraft and leased aircraft will constitute a substantial element of statement of financial position assets and liabilities, and depreciation and finance charges in the statement of comprehensive income.

(iv) Much of the internal auditors' work is likely to relate to ensuring that company policy has been complied with. Policy will relate to the authorisation for and acquisition of aircraft, and accounting for aircraft in terms of the correct classification of leases (operating or financing) and depreciation policy, for example. Company policy is likely to be extensive and detailed for such material items and external auditors will be concerned to ensure that it is both appropriate and has been complied with.

(v) It is also possible that the internal auditors' work may involve some verification of the statement of comprehensive income and statement of financial position entries at the year-end. Given the likely materiality of the amounts involved, this work will also be of interest to the external auditors.

(vi) It is possible that the internal auditors' work may also relate to the quality of aircraft, and other operational aspects of fleet management. These issues may also be relevant to the external auditors, at least insofar as they relate to compliance with laws and regulations.

(vii) In relation to maintenance, the internal auditors' work is likely to relate to the authorisation and correct accounting for maintenance expenditure (capitalisation or expensing), and on the operational side, to the quality thereof, as for fleet acquisition (above). Maintenance expenditure in the statement of comprehensive income may well be material and the work of the internal auditors is therefore of interest to external auditors.

*Trade payables and long term debt financing*

(viii) The extent of the external auditor's interest in the internal auditors' work on trade payables and long term financing will depend on the materiality of the amounts involved. Trade payables (for certain types of routine maintenance, and payables due to the service organisations, for example) may be material. Long term debt financing is very likely to be material as many airlines have substantial debt financing.

(ix) Internal audit work on trade payables is likely to involve ensuring that routine internal controls are properly designed and are operating. The external auditors may well be interested in the internal auditors' work in this area.

(x) There are substantial financial statement disclosures required for debt financing. The internal auditors' assistance with ensuring that disclosures are properly made, as well as with ensuring that any covenants have been complied with and that the accounting for the financing is appropriate, may also be helpful to the external auditors.

(b) **Quality of internal audit function: extent of reliance**

(i) The quality of the internal audit function will have a significant effect on the extent of the external auditor's reliance. If the quality of work is not adequate, reliance will not be possible, regardless of the extent and relevance of the work performed.

(ii) The firm will seek to ensure that there is an appropriate structure within the department itself, with appropriate reporting lines outside the department, preferably reporting to the audit committee.

(iii) The internal audit function has recently been expanded and there are likely to be changes in the way that it is organised. The function should have operational independence within the organisation and formal terms of reference that encompass the recent changes made.

(iv) The function should have a clearly defined set of operating procedures, as well as a work program. Proper documentation of all work performed is essential.

(v) Staff should be appropriately trained, experienced and qualified. The head of such an important department should preferably be professionally qualified.

(c) **Audit evidence: outsourced functions**

(i) Internal controls exercised by the company over in-flight catering and payroll must be properly designed and operated. The firm will seek to review documentation of controls and internal audit reports. It will seek to obtain evidence that controls have been applied.

(ii) A breach of regulations or a deterioration in the quality of catering could both have a significant effect on the financial statements, particularly if fines were payable or adverse publicity was likely. Enquiries into both areas and a review of relevant documentation provided by, for example, food licensing authorities to the company or the service organisation, and company lawyers (in relation to passenger complaints, perhaps), will be necessary.

(iii) Evidence of controls sought by the firm will include:

- controls over the selection of the service organisations selected (by competitive tendering, for example);
- evidence relating to the completeness, accuracy and timeliness of information provided to, and received from, the payroll organisation (batch summaries and exception reports, for example);
- evidence relating to the security measures taken by the payroll organisation to ensure that confidential information is kept confidential;
- evidence relating to the security measures taken by the catering organisation to ensure that health and safety standards are maintained and that no 'sabotage' of the food can take place.

chapter

# 13

# Summary of key ISAs

## Chapter learning objectives

Question 2 of the exam is always a ten mark knowledge question. At least one of the other questions will also contain a knowledge element. Knowing the key points from the audit standards is crucial to scoring well in these questions.

**200 series: General principles and responsibilities**

**ISA 200** ***Overall Objectives of the Independent Auditor and the Conduct of an Audit in Accordance with International Standards on Auditing***

Objectives of the auditor:

- To obtain reasonable assurance whether financial statements as a whole are free from material misstatement, whether due to fraud or error.
- To express an opinion on whether the financial statements are prepared, in all material respects, in accordance with a relevant financial reporting framework.
- To report on the financial statements, and communicate as required, in accordance with the auditor's findings.

Responsibilities of management:

- Preparation of the financial statements in accordance with the applicable financial reporting framework, including their fair presentation.
- Internal control necessary to enable preparation of financial statements that are free from material misstatement, whether due to fraud or error.
- To provide the auditor with:
  - access to all information relevant to the preparation of the financial statements
  - unrestricted access to persons from within the entity whom the auditor determines it necessary to obtain evidence.

Inherent limitations of audit:

Audit evidence is persuasive rather than conclusive because of:

- the nature of financial reporting
- the nature of audit procedures
- the need to conduct audit a within reasonable time and at reasonable cost.

**ISA 210** ***Agreeing the terms of audit engagements***

The auditor should accept or renew an engagement only if the preconditions for an audit are present:

- An appropriate financial reporting framework is to be applied in the preparation of the financial statements; and
- Management's acknowledgement and understanding of its responsibilities.

Contents of engagement letter:

- The objective and scope of the audit.
- The responsibilities of the auditor.
- The responsibilities of management.
- The identification of an applicable financial reporting framework.
- Reference to the expected form and content of any reports to be issued.

**ISA 230** ***Audit documentation***

Objective of documentation:

- Sufficient appropriate record of basis for audit report
- Evidence that audit planned and performed in accordance with ISAs and legal / regulatory requirements

Content - to enable an experienced independent auditor to understand:

- Nature, timing & extent of audit procedures:
  - Specific items tested.
  - Who performed work and when.
  - Who reviewed work and when.
- Results of audit procedures.
- Significant conclusions and professional judgements.

**ISA 240** ***The auditor's responsibilities relating to fraud in an audit of financial statements***

- Identify risks of material misstatement in FS due to fraud.
- Obtain sufficient appropriate evidence regarding assessed risks.

Respond appropriately to fraud or suspected fraud identified.

Fraud: intentional act involving use of deception to obtain unjust/illegal advantage.

Two types of fraud:

- Fraudulent financial reporting.
- Misappropriation of assets.

Professional scepticism: an attitude of a questioning mind; a critical assessment of audit evidence.

Audit procedures to identify:

- Appropriateness of journal entries.
- Review of accounting estimates.
- Identify significant transactions outside normal course of business.

Examples of fraud risk factors:

- High degree of competition.
- Need to obtain additional financing.
- Low morale amongst senior staff.
- Large amounts of cash on hand.

**ISA 250 *Consideration of laws and regulations in an audit of financial statements***

Auditor's responsibilities:

- Obtain general understanding of legal/regulatory framework applicable to entity.
- Obtain sufficient appropriate evidence regarding compliance with provisions of laws/regulations that may materially affect FS.

**ISA 260 *Communication with those charged with governance***

Those charged with governance:

- Those with responsibility for overseeing the strategic direction of the entity.

Matters to be communicated:

- Auditor's responsibility in relation to the FS audit.
- Planned scope and timing of audit.
- Significant findings from audit.
- Auditor's independence (listed companies).

**ISA 265 *Communicating deficiencies in internal control to those charged with governance and management***

Reporting responsibilities:

- Significant deficiencies, to those charged with governance.
- Other deficiencies, to an appropriate level of management.

What makes matters significant:

- Likelihood of material misstatement in FS.
- Susceptibility to loss / fraud of related asset.
- Volume of activity in related account balance.
- Interaction of deficiency with other deficiencies.

## 300 & 400 series: Assessment and response to assessed risks

**ISA 300 *Planning an audit of financial statements***

Objectives of planning:

- Help auditor to devote appropriate attention to important areas of audit.
- Help identify and resolve issues on a timely basis.
- Assist in selection of suitable audit team.
- Help direction and supervision of audit team.

Content of audit strategy:

- Scope of engagement (e.g. input of other auditors).
- Reporting objectives of assignment (e.g. reporting timetable).
- Nature/timing/extent of resources.

Content of audit plan:

- Risk assessment procedures.
- Detailed planned audit procedures.

**ISA 315 (Revised) *Identifying and Assessing the Risks of Material Misstatement Through Understanding the Entity and its Environment* (issued March 2012, effective for audits of financial statements for periods ending on or after December 15, 2013)**

Required understanding of entity and environment:

- Industry/regulatory factors affecting FS
- Nature of entity:
  - operations
  - ownership and governance
  - financing.
- Accounting policies.
- Objectives and strategy.

Risk:

- Audit: risk of inappropriate opinion.
- Inherent: risk of susceptibility of an assertion about a class of transaction (e.g. sales) or account balance (e.g. receivables) to material misstatement.
- Control: risk that material misstatement not detected by entity's internal control.
- Detection: risk that audit procedures do not detect material misstatements.

IT controls, risks:

- Unauthorised changes to data in master files.
- Unauthorised access to programs.
- Inappropriate manual intervention.

Assessing whether a control is relevant to audit:

- Materiality.
- Significance of related risk.
- Applicable legal/regulatory requirements.
- Nature of entity's business.

**ISA 320 *Materiality in planning and performing an audit***

Materiality: Misstatements, including omissions, are considered to be material if they, individually or in the aggregate, could reasonably be expected to influence the economic decisions of users taken on the basis of the financial statements

Performance materiality: an amount set at less than materiality for the FS as a whole, to reduce to an appropriately low level the probability that the FS as a whole are materially misstated.

Tolerable error: A monetary amount set by the auditor in respect of which the auditor seeks to obtain an appropriate level of assurance that the monetary amount set by the auditor is not exceeded by the actual misstatement in the population.

**ISA 330 The auditor's responses to assessed risks**

The auditor shall design and perform audit procedures whose nature, timing and extent are based on and are responsive to the assessed risks of material misstatement.

**Test of controls**: to evaluate operating effectiveness of controls in preventing, or detecting and correcting material misstatements at the assertion level.

**Substantive procedures**: to detect material misstatements at assertion level, comprising tests of details and analytical procedures.

**ISA 450 *Evaluation of misstatements identified during audit***

A misstatement is: A difference between the amount, classification, presentation, or disclosure of a reported financial statement item and the amount, classification, presentation, or disclosure that is required for the item to be in accordance with the applicable financial reporting framework. Misstatements can arise from error or fraud.

Requirements:

- Accumulate identified misstatements.
- Determine whether audit strategy needs to be revised.
- Communicate misstatements to appropriate level of management on a timely basis.
- Evaluate effect of uncorrected misstatements on FS.
- Request management written representation that uncorrected misstatements are not material.

**500 series: Evidence**

**ISA 500 *Audit evidence***

Characteristics:

- Appropriateness: quality, linked to relevance and reliability.
- Sufficiency: quantity, linked to quality and to risk of material misstatement.

Relevance: linked to assertions.

- Assertions:
  - Account balances: Completeness, rights and obligations, valuation, existence.
  - Transactions: Occurrence, completeness, accuracy, cut-off.

Reliability.

- Independent better than internal.
- Auditor generated better than indirectly obtained.
- Documentary better than oral.
- Originals better than photocopies.

**ISA 510 *Initial audit engagements, opening balances***

Objective: to obtain sufficient appropriate evidence whether:

(1) Opening balances are misstated.

(2) Consistent accounting policies with current year

**ISA 520 *Analytical Procedures***

Definition:

- Evaluation of financial information.
- By analysing plausible relationships.
- Among financial and non-financial data.

**ISA 530 *Audit Sampling***

Definitions:

- Audit sampling: application of audit procedures to less than 100% of population to provide auditor with reasonable basis to draw conclusions on entire population.
- Sampling risk: of unrepresentative sample.
- Non-sampling risk: of erroneous conclusion from representative sample.
- Statistical sampling: random sampling plus use of probability theory to evaluate results.

Factors increasing sample size:

- Increase in risk of material misstatement.
- Increase in tolerable misstatement.
- Increase in expected misstatement.

**ISA 540 *Auditing accounting estimates, including fair value accounting estimates and related disclosures***

Audit approach:

- Review post balance sheet events
- Test management's estimate:
  - Appropriateness of method.
  - Reasonableness of assumptions.
- Develop an independent estimate.

**ISA 560 *Subsequent events***

**Adjusting:** provide evidence of conditions existing at the balance sheet date.

**Non-adjusting:** provide evidence of conditions arising after the balance sheet date.

**ISA 570 *Going Concern***

Definition – entity viewed as continuing in business for the foreseeable future.

**ISA 580 *Written representations***

Content:

- Management responsibility for preparation of FS.
- Auditor provided with all relevant information.
- All transactions recorded in FS.
- Plans that may affect the carrying value of the assets.

## 600 series: Using the work of others

**ISA 610 (Revised) *Using the work of internal auditors* (issued March 2012, effective for audits of financial statements for periods ending on or after December 15, 2013)**

The external auditor must evaluate:

- the extent to which the internal audit function's **organisational status** and relevant policies and procedures support the **objectivity** of the internal auditors)
- the **competence** of the internal audit function
- whether the internal audit function applies a systematic and disciplined **approach**, including quality control.

They also have to plan adequate time to review the work of the internal audit function to evaluate whether:

- the work was properly planned, performed, supervised, reviewed and documented
- sufficient appropriate evidence has been obtained
- the conclusions reached are appropriate in the circumstances
- the reports prepared are consistent with the work performed.

**ISA 620 *Using the work of an auditor's expert***

The external auditor must assess an expert's:

- independence and objectivity
- competence.

The auditor must assess the expert's work including:

- the consistency of the findings with other evidence
- the significant assumptions made
- the use and accuracy of source data.

**700 series: Audit conclusions and reporting**

### ISA 700 *Forming an opinion and reporting on the financial statements*

Content of audit report:

- Title: reference to independent auditor.
- Addressee: shareholders/members.
- Introductory paragraph:
  - Entity.
  - Financial statements.
  - Reporting date.
- Management's responsibility for preparation of FS.
- Auditor's responsibility:
  - To express an opinion on FS.
  - Audit conducted in accordance with ISAs.
- Description of audit.
- Audit opinion:
  - FS prepared in accordance with IFRS.
  - FS give true and fair view.

### ISA 705 *Modifications to the audit opinion in the Independent Auditor's report*

Definitions:

- Modified: qualified, adverse or disclaimer.
- Pervasive: not confined to specific elements or representing a substantial proportion of a single element.

Modifications:

- FS as a whole not free from material misstatement
  - Material: qualified
  - Pervasive: adverse
- Unable to obtain sufficient appropriate evidence
  - Material: qualified
  - Pervasive: disclaimer

**ISA 706 *Emphasis of matter paragraphs and other matter paragraphs in the Independent Auditor's report***

Emphasis of matter: refers to matter fundamental to user's understanding of FS. Can only be used to highlight a matter already disclosed in the FS.

Other matter: refers to matters relevant to the audit, the audit report or the auditor's responsibilities.

**ISA 710 *Comparative information – corresponding figures and comparative financial statements***

Responsibilities, evaluate whether:

- Comparative information agrees to amounts presented in FS.
- Consistent accounting policies.

**ISA 720 *The auditor's responsibilities relating to other information in documents containing audited financial statements***

Responsibilities:

- Read other information to identify material inconsistencies with FS
- If inconsistencies identified:
  - If FS are wrong, propose adjustment. If refused consider modifying audit opinion.
  - If other information is wrong, propose adjustment. If refused consider:
    - referring to the matter in audit report.
    - withholding audit report.
    - resignation.

chapter

# 14

# Additional practice questions

**Test your understanding 1**

Your firm is the external auditor to two companies. One is a hotel, Tourex, the other is a food wholesaler, Pudco, that supplies the hotel. Both companies have the same year-end. Just before that year-end, a large number of guests became ill at a wedding reception at the hotel, possibly as a result of food poisoning.

The guests have taken legal action against the hotel and the hotel has taken action against the food wholesaler. Neither the hotel nor the food wholesaler have admitted liability. The hotel is negotiating out-of-court settlements with the ill guests, the food wholesaler is negotiating an out-of-court settlement with the hotel. At the statement of financial position date, the public health authorities have not completed their investigations.

Lawyers for both the hotel and the food wholesaler say informally that negotiations are 'going well' but refuse to confirm this in writing. The amounts involved are material to the financial statements of both companies.

**Required:**

(a) **Describe how ACCA's Rules of Professional Conduct apply to this situation and explain how the external auditors should manage this conflict of interest.**

**(6 marks)**

(b) **Outline the main requirements of IAS 37 Provisions, Contingent Liabilities and Contingent Assets and apply them to this case.**

**(7 marks)**

**Test your understanding 2**

Professional ethics are relevant to both external auditors and internal auditors.

You work for a medium-sized firm of Chartered Certified Accountants with seven offices and 150 employees. Your firm has been asked to tender for the provision of statutory audit and other services to Billington Travel, a private company providing discounted package holiday services in the Mediterranean. The company is growing fast and would represent a substantial amount of fee income for your firm. The finance director has explained to you that the company would like the successful firm to provide a number of different services. These include the statutory audit and assistance with the preparation of the financial statements. The company is also struggling with a new computer system and the finance director considers that a systems review by your firm may be helpful. Your firm does not have much experience in the travel sector.

**Required:**

(a) **Explain why it is necessary for external auditors to be and be seen to be independent of their audit clients.**

**(3 marks)**

(b) **With reference to the ACCA's Rules of Professional Conduct, describe the ethical matters that should be considered in deciding on whether your firm should tender for:**

(i) **the statutory audit of Billington Travel**

**(4 marks)**

(ii) **the provision of other services to Billington Travel**

**(4 marks)**

You are a student Chartered Certified Accountant and you are one of four assistant internal auditors in a large manufacturing company. You report to the chief internal auditor. You have been working on the review of the payables system and you have discovered what you consider to be several serious deficiencies in the structure and operation of the system. You have reported these matters in writing to the chief internal auditor but you are aware that none of these matters have been covered in his final report on the system which is due to be presented to management.

**Required:**

(c) **List the actions you might take in these circumstances.**

**(6 marks)**

(d) **Explain the dangers of doing nothing in these circumstances.**

**(3 marks)**

**(Total: 20 marks)**

**Test your understanding 3**

Day-to-day internal controls are important for all businesses to maximise the efficient use of resources and profitability.

Your firm has recently been appointed as auditor to Cliff, a private company that runs a chain of small supermarkets selling fresh and frozen food, and canned and dry food. Cliff has very few controls over inventory because the company trusts local managers to make good decisions regarding the purchase, sale and control of inventory, all of which is done locally. Pricing is generally performed on a cost-plus basis. Each supermarket has a stand-alone computer system on which monthly accounts are prepared. These accounts are mailed to head office every quarter. There is no integrated inventory control, sale or purchasing system and no regular system for inventory counting. Management accounts are produced twice a year.

Trade at the supermarkets has increased in recent years and the number of supermarkets has increased. However, the quality of staff that has been recruited has fallen. Senior management at Cliff are now prepared to invest in more up-to-date systems

**Required:**

(a) **Describe the problems that you might expect to find at Cliff resulting from poor internal controls.**

**(8 marks)**

(b) **Make FOUR recommendations to the senior management of Cliff for the improvement of internal controls, and explain the advantages and disadvantages of each recommendation.**

**(12 marks)**
**(Total: 20 marks)**

**Test your understanding 4**

(a) There are a number of key procedures which auditors should perform if they wish to rely on internal controls and reduce the level of substantive testing they perform. These include:

(i) Documentation of accounting and internal control systems;

(ii) Walk-through testing;

(iii) Audit sampling;

(iv) Testing internal controls;

(v) Dealing with deviations from the application of control procedures.

**Required:**

**Briefly explain each of the procedures listed above.**

**(10 marks)**

**NB: (i) to (v) above carry equal marks**

Flowers Anytime sells flowers wholesale. Customers telephone the company and their orders are taken by clerks who take details of the flowers to be delivered, the address to which they are to be delivered, and account details of the customer. The clerks input these details into the company's computer system (whilst the order is being taken) which is integrated with the company's inventory control system. The company's standard credit terms are payment one month from the order (all orders are despatched within 48 hours) and most customers pay by bank transfer. An accounts receivable ledger is maintained and statements are sent to customers once a month. Credit limits are set by the credit controller according to a standard formula and are automatically applied by the computer system, as are the prices of flowers.

**Required:**

(b) **Describe and explain the purpose of the internal controls you might expect to see in the sales system at Flowers Anytime over the:**

(i) **Receipt, processing and recording of orders.**

**(6 marks)**

(ii) **Collection of cash.**

**(4 marks)**

(c) **Describe how you would test each of the controls identified in part (b).**

**(10 marks)**

**(Total: 30 marks)**

**Test your understanding 5**

Your firm is the external auditor of Bestwood Engineering, a privately owned incorporated business, which manufactures components for motor vehicles and sells them to motor vehicle manufacturers and wholesalers. It has sales of $10 million and a profit before tax of $400,000.

The company has a new chief financial officer who has asked your advice on controls in the company's purchases and accounts payable system.

Bestwood Engineering has separate accounts, purchasing and goods received departments. Most purchases are required by the production department, but other departments are able to raise requisitions for goods and services. The purchasing department is responsible for obtaining goods and services for the company at the lowest price which is consistent with the required delivery date and quality, and for ensuring their prompt delivery.

The accounts department is responsible for obtaining authorisation of purchase invoices before they are input into the computer which posts them to the accounts payable ledger and the general ledger. The accounting records are kept on a microcomputer and the standard accounting software was obtained from an independent supplier. The accounting software maintains the accounts payable ledger, accounts receivable ledger, general ledger and payroll. The company does not maintain inventory records, as it believes the costs of maintaining these records outweigh the benefits.

The chief financial officer has explained that services include gas, electricity, telephone, repairs and short-term rental (hire) of equipment and vehicles.

**You are required to:**

(a) **describe the procedures which should be in operation in the purchasing department to control the purchase and receipt of goods.**

**(8 marks)**

(b) **describe the controls the accounts department should exercise over obtaining authorisation of purchase invoices before posting them to the accounts payable ledger.**

**(6 marks)**

(c) **explain how controls over the purchase of services, from raising the purchase requisition to posting the invoice to the accounts payable ledger, might differ from the procedures for the purchase of goods, as described in your answers to parts (a) and (b) above.**

**(6 marks)**

**(Total: 20 marks)**

**Test your understanding 6**

(a) Computer-Assisted Audit Techniques (CAATs) are used to assist an auditor in the collection of audit evidence from computerised systems.

**Required:**

**List and briefly explain four advantages of CAATs.**

**(4 marks)**

(b) Porthos, a limited liability company, is a reseller of sports equipment, specialising in racquet sports such as tennis, squash and badminton. The company purchases equipment from a variety of different suppliers and then resells this using the Internet as the only selling media. The company has over 150 different types of racquets available in inventory, each identified via a unique product code.

Customers place their orders directly on the Internet site. Most orders are for one or two racquets only. The ordering/sales software automatically verifies the order details, customer address and credit card information prior to orders being verified and goods being despatched. The integrity of the ordering system is checked regularly by ArcherWeb, an independent Internet service company.

You are the audit manager working for the external auditors of Porthos, and you have just started planning the audit of the sales system of the company. You have decided to use test data to check the input of details into the sales system. This will involve entering dummy orders into the Porthos system from an online terminal.

**Required:**

**List the test data you will use in your audit of the financial statements of Porthos to confirm the completeness and accuracy of input into the sales system, clearly explaining the reason for each item of data.**

**(6 marks)**

(c) **You are also considering using audit software as part of your substantive testing of the data files in the sales and inventory systems of Porthos.**

(i) **List and briefly explain some of the difficulties of using audit software;**

**(4 marks)**

(ii) **List the audit tests that you can program into your audit software for the sales and inventory system in Porthos, explaining the reason for each test.**

**(6 marks)**

**(Total: 20 marks)**

**Test your understanding 7**

You are currently engaged in reviewing the working papers of several audit assignments recently carried out by your audit practice. Each of the audit assignments is nearing completion, but certain matters have recently come to light which may affect your audit opinion on each of the assignments. In each case the year end of the company is 30 September 20X2.

(a) **Jones** (Profit before tax $150,000)

On 3 October 20X2 a letter was received informing the company that a customer, who owed the company $30,000 as at the year end had been declared bankrupt on 30 September. At the time of the audit it was expected that unsecured creditors, such as Jones, would receive nothing in respect of this debt. The directors refuse to change the financial statements to provide for the loss, on the grounds that the notification was not received by the statement of financial position date.

Total debts shown in the statement of financial position amounted to $700,000.

**(4 marks)**

(b) **Roberts** (Profit before tax $500,000)

On 31 July 20X2 a customer sued the company for personal damages arising from an unexpected defect in one of its products. Shortly before the year end the company made an out-of-court settlement with the customer of $10,000, although this agreement is not reflected in the financial statements as at 30 September 20X2. Further, the matter subsequently became known to the press and was extensively reported. The company's legal advisers have now informed you that further claims have been received following the publicity, although they are unable to place a figure on the potential liability arising from such claims which have not yet been received. The company had referred to the claims in a note to the financial statements stating, however, that no provision had been made to cover them because the claims were not expected to be material.

**(4 marks)**

(c) **Williams** (Net loss for the year $75,000)

Three directors of this manufacturing company owed amounts totalling $50,000 at the end of the financial year, and you have ascertained that such loans were not of a type permissible under the local legislation. These amounts had been included in the statement of financial position with other items under the heading 'Receivables collectable within one year'. The directors did not wish to disclose these loans separately in the financial statements as they were repaid shortly after the year end, as soon as they were made aware that the loans were not permissible. The directors have argued that the disclosures could prove embarrassing and that no purpose would be served by revealing this information in the financial statements.

**(4 marks)**

(d) **Griffiths** (Net profit before tax $250,000)

The audit work revealed that a trade investment stated in the statement of financial position at $500,000 had suffered a permanent fall in value of $300,000. The company admitted that the loss had occurred, but refused to make an allowance for it on the grounds that other trade investments (not held for resale) had risen in value and were stated at amounts considerably below their realisable values.

**(4 marks)**

(e) **Evans** (Net profit before tax $100,000)

This client is a construction company, currently building a warehouse on its own premises, and using some of its own workforce. The cost of labour and materials has been included in the cost of the non-current asset in the statement of financial position, the total figure being based on the company's costing records. The warehouse is almost complete and the cost shown in the statement of financial position includes direct labour costs of $10,000. However, during audit testing it was discovered that the costing records, showing the direct labour costs for the warehouse in the early part of the year, had been destroyed accidentally.

**(4 marks)**

**Required:**

**Discuss each of the cases outlined above, referring to materiality considerations and, where appropriate, relevant accounting principles and appropriate accounting standards. You should also indicate, with reasons, the kind of audit report (including the type of modification, if necessary) which you consider would be appropriate in each case.**

**You are not required to produce the full audit reports, and you may assume that all matters other than those specifically mentioned are considered satisfactory.**

**(Total: 20 marks)**

**Test your understanding 8**

Fraud and error present risks to an entity. Both internal and external auditors are required to deal with risks to the entity. However, the responsibilities of internal and external auditors in relation to the risk of fraud and error differ.

**Required:**

(a) **Explain how the internal audit function helps an entity deal with the risk of fraud and error.**

**(5 marks))**

(b) **Explain the responsibilities of external auditors in respect of the risk of fraud and error in an audit of financial statements.**

**(8 marks)**

(c) Stone Holidays is an independent travel agency. It does not operate holidays itself. It takes commission on holidays sold to customers through its chain of high street shops. Staff are partly paid on a commission basis. Well-established tour operators run the holidays that Stone Holidays sells. The networked reservations system through which holidays are booked and the computerised accounting system are both well-established systems used by many independent travel agencies.

Payments by customers, including deposits, are accepted in cash and by debit and credit card. Stone Holidays is legally required to pay an amount of money (based on its total sales for the year) into a central fund maintained to compensate customers if the agency should cease operations.

**Describe the nature of the risks to which Stone Holidays is subject arising from fraud and error.**

**(7 marks)**

**(Total: 20 marks)**

**Test your understanding 9**

Ajio is a charity whose constitution requires that it raises funds for educational projects. These projects seek to educate children and support teachers in certain countries. Charities in the country from which Ajio operates have recently become subject to new audit and accounting regulations. Charity income consists of cash collections at fund raising events, telephone appeals, and bequests (money left to the charity by deceased persons). The charity is small and the trustees do not consider that the charity can afford to employ a qualified accountant. The charity employs a part-time bookkeeper and relies on volunteers for fund raising. Your firm has been appointed as accountants and auditors to this charity because of the new regulations. Accounts have been prepared (but not audited) in the past by a volunteer who is a recently retired Chartered Certified Accountant.

**Required:**

(a) **Describe the risks associated with the audit of Ajio under the headings inherent risk, control risk and detection risk and explain the implications of these risks for overall audit risk.**

**(10 marks)**

(b) **List and explain the audit tests to be performed on income and expenditure from fund raising events.**

**(10 marks)**

**Note:** In part (a) you may deal with inherent risk and control risk together. You are not required to deal with the detail of accounting for charities in either part of the question.

**(Total: 20 marks)**

**Test your understanding 10**

You are the audit manager of Hood Enterprises, a limited liability company. The company's annual turnover is over $10 million.

**Required:**

(a) **Compare the responsibilities of the directors and auditors regarding the published financial statements of Hood Enterprises.**

**(6 marks)**

(b) An extract from the draft audit report produced by an audit junior is given below:

***Basis of opinion***

'We conducted our audit in accordance with Auditing Standards. An audit includes examination, on a test basis, of evidence relevant to the amounts and disclosures in the financial statements. It also includes an assessment of all the estimates and judgements made by the directors in the preparation of the financial statements, and of whether the accounting policies are appropriate to the company's circumstances, consistently applied and adequately disclosed.

'We planned and performed our audit so as to obtain as much information and explanation as possible given the time available for the audit. We confirm that the financial statements are free from material misstatement, whether caused by fraud or other irregularity or error. The directors however are wholly responsible for the accuracy of the financial statements and no liability for errors can be accepted by the auditor. In forming our opinion we also evaluated the overall adequacy of the presentation of information in the company's annual report.'

**Required:**

**Identify and explain the errors in the above extract.**

**Note:** You are not required to redraft the report.

**(10 marks)**

(c) The directors of Hood Enterprises have prepared a cash flow forecast for submission to the bank. They have asked you as the auditor to provide a negative assurance report on this forecast.

**Required:**

**Briefly explain the difference between positive and negative assurance, outlining the advantages to the directors of providing negative assurance on their cash flow forecast.**

**(4 marks)**

**(Total: 20 marks)**

## Test your understanding answers

### Test your understanding 1

(a) Managing conflicts of interest

ACCA's Rules of Professional Conduct state that auditors should avoid conflicts of interest (both conflicts between the firm and clients, and conflicts between clients) wherever possible. In some cases, such as these, they are unavoidable.

Full disclosure is important – both companies should be fully aware that the firm is acting for the other party.

One or both companies may object to the firm acting for the other company and the auditor may be forced to make a decision as to which company to resign from. However, this is not an attractive course of action because the audits may already have commenced and it may be difficult for one of the companies to find a new auditor, quickly.

The auditor should probably not, therefore, resign unless forced to do so – this might be prejudicial to the interests of one of the clients.

It is important in such cases that different teams of staff, and different engagement partners work on the respective audits.

Internal procedures within the firm should be set up to prevent confidential information from one client being transferred to the other and the interests of one firm damaging the interests of the other. Such procedures are sometimes known as 'Chinese Walls'.

If two completely separate offices could work on the two engagements, so much the better.

(b) IAS 37 states that a provision is a liability of uncertain timing or amount. It should only be recognised when there is a present obligation (legal or constructive) arising from past events and it is probable that a transfer of economic benefits will be required to settle the obligation and a reliable estimate of the amount can be made. If the firm can obtain sufficient appropriate audit evidence to show that Tourex and/or Pudco are likely to have to make a payment, and that the amount can be reliably estimated, a constructive obligation seems to exist and provision should be made.

IAS 37 states that a contingent liability is either a possible obligation arising from past events whose existence will be confirmed by uncertain future events outside the control of the entity or, a present obligation arising from past events that is not recognised because a transfer of economic benefits is not probable, or because the amount of the obligation cannot be measured with sufficient certainty. If Tourex and/or Pudco are uncertain as to whether a payment will have to be made, or if they are certain but the amount cannot be estimated, a contingent liability should be disclosed in the accounts.

IAS 37 states that a contingent asset is a possible asset arising from past events whose existence will be confirmed by uncertain future events outside the control of the entity. Contingent assets can be disclosed when an inflow of economic benefit is probable. When they are virtually certain, a contingency does not exist; the income may be accrued. This might apply to Tourex in its claim against the food company. It seems unlikely that there is sufficient certainty relating to the claim and therefore no disclosure should be made.

It also states that expected re-imbursements (such as those arising from insurance contracts) should be recognised only where they are virtually certain, and treated as separate assets. The net expense may be recognised in the statement of comprehensive income. If either Tourex or Pudco hold insurance against such events, and it is probable that the insurance claim will be met, a contingent asset may need to be disclosed. If there is any uncertainty, there should be no disclosure. If it is virtually certain that the claim will be met, a separate asset should be recognised.

A brief description of the nature of each class of contingent liability should be made unless the possibility of the transfer of benefits is remote. Where practical, an estimate of the financial effect, an indication of the relevant uncertainties, and the possibility of any reimbursement should be disclosed. Similar rules apply to contingent assets.

**Test your understanding 2**

(a) **Independence**

(i) It is important for external auditors to be independent of their audit clients because external auditors act on behalf of the owners of the business (normally the shareholders) and report on the financial statements prepared by the management for the benefit of shareholders.

(ii) If external auditors are not independent of their clients, for example if they hold shares in the companies that they audit, their ability to form an objective opinion on the financial statements is impaired.

(iii) External auditors must also be seen to be independent because if they are not, the owners of the business will not have confidence in the audit reports that the auditors issue.

(iv) The ACCA's Rules of Professional Conduct require that auditors are independent, and that they are seen to be independent. The Rules cover a number of areas in which the auditors' independence may be, or be seen to be, impaired.

(v) National legislation also normally requires external auditors to be independent.

(b) **Billington Travel**

(i) The statutory audit

- The Rules of Professional Conduct state that it is important that the firm is competent to undertake the audit; it must have adequate resources in terms of staff with sufficient experience in this sector. The fact that the services to be provided would constitute a substantial amount of fee income indicates that the firm might not, at present, have those resources.
- It may be appropriate to consider whether experience in this sector can be brought in, by the recruitment of additional staff.
- The firm should consider whether staff are available at the right time of year and whether the work fits in with the firm's existing obligations.
- The Rules of Professional Conduct also state that the firm must be independent of its clients; in particular, this means that it must not take too much of its fee income from one client (or group of clients).

- Generally, for non-public interest clients, the fee income (including income from additional services) should not exceed 15% of the gross practice income. If that figure is exceeded, it may be possible to consider providing some, but not all, of the services requested.

(ii) The provision of other services

- Preparation of financial statements: it is generally acceptable under the Rules of Professional Conduct for auditors to provide assistance with the preparation of financial statements for private company clients, provided that the client takes full responsibility for the accounting records and financial statements.
- It is important to know why the company needs assistance in this area and it would be preferable in the long run for the company to be able to prepare its own financial statements.
- It is important that those preparing the financial statements are independent of those performing the audit as far as possible, in order that the firm is seen to remain independent.
- Systems review: the external auditor is often well placed to provide assistance with such reviews as the firm obtains a working knowledge of systems during the course of the audit.
- However, there is always the danger that the firm finds itself in the position of having to report on a system that it has helped to improve, and it may be difficult in such circumstances to be critical of the system. This detracts from the firm's ability to remain independent, and in this case, given that it is the first year of audit and that assistance is also needed with the preparation of financial statements, it seems preferable not to tender for the systems review, this year.

(c) **Actions to be taken**

(i) It may be appropriate to discuss the matter, discreetly, with other staff members to establish whether or not it is of concern to them, as well as to you. It would be preferable to discuss the matter with persons who are known to be reliable.

(ii) If the concerns are shared, or if the other staff have no knowledge of the matter, or if you are still concerned about the matter, it may be appropriate to discuss the matter with the chief internal auditor to try and establish why the matter has not been reported, as there may be a good reason. If other staff support you in your view, it may be appropriate to take another member of staff along to the discussion.

(iii) If the chief internal auditor is able to reassure you (either that it is not necessary to report the matter, or that the matter will be reported), no further action will be necessary, although it may be useful to make a brief note of the discussion.

(iv) If you are not satisfied, or if the chief internal auditor undertakes to report the matter but does not do so within a reasonable time, the situation may be more serious and it is more important in such circumstances to make notes of any discussions. It may be appropriate to have further discussions with the chief internal auditor.

(v) If you are still not satisfied, and you consider that the matter is sufficiently serious, it may be appropriate to approach a more senior member of management to voice your concerns. You may wish to avoid this situation but it may be necessary in order to protect yourself.

(vi) On the assumption that the matter is one of internal concern to the company and there is no question of illegality, the question of reporting the matters to third parties outside the organisation does not arise.

(d) **Doing nothing**

(i) The principal danger in doing nothing lies in the possibility that you may be accused of not bringing attention to the matter or even of being actively involved in a 'cover-up'.

(ii) Professional ethics do not permit chartered certified accountants to take no action at all where serious matters are concerned and to do nothing might, in extreme circumstances, involve you in disciplinary proceedings by the ACCA, even as a student.

(iii) To do nothing might also mean that the business of the company you work for is damaged, and therefore your own employment prospects.

**Test your understanding 3**

(a) Problems expected at Cliff: poor internal control

(i) The company may experience some level of over-ordering, leading to reduced profitability as a result of inventory going past its 'best before' date

(ii) Inventory that is not well-controlled in a supermarket may result in a breach of health and safety regulations which may result in fines or even closure of the supermarkets.

(iii) There may be stock-outs leading to the potential loss of business to other supermarkets.

(iv) There may be inefficiencies as a result of a lack of central ordering system resulting from quantity discounts not being obtained.

(v) All of the problems noted above are likely to be exacerbated where local managers or staff are either inexperienced or possibly dishonest – the question states that poorer quality staff have been recruited recently.

(vi) Supermarket inventory is very easily pilfered either by staff or customers even where it is well-controlled. The lack of regular inventory counts in particular means that pilferage is very easy to hide.

(vii) There may be a lack of understanding in the business as a whole as to the availability of new products, products with high margins or other areas in which profitability might be improved.

(b) Four recommendations, explanation of advantages and disadvantages: improvements to internal control

**Recommendation 1:** that an integrated system be introduced across all supermarkets that links sales, purchases and inventory records.

*Advantages:* This would provide the company with an overall view of what inventory is held at any particular time, enable it to order centrally and reduce the scope for pilferage. It would result in reduced stock-outs and reduced inventory obsolescence.

*Disadvantages:* This would require considerable capital investment in hardware, software and training. It would also take control away from local managers which would almost certainly cause resentment.

**Recommendation 2**: the imposition of regular, or continuous inventory counting procedures together with the prompt update of inventory records for discrepancies found and investigation of the reason for the discrepancies.

*Advantages:* This would further reduce the possibility of stock-outs and provide evidence of over-ordering, which would enable purchasing patterns to be refined.

*Disadvantages:* There are costs in terms of staff time and, again, a certain level of resentment among staff who may feel that they are being 'spied on', or that they are no longer trusted. Training would also be required and additional administrative work would need to be undertaken by local managers.

**Recommendation 3**: that management accounts are produced on at least a quarterly basis, that figures relating to each supermarket are provided to head office on a monthly basis, and that an analysis is undertaken by head office on the performance of individual supermarkets and inventory lines.

*Advantages*: This would enable the company to determine which supermarkets are performing better than others. It would also enable the company to identify those inventory lines that sell well and those that are profitable.

*Disadvantages*: The production of more regular and detailed information will be time-consuming. Local managers may feel that they are unable to service the particular needs of their customers if decisions are made on a global basis; customers may feel the same way.

**Recommendation 4**: that sales price decisions are made by head office.

*Advantages*: This would enable the company to experiment with the use of 'loss leaders', for example, and to impose a degree of consistency across supermarkets to prevent inappropriate pricing decisions being taken by local managers.

*Disadvantages*: Again, loss of control at a local level is likely to result in resentment and the possible loss of good staff. What sells well in one supermarket may not do so in another. To the extent that head office have less experience of local conditions than local staff, it is possible that inappropriate pricing decisions may be made by head office.

(c) Sufficient audit evidence and audit reports

(i) The main problem for the auditors will be gaining sufficient evidence to determine whether any amounts should be provided for and/or disclosed in the financial statements of the two companies.

(ii) The lawyers refuse to provide anything other than informal evidence and this will almost certainly not be sufficient to form an audit opinion.

(iii) Unless audit evidence can be obtained elsewhere – a qualified ('except for') opinion, on the basis of being unable to obtain sufficient appropriate evidence, may be needed for both companies as the amounts involved are material.

(iv) However, it may be possible to take the view that there is a significant uncertainty, and that an explanatory paragraph referring to this significant uncertainty is therefore appropriate, rather than a qualification to the auditors' opinion, provided that the matter is adequately disclosed in the financial statements.

(v) It may be possible for the auditors to suggest to the companies that it would be very helpful for the lawyers to provide some indication as to their view of the likely outcome and the amounts involved, in order to avoid a modified opinion.

(vi) The auditors should also take note of the progress of any legal proceedings and any proceedings that may be instigated by the public health authorities as such authorities might impose significant fines, and they might even close the businesses down, which has implications for the going concern status of both.

**Test your understanding 4**

(a) **Key procedures**

(i) *Documentation of accounting and internal control systems*

Auditors document accounting and internal control systems in order to evaluate them for their adequacy as a basis for the preparation of the financial statements and to make a preliminary risk assessment of internal controls.

In very simple systems with few internal controls where auditors do not intend to perform tests of internal controls, it is not necessary to document the internal control system in detail. It is always necessary, however, to have sufficient knowledge of the business to perform an effective audit.

For large entities, where the client has already documented the system, it is not necessary for the auditors to repeat the process if they can satisfy themselves that the client's documentation is adequate.

(ii) *Walk through tests*

The purpose of walk-through tests is for the auditors to establish that their recording of the accounting and internal control system is adequate.

Auditors trace a number of transactions from source to destination in the system, and vice versa. For example, customer orders can be traced from the initial documentation recording the order, through to the related entries in the daybooks and ledgers.

It is common for walk-through tests to be performed at the same time as tests of controls, where auditors are reasonably confident that systems are recorded adequately.

(iii) *Audit sampling*

Auditors perform tests of controls and substantive testing on a sample basis in order to form conclusions on the populations from which the samples are drawn.

It is not possible in anything but the very smallest of entities to take any other approach, as testing 100% of a population may be impractical, not cost effective and not accurate because populations are too large and because of human error.

Samples can be selected in a number of ways – either statistically or on the basis of auditor judgement. In all cases, the sample selected must be representative of the population as a whole.

(iv) *Testing internal controls*

Auditors test internal controls in order to establish whether they are operating effectively throughout the period under review. If controls are operating effectively, auditors can reduce the level of substantive testing on transactions and balances that would otherwise be required.

In testing internal controls, auditors are checking to ensure that the stated control has been applied. For example, auditors may check that there is a grid stamp on a sales invoice with various signatures inside it that show that the invoice has been approved by the credit controller, that it has been checked for arithmetical accuracy, that the price has been checked, and that it has been posted to the sales ledger. The signatures provide audit evidence that the control has been applied.

Auditors are not checking to ensure that the invoice is, in fact, correct. This would be a substantive test. Nevertheless, it is possible to perform tests of control and substantive tests on the same document at the same time.

(v) *Dealing with deviations from the application of control procedures*

Where it appears that an internal control procedure has not been applied, it is necessary to form an opinion as to whether the deviation from the application of the procedure is an isolated incident, or whether the deviation represents a systematic breakdown in the application of the control procedure. This is usually achieved by selecting a further sample for testing.

If it cannot be shown that the non-application of the procedure is isolated (i.e. there are no further instances in which the control has failed), it is necessary either to find a compensating control that can be tested, or to abandon testing of controls and to take a wholly substantive approach. Where there is a breakdown in internal controls it is also necessary to reassess the auditor's preliminary risk assessment. Abandoning tests of control may place strains on the budget for the audit and auditors should always consider the possibility of compensating controls before abandoning tests of controls.

| (b) **Controls**<br>*Receipt, processing and recording* | (c) **Test of Control** |
|---|---|
| All orders taken should be recorded on a pre-numbered multi-part document generated by the computer. One part might be a copy for the customer, one might form the invoice, one might be for the despatch department and one might be retained for accounts receivable ledger purposes. Manual or computer systems should perform checks on the completeness of the sequence of pre-numbered documents at various stages. Any documents unaccounted for should be traced and investigated. | Review a sample of the sequence checks performed. |
| The computer system should apply the credit limits set by the credit controller and the system should reject any orders that exceed customer credit limits at the point at which the order is taken, so that the customer can be advised. Any override of credit limits should be authorised by the credit controller. | Try to enter an order that would put a customer over the credit limit and check that the system rejects it. |
| From time to time, there should be an independent check to ensure that the credit limits within the system are being properly calculated and properly applied to individual transactions. Similar considerations apply to prices maintained within the system. | Take a sample of prices in the system and compare to the authorised price list. |
| The computer system should also reject any order for which there are no flowers available so that orders cannot be taken for flowers that cannot be delivered. | Try to input an order for flowers which are not available to check that it is rejected. |
| All invoices should be posted to the sales daybook, the accounts receivable ledger and the accounts receivable control account automatically by the system and the accounts receivable ledger and the accounts receivable control account should be reconciled each month in order for sales and receivables records to be kept up to date. | Review the reconciliations. |

| | |
|---|---|
| There should be controls in place to deal with credit notes and other discrepancies involving the price, type or quality of flowers delivered in order to maintain the accuracy of records and customer goodwill. | Review a sample of credit notes or other adjustments made for evidence of authorisation. |
| *Collection of cash* | |
| At the end of each period, the system should produce a list of overdue receivables. There should be procedures for chasing these customers and for putting a 'stop' on accounts where amounts are significant in order to control bad debts. | Review the list of overdue receivables. Review correspondence chasing these customers. |
| When bank transfers are received from customers, they should be input into the system and matched with individual transactions and controls should ensure that the correct amounts are allocated to the correct customers and transactions. | Review the bank statement and check that all transfers have been matched with customers. |
| An exception report should be produced for any unallocated bank transfers. Exceptions should be promptly investigated. This will ensure that receivables information is accurate and up to date and that customers are not chased for amounts that have been paid. | Review the exception report. Check that all matters were resolved speedily. |
| A bank reconciliation should be performed on a monthly basis in order to ensure that the company's cash records are complete, accurate and up to date. | Review bank reconciliations. |

**Test your understanding 5**

(a) **Purchasing department – procedures to control the purchase and receipt of goods**

The controls the purchasing department should exercise over ordering and control over receipt of goods and services should include:

- For all goods ordered, there should be a purchase requisition from a user department. The purchasing department should not be permitted to raise purchase requisitions, as this would create a weakness in the division of duties. For goods required by the purchasing department, they should request another department (e.g. the accounts department) to raise a purchase requisition. Before raising the purchase requisition, the accounts department should ensure it is for goods the purchasing department require and are authorised to order.
- The purchasing department should check the purchase requisition is for goods the user department is authorised to buy or consume. If the value of the order is substantial, the purchasing department should ensure there is a need for such a large order, by checking current inventory levels and future orders to determine whether so large a quantity or value is required.
- The purchase requisition should use a standard form and be signed by an authorised signatory.
- The purchasing department should order the goods from an authorised supplier. Where there is a choice of supplier or a new supplier is required, the purchasing department should obtain the product from the supplier who provides the product or service at the best price, quality and delivery. For audit purposes, it is desirable for staff in the purchasing department to record details of the suppliers contacted, the price, delivery date and perceived quality, and the decision on which supplier was finally chosen.
- The purchasing department should raise the purchase order which should be signed by the purchasing manager. For large value purchases, a director may be required to sign the purchase order. The purchase order should be sent to the supplier, the goods received department, the user department and the accounts department. The purchasing department should ensure the goods are received on time. This may require them to contact the supplier a week before the expected delivery date to ensure they are received on time, and allow action to be taken if the delivery date is later than specified on the purchase order.

- When the goods are received, the purchasing department should receive a copy of the goods received note (GRN) from the goods received department. They should record the goods received against the order. From this information, they will be able to take action when there are short deliveries or the goods are received late. Frequently purchasing departments file purchase orders in three types of file:
  - where none of the goods have been received
  - where some of the goods ordered have been received
  - where all the goods ordered have been received (i.e. 'dead' purchase orders).
- The purchasing department may be part of the system which authorises purchase invoices. They should check the goods on the invoice are consistent with the purchase order and the price per unit is correct.
- The purchasing department should be informed about short deliveries (i.e. the quantity of goods received is less than on the purchase order or advice note) and when there are quality problems. From this information, they can contact the supplier so that corrective action is taken. Also, such details may be helpful in determining whether the supplier should be used for future orders.
- The purchasing department should be informed of situations when goods or services are received but no purchase order has been raised. With this information, the purchasing department should contact the 'offending' department and ensure that in future a purchase order is raised for all the goods they order. The supplier should be contacted and informed that an authorised purchase order must be received by them (the supplier) before any goods or services are provided by the supplier.

(b) **Controls over obtaining authorisation of purchase invoices**

- The accounts department will receive the purchase invoice, which they should record in a register.
- The invoice expense will be included on the invoice (for posting to the general ledger). The expense analysis will be checked by an independent department (e.g. the purchasing or user department).

- The accounts department will either match the purchase invoice to the goods received note and delivery note or ask the goods received department to check and authorise the purchase invoice.
- The purchasing department will be asked to confirm the goods are as described on the purchase order and the price per unit is correct.
- The user department may be asked to authorise the purchase invoice.
- An appropriate responsible official will be asked to authorise the purchase invoice.
- Provided these checks are satisfactory, the accounts department should input the invoice details into the computer which will post it to the accounts payable ledger and the general ledger.

Where there is a problem with the invoice (e.g. concerning the quantity, quality or price of the goods received) the accounts department should put the invoice in a 'hold' file. They should contact the supplier (sometimes with the help of the purchasing or user department) and try to resolve the problem. When either a credit note is received or the correct quantity and quality of goods have been received, the accounts department will get authorisation (e.g. from the purchasing department) that the situation is resolved and they should input the purchase invoice into the computer (and credit note if this is required).

Periodically, an independent person should check suppliers' statements against the balances on the accounts payable ledger. Differences between these two balances should be recorded. If the transaction which created the difference is close to the date of the check, it is probable that no action will be taken. However, older items should be investigated to ensure that action is being taken to resolve the problem.

(c) **Controls over the purchase of services**

Frequently, procedures over receiving services are less strong and less effective than those over receiving goods.

For some types of service, such as receipt of electricity, gas, water and telephone charges there may be no system for raising purchase orders. However there should be a system for reviewing these costs, by comparing them with the previous year (or period), with budget and with amounts charged by alternative suppliers. In this way, the company can ensure these services are received at the most economical cost.

For some of these services it may be possible to suggest ways in which these costs can be reduced (e.g. by turning off lights and reducing the temperature settings in winter).

Costs of gas, electricity and water can be monitored by checking the meter readings monthly and determining whether the consumption is reasonable. For telephone expenses, the system should provide information on the cost for each department, and each department manager should review his/her department's costs. A risk with telephone systems is that they can be abused by staff, who make personal telephone calls using the company's telephone system. The department managers should be made responsible for checking this abuse is kept to a minimum.

For receipt of all other services, before the service is obtained, a purchase requisition should be raised by the user department, and the purchasing department should raise a purchase order. In emergency situations, it may be acceptable to raise a purchase requisition and order after the service has been received (e.g. the repair of a vehicle which has broken down). There should be a system whereby action is taken when no purchase order has been raised for a service which has been received. In many situations when a service has been received, it is probably appropriate that the department receiving the service should issue a goods received note and send it to the purchases accounts and the purchasing departments. In this way, the same system can be used for processing receipt of services as for receipt of goods.

**Test your understanding 6**

(a) The advantages of Computer-Assisted Audit Techniques (CAATs) are that they:

- Enable the auditor to test program controls – if CAATs were not used then those controls would not be testable.
- Enable the auditor to test a greater number of items quickly and accurately. This will also increase the overall confidence for the audit opinion.
- Allow the auditor to test the actual accounting system and records rather than printouts which are only a copy of those records and could be incorrect.
- Are cost effective after they have been set up as long as the company does not change its systems.
- Allow the results from using CAATs to be compared with 'traditional' testing – if the two sources of evidence agree then this will increase overall audit confidence.

(b)

| **Test Data** | **Reason for Test** |
|---|---|
| Input of an order for a negative number of tennis racquets | Ensures that only positive quantities are accepted – tennis racquets although the company cannot despatch negative quantities anyway. |
| Input of an order for ten tennis racquets | There are reasonableness checks in the system to identify possible input errors. A warning message should appear on screen asking the customer to confirm any order for more than say two racquets. |
| Input of an order without payment details | Ensures that orders are paid for prior to despatch – being completed this also limits the number of bad debts. |
| Input of invalid inventory code | Ensures that the computer detects the invalid code and presents an error message rather than taking the nearest code and accepting that. |
| Input of invalid customer credit card details | Online checking of credit card details to the credit card company ensures that goods cannot be despatched without payment. This will also limit the number of bad debts. |

| | |
|---|---|
| Input of invalid address | Ensures that the address and post code are valid, possibly by accessing a database of valid codes. If the code is not valid an error message should be displayed. This ensures that goods are only despatched to valid addresses. |

(c) **Audit software**

(i) Difficulties of using audit software

- Substantial setup costs because the client's procedures and files must be understood in detail before the audit software can be used to access and interrogate those files.
- Audit software may not be available for the specific systems set up by the client, especially if those systems are bespoke. The cost of writing audit software to test those systems may be difficult to justify against the possible benefits on the audit.
- The software may produce too much output either due to poor design of the software or using inappropriate parameters on a test. The auditor may waste considerable time checking what appear to be transactions with errors in them when the fault is actually in the audit software.
- Checking the client's files in a live situation. There is the danger that the client's systems are disrupted by the audit program. The data files can be used offline, but this will mean ensuring that the files are true copies of the live files.

| (ii) **Audit Software** | **Reason for Test** |
|---|---|
| Calculation check of the sales day book | Ensures that the computerised sales day book has been cast correctly and helps to verify the sales balance in the financial statements. |
| Analysis of the aging of items in the inventory ledger | Help to detect inventory items which are relatively old which may need valuing at net realisable value rather than cost. |
| Selecting a sample of inventory at the end of the year as part of the physical verification | Removes bias from sample selection as well as being quicker than selecting the items manually. |
| Selecting a sample of sales invoices for checking to despatch documentation | Removes bias from sample selection as well as being quicker than selecting the items manually. |
| Checking completeness of sales invoice numbers | Ensures that all sales invoices are recorded in the sales day book. |

| | |
|---|---|
| Check that all sales invoices have been paid for | All sales are paid for on ordering, unpaid sales would be a violation of systems rules and would need to be investigated by the auditor. |
| List large credit notes (perhaps more than five racquets) for investigation by the auditor | The auditor will find reasons for the return – this is also a check on the accuracy of the ordering system – ordering errors may result in customers returning goods later. |

**Test your understanding 7**

(a) **Jones**

*Materiality*

The amount of the loss at $30,000 represents 20% of pre-tax profit and more than 4% of accounts receivable; it would therefore seem to be material in both statement of comprehensive income and statement of financial position terms, although it is clearly more material in relation to profit.

*Relevant accounting principles*

The bankruptcy of the customer indicates that the company has overstated profit and assets as at the year-end by $30,000. This letter provides evidence of a condition existing at the statement of financial position date (IAS 10). It should therefore be treated as an adjusting event. The loss should be provided for in full in the financial statements at 30 September 20X2.

*Form of audit report*

The management's refusal to adjust the accounts for the loss means that the financial statements are materially misstated. In such a case, the auditor has to make a decision as to whether the amount of the loss is 'material and pervasive' or 'material but not pervasive'. Without more facts being available, it is difficult to draw conclusions satisfactorily in this area, but on the face of it a qualified opinion would appear appropriate as the true and fair view would not be entirely destroyed if the loss were to remain unadjusted.

(b) **Roberts**

*Materiality*

The amount of $10,000 represents only 2% of the stated profit before tax of $500,000 and does not, in itself, appear to be material in terms of its impact on the financial statements. Unfortunately, however, the potential losses may be very much more significant than the figure of $10,000, since other claims are now pending, and the auditor may have to conclude that the whole legal matter is potentially material.

*Relevant accounting principles*

There is clearly a contingent liability in respect of potential claims arising from the product defect. The potential loss which is material should be accrued in the financial statements where it is probable that future events will confirm the loss and that the loss can be estimated with reasonable accuracy (except where the possibility is remote).

*Form of audit report*

There is clearly uncertainty with regard to the outcome of the pending claims and the potential liability which they represent. The auditor will have to decide whether or not the possibility of loss is likely or remote. Management has apparently chosen to ignore both the actual loss (which is not individually material) and the potential loss (which may well be material). If the auditor can be convinced that management's view is acceptable and the disclosure in the notes is adequate, then a modification may be completely avoidable. The auditor should be aware, however, that items which are not material when considered individually may well have a cumulative effect which is material in total. If the auditor does not believe that the management's view is acceptable, or does not think that the disclosure is adequate, then a qualified opinion due to a material misstatement is probably sufficient. However, if the auditor believes that the claims are likely to be successful and are likely to be substantial then it may be necessary to issue an adverse opinion.

(c) **Williams**

*Materiality*

The loans are not bad debts and so have no effect on the reported loss. However, this sort of matter cannot have the same materiality test applied to it as in the cases previously discussed in this answer. We are told that amounts owed by directors are required to be disclosed as a requirement of the local legislation. Materiality should, therefore, not be measured in relation to profit or loss for the year or the statement of financial position, but in relation to the requirements of the law. It would appear that the loans are not allowed and that Williams is materially in non-compliance with the local law.

*Relevant accounting principles*

As mentioned in the question, the loans are not allowed and disclosure should in any case be made under the local legislation. The item is required to be separately disclosed and cannot be 'hidden' as part of a figure containing other 'receivables collectable within one year'.

This also contravenes IAS 24 Related Party Disclosures, which requires transactions made with directors during the year and any related year-end balances to be fully disclosed in the financial statements.

*Form of audit report*

Given the breach of IAS 24 the lack of disclosure would lead to a misstatement. Given the nature of directors' emoluments and the fact that this contravenes local laws it is likely that this would be considered material, regardless of the size of the loans or the fact that they were repaid after the year-end. Whilst material it is unlikely that this would be considered pervasive. Therefore, unless the directors amended the financial statements, a qualified opinion would be issued.

(d) **Griffiths**

*Materiality*

The fall in value is clearly material. In fact, the auditor would probably have to view the matter as pervasive, because providing for the loss would have the effect of converting a net profit before tax of $250,000 into a loss of $50,000.

*Relevant accounting principles*

Long-term investments should be written down where there has been an impairment in value. Falls in the value of one asset must not be offset against increases in the value of another asset. Each asset has to be considered separately.

The directors should ensure adequate allowance is made for all known liabilities (expenses and losses). The accounting treatment adopted, offsetting known losses against unrealised profits, is unacceptable. As the company admits that a permanent fall in value has taken place, it should make full allowance against the loss. Further, as the other trade investments (with reputedly high realisable values) are permanent investments not held for resale, the accounting treatment adopted for them could be amended.

*Form of audit report*

As mentioned above, it is likely that the auditor would have to view the misstatement as both material and pervasive. The auditor will probably be forced to give an adverse opinion, stating that the financial statements do not show a true and fair view.

(e) **Evans**

*Materiality*

The $10,000 represents 10% of the reported net profit before tax, and so would appear to be material. However, the actual materiality of this item in relation to profit is, in fact, a somewhat judgemental matter. The auditor would probably conclude that the possible error in calculating the $10,000 was not material in relation to the profit of $100,000, since the amount of any error will probably be substantially less than the full amount included in the accounts. Further since the accounting records were only destroyed for the early part of the year, the auditor would still be able to confirm the calculations for the later part of the year. In these particular circumstances, therefore, the auditor may consider that the amount of any error (which is likely to be considerably less than $10,000) is not material.

*Relevant accounting principles*

It is perfectly acceptable for the company to add the cost of its own labour and materials in the construction of the warehouse, since these have been used to create a capital asset. This is following the 'matching' or 'accruals' concept as set out in IAS 1 and applied in IAS 16.

*Form of audit report*

The accounting treatment is generally acceptable and the amount of any error is not likely to be considered material, the auditor will probably be able to give a standard unmodified audit report.

**Test your understanding 8**

(a) **Internal audit function: risk of fraud and error**

(i) Internal audit can help management manage risks in relation to fraud and error, and exercise proper stewardship by:

- commenting on the process used by management to identify and classify the specific fraud and error risks to which the entity is subject (and in some cases helping management develop and implement that process);
- commenting on the appropriateness and effectiveness of actions taken by management to manage the risks identified (and in some cases helping management develop appropriate actions by making recommendations);
- periodically auditing or reviewing systems or operations to determine whether the risks of fraud and error are being effectively managed;
- monitoring the incidence of fraud and error, investigating serious cases and making recommendations for appropriate management responses.

(iv) In practice, the work of internal audit often focuses on the adequacy and effectiveness of internal control procedures for the prevention, detection and reporting of fraud and error. Routine internal controls (such as the controls over computer systems and the production of routine financial information) and non-routine controls (such as controls over year-end adjustments to the financial statements) are relevant.

(v) It should be recognised however that many significant frauds bypass normal internal control systems and that in the case of management fraud in particular, much higher level controls (those relating to the high level governance of the entity) need to be reviewed by internal audit in order to establish the nature of the risks, and to manage them effectively.

(b) **External auditors: fraud and error in an audit of financial statements**

(i) External auditors are required by ISA 240 *The Auditor's Responsibilities Relating to Fraud...* to consider the risks of material misstatements in the financial statements due to fraud. Their audit procedures will then be based on that risk assessment. Regardless of the risk assessment, auditors are required to be alert to the possibility of fraud throughout the audit and maintain an attitude of professional scepticism, notwithstanding the auditors' past experience of the honesty and integrity of management and those charged with governance. Members of the engagement team should discuss the susceptibility of the entity's financial statements to material misstatements due to fraud.

(ii) Auditors should make enquiries of management regarding management's assessment of fraud risk, its process for dealing with risk, and its communications with those charged with governance and employees. They should enquire of those charged with governance about the oversight process.

(iii) Auditors should also enquire of management and those charged with governance about any suspected or actual instance of fraud.

(iv) Auditors should consider fraud risk factors, unusual or unexpected relationships, and assess the risk of misstatements due to fraud, identifying any significant risks. Auditors should evaluate the design of relevant internal controls, and determine whether they have been implemented.

(v) Auditors should determine an overall response to the assessed risk of material misstatements due to fraud and develop appropriate audit procedures, including testing certain journal entries, reviewing estimates for bias, and obtaining an understanding of the business rationale of significant transactions outside the normal course of business. Appropriate management representations should be obtained.

(vi) External auditors are only concerned with risks that might cause material error in the financial statements. External auditors might therefore pay less attention than internal auditors to small frauds (and errors), although they must always consider whether evidence of single instances of fraud (or error) are indicative of more systematic problems.

(vii) It is accepted that because of the hidden nature of fraud, an audit properly conducted in accordance with ISAs might not detect a material misstatement in the financial statements arising from fraud. In practice, routine errors are much easier to detect than frauds.

(viii) Where auditors encounter suspicions or actual instances of fraud (or error), they must consider the effect on the financial statements, which will usually involve further investigations. They should also consider the need to report to management and those charged with governance.

(ix) Where serious frauds (or errors) are encountered, auditors need also to consider the effect on the going concern status of the entity, and the possible need to report externally to third parties, either in the public interest, for national security reasons, or for regulatory reasons. Many entities in the financial services sector are subject to this type of regulatory reporting and many countries have legislation relating to the reporting of money laundering activities, for example.

(c) **Nature of risks arising from fraud and error: Stone Holidays**

(i) Stone Holidays is subject to all of the risks of error arising from the use of computer systems. If programmed controls do not operate properly, for example, the information produced may be incomplete or incorrect. Inadequate controls also give rise to the risk of fraud by those who understand the system and are able to manipulate it in order to hide the misappropriation of assets such as receipts from customers.

(ii) All networked systems are also subject to the risk of error because of the possibility of the loss or corruption of data in transit. They are also subject to the risk of fraud where the transmission of data is not securely encrypted.

(iii) All entities that employ staff who handle company assets (such as receipts from customers) are subject to the risk that staff may make mistakes (error) or that they may misappropriate those assets (fraud) and then seek to hide the error or fraud by falsifying the records.

(iv) Stone Holidays is subject to problems arising from the risk of fraud perpetrated by customers using stolen credit or debit cards or even cash. Whilst credit card companies may be liable for such frauds, attempts to use stolen cards can cause considerable inconvenience.

(v) There is a risk of fraud perpetrated by senior management who might seek to lower the amount of money payable to the central fund (and the company's tax liability) by falsifying the company's sales figures, particularly if a large proportion of holidays are paid for in cash.

(vi) There is a risk that staff may seek to maximise the commission they are paid by entering false transactions into the computer system that are then reversed after the commission has been paid.

**Test your understanding 9**

(a) **Risks and implications for audit risk**

*Inherent and control risks*

(i) Charities can be viewed as inherently risky because they are often managed by non-professionals and are susceptible to fraud, although many charities and the volunteers that run them are people of the highest integrity who take a great deal of care over their work. The assessment of this aspect of inherent risk depends on each individual charity, and the areas in which it operates.

(ii) Charities are also at risk of being in violation of their constitutions which is important where funds are raised from public or private donors who may well object strongly if funds are not applied in the manner expected. Other charities and regulatory bodies supervising charities may also object. Again, the auditors will assess the level of risk. The involvement of a recently retired Chartered Certified Accountant in the preparation of accounts in the past may lower the auditor's assessed inherent risk to an extent.

(iii) Most small charities have a high level of control risk because formal internal controls are expensive and are not often in place. This means that donations are susceptible to misappropriation. Charities rely on the trustworthiness of volunteers. The auditors will assess the level of risk.

*Detection risk*

(iv) Detection risk comprises sampling risk and non-sampling risk. It is possible in this case that all transactions will be tested and therefore sampling risk (the risk that samples are unrepresentative of the populations from which they are drawn) is not present.

(v) Non-sampling risk is the risk that auditors will draw incorrect conclusions because, for example, mistakes are made, or errors of judgement are made in interpreting results, or because the auditors are unfamiliar with the client, as is the case here.

*Audit risk*

(vi) Audit risk is the product of inherent risk, control risk and detection risk and is the risk that the auditors will issue an inappropriate audit opinion. This risk can be managed by decreasing detection risk by altering the nature, timing and extent of audit procedures applied. Where inherent risk is high and controls are weak (as may be the case here) more audit work will be performed in appropriate areas in order to reduce audit risk to an acceptable level.

(b) **Audit tests – fund raising events**

(i) Attend fund raising events and observe the procedures employed in collecting, counting, banking and recording the cash. This will help provide audit evidence that funds have not been misappropriated and that all income from such events has been recorded. Sealed boxes or tins that are opened in the presence of two volunteers are often used for these purposes.

(ii) Perform cash counts at the events to provide evidence that cash has been counted correctly and that there is no collusion between volunteers to misappropriate funds.

(iii) Examine bank paying in slips, bank statements and bank reconciliations and ensure that these agree with records made at events. This also provides evidence as to the completeness of income.

(iv) Examine the records of expenditure for fund raising events (hire of equipment, entertainers, purchase of refreshments, etc.) and ensure that these have been properly authorised (where appropriate) and that receipts have been obtained for all expenditure. This provides evidence as to the completeness and accuracy of expenditure.

(v) Review the income and expenditure of fund raising events against any budgets that have been prepared and investigate any significant discrepancies.

(vi) Ensure that all necessary licences (such as public entertainment licences) have been obtained by the trustees for such events in order to ensure that no action is likely to be taken against the charity or volunteers.

(vii) Obtain representations from the trustees to the effect that there are no outstanding unrecorded liabilities for such events – again for completeness of expenditure and liabilities.

**Test your understanding 10**

(a) **Preparation of financial statements**

The directors are normally required to prepare the financial statements of the company using the appropriate law of their country and in accordance with the International Accounting Standards (IASs). The auditors are normally required to check or audit those financial statements, again in accordance with the legislation of their country and the International Standards on Auditing.

**Fraud and error**

The directors are responsible for preventing and detecting fraud and error in the financial statements, no matter how immaterial this may be. Auditors are responsible for giving an opinion on whether the financial statements show a true and fair view; in other words that the financial statements are materially correct. Auditors are not required to detect immaterial fraud or error.

**Disclosure**

The directors must ensure that there is adequate disclosure of all matters required by statute or IASs in the financial statements. The auditor will check that disclosure provisions have been complied with, and where certain disclosures have not been made, provide this information in the audit report.

### Going concern

The directors are responsible for ensuring that the company will continue in operational existence for the foreseeable future, and report to the members in the published financial statements if this is unlikely to be the case. The auditor will check the accuracy of the directors' workings and assumptions and if these are considered incorrect or inappropriate, then the audit report may be modified or qualified to bring the situation to the attention of the members of the company.

(b) **Review of audit report extract**

The basis of opinion paragraph may not meet the requirements of ISAs 700-705 for the following reasons:

The use of the term Auditing Standards is not clear, because the report does not state which auditing standards have been used. This provides uncertainty regarding the actual standard of work performed.

The assessment of estimates and judgements made by the directors normally relates to significant amounts only, rather than all of those estimates and judgements. The use of the word all implies that the audit was more thorough than it probably was. Replacing the word all with the word significant will show that there was some limit to the audit testing and that this was probably focused on material amounts only.

Stating that time was a factor in obtaining information and explanations for the audit is not correct as this implies some factor which could have been avoided and that the audit may therefore be incomplete. The auditor has to plan the audit carefully and ensure that all the information and explanations considered necessary are obtained to form an opinion, not simply stop work when time runs out.

The auditor does not confirm that the financial statements are free from material misstatement as this implies a degree of accuracy that the auditor simply cannot provide. Making the statement could also leave the auditor liable to claims from members or third parties should errors be found in the financial statements later. Rather than make such a categorical statement, the auditor provides reasonable assurance that the financial statements are free from material misstatement, which clearly implies that audit techniques are limited.

The disclaimer regarding errors appears to be useful in that it limits the auditor's liability. However, it does not belong in the basis of opinion paragraph as it appears to severely limit the basis of the auditor's opinion by stating that the directors are responsible for all errors. Directors' responsibilities are also clearly outlined in another section of the report, and this statement also appears to extend those responsibilities making the audit report overall less clear. This could also imply that the auditor has done little or no work.

As the auditor is not required to audit the whole of the annual report of a company, it is inappropriate to refer to disclosure in that report when checking overall adequacy of presentation. Adequacy of presentation can only be confirmed regarding items actually audited, which is basically the financial statements.

(c) **Positive v negative assurance**

A positive assurance report means that the auditor has carried out sufficient work to be able to state that financial information is free from material error.

A negative assurance report means that nothing has come to the attention of the auditor, which indicates the financial information being reported on has errors in it. However, the extent of the work carried out is normally less, which means that less reliance can be placed on this report.

The advantages of providing negative assurance include:

– The user of the financial information receives some comfort that the information is correct, even though that assurance is less than positive assurance.

– The report adds some credibility to the financial information because it has been reviewed by a professional accountant.

– For the preparer, the report will be more cost effective than obtaining a full positive assurance report.

# Index

# Index

## S



## T



## U



## V



## W